Global Mobility of Research Scientists

Global Mobility of Research Scientists
The Economics of Who Goes Where and Why

Edited by

Aldo Geuna

AMSTERDAM • BOSTON • HEIDELBERG • LONDON
NEW YORK • OXFORD • PARIS • SAN DIEGO
SAN FRANCISCO • SINGAPORE • SYDNEY • TOKYO

Academic Press is an imprint of Elsevier

ELSEVIER

British Library Cataloguing-in-Publication Data
A catalogue record for this book is available from the British Library

Library of Congress Cataloging-in-Publication Data
A catalog record for this book is available from the Library of Congress

ISBN: 978-0-12-801396-0

For information on all Academic Press publications
visit our website at http://store.elsevier.com/

  Working together
to grow libraries in
developing countries

www.elsevier.com • www.bookaid.org

Publisher: Nikki Levy
Acquisition Editor: J. Scott Bentley
Editorial Project Manager: Susan Ikeda
Project Managers: Nicky Carter
Designer: Mark Rogers

Typeset by TNQ Books and Journals
www.tnq.co.in

Printed and bound in the United States of America

Contents

3. International Careers of Researchers in Biomedical Sciences: A Comparison of the US and the UK

Cornelia Lawson, Aldo Geuna, Ana Fernández-Zubieta, Rodrigo Kataishi and Manuel Toselli

4. Mobility and Productivity of Research Scientists

Ana Fernández-Zubieta, Aldo Geuna and Cornelia Lawson

5. Who Leaves and Who Stays? Evidence on Immigrant Selection from the Collapse of Soviet Science

Ina Ganguli

6. China's "Great Leap Forward" in Science and Engineering

Richard B. Freeman and Wei Huang

7. Which Factors Influence the International Mobility of Research Scientists?

Silvia Appelt, Brigitte van Beuzekom, Fernando Galindo-Rueda and Roberto de Pinho

8. **Destinations of Mobile European Researchers: Europe versus the United States**

Reinhilde Veugelers and Linda Van Bouwel

9. **Appointment, Promotion, and Mobility of Bioscience Researchers in Japan**

Cornelia Lawson and Sotaro Shibayama

10. Moving Out of Academic Research: Why Do Scientists Stop Doing Research?

Aldo Geuna and Sotaro Shibayama

Contributors

Silvia Appelt Economic Analysis and Statistics Division, Directorate for Science, Technology and Innovation, Organisation for Economic Co-operation and Development (OECD), Paris, France

Roberto de Pinho Science, Technology and Innovation Indicators Unit, Ministry of Science, Technology and Innovation, Brazil

Ana Fernández-Zubieta Institute for Advanced Social Studies – Spanish Council for Scientific Research, Campo Santo de los Mártires, Córdoba, Spain

Chiara Franzoni School of Management, Politecnico di Milano, Milan, Italy

Richard B. Freeman Harvard University and NBER, Cambridge, MA, USA

Fernando Galindo-Rueda Economic Analysis and Statistics Division, Directorate for Science, Technology and Innovation, Organisation for Economic Co-operation and Development (OECD), Paris, France; IZA, Institute for the Study of Labour

Ina Ganguli University of Massachusetts, Amherst, MA, USA

Aldo Geuna Department of Economics and Statistics Cognetti De Martiis, Università di Torino, Turin, Italy; BRICK, Collegio Carlo Alberto, Moncalieri, Turin, Italy

Wei Huang Harvard University and NBER, Cambridge, MA, USA

Rodrigo Kataishi Department of Economics and Statistics Cognetti De Martiis, Università di Torino, Turin, Italy; BRICK, Collegio Carlo Alberto, Moncalieri, Turin, Italy

Cornelia Lawson Department of Economics and Statistics Cognetti De Martiis, Università di Torino, Turin, Italy; BRICK, Collegio Carlo Alberto, Moncalieri, Turin, Italy; School of Sociology and Social Policy, University of Nottingham, Nottingham, UK

Giuseppe Scellato Department of Management and Production Engineering, Politecnico di Torino, Turin, Italy; BRICK, Collegio Carlo Alberto, Moncalieri, Turin, Italy

Sotaro Shibayama Research Center for Advanced Science and Technology, University of Tokyo, Meguro-ku, Tokyo, Japan

Paula Stephan Andrew Young School of Policy Studies, Georgia State University, Atlanta, GA, USA; National Bureau of Economic Research, Cambridge, MA, USA; Department of Economics and Statistics Cognetti De Martiis, Università di Torino, Turin, Italy

Manuel Toselli Department of Economics and Statistics Cognetti De Martiis, Università di Torino, Turin, Italy; BRICK, Collegio Carlo Alberto, Moncalieri, Turin, Italy

Brigitte van Beuzekom Economic Analysis and Statistics Division, Directorate for Science, Technology and Innovation, Organisation for Economic Co-operation and Development (OECD), Paris, France

Linda Van Bouwel Faculty of Business and Economics, KU Leuven, Leuven, Belgium

Reinhilde Veugelers Faculty of Business and Economics, KU Leuven, Leuven, Belgium; Bruegel, Brussels, Belgium; CEPR, London, UK

Acknowledgments

This book is the first major result of a long research path. More than 10 years ago, during research leave at the Robert Schuman Centre, European University Institute, I started researching the mobility of academic researchers and, with my colleagues Gustavo Crespi and Lionel Nesta, wrote a paper on academic mobility from universities to firms. In 2007/2008 I was involved in the EUROCV project, financed by the PRIME research network, where we tried to assess the possibility of using the electronic curriculum vitae (CV) of European scientists to analyze their careers. After supervising Ana Fernández-Zubieta's master's dissertation, I started working with her on the EUROCV project; we both become fascinated by the possibility of using CV information to study the mobility and productivity of scientists. In that early stage we began working with engineers to try to develop a software package to codify CV information. We rather naively thought that writing the software would not take too long, enabling us to build the databases needed to address the many questions which we were coming up with based on that CV information. With the collaboration of Cornelia Lawson, who joined us in our quest in 2010, and the precious help of various coauthors, we continued along this research, which we have not yet completed. In 2013/2014 I spent a sabbatical at Stanford University, during which I managed to write a few papers and produce this book.

The complexity of the data problem and econometric analysis is not the only reason for the long gestation of this research output. Much of the time lost was related to my return to my home country (an example of international mobility, and perhaps a self-reflective incentive to study this specific aspect of mobility). In 2008 I was appointed to the position of full professor at the University of Torino, having left the University of Sussex in the United Kingdom, where I spent the first 10 years of my academic career (following completion of a PhD degree in the Netherlands and a postdoctoral period in France—more international mobility). Back in Italy, I decided to devote much more time to administrative tasks than was sensible (or would be contemplated by a rational agent keen to maximize his reputation). Some of the models we use to analyze mobility are limited by the assumption that scientists always work to do what will best benefit their careers. Sometimes, especially when scientists move back to their home countries, they might feel that priorities have changed and there is a desire to contribute to improving the scientific system in their home country: How silly this is. Overly much time can so easily be devoted to administration at the expense of research, a trap I fell into. My sincere apologies go to all my coauthors who over those years generously accepted continuous excuses for my inability to make my contribution to our common research. I am particularly grateful to Ana, Cornelia, and Sotaro, who have been tolerant of my delays caused by meetings and my other administrative commitments.

One way of keeping a researcher up to date is to involve her or him in the organization of a workshop, especially if this becomes an annual event that obliges the researcher to look over, and sometimes read thoroughly, the good number of papers submitted to the workshop. I used this strategy to keep abreast. This book owes much to all the participants and discussants at the annual "Organization, Economics and Policy of Scientific Research Workshop," which I have organized, with the support of BRICK, Department of Economics and Statistics Cognetti de Martiis, University of Torino and Collegio Carlo Alberto, since 2008. Most of the authors of the papers in this edited collection participated in at least one of these annual events. Also, the papers benefited greatly from the workshop discussions. Special thanks are due to members of the Scientific Committee, who supported the workshops and indirectly contributed to the production of a better book.

I thank all the contributors to this volume, not only for their papers but also for their comments and suggestions on each other's contributions. I acknowledge their patience in responding to my reminder emails while confessing that I was last in submitting my final paper.

Special thanks for their support in putting together this book (and for all other small achievements of my academic career) are due to two exceptional colleagues and friends: Paula Stephan and Paul A. David. Without their continuous stimulus, help, critical comments, personal support, and friendship during most of the past 20 years I would not have achieved much.

The research that led to this book was supported by several grants. Here I acknowledge the two research projects without which the book would not have been finalized: the Collegio Carlo Alberto Project "Researcher Mobility and Scientific Performance" and "An Observatorium for Science in Society based in Social Models" (SISOB), contract no. FP7-266588 of the European Commission. Finally, thanks are due to the Stanford Institute for Economic Policy Research for the support provided during my sabbatical at Stanford University.

Aldo Geuna
Torino, Italy
April 9, 2015

Introduction

On September 4, 1506, Erasmus of Rotterdam defended his doctoral dissertation in Divinity (written in Latin) at the University of Torino. Following that, he lectured for a few years at the University of Cambridge, then spent a short period in the University of Leuven before finally settling down at the University of Basel. Such a pattern was not atypical among academics in Europe during the medieval and Renaissance periods (de Ridder-Symoens, 1992, 1996). The development of national universities in the late eighteenth and the nineteenth centuries, in Europe and around the world, shaped the evolution of universities over the next 200 years and changed the pattern of going abroad for study. In these national universities teaching and research were conducted mainly in the local language, although international cooperation and interaction were continuous features. Toward the end of the twentieth century, universities experienced a new period of change, which has extended into the early twenty-first century, involving increased researcher mobility and internationalization; this is making them look more like their medieval progenitors (Geuna, 1998). Because of the diffusion of English as the lingua franca (in the medieval period it was Latin), the availability of the Internet, which has lowered the costs of international communication and collaboration (similar to the effect of mechanical movable type printing developed by Gutenberg), and the relatively peaceful historical period following the end of the Cold War, the number of international students and professors has increased significantly in the past 25 years. These flows (or movements) are not simply one way, from less advanced scientific systems to more advanced ones (brain drain); it is a much more complex phenomenon with return-to-home-country mobility and mobility from more advanced to less advanced systems. While it is true that the United States is predominant in attracting large numbers of researchers from across the world, other countries such as Australia, Canada, Sweden, Switzerland, and the United Kingdom are receiving as high or even higher shares of foreign-born researchers. Return mobility is equally important, with high shares of academic staff studying or working abroad before returning to their home countries.

It is hoped that this transformation will be accompanied by a new renaissance marked by the most talented students, scholars, and researchers finding matches with the best and most relevant institutions in which to carry out their activities. However, we know little about the effects of increased national and international mobility of students and researchers. In recent years some attempts have been made to map this phenomenon (Auriol, Misu, & Freeman, 2013; Chang & Milan, 2012; Moguerou & Di Pietrogiacomo, 2008) and analyze the individual and social returns from increased mobility. The economics of science has taken over from the quantitative sociology of science, and using insights from labor economics and organizational science has advanced our understanding of the characteristics and implications of academic mobility.

This book specifically investigates scientists' (not students') mobility within and across countries, and provides the first comprehensive analysis of this increasingly important phenomenon. The chapters in this volume adopt an applied economic perspective to the topic, while providing a continuous dialogue with work in the traditional sociology of science, which has produced much original research in this area. In an increasingly globalized world dependent on scarce knowledge inputs, a better understanding of how the localization and mobility of academic researchers contributes to the production of knowledge is crucial. What characterizes nationally and internationally mobile researchers? What are the individual and social implications of increased research scientist mobility? Is mobility a prerequisite for or the result of high scientific productivity? Does intersectoral mobility hamper or spur academic productivity? Is it sensible for governments to support researcher mobility? If so, at which stage in the academic career would some government support be most beneficial? Is a high level of job mobility a prerequisite for a productive national academic system?

Some of these questions are addressed in the chapters in this book. The 10 standalone but coordinated chapters that compose this volume draw on a set of recently developed databases covering 30 countries (including the United States, the United Kingdom, France, Germany, Italy, Japan, Russia, and China, among others) to analyze these and other questions. On the basis of a comprehensive framework to characterize and analyze mobility in science, an original set of applied methodologies is formulated to address the research questions posed above. Particular attention is devoted to the interaction between researchers' mobility and productivity on related career decisions and mobility. Chapter 1, by Fernández-Zubieta, Geuna, and Lawson, sets the scene by discussing the theoretical and empirical background to the overall analysis. Chapter 1 is not a traditional all-inclusive literature review; its aim is to highlight three important changes (internationalization, intersector mobility and collaboration, and career diversification) in the research system that make researcher mobility more relevant to the dynamics of knowledge creation and dissemination. On this basis, Chapter 1 presents a typology of researcher mobility which it uses as a tool to discuss the evidence in the literature, and provides a systemic analysis of these phenomena. It identifies unanswered research questions (some of which are addressed by the chapters in this volume) that will continue to typify this new field of research in years to come. Finally, in a didactic way, it highlights the econometric challenges associated with the analysis of academic research mobility and individual scientific productivity. The nine succeeding chapters present specific studies, most of which deal with international mobility of scientists.

Chapter 2, by Franzoni, Scellato, and Stephan, presents the first detailed analysis of mobility patterns among a large sample of over 17,000 researchers working in 16 countries in the fields of biology, chemistry, earth and environmental sciences, and materials science. Following a discussion of the main results of the GloSci survey of international mobility and migration patterns, the authors analyze the reasons for training (PhD and/or postdoctorate) and working abroad and the factors that drive the decision to return home. Their analysis of returnees to a large selection of these countries does not provide evidence of performance differences compared with those researchers who decide to stay abroad. The second part of Chapter 2 presents the results of the authors' research on the relationships between international mobility and collaboration, and performance. Franzoni, Scellato, and Stephan highlight a strong correlation between various measures of international scientific collaboration (research network) and migration, and they point to a significant share of scientists who collaborate with researchers from their country of origin. Finally, they provide evidence supporting a positive differential in the performance of foreign-born compared with nonmobile native researchers.

The chapter by Lawson, Geuna, Fernández-Zubieta, Kataishi, and Torselli (Chapter 3) provides a detailed analysis of scientific productivity for a sample of about 630 academic researchers working in the area of biomedical research in the United Kingdom and the United States. Based on a reconstruction of these researchers' full careers derived from curriculum vitae information, the chapter assesses the impact of postdoctoral experience on follow-on researcher performance in terms of both the number of and impact/quality-adjusted publications (top journals and average impact). For the United States, they find an overall performance premium and a positive postdoctoral effect in terms of average impact, especially for postdoctoral experience in a top-quality United States institution. The "US postdoctoral training" advantage is transferable geographically; the authors show that United Kingdom researchers who return to their home country after a postdoctoral period in the United States (especially at a top-quality institution) achieve publications of significantly higher average impact/quality in their later academic careers. Finally, the authors show that United States postdoctorates who remain in the United States publish more and produce publications with higher impact/quality than those who move to the United Kingdom. A surprising finding is that studying for a PhD in the United States does not increase future performance; United States students who studied for their PhD degrees in the United States ultimately publish articles with lower average impact/quality than achieved by those who moved to the United States for their postdoctoral experience.

Chapter 4, by Fernández-Zubieta, Geuna, and Lawson, looks at the relationship between mobility and productivity within the national system, paying particular attention to the other two types of mobility identified in Chapter 1: social and intersectoral mobility. Like the previous chapter, the analysis is based on full career information extracted from curriculum vitae for 171 science and engineering researchers in the United Kingdom. The study finds no evidence that mobility per se increases academic performance. A move to a higher-ranked department has a positive and weakly significant impact, whereas downward mobility reduces researcher productivity. In line with the literature, job mobility is shown to be associated with a short-term decrease in performance, arguably as a result of adjustment costs. The overall performance of researchers who move to academia from industry is not significantly different from the performance of "pure" academics; the short-term publication disadvantage suffered by researchers moving from business seems to vanish soon after joining academia.

The next three chapters look at different aspects of the brain-drain versus brain-circulation debate. Chapter 5 by Ganguli deals with the issue of self-selection of migrants in the case of the exodus of Russian scientists after the collapse of the USSR in 1991. Using a large data set of over 15,000 Russian scientists who were publishing in the top Soviet journals just before the end of the USSR, Ganguli identifies that 14% of the sample had emigrated by 2005. Emigrants tended to be men, relatively young in age, with higher than average scientific productivity. The most skilled left early in the transition period, migrating especially to the United States. These results are consistent with a positive selection bias, which increases with migration costs and the wage premium, as predicted by the theoretical framework presented in this chapter.

The chapter by Freeman and Huang (Chapter 6) studies the rapid development of the science and engineering system in China, especially since the mid-1990s. Freeman and Huang highlight how international mobility and international collaboration has allowed China to rapidly catch up with most advanced countries in science and engineering. Their study provides detailed information on the role played by international student and researcher mobility in the modernization of the Chinese university system. A combination of policies to support the outward flow of students, and in a second period, policies to incentivize return flows characterize the increased globalization of Chinese scientists. The United States has been particularly important in this process. By 2012, about 60% of Chinese students going abroad were moving to the United States and accounted for around 25% of foreign students in the United States. International collaboration measured by coauthorship confirms the special interaction between China and the United States; in 2012, slightly less than 50% of China's international collaborations were with United States authors. Finally, Freeman and Huang analyze international collaboration in more detail and provide evidence of a positive correlation between output impact measures and Chinese researchers with either international work experience or collaboration with foreign coauthors.

Appelt, van Beuzekom, Galindo-Rueda, and de Pinho's chapter (Chapter 7) also uses publications as a source of information on the location of authors and their international scientific collaboration network. They adopt an aggregate-level approach to investigating the drivers of scientist mobility over the period 1996–2011, and present a gravity model for bilateral data on international scientist mobility flows. They find that although the United States plays a dominant role in international scientist mobility, mobility flows involve many origin and destination countries. Bidirectional mobility flows are often similar in magnitude, pointing to a large share of scientists moving between more and less advanced countries. They show that the system is characterized by the circulation of scientists rather than simple outward migration. Appelt, van Beuzekom, Galindo-Rueda, and de Pinho test five exploratory models to understand the factors correlated with bilateral flows. They control for (1) geographic, economic, and scientific proximity, (2) the level of bilateral migration, (3) science, technology and industry, and economic factors, and (4) policy-related factors. They also analyze the role played by scientific collaboration and international student flows. In addition to the traditional factors related to migration, their results highlight the important role of scientific collaboration and the flow of tertiary-level students in the opposite direction, from destination to origin countries.

Mobility to the United States compared with intra-European mobility is the focus of Chapter 8 by Veugelers and Van Bouwel, who examine what drives intra-European Union and EU–US mobility, and particularly the motivations for international mobility. Using original information from a sample of some 1,000 mobile, European-born researchers who were awarded their PhD in Europe, they study what characterizes mobile researchers to the United States compared with those who choose another intra-EU destination. They show that while personal characteristics are not significant, career motivations tend to be strongly correlated to the decision to move to the United States. In particular, career progression and the opportunity to work with "star scientists" motivates researchers' moves to the United States rather than to another EU country. Chapter 8 also analyzes whether earlier intra-European student mobility affects the subsequent mobility decision of a move to the United States or within Europe. Studying for a PhD degree outside the birth country is correlated with an increased probability of inter-EU mobility; however, if the PhD award is in a country with strong scientific performance, the researcher is more likely to move to the United States.

The last two chapters are based on Japanese data and investigate research scientists' careers. Chapter 9 by Lawson and Shibayama focuses on the initial placement and successive promotion steps, from PhD training to early career job transition and international mobility, for a sample of 370 bioscience professors in Japan. Lawson and Shibayama link career steps to institutional ranking, paying particular attention to entry and careers in the seven top imperial universities in Japan. Confirming evidence from the United States, they find that the prestige of the PhD-awarding institution is the best predictor of initial placement. They also find some evidence of inbreeding being more common in prestigious institutions, and that early career job transition and international mobility are not correlated with promotion. They estimate the time to promotion, highlighting that mobility speeds promotion only if the move is associated with a promotion (usually in a lower-ranked university), and that foreign research visits decrease the time to promotion.

Chapter 10 by Geuna and Shibayama looks at a special type of mobility identified in Chapter 1: occupation mobility. It analyzes a move by an academic researcher into a position in academia that focuses on non-research activities (teaching and administration) or a move to industry. Using a new database that includes the complete cohort of 14,000 Japanese PhD graduates in hard sciences in the period 1985–1989, Geuna and Shibayama study the probability of exiting academic research. Female academics, and researchers in less prestigious universities, have a lower probability of embarking on an academic research career and tend to exit academic research more quickly after having started along this path. An academic's scientific productivity and academic network reduce the probability of moving out of a university research career but individual and institutional network effects play a role, mainly for senior researchers.

One effect of Chinese and Indian researchers, as well as researchers from other countries, leading and working at top US university laboratories, and Greek and Italian researchers, among others, heading top UK departments, is that the public funding disbursed in one country benefits another country since a significant share of the education costs (up to the undergraduate/graduate level) of foreign-born researchers are covered by public funding in their country of origin. But some of the benefits accruing to this education investment are captured by the country of origin. As long as science remains open and the benefits of science are available to all countries, international mobility and international collaboration benefit all countries. Clearly, some of the benefits from university research are more easily appropriable at the local level; however, the Internet is reducing the distance from home for diaspora communities, thereby making localization less relevant and network links more important.

REFERENCES

Auriol, L., Misu, M., & Freeman, R. (2013). *Careers of doctorate holders: Analysis of labour market and mobility indicators.* Organisation of Economic Cooperation and Development, STI Working Papers 2013/4. Paris: OECD.

Chang, W. Y., & Milan, L. M. (2012). *International mobility and employment characteristics among recent recipients of US doctorates.* Arlington: National Science Foundation. National Center for Science and Engineering Statistics.

De Ridder-Symoens, H. (Ed.). (1992). *A history of the university in Europe. Volume 1 – universities in the middle ages.* Cambridge: Cambridge University Press.

De Ridder-Symoens, H. (Ed.). (1996). *A history of the university in Europe. Volume 2 – universities in the early modern Europe.* Cambridge: Cambridge University Press.

Geuna, A. (1998). The Internationalisation of European Universities: A return to medieval roots'. *Minerva, 36,* 253–270.

Moguerou, P., & Di Pietrogiacomo, P. (2008). *Stock, career and mobility of researchers in the EU.* Luxembourg: Office for Official Publications of the European Communities.

Chapter 1

What Do We Know of the Mobility of Research Scientists and Impact on Scientific Production

Ana Fernández-Zubieta[1], Aldo Geuna[2,3], Cornelia Lawson[2,3,4]

[1]*Institute for Advanced Social Studies – Spanish Council for Scientific Research, Campo Santo de los Mártires, Córdoba, Spain;* [2]*Department of Economics and Statistics Cognetti De Martiis, Università di Torino, Turin, Italy;* [3]*BRICK, Collegio Carlo Alberto, Moncalieri, Turin, Italy;* [4]*School of Sociology and Social Policy, University of Nottingham, Nottingham, UK*

Chapter Outline

1. INTRODUCTION

The establishment of research networks and the mobility of researchers across different countries, fields, and sectors have become a major policy objective in recent years (OECD, 2008; EC, 2012). Studies of mobile inventors' social capital show that links to the original location are maintained and that knowledge flows are deeply embedded in labor mobility (Agrawal, Cockburn, & McHale, 2006, 2011; Almeida & Kogut, 1999; Breschi & Lissoni, 2003). Thus, mobility generates positive spillovers among firms (Cooper, 2001; Møen, 2005), sectors (Crespi, Geuna, & Nesta, 2007; Zucker, Darby, & Brewer, 1998), academic institutions (Azoulay, Zivin, & Sampat, 2012), and countries (Hunt & Gauthier-Loiselle, 2010; Moser, Voena, & Waldinger, 2014). The evidence also shows that university scientists can increase their individual visibility and credibility by moving to a different academic environment and improving their performance, patterns of collaboration, and career development (Azoulay et al., 2012). Therefore, both the research system and the individual researcher can benefit from mobility.

Recent developments in the research system are demanding a better understanding of the consequences of mobility across locations, sectors, and career stages. First, globalization of the research community and increasing levels of international mobility (Auriol, Misu, & Freeman, 2013; Franzoni, Scellato, & Stephan, 2012; Moguerou & Di Pietrogiacomo, 2008) and collaboration (Glanzel, Debackere, & Meyer, 2008) are making the geographical mobility of researchers more relevant to an adequate flow of knowledge across locations. Second, the importance of improved knowledge transfer between research sectors (Gassmann, Enkel, & Chesbrough, 2010; Howells, Ramlogan, & Cheng, 2012; Powell, Koput, & Smith-Doerr, 1996) calls for a stronger emphasis on moves between public and private sectors. Third, the increased number of foreign PhD students and PhD graduates joining firms, and the greater number of fixed-term academic positions and the rapid diversification of academic work roles, are requiring a better understanding of the labor markets for researchers and the career consequences of mobility (Enders, 2005; Enders & Weert, 2004; Mangematin, 2000; Stephan, 2012; Zellner, 2003).

This chapter focuses on the mobility of academic researchers across locations, sectors, and career stages; its social relevance; and its consequences for researcher performance. We propose an approach to the analysis of researcher mobility that considers multiple mobility events throughout a researcher's career (Eurobarometer, 2005). We start by reviewing the relevant literature on researcher mobility to understand its increasing importance, advantages, and disadvantages. We develop a typology of mobility events based on a life-course perspective, which allows us to present and select the more relevant mobility events during a researcher's career. We also discuss the modeling difficulties (including selection bias, unobserved heterogeneity, and reverse causality) related to analyzing the effects of researcher mobility, and we suggest ways to overcome them.

2. WHY ARE WE INCREASINGLY INTERESTED IN RESEARCHER MOBILITY?

Researchers have always moved across countries and sectors, and throughout their careers. Current research systems, however, are characterized by higher levels of internationalization and increased importance of intersector mobility and collaboration, as well as career diversification (temporariness and changes in work roles), all of which are making researcher mobility more significant to the development of the research system.

Data from the Organisation for Economic Co-operation and Development and the United Nations Educational, Scientific and Cultural Organization (UNESCO) Institute for Statistics (hereafter UIS) show a five-fold increase in foreign students worldwide between 1975 and 2012. Since 2000 alone their number has almost doubled (OECD, 2014),[1] whereas in the United States, the number of international students has increased by 32% since 2000–2001 (Institute of International Education, 2012). The trend is similar in the United Kingdom, where the number of international students in research degree programs in UK higher education institutions increased threefold between 1994/1995 and 2012/2013.[2] There is less precise and less comparable information available on the nationalities of research scientists. Moguerou and Di Pietrogiacomo (2008) show that the share of nonnational science and technology professionals without citizenship in the 27 countries of the European Union at that time increased from 1.6% to 2.4% in nine European member states between 2000 and 2006. An analysis of the mobility patterns of published authors listed on Scopus between 1996 and 2011 shows that the share of mobile authors differs among countries and regions. In Switzerland nearly 20% of authors have had a foreign affiliation, whereas in the rest of Western Europe the share is 12%, in Southern Europe it is 9%, and in the United States it is 7.4%; in China, Japan, and Brazil, however, this share is only 5% (OECD, 2013).[3] The same study shows that the United States is the most internationally connected because it is the most important destination for researchers from other parts of the world (confirmed in Franzoni et al., 2012). In the United Kingdom, one of the European countries with a high level of internationalization, Higher Education Statistics Agency data show that in 2012/2013, 28% of research-active academic staff were of a non-UK nationality.

---

1. Europe hosts about 48% of foreign students (with a large share of intra-European mobility), North America 21%, and Asia 18%. Numbers of international students in Australia, Africa, and Central and South America also have grown, showing that this is a truly global trend. More than half of all foreign students originate in Asia, with China accounting for 18.6% of international students (OECD, 2014).
2. Higher Education Statistics Agency, Students, Qualifiers and Staff data tables, https://www.hesa.ac.uk/content/view/1973/239/, [accessed 17.04.15].
3. While in Switzerland and the United States newcomers outnumber returnees, the reverse applies to the rest of Europe and Asia. A 16-country study that surveyed academics about their mobility found similar patterns but a much larger proportion of movers, perhaps because it included mobility before first publication (Franzoni et al., 2012).

At the same time, an increasing share of researchers, especially among post-doctoral researchers, is leaving academia because of a lack of available academic positions (Stephan, 2012). For instance, in the United States about 37% of doctoral graduates are employed by private-sector firms; the shares are similar for Germany (39%) and the United Kingdom (32%).[4] In Japan about 56% of all PhD students for whom destinations are known moved to take up positions outside of academia after graduating (NISTEP, 2009). Once doctorate holders join a specific sector following the completion of their PhD degree, they are primarily mobile within that sector, especially in countries with high-intensity research and development, such as Germany and the United States (OECD, 2014).

Within academia, there has been a greater shift toward employment with part-time and fixed-term contracts, particularly through an increase in positions financed by external grants. For example, in the United States the number of postdoctorates in science, engineering, and health tripled between 1990 and 2012 (NAP, 2014), whereas in colleges the share of contingent (part-time or nontenured) faculty increased to 75.5% in 2011 (from just 18.5% in 1969; Roach, 2014). In Germany the share of externally funded positions doubled between 2000 and 2010, with the majority of that increase represented by part-time positions (EFI, 2012). In the United Kingdom fixed-term, part-time contracts increased by 19% between 2011 and 2012 alone (Locke, 2014); a third of positions are now temporary, and a third are part-time. In Japan and Korea more than 50% of academic teaching staff in universities and colleges are employed through part-time contracts (Stephan, 2012; MEXT, 2012). There is also a perceived greater emphasis on activities that are outside teaching and research roles. Teichler, Arimoto, and Cummings (2013) found that 30% of academic time is spent on other tasks; compared with a 1992 survey, however, they identified only a small shift toward these other activities.

In this chapter we focus on geographical (researchers changing countries); intersectoral (researchers changing sectors, especially between the public and private sectors); and career (temporariness and changing work roles) dimensions of mobility, and highlight their consequences for individual researchers and the research system as a whole.

2.1 Geographical Dimension: International Mobility of Researchers and "Brain Circulation"

Researchers leaving their home countries traditionally was of concern to national authorities and seen as potentially diminishing their national research

---

4. For numbers see Auriol et al. (2013) for the United States, KBWN (2013) for Germany, and Vitae (2010) for the United Kingdom. The numbers are comparable to the Netherlands, Belgium, and Denmark (33–37% of all PhD holders). Employment status was measured 1.5 years after graduation for German PhDs, 3 years after graduation for UK PhDs, and in 2010 for all others regardless of year of graduation. In countries with low-intensity research and development, for example, countries in eastern and southern Europe, after higher education, the government was the most important destination sector (Auriol et al., 2013).

and economic potential. However, improved international communications and the return of nationals from abroad have caused the geographical mobility of researchers ("brain drain") to be seen as bringing possible benefits to the origin countries and the mobile researchers ("brain circulation").

Neither geographical mobility nor the possible associated effects are new phenomena. The international travels of early scientists demonstrate the historical relevance of the geographical mobility of researchers and its costs and benefits. The concept of brain drain emerged first in the 1960s in a report from the Royal Society of London on the migration of British engineers and scientists to the United States (Rhode, 1991). Brain drain now refers more broadly to the unidirectional migration of skilled workers from less developed to more developed countries or regions. The "brain drain gain" debate focuses on the benefits to receiving countries and losses for sending countries or regions. In the 1970s the laissez-passer of the "dominant," "cosmopolitan" view defended the compensation and overall efficiency of migration for economic development (Berry & Soligo, 1969; Grubel & Scott, 1977; Johnson, 1968). Some authors (e.g., Nerdrum & Sarpebakken, 2006; Patinkin, 1968; Regets, 2001) were critical of this problem being analyzed in terms of efficiency at the country level and claimed that other aspects, such as imperfections related to regional labor markets and individual opportunities for career development, as well as other levels of analysis, should be considered (Ackers, 2005; Ackers & Oliver, 2007; Gaillard & Gaillard, 1998).

While the migration of scientists is normally considered as beneficial to the host/receiving country, it can result in the displacement of home-grown researchers. For example, following a high influx of high-skilled immigrants to a firm, native science and engineering workers experience lower wages and longer career transition periods (Pekkala Kerr & Kerr, 2013). In the United States wage decreases have been observed, especially for postdoctorates, with larger entry of foreign doctoral scientists (Borjas, 2009), although there is no evidence of job displacement beyond postdoctoral positions (Stephan, 2012). Borjas and Doran (2012), studying the case of a large Soviet mathematician influx into the United States, found that American academics showed reduced publication performance and increased out-mobility in fields in which Soviet mathematicians specialized. This was perhaps a result of the academic institutional environment, which was able to support only limited growth.

The increased return of scientists to their countries of origin (Saxenian, 1999), and continued links with diasporas (Agrawal, Kapur, McHale, & Oettl, 2011), have brought a new perspective to the discussion and analysis of geographical mobility. The brain circulation concept (Johnson & Regets, 1998; Mahroum, 1998, 2000) treats geographical mobility as a two-way process that acknowledges the benefits that those leaving and those returning to sending countries bring (Ackers, 2005; Barre, Hernandez, Meyer, & Vinck, 2003; Meyer, 2001; Moguerou, 2006; Meyer & Wattiaux, 2006). For example, collaborations between Indians abroad with their communities back home have been found to increase knowledge flows from the host country to India (Agrawal et al., 2011). Ethnic knowledge flows also have been confirmed in other studies (e.g., Agrawal, Kapur, & McHale, 2008; Oettl & Agrawal, 2008), Kerr (2008) showed that a US patent with a Chinese inventor receives at least 20% more cites from Chinese patents than the average citation of a US patent.

The advancement of international communication techniques (Ding, Levin, Stephan, & Winkler, 2010) has made geographical mobility a process that sending countries can benefit from. Also, changes in the patterns and motivations of researcher mobility blur the boundary between migration and mobility (King, 2002), highlighting the importance of focusing on the return of migrants (Boeri, Brücker, Docquier & Rapoport 2012). From this perspective, a sojourn abroad is not considered a migration process with clear winners and losers (brain gain and brain drain); rather, it is considered a reciprocal process, allowing individuals and countries or regions to benefit from current collaborations and future returns (brain circulation). Survey studies of academic researchers confirm that a large share maintain collaborative links with their home countries (Baruffaldi & Landoni, 2012; Scellato, Franzoni, & Stephan, 2015), although primarily if the origin country has a large local research base and the individual moved at a career stage, such as postdoctoral work or a position, that had allowed the formation of a home country network (Scellato et al., 2015; Gibson & McKenzie, 2012). The increasing share of internationally coauthored papers (BIS, 2013; Glanzel et al., 2008) is further evidence of the importance of international collaborations for knowledge creation.[5] The chapter by Appelt et al. (Chapter 7), which is based on bilateral international scientists flows calculated from publication data for the period 1996–2011, provides support for the brain circulation view of a complex network of international mobile students and scientists with high levels of international cooperation (copublication).

Greatly improved and cheaper communication channels, the globalization of the research community, and the high relevance of international scientific networks are increasing return opportunities following geographical mobility. This suggests that geographical mobility could become even more relevant, and that countries and researchers should benefit even more in the future. This would seem to demand a broader conceptualization of geographical researcher mobility.[6]

2.2 Intersector Dimension: University-to-Business Mobility and Knowledge Transfer

The birth of "Big Science" (Price, 1963) and the necessary collaboration between governments, universities, and industries point to the relevance of intersector

---

5. The shares of internationally coauthored papers in 1991–2005 increased from 13.5% to 27.7%; 12% to 26.8%, and 9.8% to 22.4% for 15 countries in the European Union, the United States, and Japan, respectively (Glanzel et al., 2008).
6. For example, virtual mobility as the concept of multiple affiliations and honorary appointments could be considered a new specification of the geographical dimension of mobility.

collaborations for research development.[7] At that time, several authors in the sociology of science became interested in intersector job mobility. The works of Marcson (1960), Krohn (1961), Kornhauser (1962), and Hagstrom (1965) analyze the "role strain" problem caused by job transitions between an academic and a business environment, and they focus on the problem of adaptation caused by different norms and values in different research sectors. The focus has shifted more recently to researcher mobility as a mechanism for knowledge transfer between sectors.

Research scientists are particularly relevant to the dynamics of knowledge production and dissemination; much scientific knowledge is characterized by embeddedness and tacitness. Location and distance are important for explaining the innovation process, and the significance of knowledge spillovers and mobility allowing access to new knowledge is growing (Agrawal et al., 2006, 2008; Audretsch & Feldman, 2004).[8] Knowledge spillovers tend to be bounded geographically, and researcher mobility can influence this feature. So far, the knowledge spillovers literature has focused on patents (Henderson, Jaffe, & Trajtenberg, 1998; Jaffe, 1989), investments, and spinoffs (Bozeman, 2000; Mowery & Shane, 2002) as mechanisms of knowledge transfer. Rather than being "in the air," these spillovers tend to be embodied by researcher mobility (Azoulay et al., 2012). In particular, knowledge spillovers from academia to industry tend to rely on researchers' moves. In addition, spillovers from academia are stronger when embodied as researchers, which suggests the criticality of researcher mobility for the knowledge dissemination process. Azoulay et al. (2012) analyze interregional mobility patterns and their effects on knowledge dissemination for a sample of elite scientists, showing that patent-to-article and patent-to-patent citations in a scientist's location of origin decline following a move to another country, whereas article-to-article citations do not. Importantly, citations from the destination location increase after a move. These results stress the importance of location for knowledge spillovers.

However, little attention has been paid to the intersector mobility of researchers, and few papers look at the mobility of academics to industry; most focus on academic entrepreneurship (e.g., Audretsch & Stephan, 1999; Stuart & Ding, 2006; Toole & Czarnitzki, 2010). A study by Zucker, Darby, and Torero (2002) considered the mobility of academic stars to industry, on a full- or part-time basis, and founds that academics are valuable to firms and that their moves depend largely on mobility costs and the availability of other outside options. Crespi et al. (2007) looked at the sector mobility of academic inventors in the European context and found that academics with more valuable inventions are more likely

---

7. See Merton (1938) for an analysis of the socioeconomic factors in the origins of the institutionalization of science and the relationship between science and industry.

8. There is a rich literature on the importance of hiring for knowledge acquisition and firm performance (Almeida & Kogut, 1999; Agrawal et al., 2006; Ejsing et al., 2013; Herstad et al., 2015; Møen, 2005; Palomeras & Melero, 2010; Rosenkopf & Almeida, 2003; Singh & Agrawal, 2011).

to move to industry. Works by Herrera, Muñoz-Doyague, and Nieto (2010); Ejsing, Kaiser, Kongsted, and Laursen (2013); and Herstad, Sandven, and Ebensberger (2015) show that scientists who move to private firms from universities or research institutes have a positive effect on both the inputs to and outputs of firms' innovation processes. These studies show that researcher mobility is a relevant mechanism of knowledge and technology transfer, and they shed light on some of the factors that affect the probability of a move from public research to industry. These authors indicate that researchers' intersectoral mobility is crucial for the knowledge dissemination process, and it might also be important for explaining the process of dissemination via mechanisms other than patenting and licensing.

Similar to the case of geographical mobility, intersectoral mobility has been considered so far as a single (one-time, one-way) event. The increasing frequency and importance of intersectoral mobility for the dynamics of knowledge production and dissemination requires analysis that considers multiple mobility events.

2.3 Career Dimension: Temporariness and Work Role Changes

The linear career progress from PhD graduate to professor is no longer straightforward because of the existence of more part-time and short-term contracts (Blaxter, Hughes, & Tight, 1998; Stephan & Ma, 2005; Stephan, 2012). Alternative work arrangements, postdoctoral appointments, and other types of temporary employment contracts have become common in universities. These developments raise questions about their effect on researchers' career development. The "extension of the educational career ladder" (Zumeta, 1985) is a source of temporariness and uncertainty (Cruz-Castro & Sanz-Menendez, 2005; Stephan, 2012; Smith-Doerr, 2006), which can create problems for the future recruitment of researchers (Enders, 2005; Enders & Weert, 2004; Stephan, 2012). More fragmented career paths and a reduced focus on scientific research result in a lack of autonomy and fewer opportunities for specialization (Stephan, 2012; Smith-Doerr, 2006). For example, Gaughan and Robin (2004), Jonkers (2011), and Cruz-Castro and Sanz-Menendez (2011), in studies from France, Argentina, and Spain, respectively, show that postdoctoral positions delay promotion to a tenured/permanent position. This fragmentation and job insecurity could be driving promising scientists out of academia (Stephan, 2012) and could be negatively affecting scientific knowledge production and advancement in general.

The increase in temporary positions could also be an indication of a changing academic market that is requiring more flexibility in relation to a research career (Enders, 2005). Temporary positions might, then, be positive for performance and career development by enlarging networks and encouraging interdisciplinarity (Rhoten & Parker, 2004; Su, 2011; Zubieta, 2009). For example, postdoctoral stays have been shown to improve academic performance (Su, 2011) and the scientific impact of academic research (McGuinnis, Allison, & Long, 1982). These positive effects are evident in the context of the quality of the institutions hosting

	GEOGRAPHICAL	INTERSECTORAL	CAREER
(−)	Brain Drain/Displacement	Loss of Talent	Job Insecurity/Loss of Talent
(+)	Brain Circulation/ Productivity Increase	Knowledge Transfer	Labor Market Flexibility

FIGURE 1   Main advantages and disadvantages of researchers' mobility.

postdoctoral researchers (McGuinnis et al., 1982; Long, 1978). Temporary positions in the early career stage could also be positive from a job market perspective by allowing better career matches (Jovanovic, 1979; Parsons, 1991).[9] From a labor market perspective, temporary positions might reduce the cost of science. Also, temporary positions are more widespread among foreign researchers (Lan, 2012; Stephan, 2012), indicating that labor costs may be a factor (Stephan, 2012). Therefore, it is important to determine whether temporary positions are a mechanism to attract talent and to improve research capacity (as discussed in Chapter 3 by Lawson et al.), or if they work to create poorer employment conditions, which, in the long-term, could diminish national research potential (Freeman, 2006).

Researchers also are being required to take on increasingly diverse work roles (Blaxter et al., 1998; Enders, 2005; Kim & Cha, 2000), raising concerns about the consequences. Encouragement and reinforcement of knowledge transfer activities and applied research might be working to diminish other traditional academic roles and to crowd out basic research and the public dissemination of science (Blumenthal, Campbell, Anderson, Causino, & Louis, 1996; Heller & Eisenberg, 1998). Increased teaching workloads can also reduce research activity and decrease promotion opportunities (Stephan, 2012). Similarly, faculty time allocated to service and administration activities reduces the opportunities for research and thus the award of tenure and promotion (Porter, 2007). These negative effects on careers risk researchers being pushed to take up temporary employment or move out of research. However, these new work roles could also generate new projects and ideas for research and open new career opportunities for researchers. For example, Lee (2000) and Coate, Barnett, and Williams (2001) point to the importance of the bottom-up generation of ideas through teaching, consulting, and knowledge transfer activities.

Figure 1 summarizes the main advantages and disadvantages of researcher mobility along the three dimensions discussed in this section. Geographical

9. In the context of job matching, young researchers lack experience, making the return on their investment in information greater, and their probability of job mobility higher, compared with older researchers, who are more likely to have found their optimal match. Young researchers are required to experience more job changes in the search for an optimal match (Jovanovic, 1979; Parsons, 1991). In the market structure approach (Ryan, 2001), however, the labor market structure causes high mobility (turnover) among the young. The job rewards offered to young people are smaller, and it takes longer to achieve high wages. This encourages job mobility, which frequently has a negative effect.

mobility can lead to a brain drain for the sending countries and to the displacement of researchers in the receiving countries. A significant strand in the academic and policy literature, however, acknowledges the benefits from brain circulation and the positive returns to sending countries and institutions. The literature on the intersectoral mobility of researchers focuses on their role as facilitators of the knowledge transfer process, while also acknowledging that loss of talent through mobility out of academia can damage scientific research. In the context of career development, researcher mobility and higher availability of positions could introduce flexibility into the labor market and reduce the costs of research. These features also allow individual researchers to find better matches and new research directions, providing opportunities to adjust their working lives to suit their preferences, which potentially could improve the performance of the research sector. A declining academic job market with more fixed-term positions and the incompatibilities among the multiple academic work roles could, however, result in job insecurity, the loss of promising researchers, and the inability to pursue groundbreaking research, with potentially detrimental effects on science in general.

3. MOBILITY FROM A LIFE COURSE PERSPECTIVE

Although geographical, intersectoral, and career mobility are not new phenomena, changes in the research system—internationalization, increasing intersector collaboration, and diversification of career and work roles—make researcher mobility more relevant to the dynamics of knowledge creation and dissemination. New approaches to the analysis of mobility show that in order to be able to properly account for and assess these changes, it is crucial to adopt a life course perspective to the consideration of mobility because we can expect a relationship between sequential mobility experiences. For example, inferior employment prospects and increased job mobility (e.g., an increase in postdoctoral positions) among young researchers is reducing their job prospects and performance as senior researchers (Stephan & Ma, 2005). Also, Parey and Waldinger (2011), among others, suggest that there is a strong relationship between mobile researchers and previous mobility events. Therefore, it seems that there are career and mobility path dependencies. This broader approach tends both to increase the scope of analysis and to reinforce the advantages of increased researcher mobility across its dimensions: geographical, intersectoral, and career.

3.1 A Typology of Research Mobility

Mobility can be defined as a change, and types of mobility can be defined according to what is changed. First, it is important to differentiate between educational mobility and job-to-job mobility. The former refers to mobility among students, ending with the completion of a PhD; the latter refers to changing employers and includes the postdoctoral period. Student mobility has been quite well studied because of the better availability of data (Moguerou & Di Pietrogiacomo, 2008), but there exists little work on researchers' job-to-job mobility. Changes of employers can be analyzed in terms of occupational mobility (changes to occupational status) and sector mobility (changes in the sector of employment). All these mobility dimensions can be qualified by a change in geographic location (geographic mobility), by prestige (social mobility) of the sending and receiving institutions, and by subject focus (disciplinary mobility). The main types of mobility reviewed in this chapter[10] and their defining changes are listed below:

- Educational mobility: change across levels of formal education
- Job-to-job mobility: change of employer
- Occupational mobility: change of occupational status (e.g., job profile and content)
- Sectoral mobility: change in the sector of employment
- Geographic mobility: change of location
- Social mobility: change in social position
- Disciplinary mobility: change of disciplinary focus.

3.1.1 Educational Mobility

Educational mobility refers to changes in levels of formal education. Although education levels are important criteria for selecting the population for an analysis of other types of mobility (e.g., a highly skilled population), it is used primarily as an indicator of the future supply of researchers. A more refined proxy for the educational mobility of researchers is the international mobility of PhD candidates and analyses of specific mobility programs for students (e.g., Erasmus and Marie Curie programs). Analyses of these programs indicate that there is a relationship between mobile researchers and previous mobility events (e.g., Ackers, 2004, 2005). For instance, Van der Sande, Ackers, and Gill (2005), as well as Hansen (2003), show that more than 60% of Marie Curie scholarship holders had previously lived in another country.

The mobility and migration literature does not consider mobility during the early stages of education, even though this "provides the 'seeds' for future international skilled labour" (Balaz & Williams, 2004, p. 235). Mobility during education is instead used primarily to explain future mobility, for example, taking up a postdoctoral or job position in another country or institution (Ackers, 2004). Ackers (2005) suggests that it might be "more 'efficient' to address some of the issues around undergraduate mobility retrospectively" (p. 108) since a large share of mobile undergraduates will not progress to become researchers.

---

10. Employment mobility, which considers transitions between unemployment, employment, and inactivity, or changes to the proportions of full-time versus part-time employment, is generally the focus of labor economics. Employment mobility is usually measured through changes in the International Labor Organization (ILO) survey categories. Because of the small number of observations, however, ILO surveys are not appropriate for measuring researcher mobility (Moguerou & Di Pietrogiacomo, 2008).

Sretenova (2003) proposes a focus on postdoctoral or more senior scientists, that is, on job-to-job mobility, in order to study the mobility of research scientists.

3.1.2 Job-to-Job Mobility

Job-to-job mobility refers to a move from one employer to another. Research scientists tend to move more to improve their opportunities for research and move less to achieve greater economic rewards. For example, research scientists use job mobility to access the best scientific equipment and scientific teams (Martin-Rovet, 2003), and to improve their career prospects either at home or abroad (Ackers, 2005). In particular, a job move to another country is frequently linked to academic career progression and performance (e.g., Ackers, 2005). In addition, other characteristics of the national academic labor market—for example, a transparent and meritocratic recruitment system with a clear promotion system linked to "objective" evaluation procedures that reward excellence—have been shown to drive job mobility among research scientists (Ackers, 2005; Fernandez-Zubieta & van Bavel, 2011; Sockanathan, 2004). Although researcher mobility in the United States is associated with scientific merit and is encouraged by universities, many European countries are characterized by academic inbreeding and a reluctance among academics to move (Stephan, 2012). For example, over 59% of university professors in Spain were awarded chairing positions by their PhD-awarding institutions (Cruz-Castro & Sanz-Menendez, 2011). The importance of social ties in achieving promotion is very high and further reduces the probability of mobility (Pezzoni, Sterzi, & Lissoni, 2012; Zinovyeva & Bagues, 2015).

3.1.3 Occupational Mobility

Occupational mobility refers to changes in individual occupational status. Occupational mobility is usually measured by changes in International Standard Classification of Occupations (ISCO) categories. This criterion cannot, however, be applied to researchers because most job changes would not result in a change in ISCO category. Thus, we need to consider other substantial changes in job profiles and job content in order to analyze researchers' occupational mobility. Career progression is a driver of occupational mobility. Changes within the academic career, for example, promotion from assistant professor to associate and then full professor, are usually associated with positive changes in job profile and job content and provide access to additional resources. Therefore, job changes that result in a promotion could be considered a proxy for occupational mobility. A considerable number of studies have focused on the determinants of academic promotion, showing the importance of a higher rank to enable full access to resources and institutional advantages (e.g., Long, Allison, & McGinnis, 1993). In addition, gender discrimination in academia has been shown to operate through promotion (Ginther & Hayes, 2003; McDowell, Singell, & Stater, 2006; Ginther & Kahn, 2004). Occupational mobility can also be used to assess other types of mobility. For example, Oswald and Ralsmark (2008) show that 75% of associate professors in the top 10 economic departments among US universities did their first degree outside the United States; that is, they engaged in a type of educational mobility.

Occupational mobility also captures the transition from research-active to research-inactive academics. In a typical academic career, researcher time is split among research, teaching, and administration/service. However, not all scientists are involved in doing administration or teaching activities, and not all teachers engage in research. While all PhD holders conduct some research at the start of their careers, some might have decided or been pushed to abandon research and focus on teaching, administration, or (technical) support tasks (see Chapter 10 by Geuna and Shibayama, for a study of occupational mobility in Japan).

3.1.4 Sectoral Mobility

Sectoral mobility refers to job changes that involve a move to a new position (research-related or not) in a company or a public research organization, or return mobility from nonacademic sectors into academia. In particular, mobility from academia to business is considered one of the most important occupational changes for a research scientist. Different sectors have different evaluation and recognition systems, and mobility between them could have different effects on a research career. Since the study by Kornhauser published in 1962, more recent studies have examined the different drivers and effects of a move from academia to industry (Crespi et al., 2007; Herrera et al., 2010, 2015; Zucker et al., 2002), to a public research center (Ponomariov & Boardman, 2010), to government, and to other not-for-profit organizations (Su & Bozeman, 2009). For example, Hottenrott and Lawson (2014) showed that scientific researchers in research-intensive university departments are equally or more likely to move to industry than to remain in academia; a focus on contract research, however, is more closely associated with a move to a public or government research center or a small firm.[11] In terms of the individual level effects of a move out of academia, Toole and Czarnitzki (2010) found that US academics who left academia to start their own firms experienced a decline in research performance.

However, mobility back to academia and experience in other sectors have been understudied. Previous industry experience and intersectoral affiliations might provide substantial benefits for researchers and universities because they are conducive to network creation and may allow those scientists to bridge between sectors. Indeed, Dietz and Bozeman (2005) found a positive effect of industry experience on patent outcomes, implying that the researchers involved have a stronger footing in commercially driven research, which may also benefit university research. Lin and Bozeman (2006) showed that previous industry experience also has a

11. De Graaf and van Der Wal (2008) suggest that small businesses are more similar to small government organizations than to large business.

positive impact on the productivity of academics affiliated with research centers if the institutional conditions are appropriate. Ponomariov and Boardman (2010) extended these benefits to include academics affiliated with new collaborative research centers and showed that this affiliation enhances scientific production, as well as cross-discipline and cross-sector collaborations. Fernandez-Zubieta et al. (Chapter 4) show that, following a short period of adjustment, the publication performance of researchers with previous job experiences in the private sector is equal to that of researchers who have always worked in academia. Previous industry experience and intersectoral affiliations could provide benefits to researchers and universities by enabling more wide-ranging networks and bridging between sectors. These findings indicate that research scientists are able to adjust to new sectoral demands. Although we observe different values within sectors, De Graaf and van Der Wal (2008), in a study of 60 switchers between the public and private sectors in the Netherlands, found that the values espoused by public-to-private and private-to-public switchers were similar.

3.1.5 Geographic Mobility

Geographic mobility refers to a move from one location to another, involving different countries or different regions. Analyses of geographic mobility in the migration literature focus mainly on the direction and volume of labor flows. The availability of data on international flows is higher at the student and tertiary education levels (Moguerou & Di Pietrogiacomo, 2008). Thus, levels of international mobility of research students and highly skilled workers with tertiary education are among the most frequent indicators of the geographic mobility of researchers (Guellec & Cervantes, 2002).[12]

Based on the construction of ad hoc databases, a few recent papers have analyzed the international mobility of researchers and its impact on their performance, careers, and networks. In a study of mobile scientists in 16 countries, Franzoni, Scellato, and Stephan (2014) found that foreign academics and those who spent extended periods abroad achieve publications with a higher impact.[13] Positive performance effects for international stays also occur in relation to postdoctoral stays of UK scientists (Zubieta, 2009). For a sample of Spanish researchers, however, Cañibano, Otamendi, and Andújar (2008) showed that international mobility results in better access to international funding and networks but does not improve publication or patenting performance. Lawson and Shibayama (Chapter 9) also provide mixed evidence. They found that Japanese bioscience professors who experienced international stays are promoted sooner,

[handwritten margin note: but needs more specific clarification on how research students are related to geo-mobility of researchers]

[handwritten margin note: benefit of mobility to researchers on individual level]

---

12. The population of Human Resources for Science and Technology includes people who completed tertiary level education in a science and technology field of study or those employed in an S&T occupation, which usually requires tertiary-level qualifications. The data sources used to measure these populations, such as labor force surveys, international education statistics, and census data, do not usually allow a clear breakdown.

13. See also Franzoni et al. (Chapter 2).

but only if they were already employed through permanent contracts. On the other hand, international mobility can result in the loss of social ties (Heining, Jerger, & Lingens, 2007) and difficulties related to incorporating the knowledge acquired abroad (Melin, 2005), which may explain the difficulties of reentry and delayed promotion observed by Cruz-Castro and Sanz-Menendez (2011) and Jonkers (2011) for Spain and Argentina, respectively.

Differences might also exist in the population that emigrates and between the sending and receiving countries. For example, Borjas and Doran (2012) and Gaule and Piacentini (2013) found higher performance among Russian and Chinese emigrants to the United States compared with the native population, whereas Hunter, Oswald, and Charlton (2009) found no differences in the performance of UK emigrants to the United States and domestic US scientists. In the latter case, it might be that the United States does not attract the best talent since the UK can compete on equal terms for talented researchers. Using data on Nobel laureates in chemistry, medicine, and physics, Weinberg (2009) showed a positive trend in US leadership in science, and the capacity to attract the best researchers, compared with a declining trend in Germany and a slightly declining pattern in UK science. Levin and Stephan (1999) found that highly productive scientists are disproportionately drawn from the foreign-born and foreign-educated populations in the United States.

Motivations for researchers to move to a different country are important for understanding researchers' behavior. The available evidence highlights that research-related reasons, such as working on interesting research topics, the quality of the receiving institution, and career prospects, dominate (De Grip, Fouarge, & Sauermann, 2009; Ivancheva & Gourova, 2011). Franzoni et al. (Chapter 2), based on a sample of more than 45,000 researchers working in 16 countries, confirm that career prospects and research quality are the main drivers of researcher emigration, whereas salary plays a minimal role. They also report that personal or family reasons are the most important
[...] ng a sample of about 1000 European-
[...], Veugelers and van Bouwel (Chapter
[...] ore strongly related to EU–US mobil-
[...] and PhDs with previous experience of
[...] move within Europe compared with

[handwritten margin notes: → support my finding developed countries are less motivated]

[handwritten margin notes: → support my finding that foreign-bo are overrep in research in U.S.A.]

[handwritten margin notes: explain stay or return]

[handwritten overlay note: Many studies focus on researchers' choice of stay or return on individual-level]

3.1.6 Social Mobility

Social mobility refers to changes in social status. Science is a social system in which resources tend to accumulate among a few individuals and a few institutions (Merton, 1968). Social systems are structured in ways that limit movements across social strata, which means that individuals and groups move down or, less often, up the socioeconomic scale in terms of property, income, or status. Thus, a researcher who joins a high-quality department could be considered to be upwardly mobile, whereas a researcher who joins a lower-quality

[handwritten note at bottom: This can be a future research direction → social strata in int. student mobility and academic collaboration]

department could be considered downwardly mobile. Since movements up and down are associated with different access to resources and peers, social mobility aspects are relevant to an analysis of researcher mobility and its effects. Allison and Long (1990) addressed the effects of departmental affiliation on research productivity for a sample of 179 job changes and found that researchers who move upward show increased publication and citation rates, whereas those who move downward experience a decrease in productivity. Fernandez-Zubieta et al. (Chapter 4) confirm the importance of qualifying mobility according to the quality of the sending and receiving departments, and they show that mobility downward into a lower-quality department can decrease the mobile researcher's academic performance. Similarly, Kahn and MacGarvie (in press) showed that researchers obliged by visa restrictions to leave the United States and return to a low-income country publish less than a matched researcher who is able to remain in the United States. Thus, social mobility across country boundaries is observed.

that's why we need to control for country dummies

3.1.7 Disciplinary Mobility

Demands of career progression on mobility are sometimes driven by discipline (Mahroum, 1998), and therefore it is necessary to check the drivers and consequences of mobility across disciplines. Disciplinary mobility refers to a move from one discipline to another, or a move among subfields within a discipline. It applies mostly to a research scientist who joins a department with a different disciplinary focus or joins an interdisciplinary research center (Aboelela et al., 2007). Disciplinary mobility can be used to study the emergence of a new discipline (Basu & Dobler, 2012; Lawson & Soos, 2014); this type of mobility occurs among researchers searching for new, promising areas that could lead to significant new findings (Gieryn, 1978). However, Borjas and Doran (2012) showed that disciplinary mobility can also be caused by supply shocks; American mathematicians moved away from fields that received larger numbers of Soviet immigrants. Disciplinary mobility often is accompanied by other types of mobility. For example, Garvey and Tomita (1972) found that research scientists moved to a new field primarily because of the conclusion of a project or a change of institution.

3.2 Researcher Mobility from a Life Course Perspective

As Section 3.1 shows, mobility types are not mutually exclusive. For example, a researcher's job change may require relocation to a different country, and this combines job-to-job and geographic mobility. One of the challenges involved in analyzing mobility from a life course perspective, which accounts for diverse mobility events throughout a researcher's career, is to select the changes that are the most relevant and apply the other dimensions of mobility. This implies that we need to establish a basic researcher trajectory and select the most relevant changes that occur.

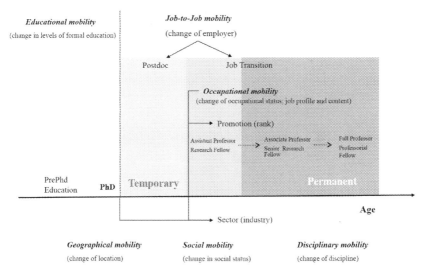

FIGURE 2   Researcher mobility from a life course perspective.

Figure 2 depicts the trajectory and most relevant mobility events in a research-er's career that we discussed above. For a researcher, successful completion of doctoral studies is generally the starting point of a researcher career and allows educational and job mobility dimensions to be clearly differentiated.[14] After being awarded a PhD degree, many research scientists take up postdoctoral positions; some then move on to a tenure-track/tenured or permanent position, whereas others leave academia. The difference between a post-PhD, non-ten-ure-track (fixed term with no prospect of permanent employment), tenure track (fixed-term with the prospect of permanent employment), and tenured position (permanent) helps to establish a clear difference within job-to-job mobility: "postdocs" and "job transition." The distinction between tenured (and tenure-track) and non-tenure-track (or permanent and nonpermanent) job changes is supported for several reasons. Tenured positions have a clear institutional ascrip-tion, job profile, and access to resources. Furthermore, the increasing number and concatenation of postdoctoral and temporary research positions reinforces the need to treat job mobility among tenured and nontenured academic staff differently since many temporary positions lead to involuntary job mobility. Job-to-job mobility of tenured/permanent academics is (mostly) the result of an individual choice, not a necessity. In the case of comparisons among interna-tional samples, institutional differences may hinder the proper identification of

---

14. A researcher can also have pre-PhD work experience. These events can be controlled for by including variables that indicate whether a researcher was employed before PhD completion. This is especially relevant if the researcher has pre-PhD work experience in industry since the job content is different.

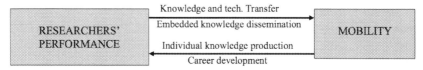

FIGURE 3 Researchers performance and mobility relationship.

comparable permanent positions. For this type of analysis it is better to consider only associate and full professors as permanent/tenured positions, in line with evidence presented by Lawson et al. in Chapter 3.

4. THE CHALLENGES RELATED TO ANALYZING RESEARCHER MOBILITY WITHIN A LIFE COURSE PERSPECTIVE

Changing job positions and collaborating with other researchers and sectors is part of an academic career. Researcher mobility is affected by different national science and technology policies, and human resources management practices, and labor markets promote different research trajectories (Gaughan & Robin, 2004). Mobility can become a system requirement, thereby creating more mobility (Mahroum, 2000).

An individual-level analysis of research mobility from a life course perspective allows simultaneous characterization of different mobility events and checking of their effect on academic performance, taking into account national and field-specific characteristics. Analyzing mobility from a life course perspective can also help to clarify the direction of causality between researcher performance and mobility (see Figure 3). For example, the effect of job mobility on a senior researcher's academic performance might be determined by earlier mobility experience and academic performance as a young researcher. Thus, the relationship between researcher mobility and productivity could go in both directions.

There is theoretical support for and empirical evidence pointing in both directions. Some studies show that mobility improves academic performance. For example, Franzoni et al. (2014) found that geographically mobile researchers show superior academic performance compared with nonmobile ones, even taking into account positive selection mechanisms in migration processes. Cañibano et al. (2008) found no evidence of a positive effect of mobility on academic performance but did not focus on job-to-job mobility[15] or the quality of performance. Dietz and Bozeman (2005) considered the effect of researcher's time spent in industry on performance and found a positive effect of years spent outside academia on patent productivity.

---

15. Cañibano et al. (2008) analyzed "stays," differentiating between short (less than a month) and long (more than 1 month) stays, pre- and postdoctoral periods, and the number of countries and centers in which the researcher has worked.

However, these results could be biased by migrants' self-selection. The economic literature on the assimilation of immigrants suggests that there are positive self-selection effects, such as immigrants being more talented, more entrepreneurial, and less risk averse (Borjas, 1985; Chiswick, 1978; LaLonde & Topel, 1992). Ganguli (Chapter 5), based on a large sample of Russian scientists, shows that after the collapse of the Soviet Union migration was characterized by positive selection, and, as economic theory suggests, this positive selection increased with migration costs and the wage premium. Higher productivity is also likely to affect intersector mobility. There is evidence that individual performance increases the likelihood of moving from academia to industry. For example, "star scientists" are more likely to have part-time appointments or affiliations with industry (Zucker et al., 2002), or to leave academia to start their own companies (Toole & Czarnitzki, 2010).

Because of this bidirectional relationship of mobility performance, some, such as Hoisl (2007), analyzed simultaneously mobility and productivity and found that a move increases productivity but that increased productivity decreases the probability of moving. This seems to support the productivity-enhancing mechanism predicted by job-matching theory. Evidence in the academic environment is less frequent, but Fernandez-Zubieta, Geuna, and Lawson (2015b) suggest that a productivity-enhancing effect is not confirmed if the analysis is limited to domestic moves.

In light of the evidence of the different effects for different mobility types, the bidirectional relationship of mobility and productivity, and the dynamic nature of these variables, an econometric analysis should address potential biases when estimating causal links (e.g., omitted variables, reverse causality, measurement error, sample selection) and find ways to overcome them. A few of the chapters in this volume take this approach. For example, the chapter by Fernandez-Zubieta et al. (Chapter 4) shows that job experiences per se do not increase academic performance and that job mobility to a better department has a positive weakly significant impact, whereas downward mobility reduces academic performance. In addition, job mobility is always associated with a short-term decrease in performance. The relationship between mobility and research productivity not only changes across different types of mobility but also across diverse career moves. Lawson et al. (Chapter 3) indicate that work experience in the US labor market provides a performance premium and that postdoctoral experience in a top-quality US institution adds a quality premium—both effects that are geographically transferable.

4.1 Problem of Biases when Estimating Causal Effects

Econometric research and methods have to deal with the recurrent problem of biases (Heckman, 1979) when estimating causal effects (e.g., omitted variables, reverse causality, measurement error, sample selection). To measure mobility and its impact on productivity, the model needs to include information on a researcher's characteristics and the job, as well as the match between the two, in order to address selection into mobility (Osberg, Mazany, Apostle, & Clairmont, 1986). Biographical information, such as a researcher's age, sex, and household structure, are as important as information on prior mobility events, research ability, and researcher's expectations about mobility outcomes. Job characteristics models should include details on teaching hours, capital availability, and job satisfaction. The model should also include some measures for the structure of the academic market. These data are difficult to obtain, and thus selection bias is difficult to resolve. From a life course perspective, there are additional problems related to personal and job characteristics that may change over time and affect selection into mobility and its effect on productivity. First, personal characteristics change over time. As already mentioned, younger researchers are more likely to move because they are less likely to have found their optimal conditions or optimal match. However, mismatch, which is likely in the case of early job changes, does not increase productivity and might result in decreased productivity.[16] Thus, job mobility should have a stronger positive effect on the productivity of older researchers since information on researchers' performance and characteristics increases with career progression. Also, researchers' family situations change over time, as do job characteristics and the motivations for job mobility. Teaching commitments and capital availability could change every academic year, which can affect a researcher's productivity and her willingness to move. Similarly, the structure of the academic labor market is subject to change. In the United Kingdom, the research assessment exercise resulted in changing measures for the assessment of research quality, and this has affected the requirements of the academic profession and the competition between universities for the best staff.

Therefore, when estimating the effect of mobility on productivity, standard regression estimates are biased since unobserved personal attributes are correlated with both the variable of interest and the independent variable. Mobile researchers might seem to be more productive than the comparison group, but this effect might be caused by the variable of interest (mobility) or by other variables (e.g., ability, greater motivation) in the mobile group, for which data are not available and thus are not controlled for. Assuming that only the most promising and productive researchers are offered positions and are able to move introduces two elements that need to be solved: (1) reverse causality, that is, the probability of moving depends on past productivity (the variable of interest is not exogenous), and (2) omitted variables, that is, the ability to do research (and be productive) influences both the probability of being offered a position and research productivity. Then the challenge is to isolate the effect of the omitted variable and to resolve the reverse causality problem.

In an ideal setting social scientists want to study the effect of mobility in an experiment that randomly assigns researchers to a mobile or an immobile group,

---

16. See footnote 10.

thereby exploiting an exogenous source of variation in the explanatory variable to analyze the effect of mobility on productivity. A natural experiment sets an exogenous and abrupt change in the group under scrutiny: for example, a university department that is unexpectedly closed, forcing all researchers to move (assuming that the closure was not caused by their productivity). Then the possible causal link of productivity on mobility can be controlled for by using this external shock as an instrument or by defining an unaffected control group. Moser et al. (2014) used the dismissal of Jewish scientists from Nazi Germany as a natural experiment to address the endogeneity problem in an analysis of mobility to the United States. Similarly, Borjas and Doran (2012) used the collapse of the Soviet Union as an external shock to measure mobility and productivity. Alternatively, when treatment effectively is random, the regression discontinuity (RD) design can be used (Imbens & Lemieux, 2008). This assumes that the value of a treatment predictor is on either side of a fixed threshold. This design can be applied to situations in which an administrative body sets transparent rules for treatment and defines a cut-off point because of resource restrictions. The RD design was implemented originally by Thistlewaite and Campbell (1960), who analyzed the impact of scholarships based on observed test scores on future outcomes and compared the group that just passed with the group that just failed. In the case of mobility, the RD design is particularly useful to assess PhD student/postdoctoral mobility if places are determined by a placement test/assessment (such as in the case of the European Commission Marie Skłodowska-Curie grants) or participation in research visit programs when these are determined by a stringent set of criteria (e.g., the Fulbright Program). In the case of job-to-job mobility, the RD design is difficult to implement because assignment to treatment is not based on program participation or observable selection criteria.

Thus, natural experiments and quasi-randomized assignment represent rare events that allow for advanced econometric exercises but are of little relevance to policy to investigate the importance of job-to-job mobility. If the interest is in analyzing common patterns of mobility in science, we need to develop econometric models that address differently intrinsic problems of heterogeneity, endogeneity, and selectivity. Since mobility cannot be randomized, the most common solution in econometric analysis is to control for confounding factors, for example, sex, age, and past productivity. Standard models, however, do not adjust for confounding if the treatment—in our case mobility—varies over time (Robins, 1999). Thus, controlling for, for instance, past values of productivity that affect later mobility but that also may be affected by earlier mobility can lead to biased estimates because we control for the pathway that is hypothesized to lead to higher productivity. A second solution would be to use fixed-effects estimators that remove individual unobservable, time-invariant differences between mobile and immobile researchers. They do not, however, adjust for unobserved, time-varying confounding and thus might still result in a spurious correlation between mobility and publications (Robins, 1999).

We need to discuss other research designs able to deal with reverse causality and selection processes, such as instrumental variables (cf. Wooldridge, 2010) and treatment effects (cf. Wooldridge, 2006). Instrumental variables are variables that affect the regressor causing the bias but do not affect the variable under scrutiny. When analyzing the effect of mobility on productivity, instrumental variables for mobility are those variables that affect mobility but not productivity. Finding plausible instruments is very difficult, however, especially in the case of mobility and productivity; one researcher's instrument might be another researcher's hypothesized cause of publication. Addressing the causality between inventor mobility and productivity, Hoisl (2007) proposed a simultaneous relationship: They considered "city size" as an instrument for mobility in the productivity equation and "external sources of knowledge" as an instrument for productivity in the mobility equation. Toole and Czarnitzki (2010) used lagged regional variables as an instrument in their productivity equations for joining or founding a firm. While these instruments might explain mobility opportunities to business firms without effecting productivity, they are less convincing in the academic context. Researchers in larger or more dynamic cities may have both more employment opportunities and proximity to more peers, which may also affect their productivity. A positive effect of mobility on publications may simply be a spurious relation caused by access to larger networks. However, instruments beyond regional indicators are difficult to identify and measure.

We propose six instruments for voluntary mobility of permanent academic staff. We consider these instruments feasible, although they are likely to involve extensive data compilation.

1. Dahl and Sorenson (2010) showed for a sample of Danish scientists and engineers, and Gibson and McKenzie (2011) showed for a sample of migrants from three Pacific countries, that both are highly skilled, value proximity to family and friends, and are willing to forgo a part of their incomes to live closer to home. Franzoni et al. (2012) confirmed that family ties are an important motivation for research-active scientists to return to their home countries. Therefore, we propose the distance to one's place of birth and the distance to the city of undergraduate education as the first set of instruments. Researchers who live farther away from home are more likely to move since the social costs associated with a move are lower. Distance from home should not affect productivity, although this cannot be ruled out since close family may provide help with childcare, which in turn could affect productivity.

2. Our second instrument is the number of available job openings. Job openings directly affect the opportunities for receiving job offers and accepting an offer. Detailed information on available positions in a given year, field, and ranking could act as instruments for mobility and should not affect productivity unless they represent an overall increase in capital available to universities.

3. Third, we suggest using researchers' foreign language proficiency. Language proficiency is assumed to be correlated to a researcher's interest in other cultures and could indicate a higher propensity to be mobile without affecting productivity. Gibson and McKenzie (2011) confirmed that highly able students who study a foreign language are more likely to emigrate.

individual-level studies

4. Previous papers have used migration during childhood (Franzoni et al., 2012) or participation in international exchange programs during undergraduate studies (Parey & Waldinger, 2011) as instruments for later migration. Franzoni et al. (2012) conceded that their instrument is valid only if early migration happens irrespective of investment in education and parents' wealth. Gibson and McKenzie (2011), however, showed that when controlling for education and parents' characteristics, migration during childhood has no effect on later migration.

5. Gibson and McKenzie (2011) found weak evidence that a spouse with a foreign nationality reduces the propensity to return to the home country. Family characteristics such as spouse's background (in terms of profession or distance to home) or children's age might explain mobility. Researchers' with school-age children are expected to move less. While young children can have a performance-hampering effect for female researchers, school-age children do not significantly affect performance (Stack, 2004) and could present a possible instrument.

6. Finally, to control for individual time-varying characteristics that might affect mobility, it is possible to compute a performance mismatch instrument based on the idea that rising star scientists might have incentives to leave departments that are in a relative productivity decline. A scientist with increasing productivity located in a department that is experiencing an overall decrease in performance will have not only a higher incentive to move out but also more opportunities.

Fernandez-Zubieta et al. (2015b) presented the results of estimates using instruments 1 and 6.

In the absence of natural experiments and instruments, we can address the problem of reverse causality by modeling the likelihood of being treated. Thus, we can account for selection into mobility based on observable characteristics before mobility. Among the important selection criteria that should be considered when matching academics are age, experience, contract type, past productivity, prior mobility events, family-related factors, and reputation factors. The sample should be split into a treated group and an untreated control group. Treatment effect methods assume that each individual has potentially two outcomes dependent on treatment. Thus, by assuming that the treatment and control groups are alike, we can estimate a causal effect. Selection of observable characteristics is achieved through propensity score matching (PSM) (Rosenbaum & Rubin, 1983). PSM allows the propensity of each individual to be mobile to be modeled and a control group to be created based on propensity scores.[17] If treatment, confounding variables, and outcome variables vary over time, estimates based on PSM may be biased (Robins, 1999). Various researchers have

---

17. Other matching techniques are Mahalanobis matching and coarsened exact matching (Blackwell, Iacus, King, & Porro, 2009).

proposed inverse probability of treatment weights to deal with this problem (e.g., Hernan, Brumback, & Robins, 2001; Robins, 1999; Robins, Hernan, & Brumback, 2000). Inverse probability of treatment weights allows average treatment effects to be estimated even if confounding variables predict publications and mobility, and are themselves predicted by past mobility. Thus, they allow us to consider past publication and past mobility events for estimating selection into mobility. The problem of matching based on observable characteristics is that the likelihood of being mobile also depends on unobservable characteristics. Therefore matching can reduce endogeneity concerns but not eliminate them (Heckman & Navarro-Lozano, 2004).

5. CONCLUSION

Academic mobility is not a new phenomenon. Since universities began to flourish in Medieval Europe, academics have moved across institutions, acquiring new knowledge and social connections and bringing and diffusing their knowledge to new colleagues and students. In recent years scientists' mobility has increased significantly and has been associated with major changes in research systems. In this chapter we identified and discussed mobility along three main dimensions: internationalization, increasing intersector collaboration, and diversifying career and work roles. The literature on the mobility of researcher scientists is scarce because of a lack of reliable data to trace scientists along their careers. However, we have highlighted some overall trends and discussed some individual and social advantages and disadvantages of researcher mobility.

The literature review suggests that to properly analyze the effect of mobility in the current evolving research system, it is necessary to consider multiple mobility events and short- and long-term return opportunities (not just to consider mobility as a one-time, one-way process). A life course perspective should be adopted to assess properly the positive or negative effects of increased researcher mobility.

We highlighted that mobility analysis requires identification and selection of the most relevant mobility events in a researcher's career. We presented a typology of mobility that differs between educational, job-to-job, occupational, sectoral, geographic, social, and disciplinary mobility, as well as a researcher's career trajectory, which allowed us to select job-to-job mobility as the main mobility type in a researcher's career and to consider the other mobility types across it. We emphasized the need for clear differentiation of job changes among researchers in permanent positions versus nontenured, nonpermanent positions when analyzing the impact of mobility on productivity. The analysis of job positions at the individual level allows analysis of the relationship between different types of mobility, academic markets, and researcher careers.

We reviewed the different research designs able to deal with biases, such as unobserved heterogeneity, endogeneity, reverse causality, in order to study the causal links between mobility and researchers' productivity. We considered the advantages and disadvantages of these methods—natural experiments, quasi-randomized assignment, instrumental variables, and treatment effects—and discussed some possible instruments.

There are several reasons for adopting a life course perspective (sequentialist approach) to study mobility and to overcome some of its limitations. First, changes in the research system require an analysis of mobility that does not consider mobility as a one-time, one-way event. Second, there might be a relationship between diverse mobility experiences, for example, deterioration of young researchers' employment prospects and increased job-mobility (*précarité*) among young researchers (e.g., increased number of postdoctoral positions), that might decrease job prospects and performance for a senior researcher (mobility path dependence). Third, the prospect of increased availability of longitudinal data sets encourages the analysis of mobility using a life course perspective and addresses biases when analyzing causal links. Finally, the strong policy interest in mobility requires tools able to evaluate properly the outcomes of these policies.

ACKNOWLEDGMENTS

The authors thank Paula Stephan for her helpful comments when drafting this chapter. Financial support from the European Commission (FP7) Project "An Observatorium for Science in Society based in Social Models – SISOB" (contract no. FP7 266588) and the Collegio Carlo Alberto Project "Researcher Mobility and Scientific Performance" is gratefully acknowledged. Ana Fernandez-Zubieta acknowledges financial support from the JAE-Doc "Junta para la Ampliación de Estudios" Program, which is cofinanced by Social Structure Funds (SSF).

REFERENCES

Aboelela, S. W., Larson, E., Bakken, S., Carrasquillo, O., Formicola, A., Glied, S. A., et al. (2007). Defining interdisciplinary research: conclusions from a critical review of the literature. *Health Services Research, 42*, 329–346.

Ackers, H. L. (2004). Managing relationships in peripatetic careers: scientific mobility in the European Union. *Women's Studies International Forum, 27*, 189–201.

Ackers, H. L. (2005). Moving people and knowledge, the mobility of scientists within the European Union. *International Migration, 43*, 99–129.

Ackers, H. L., & Oliver, E. (2007). From flexicurity to flexsecquality? The impact of the fixed-term contract provisions on employment in science research'. *International Studies of Management and Organization, 37*(1), 53–79.

Agrawal, A., Cockburn, I., & McHale, J. (2006). Gone but not forgotten: knowledge flows, labor mobility, and enduring social relationships. *Journal of Economic Geography, 6*, 571–591.

Agrawal, A., Kapur, D., & McHale, J. (2008). How do spatial and social proximity influence knowledge flows? Evidence from patent data. *Journal of Urban Economics, 64*, 258–269.

Agrawal, A., Kapur, D., McHale, J., & Oettl, A. (2011). Brain drain or brain bank? The impact of skilled emigration on poor-country innovation. *Journal of Urban Economics, 69*, 43–55.

Allison, P. D., & Long, J. S. (1990). Departmental effects on scientific productivity. *American Sociological Review*, 469–478.

Almeida, P., & Kogut, B. (1999). Localization of knowledge and the mobility of engineers in regional networks. *Management Science, 45*, 905–917.

Appelt, S., van Beuzekom, B., Galindo-Rueda, F., & de Pinho, R. (Chapter 7). Which factors influence the international mobility of research scientists? In A. Geuna (Ed.), *Global mobility of research scientists: The economics of who goes where and why*. Amsterdam: Elsevier.

Audretsch, D. B., & Feldman, M. P. (2004). Knowledge spillovers and the geography of innovation. *Handbook of Regional and Urban Economics, 4*, 2713–2739.

Audretsch, D. B., & Stephan, P. (1999). How and why does knowledge spill over in biotechnology. In D. B. Audretsch, & R. Thurik (Eds.), *Innovation, industry evolution, and employment* (pp. 216–229). Cambridge: Cambridge University Press.

Auriol, L., Misu, M., & Freeman, R. (2013). *Careers of doctorate holders: Analysis of labour market and mobility indicators*. Organisation of Economic Cooperation and Development, STI Working Papers 2013/4. Paris: OECD.

Azoulay, P., Zivin, J. S., & Sampat, B. (2012). The diffusion of scientific knowledge across time and space: evidence from professional transitions for the superstars of medicine. In J. Lerner, & S. Stern (Eds.), *The rate and direction of inventive activity revisited* (pp. 107–155). Chicago, IL: University of Chicago Press.

Balaz, V., & Williams, A. (2004). Been there done that: International student migration and human capital transfers from the UK to Slovakia. *Population, Place and Space, 10*(3), 217–237.

Barre, R., Hernandez, V., Meyer, J. B., & Vinck, D. (2003). *Scientific diasporas: How can developing countries benefit from their expatriate scientists and engineers?* Paris: Institut de recherche pour le développement (IRD).

Baruffaldi, S. H., & Landoni, P. (2012). Return mobility and scientific productivity of researchers working abroad: the role of home country linkages. *Research Policy, 41*, 1655–1665.

Basu, A., & Dobler, R. W. (2012). 'Cognitive mobility' or migration of authors between fields used in mapping a network of mathematics. *Scientometrics, 91*(2), 353–368.

Berry, R. A., & Soligo, R. (1969). Some welfare aspects of international migration. *Journal of Political Economy, 77*, 778–794.

Blackwell, M., Iacus, S., King, G., & Porro, G. (2009). Coarsened exact matching in stata. *The Stata Journal, 9*(4), 524–546.

Blaxter, L., Hughes, C., & Tight, M. (1998). Telling it how it is: accounts of academic life. *Higher Educational Quarterly, 52*, 300–315.

Blumenthal, D., Campbell, E., Anderson, M., Causino, N., & Louis, K. (1996). Withholding research results in academic lifescience: evidence from a national survey of faculty. *Journal of The American Medical Association, 277*, 1224–1228.

Boeri, T., Brücker, H., Docquier, F., & Rapoport, H. (2012). *Brain drain and brain gain: The global competition to attract high-skilled migrants*. Oxford: Oxford University Press.

Borjas, G. (1985). Assimilation, changes in cohort quality, and earnings of immigrants. *Journal of Labor Economics, 4*, 463–489.

Borjas, G. (2009). Immigration in high-skill labor markets the impact of foreign students on the earnings of doctorate. In R. Freeman, & D. Goroff (Eds.), *Science and engineering careers in the United States: An analysis of markets and employment* (pp. 131–162). Chicago: University of Chicago Press.

Borjas, G., & Doran, K. (2012). The collapse of the soviet union and the productivity of American mathematicians. *Quarterly Journal of Economics, 127*(3), 1143–1203.

Bozeman, B. (2000). Technology transfer and public policy: a review of research and theory. *Research Policy, 22*, 627–655.

Breschi, S., & Lissoni, F. (2003). *Localised knowledge spillovers revisited*. CESPRI Working Paper No. 142. Milan: Bocconi University.

Business, Innovation and Skills (BIS). (2013). *International comparative performance of the UK research base*. London: Department for Business, Innovation and Skills.

Cañibano, C., Otamendi, J., & Andújar, I. (2008). Measuring and assessing researcher mobility from CV analysis: the case of the Ramón y Cajal programme in Spain. *Research Evaluation, 17*, 17–31.

Chiswick, B. (1978). The effect of Americanisation on the earnings of foreign-born men. *Journal of Political Economy, 86*, 897–921.

Coate, K., Barnett, R., & Williams, G. (2001). Relationships between teaching and research in higher education in England. *Higher Education Quarterly, 55*, 158–174.

Cooper, D. P. (2001). Innovation and reciprocal externalities: Information transmission via job mobility. *Journal of Economic Behaviour and Organization, 45*, 403–425.

Crespi, G., Geuna, A., & Nesta, L. L. J. (2007). The mobility of university inventors in Europe. *Journal of Technology Transfer, 32*, 195–215.

Cruz-Castro, L., & Sanz-Menendez, L. (2005). The employment of PhDs in firms: trajectories, mobility and innovation. *Research Evaluation, 14*(1), 57–69.

Cruz-Castro, L., & Sanz-Menendez, L. (2011). Mobility versus job stability: assessing tenure and productivity outcomes. *Research Policy, 39*, 27–38.

Dahl, M. S., & Sorenson, O. (2010). The social attachment to place. *Social Forces, 89*(2), 633–658.

De Graaf, G., & van Der Wal, Z. (2008). On value differences experienced by sector switchers. *Administration & Society, 40*(1), 79–103.

De Grip, A., Fouarge, D., & Sauermann, J. (2009). *What affects international migration of European science and engineering graduates?* Bonn: IZA Discussion Paper no. 4268.

Dietz, J. S., & Bozeman, B. (2005). Academic careers, patents, and productivity: Industry experience as scientific and technical human capital. *Research Policy, 34*, 349–367.

Ding, W. W., Levin, S. G., Stephan, P. E., & Winkler, A. E. (2010). The impact of information technology on scientists' productivity and collaboration patterns. *Management Science, 56*, 1439–1461.

Ejsing, A. K., Kaiser, U., Kongsted, H., & Laursen, K. (2013). The role of university scientist mobility for industrial innovation. *Bonn: IZA Discussion Paper, 7470*.

Enders, J. (2005). Border crossings: research training, knowledge dissemination and the transformation of academic work. *Higher Education, 49*, 119–133.

Enders, J., & Weert, E. (2004). Science, training and career: changing modes of knowledge production and labour markets. *Higher Education Policy, 17*, 135–152.

Eurobarometer. (2005). *Mobility in Europe. Analysis of the 2005 Eurobarometer survey on geographical and labour market mobility*. Dublin: European Foundation for the Improvement of Living and Working Conditions.

European Commission (EC). (2012). *Excellence, equality and entrepreneurialism building sustainable research careers in the European research area*. Luxembourg: Publications Office of the European Union.

Expertenkommission Forschung und Innovation (EFI). (2012). *Gutachten zu Forschung, innovation und technologischer Leistungsfähigkeit Deutschlands*. Berlin: EFI.

Fernandez-Zubieta, A., Geuna, A., & Lawson, C. (Chapter 4). Mobility and productivity of research scientists. In A. Geuna (Ed.), *Global mobility of research scientists: The economics of who goes where and why*. Amsterdam: Elsevier.

Fernandez-Zubieta, A., Geuna, A., & Lawson, C. (2015b). Productivity pay-offs from academic mobility: should I stay or should I go? *R&R in Industrial and Corporate Change*.

Fernandez-Zubieta, A., & van Bavel, R. (2011). *Barriers and bottlenecks to making research careers more attractive and promoting mobility*. Luxembourg: Office for Official Publications of the European Communities.

Franzoni, C., Scellato, G., & Stephan, P. (2012). Foreign-born scientists: mobility patterns for 16 countries. *Nature Biotechnology, 30*(12), 1250–1253.

Franzoni, C., Scellato, G., & Stephan, P. (2014). The mover's advantage: the superior performance of migrant scientists. *Economics Letters, 122*(1), 89–93.

Franzoni, C., Scellato, G., & Stephan, P. (Chapter 2). International mobility of research scientists: lessons from GlobSci. In A. Geuna (Ed.), *Global mobility of research scientists: The economics of who goes where and why.* Amsterdam: Elsevier.

Freeman, R. B. (2006). Does globalization of the scientific/engineering workforce threaten US economic leadership? In A. Jaffe, J. Lerner, & S. Stern (Eds.), *Innovation policy and the economy* (Vol. 6) (pp. 123–158). Cambridge, MA: The MIT Press.

Gaillard, A. M., & Gaillard, J. (1998). The international circulation of scientists and technologists. *Science Communication, 20,* 106–116.

Ganguli, I. (Chapter 5). Chinas 'Great Leap Forward' in science and engineering. In A. Geuna (Ed.), *Global mobility of research scientists: The economics of who goes where and why.* Amsterdam: Elsevier.

Garvey, W., & Tomita, K. (1972). Continuity of productivity by scientists in the years 1968–71. *Social Studies of Science, 2,* 379–383.

Gassmann, O., Enkel, E., & Chesbrough, H. (2010). The future of open innovation. *R&D Management, 40*(3), 213–221.

Gaughan, M., & Robin, S. (2004). National science training policy and early scientific careers in France and the United States. *Research Policy, 33*(4), 109–122.

Gaule, P., & Piacentini, M. (2013). Chinese graduate students and US scientific productivity. *Review of Economics and Statistics, 95*(2), 698–701.

Geuna, A., & Shibayama, S. (Chapter 10). Moving out of academic research: why scientists stop doing research. In A. Geuna (Ed.), *Global mobility of research scientists: The economics of who goes where and why.* Amsterdam: Elsevier.

Gibson, J., & McKenzie, D. (2011). The microeconomic determinants of emigration and return migration of the best and brightest: evidence from the Pacific. *Journal of Development Economics, 95*(1), 18–29.

Gibson, J., & McKenzie, D. (2012). The economic consequences of 'brain drain' of the best and brightest: microeconomic evidence from five countries. *Economic Journal, 122,* 339–375.

Gieryn, T. (1978). Problem retention and problem change in science. *Sociological Inquiry, 48,* 96–115.

Ginther, D. K., & Hayes, K. J. (2003). Gender differences in salary and promotion for faculty in the humanities 1977–95. *Journal of Human Resources, 38*(1), 34–73.

Ginther, D. K., & Kahn, S. (2004). Women in economics: moving up or falling off the academic career ladder? *Journal of Economic Perspectives, 18,* 193–214.

Glanzel, W., Debackere, K., & Meyer, M. (2008). 'Triad' or 'Tetrad'? On global changes in a dynamic world. *Scientometrics, 74*(1), 71–80.

Grubel, H. G., & Scott, A. (1977). *The brain drain. Determinants, measurement and welfare effects.* Waterloo, Ont: Wilfrid Laurier University Press.

Guellec, D., & Cervantes, M. (2002). *International mobility of highly skilled workers: From statistical analysis to policy formulation. International mobility of the highly skilled.* Paris: OECD. 71–98.

Hagstrom, W. O. (1965). *The scientific community.* New York: Basic Books.

Hansen, W. (2003). *Brain drain: Emigration flows for qualified scientist.* Brussels: European Commission/MERIT.

Heckman, J. (1979). Sample selection bias as a specification error. *Econometrica*, *47*, 153–161.

Heckman, J., & Navarro-Lozano, S. (2004). Using matching, instrumental variables, and control functions to estimate economic choice models. *Review of Economic Statistics*, *86*(1), 30–67.

Heining, J., Jerger, J., & Lingens, J. (2007). Success in the academic labour market for economics – the German experience. *Regensburg: Regensburger Diskussionsbeiträge zur Wirtschaftswissenschaft* (422).

Heller, M. A., & Eisenberg, R. S. (1998). Can patents deter innovation? The anticommons in bio-medical research. *Science*, *280*, 698–701.

Henderson, R., Jaffe, A., & Trajtenberg, M. (1998). Universities as a source of commercial technology: a detailed analysis of university patenting, 1965–1988. *Review of Economics and Statistics*, *80*(1), 119–127.

Hernan, M. A., Brumback, B., & Robins, J. M. (2001). Marginal structural models to estimate the joint causal effect of non-randomized treatments. *Journal of the American Statistical Association*, *96*, 440–448.

Herrera, L., Muñoz-Doyague, M. F., & Nieto, M. (2010). Mobility of public researchers, scientific knowledge transfer, and the firm's innovation process. *Journal of Business Research*, *63*(5), 510–518.

Herstad, S. J., Sandven, T., & Ebensberger, B. (2015). Recruitment, knowledge integration and modes of innovation. *Research Policy*, *44*, 138–153.

Hoisl, K. (2007). Tracing mobile inventors. The causality between inventors mobility and inventor productivity. *Research Policy*, *36*, 619–636.

Hottenrott, H., & Lawson, C. (2014). *Flying the nest: How the home department shapes researchers' career paths*. Turin: LEI & BRICK Working Paper 09/2014.

Howells, J., Ramlogan, R., & Cheng, S. (2012). Innovation and university collaboration: paradox and complexity within the knowledge economy. *Cambridge Journal of Economics*, *36*(3), 703–721.

Hunter, R. S., Oswald, A. J., & Charlton, B. G. (2009). The elite brain drain. *The Economic Journal*, *119*(538), 231–251.

Hunt, J., & Gauthier-Loiselle, M. (2010). How much does immigration boost innovation? *American Economic Journal Macroeconomics*, *2*(2), 31–56.

Imbens, G., & Lemieux, T. (2008). Regression discontinuity designs: a guide to practice. *Journal of Econometrics*, *142*, 615–635.

Institute of International Education. (2012). *International students in the US*. http://www.iie.org/opendoors.

Ivancheva, L., & Gourova, E. (2011). Challenges for career and mobility of researchers in Europe. *Science and Public Policy*, *38*(3), 185–198.

Jaffe, A. (1989). Real effects of academic research. *American Economic Review*, *79*, 957–970.

Johnson, H. G. (1968). An 'internationalist' model. In A. Walter (Ed.), *The brain drain* (pp. 69–91). New York: The Macmillan Company.

Johnson, J. M., & Regets, M. C. (1998). *International mobility of scientists and engineers to the United States. Brain drain or brain circulation?* Arlington, VA: NSF-98-316.

Jonkers, K. (2011). Mobility, productivity, gender and career development of Argentinean life scientists. *Research Evaluation*, *20*(5), 411–421.

Jovanovic, B. (1979). Job matching and the theory of turnover. *The Journal of Political Economy*, *87*(5), 972–990.

Kahn, S., & MacGarvie, M. J. How important is US location for research in science? Review of Economics and Statistics (in press).

KBWN (Konsortium Bundesbericht Wissenschaftlicher Nachwuchs). (2013). *Bundesbericht wissenschaftlicher nachwuchs 2013*. Bielefeld: W. Bertelsmann Verlag.

Kerr, W. (2008). Ethnic scientific communities and international technology diffusion. *Review of Economics and Statistics*, *90*(3), 518–537.

Kim, Y., & Cha, J. (2000). Career orientations of R&D professionals in Korea. *R&D Management*, *30*(2), 121–137.

King, R. (2002). Towards a new map of European migration. *International Journal of Population Geography*, *8*, 89–106.

Kornhauser, W. (1962). *Scientists in industry: Conflict and accommodation*. Berkeley, CA: University of California Press.

Krohn, R. C. (1961). The institutional location of the scientist and his scientific values. *I.R.E. Transactions on Engineering Management*, *8*, *133–138*.

LaLonde, R., & Topel, R. (1992). The assimilation of immigrants in the U.S. Labor Market. In G. Borjas, & R. Freeman (Eds.), *Immigration and the workforce* (pp. 67–92). Chicago, IL: NBER,/University of Chicago Press.

Lan, X. (2012). Permanent visas and temporary jobs: evidence from postdoctoral participation of foreign PhDs in the United States. *Journal of Policy Analysis and Management*, *31*(3), 623–640.

Lawson, C., Geuna, A., Fernandez-Zubieta, A., Katahisi, R., & Toselli, M. (Chapter 3). International careers of researchers in biomedical sciences: a comparison of the US and the UK. In A. Geuna (Ed.), *Global mobility of research scientists: The economics of who goes where and why*. Amsterdam: Elsevier.

Lawson, C., & Shibayama, S. (Chapter 9). International careers of researchers in biomedical sciences: a comparison of the US and the UK. In A. Geuna (Ed.), *Global mobility of research scientists: The economics of who goes where and why*. Amsterdam: Elsevier.

Lawson, C., & Soos, S. (2014). *A thematic mobility measure for econometric analysis*. Turin: LEI & BRICK Working Paper 02/2014.

Lee, Y. (2000). The sustainability of university-industry research collaboration: an empirical assessment. *Journal of Technology Transfer*, *25*(2), 111–133.

Levin, S., & Stephan, P. (1999). Are the foreign born a source of strength for US Science? *Science*, *285*, 1213–1214.

Lin, M. W., & Bozeman, B. (2006). Researchers' industry experience and productivity in university–industry research centers: a "scientific and technical human capital" explanation. *Journal of Technology Transfer*, *31*(2), 269–290.

Locke, W. (2014). *Shifting academic careers: Implications for enhancing professionalism in teaching and supporting learning*. York: Higher Education Academy.

Long, J. S. (1978). Productivity and academic position in the scientific career. *American Sociological Review*, *43*, 889–908.

Long, J. S., Allison, P. D., & McGinnis, R. (1993). Rank advancement in academic careers: sex differences and the effects of productivity. *American Sociological Review*, 703–722.

Mahroum, S. (1998). Skilled labour. *Science and Public Policy*, *26*(1), 17–25.

Mahroum, S. (2000). Scientific mobility: an agent of scientific expansion and institutional empowerment. *Science Communication*, *21*, 367–378.

Mangematin, V. (2000). PhD job market: professional trajectories and incentives during the PhD. *Research Policy*, *29*(6), 741–756.

Marcson, S. (1960). *The scientist in American Industry*. Princeton, NJ: Princenton University Press.

Martin-Rovet, D. (2003). *Opportunites for outstanding young scientists in Europe to create an independent research team*. Strasbourg: European Science Foundation.

McDowell, J. M., Singell, L. D., & Stater, M. (2006). Two to tango? Gender differences in the decisions to publish and coauthor. *Economic inquiry*, *44*(1), 153–168.

McGuinnis, R., Allison, P., & Long, S. J. (1982). Postdoctoral training in biosciences: allocation and outcomes. *Social Forces*, *60*(3), 701–722.

Melin, G. (2005). The dark side of mobility: negative experiences of doing a postdoc period abroad. *Research Evaluation*, *14*(3), 229–237.

Merton, R. K. (1938). Science, technology and society in seventeenth-century England. *Osiris*, *4*, 360–632.

Merton, R. K. (1968). The matthew effect in science. *Science*, *159*, 56–63.

Meyer, J. B. (2001). Network approach versus brain drain: lessons from the diaspora. *International Migration Quarterly Review*, *39*, 91–110.

Meyer, J. B., & Wattiaux, J. P. (2006). Diaspora knowledge networks: vanishing doubts and increasing evidence. *International Journal of Multicultural Societies*, *8*(1), 4–24.

Ministry of Education, Culture, Sports, Science and Technology (MEXT). (2012). *Statistical abstracts 2012 edition 1.9 universities and junior colleges*. Tokyo: MEXT. Available online: http://www.mext.go.jp/english/statistics/1302965.htm. [accessed 10.10.14].

Møen, J. (2005). Is mobility of technical personnel a source of R&D spillovers? *Journal of Labor Economics*, *23*, 81–114.

Moguerou, P. (2006). *The brain drain of PhDs from Europe to the United States. What we know and what we would like to know*. Florence: European University Institute, RSCAS No. 2006/11.

Moguerou, P., & Di Pietrogiacomo, P. (2008). *Stock, career and mobility of researchers in the EU*. Luxembourg: Office for Official Publications of the European Communities.

Moser, P., Voena, A., & Waldinger, F. (2014). German-jewish ÉMIGRÉS and US Invention. *American Economic Review*, *104*, 3222–3255.

Mowery, D. C., & Shane, S. (2002). Introduction to the special issue on university entrepreneurship and technology transfer. *Management Science*, *48*, v–ix.

National Academies Press (NAP). (2014). *The postdoctoral experience revisited*. Washington DC: National Academies Press.

Nerdrum, L., & Sarpebakken, B. (2006). Mobility of foreign researchers in Norway. *Science and Public Policy*, *33*, 217–229.

NISTEP (National Institute of Science and Technology Policy). (2009). Career Trends Survey of Recent Doctoral Graduates. NISTEP Report no. 126, National Institute of Science and Technology Policy, Tokyo (in Japanese).

Oettl, A., & Agrawal, A. (2008). International labor mobility and knowledge flow externalities. *Journal of International Business Studies*, *39*, 1242–1260.

Organisation for Economic Cooperation and Development (OECD). (2008). *The global competition for talent: Mobility of the highly skilled*. Paris: Directorate for Science Technology and Industry, OECD.

Organisation for Economic Cooperation and Development (OECD). (2013). *OECD science, technology and Industry Scoreboard 2013*. Paris: OECD.

Organisation for Economic Cooperation and Development (OECD). (2014). *Indicator C4: Who studies abroad and where? In education at a Glance 2014: OECD indicators*. Paris: OECD.

Osberg, L., Mazany, L., Apostle, R., & Clairmont, D. (1986). Job mobility, wage determination and market segmentation in the presence of sample selectivity bias. *Journal of Economics*, *19*(2), 319–346.

Oswald, A. J., & Ralsmark, H. (2008). *Some evidence on the future of economics*. Warwick: Warwick Economic Research Papers No. 841.

Palomeras, N., & Melero, E. (2010). Markets for inventors: learning-by-hiring as a driver of mobility. *Management Science*, *56*(5), 881–895.

Parey, M., & Waldinger, F. (2011). Studying abroad and the effect on international labor market mobility. *The Economic Journal*, *121*(551), 194–222.

Parsons, D. (1991). The job search behavior of employment youth. *Review of Economic Statistics*, *73*(4), 597–604.

Patinkin, D. (1968). A 'nationalist' model. In W. Adams (Ed.), *The brain drain* (pp. 92–108). New York: The Macmillan Company.

Pekkala Kerr, S., & Kerr, W. R. (2013). Immigration and employer transitions for STEM workers. *American Economic Review*, *103*(3), 193–197.

Pezzoni, M., Sterzi, V., & Lissoni, F. (2012). Career progress in centralized academic systems: social capital and institutions in France and Italy. *Research Policy*, *41*(4), 704–719.

Ponomariov, B. L., & Boardman, P. C. (2010). Influencing scientists' collaboration and productivity patterns through new institutions: university research centers and scientific and technical human capital. *Research Policy*, *39*(5), 613–624.

Porter, S. R. (2007). A closer look at faculty service: what affects participation on committees? *The Journal of Higher Education*, *78*(5), 523–541.

Powell, W. W., Koput, K. K., & Smith-Doerr, L. (1996). Inter-organisational collaboration and the locus of innovation: network learning in biotechnology. *Administrative Science Quarterly*, *41*, 116–145.

Price, D. (1963). *Little science, big science*. New York: Columbia University Press.

Regets, M. (2001). Research and policy issues in high-skilled international migration: a perspective with data from the United States. In *Innovative people: Mobility of skilled personnel in national innovation systems* (pp. 243–260). París: OECD.

Rhode, B. (1991). *East-West migration/brain drain*. Brussels: European Co-Operation in the Field of Scientific and Technical Research (COST), CEE.

Rhoten, D., & Parker, A. (2004). Risks and rewards of an interdisciplinary research path. *Science*, *306*(5704), 2046.

Roach, R. (February 6, 2014). Part-time professors represented among the working poor. *Diverse: Issues in Higher Education*.

Robins, J. M. (1999). Association, causation, and marginal structural models. *Synthese*, *121*, 151–179.

Robins, J. M., Hernan, M. A., & Brumback, B. (2000). Marginal structural models and causal inference in epidemiology. *Epidemiology*, *115*, 550–560.

Rosenbaum, P., & Rubin, D. (1983). The central role of the propensity score in observational studies for causal effects. *Biometrika*, *70*, 41–55.

Rosenkopf, L., & Almeida, P. (2003). Overcoming local search through alliances and mobility. *Management Science*, *49*, 751–766.

Ryan, P. (2001). The school-to-work transition: a cross-national perspective. *Journal of Economic Literature*, *34*, 34–92.

Saxenian, A. L. (1999). *Silicon valley's new immigrant entrepreneurs*. San Francisco, CA: Public Policy Institute of California.

Scellato, G., Franzoni, C., & Stephan, P. (2015). Migrant scientists and international networks. *Research Policy*, *44*(1), 108–120.

Singh, J., & Agrawal, A. (2011). Recruiting for ideas: how firms exploit the prior inventions of new hires. *Management Science*, *57*, 129–150.

Smith-Doerr, L. (2006). Stuck in the middle: doctoral education ranking and career outcomes for life scientists. *Bulletin of Science, Technology & Society*, *26*(3), 243–255.

Sockanathan, A. (2004). Conceptualising and rewarding excellence in the UK: The role of research assessment. CSLPE Research Report 2004-17, University of Leeds.

Sretenova, N. (2003). Scientific mobility and 'brain drain' issues in the higher education sector in Bulgaria. CSLPE Research Report 2003, University of Leeds.

Stack, S. (2004). Gender, children and research productivity. *Research in Higher Education, 45*(8), 891–920.

Stephan, P. (2012). *How economics shapes science.* Cambridge, MA: Harvard University Press.

Stephan, P., & Ma, J. (2005). The increased frequency and duration of the postdoctorate career stage. *American Economic Review, 95,* 71–75.

Stuart, T. E., & Ding, W. W. (2006). When do scientists become entrepreneurs? The social structural antecedents of commercial activity in the academic life sciences. *American Journal of Sociology, 112*(1), 97–144.

Su, X. (2011). Postdoctoral training, departmental prestige and scientists' research productivity. *The Journal of Technology Transfer, 36,* 275–291.

Su, X., & Bozeman, B. (2009). Dynamics of sector switching: Hazard models predicting changes from private sector jobs to public and nonprofit sector jobs. *Public Administration Review, 69*(6), 1106–1114.

Teichler, U., Arimoto, A., & Cummings, W. K. (2013). *The changing academic profession.* Dordrecht: Springer.

Thistlewaite, D. L., & Campbell, D. T. (1960). Regression-discontinuity analysis: an alternative to the ex post facto experiment. *Journal of Educational Psychology, 51,* 309–317.

Toole, A. A., & Czarnitzki, D. (2010). Commercializing science: Is there a university "brain drain" from academic entrepreneurship? *Management Science, 56,* 1599–1614.

Van der Sande, D., Ackers, L., & Gill, B. (2005). *Impact assessment of the marie curie fellowships under the 4th and 5th framework programmes of research and technological development of the EU (1994–2002).* Brussels: European Commission.

Veugelers, R., & van Bouwel, L. (Chapter 8). Destinations of mobile European researchers: Europe versus the United States. In A. Geuna (Ed.), *Global Mobility of Research Scientists: The Economics of Who Goes Where and Why.* Amsterdam: Elsevier.

Vitae. (2010). *What do researchers do? Doctoral graduate destinations and impact three years on 2010.* Cambridge: Vitae/CRAC.

Weinberg, B. A. (2009). An assessment of British science over the 20th century. *Economic Journal, 119,* F252–F269.

Wooldridge, B. A. (2006). *Introductory econometrics: A modern approach* (3rd ed.). Cincinnati, OH: South-Western College Publishing.

Wooldridge, B. A. (2010). *Econometric analysis of cross section and panel data* (2nd ed.). Cambridge, MA: MIT Press.

Zellner, C. (2003). The economic effects of basic research: evidence for embodied knowledge transfer via scientists' migration. *Research Policy, 32,* 1881–1895.

Zinovyeva, N., & Bagues, M. (2015). The role of connections in academic promotion. *American Economic Journal: Applied Economics, 7*(2), 264–292.

Zubieta, A. (2009). Recognition and weak ties. Is there a positive effect of postdoctoral positions in academic performance and career development? *Research Evaluation, 18*(2), 105–115.

Zucker, L. G., Darby, M. R., & Brewer, M. B. (1998). Intellectual human capital and the birth of U.S. biotechnology enterprises. *American Economic Review, 88,* 290–306.

Zucker, L. G., Darby, M. R., & Torero, M. (2002). Labor mobility from academe to commerce. *Journal of Labor Economics, 20,* 629–660.

Zumeta, W. (1985). *Extending the educational career ladder: The changing quality and value of postdoctoral study.* Lexington, MA: Lexington Books.

Chapter 2

International Mobility of Research Scientists: Lessons from GlobSci

Chiara Franzoni[1], Giuseppe Scellato[2,3], Paula Stephan[4,5,6]

[1]*School of Management, Politecnico di Milano, Milan, Italy;* [2]*Department of Management and Production Engineering, Politecnico di Torino, Turin, Italy;* [3]*BRICK, Collegio Carlo Alberto, Moncalieri, Turin, Italy;* [4]*Andrew Young School of Policy Studies, Georgia State University, Atlanta, GA, USA;* [5]*National Bureau of Economic Research, Cambridge, MA, USA;* [6]*Department of Economics and Statistics Cognetti De Martiis, Università di Torino, Turin, Italy*

Chapter Outline

1. INTRODUCTION

Circulation of the skilled workforce is a global phenomenon, especially characteristic of talented individuals who are highly productive and command a wage premium (Gibson & McKenzie, 2012). Moreover, workers, especially high-skilled ones who have experienced mobility in the past, have a higher propensity to move than natives who have never experienced mobility, not only because they are less tied to the latest location but also because they are more responsive to new windows of opportunities emerging in a different location (Kerr & Lincoln, 2010). It is thus not surprising that national science and innovation systems compete not only to attract the best and brightest but also to retain national talent and to attract back those who have left for study or work abroad (Hunter, Oswald, & Charlton, 2009).

In many cases mobility is motivated by the opportunity to receive higher compensation (Hunter et al., 2009). But scientists are not only motivated by money. Scientists respond to incentives in the form of recognition, intellectual curiosity, and the freedom to perform research (Sauermann & Roach, 2010; Stephan & Levin, 1992). This means that scientists may move in order to work in a setting where they perceive that they can be more productive (Stephan, Franzoni, & Scellato, 2015). For example, mobility can provide access to special equipment or facilities or the opportunity to work with teams of experts in one's own research area. Countries that provide strong support for scientific research can thus expect to attract immigrants. The labor market also plays a role in mobility decisions. In many countries academic job markets are strongly regulated and recruiting and promotion systems change only rarely and by acts of law (Franzoni, Scellato, & Stephan, 2011), making some destinations more or less appealing than others. Moreover, not all destination countries are equally welcoming to immigrants. For example, immigration policies are extremely restrictive in Japan for virtually any type of migrant. By way of contrast, several countries have policies designed to attract high-skilled migrants that include easier visa procedures, fiscal benefits, and special recruiting packages. For a number of years, Canada, for example, had an immigration system that favored the entry of migrants with high skills, as did Australia. The European Union (EU) since 2011 implemented the "blue card" policy to facilitate entry of high-skilled migrants.

Other countries are less focused on attracting immigrants and more focused on convincing nationals who have emigrated to return to the motherland. India is discussing the creation of foreign-based contact points to encourage the recruitment of natives working abroad. China has created programs designed to attract natives back to China, either as visitors or in permanent positions (Stephan, 2012).

These, as well as other factors, contribute to the degree to which countries likely differ in the international composition of the highly skilled workforce. Yet comparisons across countries prove difficult. Few governments track the international mobility of the scientific workforce (especially the movement of natives), and there is virtually no data that allow for consistent comparisons of mobility patterns across countries among the PhD trained. Organisation for Economic Co-operation and Development countries, for example, collect data on recipients of tertiary degrees by immigration status, but the data do not allow one to distinguish between those with PhDs versus other tertiary degrees; nor do they allow one to distinguish by field of study. As a result, what we know is at best country specific. For example, data collected by the National Science Foundation of the United States show that approximately half of all PhDs awarded in science and engineering in the United States go to the foreign born (Stephan, 2010, 2012). More than two-thirds of temporary residents who receive PhDs in science and engineering in the United States work in a research capacity while in graduate school.[1] Moreover, approximately 60% of postdoctoral fellows in the US were on a temporary visa and approximately 42% of those with a doctoral degree working in a science and engineering occupation in the US were born outside the US.

GlobSci was designed to provide consistent cross-country data on active researchers. It surveyed 47,304 researchers in the four scientific disciplines of biology, chemistry, earth and environmental sciences, and materials science working or studying in 16 countries during February–June 2011. Researchers were randomly selected on the basis of being a corresponding author of an article published in 2009 in a journal related to one of the four fields (referred to here as the "focal article"). The social sciences and humanities were not sampled. Thus by design, the survey studies research-active scientists, excluding early career scientists who have yet to publish and scientists who have, in all likelihood, ceased being research active. The four fields were selected because of the high likelihood (95% or more) that published articles in these fields contained an e-mail address for the corresponding author. Journal selection was stratified by four classes of Impact Factor (IF). As such, the sample reflects authors who contributed in each of the four ranks of journals. It does not necessarily reflect the relative distribution of the entire scientific population. Countries included were Australia, Belgium, Brazil, Canada, Denmark, France, Germany, India, Italy, Japan, Netherlands, Spain, Sweden, Switzerland, the United Kingdom, and the United States. In the subsequent sections we refer to this set of countries as "core." Collectively, the 16 core countries produce about 70% of all articles published in these fields. Country of origin was determined by asking the respondents to report their country of residence at age 18. This allows us to neutralize the incidence of those foreign born who came to a country during childhood, and whose migration decision depends on family choices rather than on their own. International mobility was defined as migrating away from one's country of origin for purposes of study or work or for taking a postdoc or job position of at least 12 months.

---

1. Black & Stephan (2010) find that graduate students constitute 29.3% of the first authors of papers published in Science; 40.7% of first authors are postdocs. Using data supplied by Bill Kerr, they infer ethnicity of the first and last name of the authors, finding that 58.5% of the graduate students and 54.4% of the postdocs have names that are neither "English" nor "European."

Panelists were invited to participate by e-mail. The invitation letter and survey was fielded in English. Both were available in six other languages, as well. The overall response rate is 40.6%. The response rate, conditional on completing the entire survey, is 35.6%.[2] Response rate bias appears quite modest and is discussed in Supporting Information in Franzoni, Scellato, & Stephan (2012b). The sampling strategy and procedure is discussed in Franzoni et al. (2012b) as well. China was initially included in the survey. However, a low response rate of less than 5% for a test sample of Chinese addresses suggested that respondents were either not receiving the invitation or had problems responding to the invitation. We encountered somewhat similar problems in a later effort to survey scientists in South Korea. Based on these test samples, we decided not to survey researchers residing in either China or South Korea.

This chapter summarizes findings of empirical analyses based on data collected through the GlobSci Survey. We have organized the chapter to report information concerning the patterns of international composition (Section 2), the characteristics and intentions of those who may return (Section 3), the role played by the internationally mobile researchers in research networks (Section 4), and the performance of the internationally mobile (Section 5). The analysis summarizes findings on issues such as:

- The incidence of foreign born, returnees, and nonmobile natives across countries
- The incidence of temporary visits abroad among otherwise nonmobile natives across countries
- The main source countries supplying foreign-born talent
- The motivation for the decision to study or work abroad
- The share of natives working abroad with the intent to return to their country of birth
- The reasons natives give for returning and the performance of returnees versus foreign-based compatriots
- The role mobile scientists play in international networks
- The degree to which there is a performance premium attached to mobility

The analyses concerning temporary visits abroad and performance of returnees compared to foreign-based compatriots are presented here for the first time. Other results have been reported in prior publications and are offered here in summary form. We refer readers to the prior publications for complete coverage.

---

2. Most Web-based surveys have a response rate of 10–25% (Sauermann & Roach, 2013). Our reported response rates do not take into account undelivered invitations due to such things as incorrect e-mail address, retirement, or death and consequently underestimate the response rate of those receiving invitations. Undelivered e-mails generally account for between 3% and 6% of a sample in the US (Sauermann & Roach, 2010; Walsh, Cho, & Cohen, 2005).

2. INTERNATIONAL MOBILITY PATTERNS[3]

2.1 Incidence of Nonmobile Natives, Returnees, and Foreign Born in the 16 Core Countries

In our survey, four types of international experience qualify for the status of internationally mobile as of 2011: First, having an experience of non-PhD study outside the origin country (such as a BA, MA, laurea, or equivalent); second, having either received a PhD degree or currently being enrolled in a PhD program (or doctorate education or equivalent) outside the country of origin; third, having taken a postdoctoral appointment or currently holding a postdoctoral position outside the country of origin; and fourth, having taken a job or currently holding a job outside the country of origin. For reasons of methodological conservativeness, stays of less than 12 months are not classified as an international experience. Visiting periods of six or more months are coded separately, as explained in the section that follows.

In order to analyze international mobility patterns, we partition the research-active workforce of each of the 16 countries into three groups defined as follows: (1) Nonmobile Natives, that is, natives of a country who declared no prior experience of work or study abroad at the time the survey was administered; (2) Returnees, that is, natives of a country who declared a prior experience of work or study abroad and were residing in the country of origin at the time the survey was administered; and (3) Foreign Born, that is, immigrant scientists whose country of origin differs from the country in which they were working or studying at the time the survey was administered. Status number one corresponds to native scientists who trained in their country and who had never trained or taken a position outside the country. Categories two and three correspond to the internationally mobile scientists. These individuals share at least one experience of study or work away from their country of origin for a year or more. The two groups differ, however, with respect to their country of origin. Individuals in group two have subsequently returned home and, therefore, responded to our survey from the origin country. Individuals in group three are either still mobile or have permanently resettled away from their country of origin. Combined, the three groups represent all scientists working in a specific country in 2011. Cross-country comparisons are discussed here. Patterns of migration of national scientists are discussed in the next subsection.

We report the composition of the international workforce across the 16 countries in Columns 1–4 of Table 1, which draws in part on our prior work (Franzoni, Scellato, & Stephan, 2012b). The data reveal considerable country variation in the international background of research-active scientists. Italy, Japan, and the US are the three countries where more than half of the workforce is composed of natives with no experience abroad (Column 2). The incidence in Belgium and Brazil is just shy of 50%. At the other extreme, are the countries of Switzerland (13.9%), Canada (23.3%), and Australia (25.3%).

---

3. Section 2 is drawn in part from Franzoni et al. (2012b) and from Stephan et al. (2015).

TABLE 1 Incidence of Foreign Born, Returnees, and Natives Nonmobile Across 16 Countries

Country of Work or Study in 2011 Obs. 17,182 (number)	Incidence of Nonmobile Natives (%)	Incidence of Returnees (After Studying or Working Abroad) (%)	Incidence of Foreign Born (%)	Countries Supplying 10% or More of Foreign Workforce (%)	Share of Nonmobile Natives that Had Temporary Visits Abroad (At least 6 months) (%)
Australia (629)	25.3	30.2	44.5	UK (21.1) China (12.5)	16.4
Belgium (253)	49.4	32.4	18.2	Germany (15.2) France (15.2) Italy (13.0)	21.6
Brazil (702)	49.6	43.3	7.1	Argentina (16.0) France (14.0) Columbia (12.0) Peru (12.0)	15.8
Canada (902)	23.3	29.8	46.9	UK (13.5) US (13.5) China (10.9)	16.7
Denmark (206)	41.3	36.9	21.8	Germany (24.4)	36.5
France (1380)	38.9	43.8	17.3	Italy (13.8)	12.3
Germany (1187)	41.9	34.9	23.2	None	18.3
India (525)	41.3	57.9	0.8	a	15.7
Italy (1792)	69.7	27.3	3.0	France (13.0) Germany (11.1) Spain (11.1)	35.4

Japan (1707)	57.7	37.3	5.0	China (33.7), South Korea (11.6)	26.1
Netherlands (347)	46.1	26.2	27.7	Germany (14.6), Italy (12.5)	24.4
Spain (1185)	37.4	55.3	7.3	Argentina (12.6), France (10.3), Italy (10.3)	36.0
Sweden (314)	33.4	29.0	37.6	Germany (11.9), Russian Fed. (10.2)	18.1
Switzerland (330)	13.9	29.4	56.7	Germany (36.9)	21.7
UK (1205)	39.2	27.9	32.9	Germany (15.2), Italy (10.4)	12.1
US (4518)	52.3	9.3	38.4	China (16.9), India (12.3)	12.6

[a]Virtually zero observations.

Two countries stand out with regard to the percentage of natives who had a prior experience of work or study abroad but who later returned to the origin countries (Column 3). These are India and Spain, where the returnees make up more than 55% of active researchers. Brazil and France are distant seconds, with approximately 43% of the workforce reporting mobility for study or work prior to returning.

Switzerland is the country with the highest incidence of foreign born in the workforce (Column 4); more than one out of two living in Switzerland in 2011 were outside the country at age 18. Canada is a distant second with about 47%, followed closely by Australia (44%). The foreign born represent approximately 38% in the US and Sweden. A number of countries have an extremely low percent of foreign scientists studying or working in the country. India has virtually zero foreign scientists studying or working in country, Italy has a scant 3.0%, and Japan has 5.0%. Brazil with 7.1% and Spain with 7.3% are not that dissimilar from India, Italy, and Japan.

For many countries, "neighbors" are the most likely source of immigrants (Column 5). For example, Germany is the most likely country of origin of immigrant scientists in the Netherlands as well as immigrant scientists studying or working in Belgium, Denmark, Sweden, and Switzerland. Argentina, Columbia, and Peru are important source countries for those working or studying in Brazil. The United States is a major source country for foreigners working or studying in Canada. The most likely countries of origin for foreign scientists working or studying in Japan are China and South Korea. Cultural/language ties also matter. The UK is the top source country for Australia and is tied for top place as the source country for foreigners in Canada; Argentina is the major source country for Spain. But geography and language do not always dominate. The top source country for the US is China. The top source country for the UK is Germany, followed by Italy.

The data presented in Columns 1–5 of Table 1 exclude temporary periods of international mobility that occur, for example, when a scientist visits an institution in a foreign country for a sabbatical or to conduct research for a period of at least six months without enrolling in a program or taking a formal employment position in the country of destination. In the GlobSci survey, we also asked whether a scientist had experienced visiting periods abroad such as those just mentioned, which lasted at least six months. Column 6 of Table 1 provides the computed share of nonmobile natives who reported having experiences of temporary visits of at least six months. More than one in three scientists from Denmark, Spain, and Italy who did not report mobility for study or work reported having at least one visiting period abroad. The share is about one in four for the nonmobile in Japan and in the Netherlands and one in five for the nonmobile in Belgium and Switzerland, followed by Germany and Sweden, where about 18% of nonmobile natives had visiting periods abroad. Among the nonmobile, the least likely to have visited outside the country are those in the UK, France and the US.

2.2 Migration Patterns of National Scientists Across 16 Countries

The GlobSci survey not only provides information on the international experiences of the workforce but also allows us to measure the migration patterns of nationals of the 16 core countries, as long as this migration occurred in one of the other 16 core countries. This information is summarized in Table 2 for the 15,115 respondents who lived in a core country at age 18 and were in a core country in 2011. To correct for the fact that response rates varied by country, probability weights have been used to compute the reported rates (see Franzoni, Scellato, & Stephan, 2012b, p. 1251 and SI for details).

We again find considerable variation in the percentage of native scientists who were studying or working abroad. Not surprisingly, India heads the list with 39.8% of native scientists working or studying outside the country in 2011. But the country that has the second highest rate of nationals abroad is Switzerland, with approximately one-third of its residents studying or working abroad in 2011. The Netherlands and the UK are next, with approximately one in four of their natives studying or working outside of country. The country with the lowest percentage of nationals abroad is Japan (3.1%), but the United States is a close second at 5.0 %, followed by Brazil and Spain.

There is considerably less variation in the country of destination (Column 2 of Table 2). Indeed, the top destination country for emigrants from all countries except Belgium and Denmark is the United States. The most likely destination country for Belgian scientists is France, and the most likely destination country of Danish scientists is the UK, but even in these cases the US is the second most likely destination country. The most likely country of destination for US nationals at age 18 is Canada.

2.3 Reasons to Migrate △

Scientists who moved for work or postdoctoral study were asked to evaluate on a five-point scale the importance of 14 possible reasons for their decision to have come to their current country (Franzoni et al., 2012b, p. 1252). The scale was valued as going from "totally unimportant" (score=1) to "extremely important" (score=5), with the intermediate point being "neither important nor unimportant" (score=3). Some of the reasons reflect pecuniary benefits, such as better wages and better fringe benefits. Some reflect personal preferences/concerns ("family or personal reasons"; "appeal of life style"). Others reflect policies of the destination country that affect the quality of research undertaken and, related, the availability of resources for research ("opportunity to improve my future career prospects"; "outstanding faculty, colleagues or research team"; "excellence/prestige of the foreign institution in my area of research"; "better research infrastructure and facilities"; "greater availability of research funds"). Several take home conclusions

TABLE 2 Migration Patterns Across Natives of 16 Countries

Country of Origin at Age 18 Obs. 15,115 (number)	Share Currently Outside the Country (%)	Destination Countries with More Than 10% of Natives Abroad (%)
Australia (418)	18.3	US (45.8)
		UK (24.7)
Belgium (261)	21.7	France (30.0)
		US (20.0)
		UK (10.2)
Brazil (700)	8.3	US (34.0)
		Canada (15.7)
		Germany (15.5)
Canada (613)	23.7	US (70.1)
Denmark (183)	13.3	UK (37.5)
		US (36.4)
France (1303)	13.2	US (22.8)
		UK (14.5)
		Canada (14.0)
Germany (1254)	23.3	US (29.5)
		Switzerland (19.1)
		UK (18.0)
India (806)	39.8	US (75.1)
Italy (1938)	16.2	US (25.0)
		UK (19.7)
		France (15.5)
		Germany (10.7)
Japan (1676)	3.1	US (51.4)
Netherlands (339)	26.4	US (22.9)
		UK (19.5)
		Germany (18.8)
Spain (1175)	8.4	US (31.0)
		Germany (16.2)
		UK (15.5)
		France (14.1)
Sweden (226)	13.9	US (23.8)
		UK (13.8)
		Germany (11.5)
Switzerland (209)	33.1	US (34.2)
		Germany (29.5)
UK (1090)	25.1	US (46.9)
		Canada (16.6)
		Australia (16.6)
US (2924)	5.0	Canada (32.2)
		UK (16.3)
		Australia (10.1)
		Germany (10.0)

TABLE 3 Description of Factors in Decision to Work Abroad (Scale 1: Totally Unimportant, 5: Extremely Important)

Item	Score
Opportunity to improve my future career prospects	4.30
Outstanding faculty, colleagues, or research team	4.25
Excellence/prestige of the foreign institution in my area of research	4.15
Opportunity to extend my network of international relationships	3.90
Better research infrastructures and facilities	3.80
Appeal of the life style or international experience	3.75
Opportunity to improve my future job prospects in the country where I lived when I was 18	3.65
Greater availability of research funds	3.60
Better quality of life	3.05
Better wage/monetary compensation	2.95
Few or poor job opportunities in the country where I lived when I was 18	2.60
Better working conditions (vacations, hours of work, ...)	2.45
Family or personal reasons	2.40
Better fringe benefits (parental leaves, pension, insurance, ...)	2.35

See Franzoni et al. (2012b).

stand out when we analyze these data. First, for any specific reason there is virtually no variation across country in response, suggesting that reasons for emigrating are reasonably consistent across countries. Second, the quality of research undertaken in the host country and the quality of its scientific institutions play a large role in drawing scientists to a country: The "opportunity to improve my future career prospects" and the presence of "outstanding faculty, colleagues or research team" trump all other reasons, (see Table 3 for summary data), followed by "Excellence/prestige of the foreign institution in my area of research" and the "opportunity to extend my network of international relationships" in third and fourth place. Third, pecuniary reasons play a minimal role in attracting mobile scientists. Fourth, personal preferences/concerns are of minimal importance compared to other factors in the decision to move to the host country.

Those who went abroad for PhD study were asked to evaluate 10 factors underlying their decision to study abroad, using the same five-point scale. The 10 factors are listed in Figure 1[4] and discussed in more detail in Stephan et al. (2015). Three of the variables included in the list reflect the policies and the level of resources in the home country that can affect emigration for advanced study: fellowship obtained from the origin country, career prospects at home, and lack of good PhD programs. The first is specifically designed to encourage study abroad; the third, reflecting the absence of resources, encourages study abroad by default. The second variable reflects labor market policies and practices in the home country that place a high value on study outside

---

4. The sample is restricted to those who received their PhD in 2000 or later.

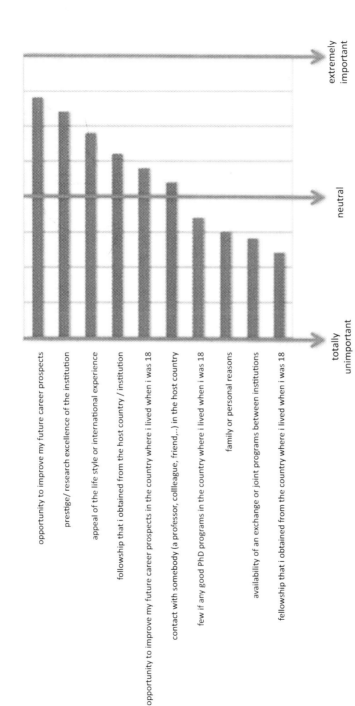

FIGURE 1 Description of factors in decision to study abroad.

the country. Three variables reflect policies and resources of the host country that either directly or indirectly encourage immigration for advanced study: prestige of the host institution, fellowship obtained from the host country, and career prospects in the host country. The latter, which is differentiated from career opportunities in the home country, reflects both the labor market for scientists in the host country (as well as other third countries) and visa policies in the host country. The other two variables involve relationships between either individuals or institutions in the home and host country.

The responses suggest that science policy in the host country plays an important role in the decision to study abroad—both the career and prestige variables are reported as "important." Two other variables have mean scores considerably above "neutral": the fellowship offered by the host country and the lifestyle in the host country. The first of these relates to active science policies on the part of the host country; the second does not. Four have mean scores indicating that respondents on average score the factors as lying between being totally unimportant and neutral. The four are: family reasons, the availability of an exchange program, the fellowships offered by the origin country to study abroad, and the lack of a good PhD program. The latter three depend in part on policies and resources of the home country. Combining these results with the above results concerning reasons for working abroad leads to the conclusion that science policy in the host country plays an important role in the decision to go to a different country for either study or work. In other work not shown here, we introduce three characteristics of the educational and research environment of the country into the analysis: the number of institutions ranked in the top 400 by World University Rankings; the percentage of GDP spent on higher education, research and development (HERD), and the H-index, a measure of highly cited publications authored in country. We find that two of the three measures are correlated significantly with the percentage in a country who are foreign born and received their PhD in country, additional evidence suggesting that science policy in the host country plays an important role in drawing immigrants to a country.

3. RETURN

In the prior section we have highlighted the incidence of natives who had been abroad and subsequently returned home and the incidence of nationals of a country who are currently out of country for work or study. Three logical questions follow: What proportion of those who are currently abroad may return in the future? What characterizes those who indicate they will return? What reasons do returnees give for returning, and is there negative selection among those who return?

3.1 Who May Return in the Future and Why

The GlobSci survey asked those who were studying or working away from their country of origin whether they intended to return some time in the future. The answers to this question were reported in Franzoni et al. (2012b, p. 1252).

TABLE 4 Answers to the Question: "Is It Possible that You Return in the Future?" By Country of Residency at Age 18 in Descending Order of Percent Answering "Yes"

Country	Yes	Depends on Job Opportunities	Perhaps Part-time or at End of Career	No or After Retirement
Sweden	38%	15%	12%	35%
Canada	35%	36%	10%	19%
Switzerland	32%	41%	9%	18%
Germany	31%	40%	10%	19%
USA	31%	27%	8%	34%
France	27%	42%	7%	24%
Brazil	27%	19%	20%	34%
Spain	26%	36%	19%	19%
Australia	24%	32%	8%	36%
Japan	23%	48%	9%	20%
Netherlands	23%	47%	10%	20%
India	22%	21%	26%	31%
Belgium	19%	30%	15%	36%
Denmark	17%	33%	22%	28%
Italy	15%	42%	15%	28%
UK	13%	29%	13%	45%

See Franzoni et al. (2012b).

Migrants from Sweden and Canada were the most likely to report that they will return home at some time in the future, with more than one in three answering affirmatively (see Table 4). Conversely, less than one in five of the migrant scientists from the UK, Italy, Denmark, and Belgium state that they plan to return at some time in the future. A considerable proportion of Indians working outside the country are less likely than the average emigrant to report that they plan to return. Emigrants from several countries place conditions on whether or not they will return. Close to one out of two from the Netherlands and Japan, for example, and about four out of 10 from five other countries (Italy, Spain, France, Germany, and Switzerland) indicate that their return depends on job opportunities. Job prospects figure less importantly in the possible return for emigrants from other countries, with those from Sweden, Brazil, and India placing the least emphasis on job prospects. A comparatively larger share of scientists from India state that they may go back either to take a part-time position or toward the end of their career.

3.2 What Reasons Do Returnees Give for Returning and Is There Negative Selection?

We asked returnees (e.g., nationals who were in the origin country at the time they took the survey and reported having studied or worked abroad in the past) to rate the importance of 12 reasons played in their decision to return. The answers are given in Figure 2, in descending order of rated importance. "Personal or family reasons" is the single most important factor reported as a motivation for return. The importance of personal and family reasons is invariant across all 16 countries of origin.[5] Four other factors are reported as moderately important. These are: better quality of life, better job opportunities or career prospects, outstanding faculty, and prestige of the home institution. The factor reported as the least important is visa or immigration constraints. The weight that respondents place on these various factors suggests that while policies that affect job prospects and working conditions in the home country play a role in bringing migrants home, personal and family reasons are paramount.

reasons of return

A question of interest is whether the productivity of those who return differs from the productivity of compatriots who remain abroad. Unfortunately, stated reasons to return may be subject to reporting bias in this respect. For example, it is possible that scientists overstate the importance of family and personal reasons and understate the importance of career problems, such as their failure to keep up in the international arena, when stating factors that explained their return. Given that migration usually occurs disproportionately from countries with a relatively weak science base to countries with a relatively strong science base, there are reasons to believe that emigrants are positively selected and returnees are conversely negatively selected, in the sense that these may be the "worst" of the "best" (Borjas & Bratsberg, 1996; Dustmann, Fadlon, & Weiss, 2011).

To investigate further on this issue, we analyze responses from GlobSci. We restrict the sample to academics who were natives of a core country and who had been studying or working abroad. There are 6,529 observations in our sample that meet these criteria. We compare the performance of those who had returned at the time they took the survey (in 2011) to the performance of the compatriots who were still abroad in 2011. We used the average IF of the journal in which the focal article was published as a measure of performance and total citations to focal articles for comparison. Table 5 reports the average IF by country and return status in 2011.[6]

In 12 of the 16 countries, returnees exhibit comparable performance to their compatriots who remained abroad in 2011. In Brazil, India, and Italy, returnees on average do not perform as well as their compatriots who have remained abroad, suggestive that negative selection might have occurred in these countries. Belgium displays a similar pattern, but the difference is only significant at 90% confidence level. The overall sample reflects the highlighted differences. Other factors, of course, could contribute to the difference, such as fewer research facilities and funding for research available to the returnees in their origin country. To partly

U.S. keeps best of developing cnts but not developed countries

5. See the Supporting Information to Franzoni et al. (2012b) for single-country scores.
6. The impact factor has been rank normalized using the procedure of Pudovkin & Garfield (2004) to minimize the potential incidence of diverse composition in subject categories across the two samples.

▲ *diaspora expatriate researchers have higher productivity than return*

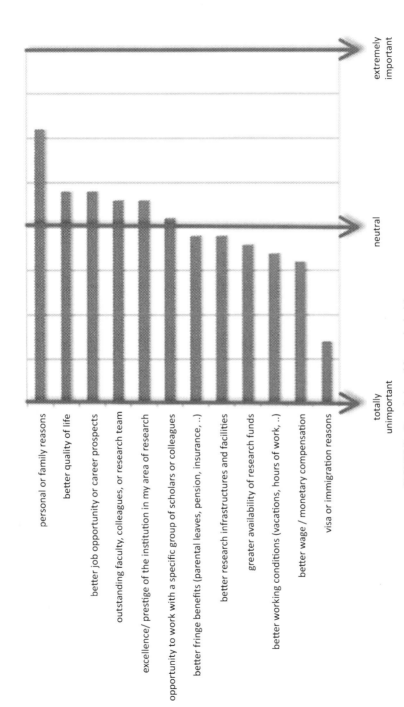

FIGURE 2   Description of factors in decision to return.

TABLE 5 Performance, Measured by Impact Factor, of Academics by Return Status in 2011

Country of Origin	Returnees	Abroad	Mean Diff (St. err.)	
Australia	0.772	0.767	0.005	0.032
Belgium	0.753	0.813	−0.060	0.036*
Brazil	0.566	0.720	−0.154	0.042***
Canada	0.747	0.721	0.026	0.025
Denmark	0.755	0.818	−0.062	0.051
France	0.802	0.787	0.015	0.019
Germany	0.778	0.796	−0.019	0.016
India	0.658	0.726	−0.068	0.020***
Italy	0.741	0.800	−0.059	0.019***
Japan	0.727	0.732	−0.006	0.036
Netherlands	0.795	0.806	−0.011	0.031
Spain	0.749	0.749	−0.001	0.026
Sweden	0.782	0.802	−0.019	0.045
Switzerland	0.797	0.794	0.002	0.034
UK	0.770	0.771	−0.002	0.018
USA	0.765	0.799	−0.034	0.022
Average (weighted)	0.747	0.772	−0.026	0.005***

Observations: 6529 national academics with international experience. * $p \leq 0.1$; *** $p \leq 0.01$.

isolate this effect from potential confounds, we run a multivariate analysis, where we control for the country of current work or study, which affects the level of resources (facilities, grants, etc.) to which scientists have access in their current location (see the Appendix to Franzoni, Scellato & Stephan, 2012a). When we do so, we find the coefficient of the "return" variable to be inconsistent with negative selection, net of the controls. When we measure citations to the focal article, rather than the IF of the journal in which the focal article was published, we find a similar result. In this case, we do, however, find a "decay" effect indicating that the longer a returnee has been back in the origin country, the less likely is the focal article to be cited, compared to the focal paper of those who remained abroad. The effect, however, is moderate in magnitude—for each additional year spent in the home country after returning, the average scientist receives 0.10 fewer citations. In other words, 10 years after returning, scientists who are back in their country of origin receive about one citation less to the focal article than those received by compatriots who have remained abroad.

In sum, we find no compelling evidence that returnees on average are adversely selected among internationally mobile scientists. This suggests that individuals who report returning for family or lifestyle reasons are, in all likelihood, not doing so as a face-saving gesture. The lack of a performance differential also suggests that the premium associated with international experience survives return with a modest decay rate, despite the fact that many of the returnees work in what are likely to be less favorable environments. Clearly, this analysis is merely suggestive; this result would benefit from further investigation.

4. INTERNATIONAL MOBILITY AND RESEARCH NETWORKS

The last three decades have witnessed an increase in the extent of international scientific collaboration (Wagner & Leydesdorff, 2005). Research teams are becoming larger and a growing proportion of teams are established between scientists based at different institutions and in different countries (Gazni, Sugimoto, & Didegah, 2012; Jones, Wuchty, & Uzzi, 2008; Wuchty, Jones, & Uzzi, 2007). For example, in the US, the foreign share of internationally coauthored papers increased steadily from about 5.1% per year during the 1980s to about 7.4% during the 1990s, with the increase being driven primarily by collaborations with Asian and European institutions (Adams, Black, Clemmons, & Stephan, 2005). The share of European papers coauthored with US-based researchers increased from 5.9% in 1985 to 9.5% in 1995, while papers coauthored with Japan-based researchers increased from 0.5% to 1.3%, and those with researchers based in Canada from 0.9% to 1.6% (Georghiou, 1998).

Numerous factors have been noted as contributing to the trend, from policy "push" initiatives to advances in technologies that foster remote collaborations (Ding, Levin, Stephan, & Winkler, 2010) to the rising importance of large equipment in science. Without denying the relevance of any of these factors, we drew on GlobSci data to investigate the relation between migration and network formation. Although we cannot use the data to infer a causal relation (in other words we do not know whether migration caused the international networks or vice versa), our data analysis provides compelling evidence that mobile scientists have a higher propensity to participate in international networks and that they see international networking as a main result of their mobility experience (Scellato, Franzoni, & Stephan, 2015).

The first piece of evidence comes from using the GlobSci data to examine the share of internationally coauthored papers by the mobility status of the correspondent author. This evidence is based on the randomly selected focal papers used to generate the panels of surveyed researchers. The data are computed for the restricted subsample of academic researchers. As can be seen from Figure 3, the incidence of international collaboration on the focal paper is lowest for nonmobile natives. It is the highest for the foreign born. Returnees have a lower incidence compared to foreign born but a significantly higher incidence than native nonmobile.

The second piece of evidence comes from the survey itself, which asked respondents to report the scope of their international research network based on research collaborations during the past two years. Table 6 shows nonmobile natives to be the most likely to report no international collaborations in the past two years. The distribution of the number of countries with which the foreign born and returnees have had a collaborator is almost the same. About half have collaborated with scientists in two to four countries and more than one-fifth have collaborated with scientists in four or more countries.

An interesting finding from GlobSci data is that a substantial number of collaborations that the foreign born engage in occur with individuals who have

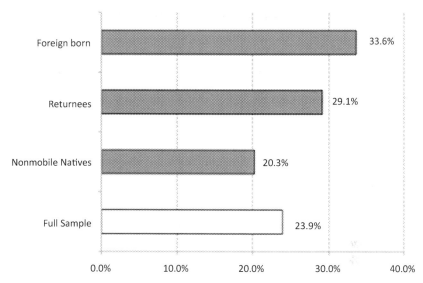

FIGURE 3   Incidence of internationally coauthored papers by mobility status of corresponding author.

TABLE 6 Size of the International Research Network Related to the Activities in the Past Two Years by Mobility Status of Respondents

	International Network Size (% of Respondents)			
	Full Sample	Foreign Born	Returnees	Nonmobile
No international collaborations	19.08	14.06	14.26	24.36
Small network (1 country)	18.71	17.59	17.28	19.91
Medium network (2–4 countries)	43.69	47.53	47.02	40.02
Large network (more than 4 countries)	18.53	20.82	21.45	15.72

See Scellato et al. (2015).

some links with the home country. These links could be with scientists who currently reside in the home country or with scientists from the same country of origin who are expats to a third country. This can be seen in Table 7, which shows the incidence, by country of current work or study of the foreign born who declare having a research collaboration with researchers located in their origin country (Columns 1 and 2) or with researchers from their origin country who

TABLE 7 Percentage of Foreign-Born Academics, by Country of Work or Study in Year 2011, Who Report Collaboration with Researchers Currently Based in Their Country of Origin (1 and 2) and with Researchers from the Same Origin Country Who Have Emigrated (3)

Current Country	Percentage of Foreign-Born Researchers Who Collaborate with Nationals in the Origin Country		Percentage of Foreign-Born Researchers Who Collaborate with Nationals Who Have Migrated to a Different Country
	1	2	3
	From Any Origin Country	From Noncore Origin Countries[a]	From Any Origin Country
Australia	46.1	42.6	26.29
Belgium	55.6	16.7	22.86
Brazil	29.3	34.5	12.20
Canada	35.8	27.5	19.44
Denmark	33.3	27.3	33.33
France	57.7	48.9	17.91
Germany	39.0	35.7	17.84
Italy	56.8	63.2	20.45
Japan	43.5	39.6	11.29
Netherlands	53.4	40.0	28.77
Spain	38.0	28.6	18.31
Sweden	56.7	44.7	17.78
Switzerland	50.3	39.3	26.38
UK	44.0	34.0	21.87
USA	37.4	35.1	16.96
TOT	41.7	35.9	19.29

[a]Core countries are those appearing in the table; noncore are all others.

migrated to a third country (Column 3). By way of example, 44% of foreign-born researchers based in the UK in 2011 report that they have an international collaboration with someone currently based in their origin country. Among all of the foreign born, the percentage who collaborate with scientists at home, regardless of country of origin, is 41.7. When we focus exclusively on foreign born from noncore countries such as Russia, Pakistan, Iran, South Korea, and China, the percentage declines to 35.9 (Column 2). There are, however, important exceptions. In the case of the US, we observe a relatively smaller reduction in the percentage when we restrict the analysis to foreign natives of noncore countries. This likely reflects the large number of Chinese and Korean scientists studying and working in the US. In the case of Brazil and Italy we actually see an increase.

TABLE 8 Incidence of Scientific Collaboration Between Foreign Born from the Same Country of Origin Working at the Same Institution, by Country of Work or Study in Year 2011

Current Country	In My Place of Employment I Work with At least One Person Who Is from My Country of Origin
Australia	34.05%
Belgium	40.00%
Brazil	31.71%
Canada	25.83%
Denmark	43.33%
France	32.34%
Germany	32.86%
Italy	27.27%
Japan	37.10%
Netherlands	26.03%
Spain	45.07%
Sweden	24.44%
Switzerland	44.17%
UK	26.24%
US	23.91%
TOT	28.25%

As noted above, the data also allow us to analyze the relationship between international mobility and research networks by looking at the propensity of foreign-born scientists to have a collaboration with researchers from their country of origin who have moved to a third country (Column 3). The aim is to capture a diaspora effect behind the higher collaboration propensity of the foreign born. The data reveal that a nonnegligible share of the foreign born collaborate with a community of expatriates from their origin country living in a third country (diaspora effect)—on average 19.3%, with a minimum of 11.9% for foreign born who are currently working in Japan and a maximum of 33.3% for foreign born currently working in Denmark.

We also analyze the relationship between international mobility and research networks by looking at the propensity of foreign-born scientists to have a collaboration with researchers from their country of origin currently based in the same institution as the respondent's. The data reported in Table 8 reveal that a considerable share of mobile researchers report collaborations with someone from their home country in their current place of employment or study. The overall findings suggest that personal/cultural links matter in explaining patterns of collaboration.

Survey participants with a migration experience were also asked to rate on a five-point scale their perception of the impact of international mobility on a number of dimensions. A summary of the results for returnees and foreign born is found in Table 9. We see that on average, both returnees and foreign-born researchers assign the highest average value to the item "enlarging my research network," followed by "learning new techniques/theories." This is consistent with the hypothesis that international mobility has a nonnegligible impact on fostering

TABLE 9 The Perceived Impact of International Mobility for Returnees and Foreign Born. 1–5 Scale: Totally Unimportant (1)–Extremely Important (5)

	Returnees	Foreign Born
Enlarging my research network	4.19	4.35
Establishing a stable research cooperation with teams/scholars located abroad	3.71	4.02
Entering into new fields of research	3.90	4.08
Learning new techniques/theories	4.12	4.17
Improving my capability to publish in high-tier journals	3.68	3.93
Improving my wage and earning possibilities	2.72	3.41
Improving my career prospects	3.89	4.08
Establishing better contacts with industrial partners	2.15	2.67
Improving my ability to raise research funds	3.16	3.65

the international openness of the research systems of both source and destination countries. Notably, items related to economic and pecuniary benefits from international mobility receive on average lower ratings than career measures. This suggests that high-skilled migration patterns—at least in the case of scientists—cannot be fully captured by underlying theoretical models that predict mobility primarily on the basis of wage differentials, but rather that factors that contribute to research productivity play a large role in determining mobility.[7]

In order to capture the net effects of mobility status on research networking, we have treated individual-level data with econometric models that account for field and country characteristics, as well as for individual attributes such as gender and age (Scellato et al., 2015). More specifically, we measure the scope of the international network by creating three discrete ordered variables of NETWORK SIZE that take the value of 1 for those with no international collaborations in the past two years, 2 for those with collaborations in just one country, 3 for those with collaborations in two to four countries, and 4 for those with collaborations in five or more countries. These levels of the ordered discrete dependent variable correspond to the thresholds used in Table 6 to identify, respectively, no international network, small network, medium network, and large network. Complete results can be found in Scellato et al. (2015).

The models compare the collaboration patterns of the foreign born and returnees to the collaboration patterns of natives who never experienced international mobility. The basic findings with regard to mobility are that those who have never experienced international mobility are the least likely to collaborate.

---

7. Recall that when returnees were asked to evaluate reasons for returning to their native country, the factor that received the highest score related to personal or family reasons rather than economic factors or career prospects in the country of origin.

Among those who have experienced mobility, the foreign born who are working in country have more extensive international collaborations than do the natives who have returned.[8] For example, foreign born have, *ceteris paribus*, a 7.12% higher likelihood of having a large research network (collaborators in more than four countries) than native nonmigrants. The same marginal effect is 5.5% for returnees. The larger network scope of foreign born versus returnees is statistically significant at 99% level. The characteristics of sending countries can affect such differences in international collaborations. In order to address this issue, we have examined whether collaborations are more likely among migrants from countries with relatively strong science bases (using H-indexes). Results indicate that foreign born who come from a country with a relative higher scientific level outperform the local nonmigrant. On the contrary, foreign born from countries with a lower H-index do not significantly outperform returnees although they do significantly outperform native nonmigrant researchers (Scellato et al., 2015).

We further analyze the data to see whether or not the effect depends on the kind of international experience, that is, whether those who migrated for reasons of study have the same propensity to establish international networks as those who migrated after training. In order to do so, we break down the results by entry point in the destination country and focus exclusively on collaboration patterns of the foreign born. We find that those who trained outside the country before entering have larger international collaborative networks. The finding suggests that the "foreigner premium" effect is driven primarily by migrant researchers with previous training or work experience outside of the destination country, that is, by individuals who likely had a rich knowledge network prior to entering the destination country. Immigrants who come for a postdoctoral position represent a clear example of this typology of researchers. These findings are consistent with the idea that, at the time of migration, senior scientists have more social capital with other scholars than do scientists who migrate during the training process and have yet to form a professional network.

It is important to stress that our research design does not permit us to establish causality. For example, it is plausible that the internationally mobile had a somewhat superior capacity to form an international network before moving. If this were the case, international networks would be a cause, not a consequence, of mobility. Thus, the evidence that we report is merely suggestive and can be consistent with both causality and reverse causality. Below, we discuss that this is certainly a topic deserving further research. In either case, our results suggest that policies

---

8. The model includes a number of author-specific variables, such as age, a dummy variable for gender, a dummy variable for whether the respondent has a job position that allows full research independence, that is, professorship, and a self-reported indicator on a 1–5 scale of the average importance of research collaboration in the specific scientific subfield of the respondent. We also include dummies that represent the disciplinary field of the scientist as well as dummies for the country of residence in 2011 and a set of three dummies representing the work environment (university, public research institution, other nonprofit institutions).

that promote the international mobility of students and postdoctoral scholars, such as the European Erasmus and Marie Curie programs, can foster international collaboration. It also suggests that policies to attract scientists who trained or worked outside the country can foster international collaborations. The Ramon y Cajal program in Spain is an example of such a program. The program, which is not limited to Spaniards, provides funds to individuals who obtained their PhD degree in the last 10 years and have carried out research abroad for at least two years or received their PhD abroad two or more years before the call.[9] Policies designed to attract emigrant scientists back to the country of origin and to promote the exchange and communication of nationals abroad with the homeland can also encourage collaboration. Examples include policies in China and India, which offer high salaries to returnees as well as visiting positions. New Zealand has promoted policies to facilitate communication and cooperation between New Zealanders abroad (particularly in Australia) and scientists who are working in country (Davenport, 2004).

5. INTERNATIONAL MOBILITY AND PERFORMANCE

Policies that foster mobility such as visa reforms and special packages for international scientists are predicated on the assumption that the foreign born outperform nonmobile scientists. Thus, a question of clear importance is whether mobility is, indeed, related to the performance of scientists. Collaboration, which we discussed in the prior section, is but one component of how this performance premium could be effectuated. Another reason to think that mobility can foster productivity is that the tacit component of knowledge embedded in individuals places migrant scientists in a position of arbitrage where they can exploit rich or unique knowledge sets (Agrawal, Kapur, McHale, & Oettl, 2011; Saxenian, 2005). Mobility can also enhance productivity because of specialization. Jones (2008) maintains that the specialized skills owned by high-skilled human capital deploy their full value when surrounded by complementary specialty skills. Matching is especially relevant in the academic labor market where productivity depends on the opportunity to work jointly with a team (Stephan, 2012) and many areas of research require dedicated laboratories and special equipment that exist in only a limited number of settings. The connection between mobility and performance can also be an artifact of selection—other things equal, only more able and thus more productive scientists can have mobility options, making nonmobile scientists adversely selected (Borjas, 1994; Ganguli, 2015; Gibson & McKenzie, 2012; Grogger & Hanson, 2011).

At the time the GlobSci survey was conducted, empirical evidence on the correlation of mobility and performance in science was scant at best. Moreover, to the best of our knowledge, no prior work had attempted to disentangle selection

---

9. See http://icc.ub.edu/index.php?m=job&c=ramon_cajal&op=frm_ramon_cajal. Accessed April 13, 2015.

and treatment effects. Studies generally were limited to the foreign born in the US (Stephan & Levin, 2001) and focused on those who made exceptional contributions (Hunter et al., 2009). In a few instances, studies had looked at specific populations (Gaulé & Piacentini, 2013). More recent work, such as that by Freeman & Huang (Chapter 6), has examined the role of diversity, finding that papers with a greater ethnic mix are more highly cited; work by Fernández-Zubieta, Geuna, Kataishi, Lawson, & Toselli (Chapter 3) finds that those who receive their PhD outside the US but work in the US in the biomedical sciences are more productive than those who do not.

5.1 Performance of Migrants

We use GlobSci data to provide comprehensive evidence on the performance of scientists by mobility status across a large sample of countries. For the purpose of this analysis, we restrict the sample to academic scientists and look at the performance measured in terms of the IF of the journal in which the focal article was published, as well as the rank-normalized IF, which accounts for potential biases due to averaging across different subject categories (Pudovkin & Garfield, 2004). The statistics are illustrated in Figure 4. We see that the mean IF of the foreign born is higher than that of native nonmobile researchers and also higher than that of the returnees, although the difference between the last two groups is not large. The performance differentials in terms of rank-normalized IF are quite minimal. Nonetheless, both the foreign born and the returnees

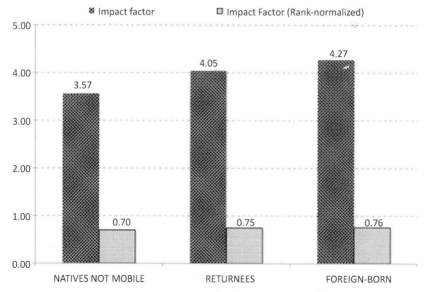

FIGURE 4 Performance by mobility status*.

outperform nonmobile natives (differences are significant at 99%), while there appears to be no statistically significant difference between the performances of the foreign born and those of the returnees.

5.2 Migration Premium

In our 2014 article (Franzoni, Scellato & Stephan, 2014), we exploited the richness of the GlobSci dataset to further examine the observed positive differential in the performance of foreign born compared to the nonmobile natives. We estimated a multivariate model to compare the relative performance of migrant and domestic scientists working in 2009 in the same research system and fields net of the effect of potentially confounding factors. These included a set of individual characteristics (age, gender, status of trainee (PhD student), H-index of the country of origin[10]) and a set of characteristics of the focal paper (number of coauthors, international coauthorship, and newness of the research area as reported by the respondent). All models also controlled for field and country of current affiliation. Controls for past experience as a temporary visitor were included in additional estimates but were not statistically significant and were omitted. Our estimates showed that, compared to domestic scientists (with or without international experience), migrant scientists published their focal article in journals having an IF that is 1.07 points higher (Franzoni et al., 2014). When we compared mobile scientists to domestic scientists who have never had an international experience, the estimated performance premium increased to 1.17 of IF.

To disentangle the effect of treatment from those of selection, we instrumented the migration events that, for our respondents, occurred for reasons of work or study after the age of 18 using migration events that occurred during childhood. The rationale for the instrument is that migration in childhood is likely not affected by individual skills (exogenous) but instead reflects parental decisions, rather than choices of the respondent. After instrumenting, the existence of a positive treatment effect of migration remains, suggesting that migrants perform at a higher level than domestic scientists with or without prior experience of international mobility and that the superior performance is in part a consequence of migrating. We can only offer hypotheses as regards why migration leads to a boost in performance. It is possible, for example, that this occurs due to matching, that is, because mobile scientists place themselves in settings where they can be more productive due to specialized skills or equipment that exists only in specific locations (Jones, 2008), or it is possible that a more diverse knowledge or ethnic mix boosts the creative outcomes (Freeman & Huang, 2015).

---

10. H-index by country and by subject category, computed for all publications in 1996–2010. Source: SCImago Journal and Country Rank. Retrieved from http://www.scimagojr.com on April 18, 2012.

6. CONCLUSIONS

6.1 Summary of Results

The GlobSci survey helps inform our understanding of the mobility of scientists working and studying in 16 countries in four fields. In terms of general patterns, we find that countries vary considerably in the extent to which they are characterized by the presence of internationally mobile scientists as well as the extent to which their residents go abroad for study or work. The country that is the most porous in terms of immigration is Switzerland; a close second is India in terms of emigration of its residents for study or work. The country that is least porous in terms of immigrants is India. Italy is a close second. The US is a contender to Japan for being least likely for researchers to emigrate for study or work. The majority of our analysis has focused on stays of a year or more for study or work. The GlobSci survey, however, also asked whether respondents made visits of six months or longer outside their native country that were not related to employment or study. Stays related to sabbaticals are an example of such visits. When we examine these responses, we find that short-term mobility for visiting periods appears to be a relatively popular phenomenon among nonmobile natives of several European countries.

We have also used the survey to study factors that lead individuals to go abroad for PhD and postdoctoral study, focusing particularly on why individuals come to the US versus go to another country (Stephan et al., 2015). The primary reasons that individuals, regardless of country of origin, give for their decision to go abroad is the "opportunity to improve my future career prospects" and the presence of "outstanding faculty, colleagues or research team." "Excellence/ prestige of the foreign institution in my area of research" and the "opportunity to extend my network of international relationships" are in third and fourth place. Regardless of country, respondents list family reasons or fringe benefits last. These findings suggest that policies in the host country that support research play a significant role in drawing individuals to study in a country. They also suggest that respondents see coming to the US as an important way to build their careers—either in the US or a third country. These findings are consistent with those related to why respondents report going abroad for work (see Table 3).

The likelihood of return varies considerably depending on the origin country, but for some countries the return of natives appears conditional on future job prospects in the country of origin. In all 16 countries in our sample, those who had returned after studying or working abroad state that the most important reason behind the decision to return was family or other personal reasons. The second most important reason was a better lifestyle. None of the policy variables was scored highly by returnees, suggesting that science policy in the home country plays a backseat role in the decision to return. When we investigated the performance of the returnees compared to those of compatriots who remained abroad, we found that, on average, returnees perform at the same level as their compatriots who remained abroad, after controlling for the differentials due to the country of current work. This appears to be consistent with the view that return is more about family and life quality reasons and less about the lack of skills to compete in the international job market. We did find a decay rate in citations experienced by those who returned after several years, but the magnitude is modest.

We have found robust evidence of a higher propensity of foreign-born researchers to set up large international research networks compared to natives, be these nonmobile or returnees. The results are consistent across the 16 analyzed host countries. We find that this higher propensity depends upon the career stage at the time of entry, suggesting that the social capital that one brings with oneself affects the depth of the network. Migrants who originally came for study tend to have the smallest networks. Those with the largest network came for work.

We also find that international mobility is correlated with performance, with nonmobile natives performing at a lower level than the foreign born and returnees performing somewhere closer to the foreign born. Moreover, we find that the superior performance of the foreign born persists after controlling for several potentially confounding factors. More importantly, it persists after instrumenting for migration, suggesting that the premium is not entirely due to positive skill bias of the mobile.

Our findings with regard to productivity have at least two important implications for scholars and policy makers. First, they corroborate the validity of policies aimed at facilitating increased brain exchange across countries. Such policies include easier immigration procedures for high-skilled human capital (Shen, 2013), and policies aimed at harmonizing the international job market for research (Franzoni et al., 2011). Second, our findings that the positive effects of migration persist having controlled for selection suggest that brain migration is not a zero-sum game in the sense that the benefits that accrue to the destination country do not necessarily come at the expense of the sending country, and that there are conversely positive externalities to be gained by promoting mobile scientists to work with domestic scientists. These findings are complementary to those reported with regard to collaboration, which suggests that research networks are portable and that both the returnees and the diaspora network of nationals abroad can enhance the networks at the benefit of the sending countries.

6.2 Future Research

We are aware that we have but scratched the surface of topics that can be investigated using the GlobSci data and that we alone will never be able to explore all of the research opportunities that the data provide. For this reason, the data will be made available for public use beginning in summer 2015. Areas for future research that readily come to mind include examining whether the relationship between productivity and mobility holds for those who make international temporary visits, such as a sabbatical or a short-term stay, which are common in academia. Similar questions could be raised with regard to the scope of the respondents' international networks. The data could also be used to examine whether the reason for migrating (PhD study, postdoctoral training, a job) relate to the performance premium that was found for migrants. It can also be used to investigate the propensity to migrate by gender. Another area for future research involves adopting the same survey methodology to study mobility patterns of scientists in Korea and China. Although the data would not be for the same period, they would allow for some comparison across countries that we were unable to sample with GlobSci.

Our analysis showed evidence of a large international network of the returnees. However, in our work, we did not address causality. We also did not take into account the time dimension. Since mobility occurs now more frequently than in the past, it is possible that our results are driven primarily by recent returnees. We did not investigate if the capability of migrants to keep their international contacts active diminishes over time or even vanishes after some time. Further research on GlobSci data and on other data sources could potentially shed light on such relevant issues.

Another area of promising research would be the processes that likely lead to our observation of the superior performance of migrant scientists. Here we suggested specialty matching and knowledge recombination as potential motives. Additional reasons for the performance differential to be investigated in future research include individual cognitive processes and teamwork and dispersed collaborations. More research is also needed to understand the nature and extent of spillovers that the migrants' networks could potentially provide to the origin country. It is possible that these networks are effective in providing information, resources, connections, or even access to infrastructures.

Finally, our results corroborate the view that policies in support of the international mobility, such as policies to sponsor mobility or return, may be effective in increasing the performance of scientists both in terms of scientific quality and in terms of international networking. Our results, however, suggest that the impact of policies may be moderated by the characteristics of the scientist and/or by the type of foreign experience and may produce their effects disproportionally in the country of origin or in the country of destination. Future research should be directed to assess more precisely the impact of diverse types of policies and the conditions that moderate their efficacy.

REFERENCES

Adams, J. D., Black, G. C., Clemmons, J. R., & Stephan, P. E. (2005). Scientific teams and institutional collaborations: evidence from U.S. universities, 1981–1999. *Research Policy, 34*, 259–285.

Agrawal, A., Kapur, D., McHale, J., & Oettl, A. (2011). Brain drain or brain bank? The impact of skilled emigration on poor-country innovation. *Journal of Urban Economics, 69*, 43–55.

Black, G., & Stephan, P. (2010). The role of foreign graduate students and postdoctoral scholars. In C. Clotfelter (Ed.), *American universities in a global market* (pp. 129–161). National Bureau of Economic Research, Chicago: University of Chicago Press.

Borjas, G. J. (1994). The economics of immigration. *Journal of Economic Literature, 32*(4), 1667–1717.

Borjas, G. J.& Bratsberg, B. (1996). Who leaves? The outmigration of the foreign-born. *The Review of Economics and Statistics*, *78*(1), 165–176.

Davenport, S. (2004). Panic and panacea: brain drain and science and technology human capital policy. *Research Policy*, *33*, 617–630.

Ding, W. W., Levin, S. G., Stephan, P. E., & Winkler, A. E. (2010). The impact of information technology on academic scientists' productivity and collaboration patterns. *Management Science*, *56*(9), 1439–1461.

Dustmann, C., Fadlon, I., & Weiss, Y. (2011). Return migration, human capital accumulation and the brain drain. *Journal of Development Economics*, *95*, 58–67.

Fernández-Zubieta, A., Geuna, A., Kataishi, R., Lawson, C., & Toselli, M. (2015). International Careers of Researchers in Biomedical Sciences: A Comparison of the US and the UK. In A. Geuna (Ed.), *Global Mobility of Research Scientists*. Amsterdam: Elsevier (Chapter 3).

Franzoni, C., Scellato, G., & Stephan, P. (2011). Changing incentives to publish. *Science*, *333*, 702–703.

Franzoni, C., Scellato, G., & Stephan, P. (2014). The mover's advantage: the superior performance of migrant scientists. *Economics Letters*, *122*, 89–93.

Franzoni, C., Scellato, G., & Stephan, P. (2012b). Foreign-born scientists: mobility patterns for 16 countries. *Nature Biotechnology*, *30*, 1250–1253.

Franzoni, C., Scellato, G., Stephan, P. (2012a). *The mover's advantage: Scientific performance of mobile academics*. NBER Working paper n. w18577. Available at http://www.nber.org/papers/w18577.

Freeman, R. B., & Huang, W., (2015). China's "Great Leap Forward" in Science and Engineering. In A. Geuna (Ed.), *Global Mobility of Research Scientists*. Amsterdam: Elsevier (Chapter 6).

Ganguli, I. (2015). Who leaves and who stays? Evidence on immigrant selection from the collapse of Soviet science. In A. Geuna (Ed.), *Global Mobility of Research Scientists*. Amsterdam: Elsevier (Chapter 5).

Gaulé, P., & Piacentini, M. (2013). Chinese graduate students and U.S. scientific productivity. *Review of Economics and Statistics*, *95*(2), 698–701.

Gazni, A., Sugimoto, C. R., & Didegah, F. (2012). Mapping world scientific collaboration: authors, institutions, and countries. *Journal of the American Society for Information Science and Technology*, *63*(2), 323–335.

Georghiou, L. (1998). Global cooperation in research. *Research Policy*, *27*, 611–626.

Gibson, J., & McKenzie, D. (2012). The economic consequences of 'brain drain' of the best and brightest: microeconomic evidence from five countries. *The Economic Journal*, *122*, 339–375.

Grogger, J., & Hanson, G. H. (2011). Income maximization and the selection and sorting of international migrants. *Journal of Development Economics*, *95*, 42–57.

Hunter, R. S., Oswald, A. J., & Charlton, B. G. (2009). The elite brain drain. *The Economic Journal*, *119*, F231–F251.

Jones, B. (2008). *The knowledge trap: Human capital and development, reconsidered*. NBER. Working paper #14138. Available at http://www.nber.org/papers/w14138. Accessed 01.09.13.

Jones, B. F., Wuchty, S., & Uzzi, B. (2008). Geography, and stratification in science. Multi-university research teams: shifting impact. *Science*, *322*, 1259–1262.

Kerr, W. R., & Lincoln, W. F. (2010). The supply side of innovation: H-1B visa reforms and U.S. Ethnic invention. *Journal of Labor Economics*, *28*(3), 473–508.

Pudovkin, A. I., & Garfield, E. (2004). Rank-normalized impact factor: a way to compare journal performance across subject categories. *Proceedings of the 67th Annual Meeting of the American Society for Information Science &Technology*, *41*, 507–515.

Sauermann, H., & Roach, M. (2010). A taste for science? PhD scientists' academic orientation and self-selection into research careers in industry. *Research Policy, 39*(3), 422–434.

Sauermann, H., & Roach, M. (2013). Increasing web survey response rates in innovation research: an experimental study of static and dynamic contact design features. *Research Policy, 42*(1), 273–296.

Saxenian, A. (2005). From brain drain to brain circulation: transnational communities and regional upgrading in India and China. *Studies in Comparative International Development, 40*(2), 35–61.

Scellato, G., Franzoni, C., & Stephan, P. (2015). Migrant scientists and research networks. *Research Policy, 44*(1), 108–120.

Shen, H. (2013). US Senate backs immigration plan. *Nature, 499,* 17–18.

Stephan, P. (2010). The I's have it: immigration and innovation, the perspective from academe. In J. Lerner, & S. Stern (Eds.), *Innovation policy and the economy* (Vol. 10) (pp. 84–127). National Bureau of Economic Research, Chicago: University of Chicago Press.

Stephan, P. (2012). *How economics shapes science*. Cambridge, MA: Harvard University Press.

Stephan, P., Franzoni, C., & Scellato, G. (2015). International competition for PhDs and postdoctoral scholars: what does (and does not) matter. In W. Kerr, J. Lerner, & S. Stern (Eds.), *Innovation, policy and the economy* (Vol. 15). MIT Press.

Stephan, P. E., & Levin, S. G. (1992). *Striking the mother lode in science: The importance of age, place, and time*. Oxford University Press.

Stephan, P. E., & Levin, S. G. (2001). Exceptional contributions to U.S. science by the foreign-born and foreign-educated. *Population Research Policy Review, 20*(1–2), 59–79.

Wagner, C. S., & Leydesdorff, L. (2005). Network structure, self-organization, and the growth of international collaboration in science. *Research Policy, 34,* 1608–1618.

Walsh, J. P., Cho, C., & Cohen, W. (2005). View from the bench: patents and material transfers. *Science, 309,* 2002–2003.

Wuchty, S., Jones, B. F., & Uzzi, B. (2007). The increasing dominance of teams in the production of knowledge. *Science, 316,* 1036–1039.

Chapter 3

this study focuses on mobility to US. and U.K., how they attract and attain researchers, not like my study focusing on the sender countries

International Careers of Researchers in Biomedical Sciences: A Comparison of the US and the UK

Cornelia Lawson[1,2,3], Aldo Geuna[1,2], Ana Fernández-Zubieta[4], Rodrigo Kataishi[1,2], Manuel Toselli[1,2]

[1]*Department of Economics and Statistics Cognetti De Martiis, Università di Torino, Turin, Italy;* [2]*BRICK, Collegio Carlo Alberto, Moncalieri, Turin, Italy;* [3]*School of Sociology and Social Policy, University of Nottingham, Nottingham, UK;* [4]*Institute for Advanced Social Studies – Spanish Council for Scientific Research, Campo Santo de los Mártires, Córdoba, Spain*

Chapter Outline

1. INTRODUCTION

In the last 30 years, biomedical sciences have become a fundamental area of research in national scientific research portfolios (Adams, 1998; Glover et al., 2014). Despite increased scientific production in countries in Asia and continental Europe, the US and the UK remain the leaders of the field (BIS, 2013; Glanzel, Debackere, & Meyer, 2008; Hu & Rousseau, 2009; Webster, 2005; Wu, 2004[1]). For example, in a comparison of 10 countries, the scientific production of the UK and the US show the highest averages for normalized citation rates for the period 1996–2006 (Hu & Rousseau, 2009).[2]

foreign researchers increase

Biomedical sciences, like other scientific fields (Auriol, Misu, & Freeman, 2013; OECD, 2008), are characterized by increased internationalization of their human resources and collaboration patterns (NIH, 2012). In the US, foreign citizens represent an important part of the biomedical science workforce (Stephan, 2012), and their share has increased more rapidly compared to the share of nationals (NIH, 2012). Growing internationalization is evident at all research levels starting from PhD students and postdocs to full professor in the US, and similar trends are observed in the UK (BIS, 2013; Sastry, 2005).

The world's top researchers tend to move (e.g., as undergraduate students, PhD students, postdoctoral researchers, or workers with permanent contracts) to countries with strong research systems, with the result that their mobility is an indication of the attractiveness of a country (Hunter, Oswald, & Charlton, 2009) or institution (Oyer, 2007). Despite the importance of this globally mobile workforce, we have little information on the role of foreign-trained and other types of mobile researchers since they are not accounted for systematically across different researcher populations (Ghaffarzadegan, Hawley, & Desai, 2013; NIH, 2012).

US and other developed countries

The US and the UK show similarities and differences in their academic markets. Both academic systems are highly international (BIS, 2013; NIH, 2012; Ziman, 1991) and competitive (Stephan, 2012). Students do not tend to join the staff in their degree-awarding institution after completing their PhD research, in either the US[3] or the UK (Horta, Veloso, & Grediage, 2010; Navarro & Rivero, 2001). The promotion system, the race for positions at the most prestigious institutions (Hoare, 1994), and other systems of evaluation, such as the Research

---

1. Webster, Lewison, & Rowlands (2003) not only showed the strength of the UK as the second highest producer of papers in the field of biomedicine, but also noted that Japan overtook the UK in terms of number of articles in the latest years of the period analyzed (1989–2002). BIS (2013) gives further support for the strength of the UK and the US in the field, especially in terms of citation impact. Still, it also reports an increased performance in emerging science markets (especially China, which moves to second place behind the US in terms of article numbers), resulting in a slight decline of overall importance (based on world article share) of the US and the UK in the period 2002–2012. Both still dominate in terms of field-weighted citation impact, which increases during the same period.
2. These are: the US, UK, France, Germany, Italy, Japan, South Korea, China, Singapore, and India.
3. Although some inter-elite inbreeding might occur in the US (see Burris, 2004; Eisenberg & Wells, 2000) and possibly also in the UK.

Evaluation Framework (REF), make the UK academic system more competitive *difference* than other academic systems in Europe. In the US, academic salaries vary more than in the UK where there is a higher level of standardization in salary scales, although salary diversification has increased substantially since the early 2000s.

In this context, this chapter studies the relationship between mobility patterns and academic performance with particular attention to international (transatlantic) mobility, for a sample of 619 US and UK biomedical researchers (327 from the US and 292 from the UK). We carry out a descriptive analysis of labor markets of these countries, paying particular attention to their mobility patterns, and we assess whether postdoctoral stays grant a performance premium, considering international and educational mobility patterns. The BIOMEDMOB database, built from CV information, includes detailed personal information, employment patterns, and publishing activities of mobile and immobile researchers for the period 1956–2012.

The two samples analyzed are quite similar in terms of mobility patterns, once country specificities are considered. We find that US-based researchers achieve higher performance than UK-based researchers, however, the gap between the two has narrowed. US postdoctoral training implies a quality premium for researchers' performance, which is highest for those that completed a postdoc at a top US institution. We also find that this US postdoc premium transfers geographically, that is, researchers working in the UK having completed a US postdoc (especially at a top institution) publish in journals with higher average impact. We also find some evidence that the US is able to not only attract top researchers worldwide at postdoctoral and tenure level, and give them research advantages, but is also able to retain the best researchers who go to the US for their postdoctoral training.

The chapter is structured as follows. Section 2 analyses mobility patterns in biomedical science; Section 3 discusses the theoretical background and presents the hypothesis. Section 4 presents the BIOMEDMOB dataset and a descriptive analysis of career and mobility. Section 5 reports the econometric results, and Section 6 concludes the chapter.

2. CAREERS AND MOBILITY IN BIOMEDICAL SCIENCE

Scientists tend to move internationally to countries with strong research systems (Freeman, 2006; OECD, 2008; Weinberg, 2009). In the US, the number of international students - mostly undergraduates - has increased by 32% since 2000–2001 (Institute of International Education, 2012). The trend is similar in the UK, making it the country with the largest populations of foreign PhD students in Europe. For instance, in 2012, 47% of PhD students in the UK came from abroad[4] (Eurostat, 2012).

---

4. Only Liechtenstein (86.8%), Luxembourg (84.1%), and Switzerland (50.7%) have higher percentages in Europe (Data on the second stage of tertiary education leading to an advanced research qualification – ISCED level 6).

Countries and research institutions pay attention to the inflows and outflows of the research workforce since these are measures of how effectively they are competing in the "global war for talent" (Chambers, Foulon, Handfield-Jones, Hankin, & Michaels, 1998). The 2012 United States House of Representative legislation allows an additional 55,000 green cards for the highest-qualified foreign graduates from American universities in science, technology, engineering, and mathematics (STEM) fields, which demonstrates the interest of the government in retaining this highly international workforce.[5]

The US and the UK are characterized by increasing internationalization of their workforce, a trend that applies especially to the biomedical field. In the 30 years 1978–2008, the number of PhDs in biomedical fields in the US more than tripled, from around 11,000 to more than 35,000 (FASEB, 2013). The number of doctorates awarded in biomedical fields also increased in the UK, with a threefold increase between 1994/95 and 2012/13, from 1114 to 3365.[6] In both countries the number of foreign doctoral students has increased significantly (the growth in European Union (EU) students has been particularly important for the UK). Academic employment has also increased, but at a lower rate and in the form of nonpermanent positions, encouraging young researchers to look for postdoc positions and other employment opportunities in other sectors (NIH, 2012, p. 25).[7] The number of postdocs in biological science[8] in the US has increased from 7083 in 1980 to 21,537 in 2010, accounting for 34% of all postdocs in science, engineering, and health in 2010 (GSS, 2013). Ghaffarzadegan et al. (2013), using FASEB data, estimate growth in international postdocs in the field at 400% between 1985 and 2009. In the UK, the share of foreign academics in the field increased slightly from 28% in 2007–2008 to 31% in 2012–2013.[9] Foreign postdoc researchers with temporary contracts in the UK also increased in that period, from 46% to 50%.[10]

The increasing biomedical workforce, including more international workers employed on a temporary basis looking for employment in nonacademic sectors, has raised policy concerns about the increasing temporariness of the biomedical

---

5. In 2014 in the US, a proposal was put forward for a rule change that might improve opportunities for the employment of highly skilled aliens. It would offer Employment Authorization Cards (EAD) to some H4 visa holders and make it easier for outstanding foreign professors and researchers to acquire an EB-1 visa. H4 visas are issued by the US Citizenship and Immigration Services (USCIS) to immediate family members of an H-1B visa holder, which allows US employers to employ foreign workers in specialty occupations on a temporary basis.
6. HESA Students, Qualifiers and Staff data tables, https://www.hesa.ac.uk/content/view/1973/239/.
7. SRD data for 2010 for the field of biology (including agriculture, environmental life sciences) shows that from a total of 83,500 employed doctoral scientists and engineers in four-year educational institutions, 38.8% were tenured, 14.8% on tenure track, and 13.5% nontenure track (http://ncsesdata. nsf.gov/doctoratework/2010/html/SDR2010_DST20.html).
8. We consider data on 'biological sciences' for the US as this field category is more similar to the one used for the UK. 'Health' fields were not included due to different categorizations in the data sources used.
9. Extracted from HESA database, September 2014.
10. Extracted from HESA database, September 2014.

workforce. The report published by the NIH (2012) highlights the increasing number of temporary contracts and recommends reducing the duration of post-doctoral positions. Postdoctoral positions could be an opportunity for research development (Gentile et al., 1989; Levey et al., 1988; Steiner, Lanphear, Curtis, & Vu, 2002; Su, 2011), a solution for researchers unable to find a permanent position (Zumeta, 1985) or for those with visa restrictions (Lan, 2012).[11] However, as the NIH report suggests, the lack of information on postdocs and other mobile workforces in the field (such as foreign trained) makes it difficult to determine the effect of the increasing number of postdocs and other changes at a systemic level.[12] To contribute to this debate, in the empirical sections of this chapter, we use individual-level data on researchers' careers to investigate mobility patterns of academics based in the US or the UK and analyze the effects of postdoctoral training on research performance. This will allow us to identify whether career paths differ between researchers in the two countries and whether postdoctoral mobility pays off in terms of research performance.

3. INTERNATIONAL MOBILITY, CAREER PROGRESSION, AND RESEARCH PERFORMANCE

Scientists tend to move to another country for research-related reasons. The self-selection mechanisms that operate in the migration process[13] might also be research related, which could affect their future prospects (Fernández-Zubieta, Geuna, & Lawson, (Chapter 4)). Ackers (2005) suggests that long-term mobile researchers could be considered "knowledge migrants" since they tend to be more interested in opportunities for career advancement than in purely economic reasons. Nerdrum & Sarpebakken (2006) point to the mobility of researchers as driven by research factors, such as keeping updated or searching for sources of inspiration, as well as "curiosity driven" (Mahroum, 1998; Stephan & Levin, 1992). These research-related factors appear to promote mobility and are found to be more important than family-related issues across countries (Ivancheva & Gourova, 2011).[14] Research-related factors appear important also for the decision to return to the country of origin (Thorn & Holm-Nielsen, 2008).

---

11. Most postdocs in the broadly defined biomedical fields are in the US on temporary visas. In 1980, 35% of all US postdocs in science, engineering, and health were in the country on temporary visas; this figure was 53% in 2010 (own calculations based on NSF data).
12. Foreign trained are not accounted for systematically across research populations (students, post-docs, researchers working in academia or industry).
13. The economic literature on the assimilation of immigrants (Borjas, 1985; Chiswick, 1978; LaLonde & Topel, 1992) suggests that there are positive self-selection effects (Chiswick, 1978), immigrants being more talented, more entrepreneurial, and more risk averse. These items also affect the decision of migrants to stay in a country or to return home. Analysis of the return decisions of migrants indicates that foreigners who remain in the country might be the best or the worst of the group (Borjas, 1985; Borjas & Bratsberg, 1996; Dustmann, 2003; Grogger & Hanson, 2011).
14. The countries studied were Austria, Bulgaria, Cyprus, Czech Rep., Greece, Hungary, Slovakia, and Switzerland.

However, Franzoni, Scellato, & Stephan (2012) indicate that while professional reasons are dominant for the decision to take a postdoc abroad, family-related reasons are important for explaining the return mobility of foreign scientist to their home countries.

Thus, researchers' outward mobility and return mobility are affected by research-related considerations that operate through selection mechanisms and matching processes. These may differ at different career stages. A researcher (student) can enter a foreign country at various career stages: (1) education (BA, MA, PHD); (2) postdoc; and (3) job (first untenured job or senior tenured position). Research-related factors that explain the decision to move might become more important as the career progresses and may affect the research performance of researchers. Positive efficiency-enhancing effects depend on the availability of information to allow optimal matching (Jovanovich, 1979; Mortensen, 1986).[15] In addition, specific individual and institutional selection mechanisms might operate in the case of foreign researchers, which might enhance research performance due to the increased level of information required by and about this group.

The level of information held by the researchers on the research system and the institutions (and the ability to make the right choices) differs at different career stages. A PhD student, compared to a postdoc, lacks an adequate level of information on the research system and institutional quality. Postdoctoral researchers are more experienced and can be expected to be better informed about the institutions and the advantages and opportunities available. David (1992) and Mangematin (2000) suggest that PhD students have to make choices when they have little information about their future careers. A postdoctoral-level researcher should be more able to recognize the "invisible colleges" (Crane, 1972) and, therefore, more able to make the "right choice" in research terms.

Similarly, the level of research-related information that research institutions have and require about their candidates changes significantly across career stages. In the early career stage, information on research achievements is scarce, making other nonresearch factors or nonindividual research factors, such as the quality of the BA/MA awarding institution, an important source of information for the hiring institution (Baldi, 1995; Long, 1978). However, institution-level foreign education credentials are more difficult for home institutions to differentiate, providing less added information for the selection. An institution considering hiring a postdoc, however, has to rely upon proven publication performance and other research-related activities carried out during the PhD research process as more reliable source of information about the latent quality of the candidate.

Based on this reasoning of increasing availability of research-related information along the career path, and individual and institutional selection

---

15. See Franzoni, Scellato, & Stephan (2014) for performance premium of migrants controlling for positive selection into migration.

mechanisms of foreigners, we can expect that international mobility will result in a better match (in terms of future performance) at a postdoctoral level compared to PhD level.

Postdoctoral research training can be either a stepping-stone in a scientific career or a sign of "job queuing" for a better position, risking the scientist losing momentum (NRC, 2012; Zumeta, 1985). There is some evidence that a postdoc improves academic performance (Meng & Su, 2010; Su, 2011) and the scientific impact of the individual's work (McGuinnis, Allison, & Long, 1982). There is evidence also that foreigners are more productive than their native US peers (Corley & Sabharwal, 2007; Lee, 2004; Stephan & Levin, 2007). Taking this evidence together might suggest that the effect of going to a leading scientific country to undertake a postdoc will have a positive effect on academic performance. However, foreign nationals appear also to be more likely to undertake postdoctoral positions because of the poor availability of other employment opportunities (Corley & Sabharwal, 2007), thereby increasing the length of their postdoctoral period (Stephan & Ma, 2005). Also, researchers that undertake a postdoc in a foreign leading scientific country appear to have important research advantages (due to selection processes and high motivation) that allow them to benefit more from a postdoctoral stay in terms of research performance but also risk the disadvantage of precarious research markets that could then diminish these research advantages. Studies of the academic job market also show that the quality of the institution providing the training affects the institutional selection process and influences future career performance (Long, 1978; McGuinnis et al., 1982). Being trained at a top-quality institution might grant postdocs additional research advantages that, in the case of foreign nationals, might help to overcome the disadvantages and lead to a successful stay in terms of academic performance.

4. DATA DESCRIPTION

Our sample is drawn from researchers (Principal Investigators (PI) and/or Coinvestigators (CO-I)) that received funding from the two most important public funding agencies for biomedicine in each country: the Biotechnology and Biological Sciences Research Council (BBSRC) in the UK and the National Institutes of Health (NIH) in the US. This sample frame allows us to identify research-active academic scientists in biomedical fields although it might exclude scientists who are funded exclusively by private foundations. Annex 1 provides a description of the data construction and response analysis.

Curricula vitae (CVs) were collected from researchers' websites and by e-mail and used to construct the careers of our sample of biomedical scientists. CVs were coded by hand. Personal details, education history, and career paths up to 2012 were recorded. We excluded academics with incomplete career data, those who had retired within the five years prior to 2012, and those who had not achieved a permanent academic position by 2012. We also excluded researchers with medical degrees since they face a very different labor market.[16] The final version of the BIOMEDMOB database, which includes only comparable researchers in the UK and the US for which we have complete career and publication information, comprises 292 UK- and 327 US-funded academics for the period 1956–2012. In the following, we present the descriptive statistics for our final sample of 619 researchers relating to basic demographic information, careers, and mobility. We compare the UK and the US samples, highlighting similarities and a few interesting differences.

4.1 Basic Demographic Information

A total of 22% of researchers in the sample are women; the average age is 53 in 2012; 77% are US or UK citizens; 81% studied for a US or UK undergraduate degree; 86% were awarded a PhD degree by a US or UK institution (average year of BA award is 1980 and PhD 1985). The average researcher was appointed to a first academic position (tenure or tenure-track) in 1990.

There are some differences between the US and the UK samples. Table 1 presents the basic demographic information. Researchers in the US are 2.65 years older, completed their BA and entered their first academic job approximately 2.5 years earlier. However, if we consider three years as the time period for an academic cohort, we can claim that the two samples are not significantly different. The statistics show that most academics working in the UK and US were previously educated there at undergraduate and PhD levels, with a slightly higher share for the US at PhD level. Country of birth is available only for 372 researchers; in this smaller sample, the share of foreigners is similar for both countries.

Table 2 analyzes countries of BA and PhD education in more detail. We are interested in particular in US–UK educational mobility. Approximately 17% of the UK sample moved to the UK from abroad for their undergraduate education, while the same share is 21% in the case of the US. Only 2.6% of academics working in the UK obtained their BA in the US; similarly, 3.5% of researchers working in the US completed their BA in the UK. The share of researchers with foreign PhD education is similar to that with BA education in the case of the UK but lower for the US, with only 11% of researchers working in the US having completed their PhD abroad. Transatlantic PhD education mobility is higher, with US-to-UK mobility reaching 6% and UK-to-US mobility 4.4%. The composition of the category "Other" shows important differences across samples, with prominent countries of undergraduate degree being Germany (14.9%), Australia (12.8%), Canada (8.5%), and New Zealand (8.5%) in the UK sample, and China (18.5%), Canada (12.3%), India (9.2%), and Germany (7.7%) in the US sample. PhD-level education shows a high concentration in terms of degree-awarding countries, with the US accounting for 35% of foreign PhDs in the UK sample

---

16. This exclusion is also necessary to make the BBSRC and NIH samples more comparable since the former is less likely to include medical doctors.

TABLE 1 Demographic Information (In Year 2012 or Last Year in Data)

	UK				US				Mean Diff
	Mean	SD	Min	Max	Mean	SD	Min	Max	
Female	0.22	0.41	0	1	0.22	0.41	0	1	ns
Age in 2012[a]	51.97	8.40	35	71	54.60	10.84	37	89	***
Born in the UK[b]	0.77	0.29	0	1					
Born in the US[b]					0.77	0.42	0	1	ns[d]
BA in the UK[c]	0.83	0.38	0	1					
BA in the US[c]					0.78	0.41	0	1	ns[d]
PhD in the UK[a]	0.83	0.37	0	1					
PhD in the US[a]					0.89	0.31	0	1	*[d]
Year BA[c]	1981.78	8.68	1962	1999	1979.39	10.90	1943	1997	***
Year PhD[a]	1986.54	9.07	1967	2006	1985.68	11.36	1950	2004	ns
Year start career	1991.49	9.93	1968	2011	1989.01	11.92	1956	2008	***
N	292				327				

*** p<0.01, ** p<0.05, * p<0.1.
aAge is missing for nine and PhD for six academics.
bCountry of birth is only known for 372 academics (186 UK and 186 US).
cBA information is missing for 19 academics.
dCompared to row above.

TABLE 2 Country of BA and PhD across UK–US Sample

Sample		BA				PhD			
		UK	US	Other	Total	UK	US	Other	Total
UK	N	226	7	40	273	236	17	30	283
	%	82.8	2.6	14.6	100	83.4	6.0	10.6	100
US	N	11	249	57	317	14	283	22	319
	%	3.5	78.5	18	100	4.4	88.7	6.9	100

and UK accounting for 37% of foreign PhDs in the US sample, followed by Australia, Germany, and the Netherlands with about 8%, respectively, in the UK and by Germany (11.4%), Canada (8.6%), and Switzerland (8.6%) in the US.

4.2 Postdoc Mobility

Table 3 presents detailed comparative information on academic mobility. All variables are dummies except for the number of job–job changes, which has a maximum value of four in the UK sample and six in the US sample with a mean of 0.78 for both countries. On completion of their PhD studies, 81% of researchers did a postdoc.[17] In both systems postdocs are very prevalent, with 84% of researchers in the UK and 80% of researchers in the US, respectively. UK academics are more likely to have done their postdoc abroad with 41% completing a postdoc in the US or some other country, compared to 11% having completed a postdoc abroad in the case of the US. The main postdoc country for UK-based scientists is the US with 26% of the total UK sample having completed a postdoc there, while only 4% of US-based academics did their postdoc in the UK. The same academic can undertake a postdoc in more than one country, for example, 62 BBSRC researchers did a postdoc in the UK and abroad. This is less common in the US sample where multiple postdocs tend to be in different universities in the US.

4.3 International and Career Mobility

The second part of Table 3 presents a detailed set of statistics concerning job changes after the postdoc (job–job mobility). Based on CV information, we reconstruct the mobility paths of researchers from their career start (the year of their first job after PhD or after the postdoc for those with postdoc experience[18]) until 2012.

Most researchers are job–job mobile (51%) with no significant difference between the UK and the US; on average, researchers move between jobs 0.8 times in both countries. International job–job mobility (change of job that involves migrating to a different country) is much lower, dropping to 7% for the US sample and 17% for scientists working in the UK. When we exclude intra-European mobility for the UK sample, 13% of researchers still had international job experience during their career, indicating a higher internationalization for the UK sample compared to the US (connections

---

17. For the UK sample, a postdoc is defined as a postdoctoral position or a research fellow appointment of less than five years. We considered research fellow positions of at least five years equivalent to lecturer, as they indicate a long-term relationship with the university, equivalent to a probation period (see also Fernández-Zubieta et al., (Chapter 4)). For the US, postdoc is as assigned on the CV.
18. In the US sample, about 95% of these are tenure-track or tenure-track equivalent positions. In the UK sample, the first position is normally a lecturer appointment, but also research fellowships of more than five years and teaching contracts that are renewed on a rolling basis.

TABLE 3 Postdoc, International and Career Mobility

	UK		US		
	Mean	SD	Mean	SD	Mean Diff
Postdoc	0.84	0.37	0.80	0.40	Ns
Postdoc in UK[a]	0.64	0.48	0.04	0.20	
Postdoc in US[a]	0.26	0.44	0.74	0.44	
Postdoc in others[a]	0.19	0.39	0.07	0.26	***
Job–job mobile	0.52	0.50	0.49	0.50	Ns
Times job–job mobile	0.78	0.95	0.78	1.02	Ns
International mobility (cross-border)	0.17	0.37	0.07	0.25	***
International mobility (EU as one)	0.13	0.34	0.07	0.25	***
International mobility (UK to US)[b]	0.02	0.14	0.02	0.13	
International mobility (US to UK)[b]	0.05	0.21	0.01	0.08	
Sector mobility (Industry—HEI/PRO)[c]	0.05	0.23	0.04	0.19	Ns
Sector mobility (PRO-HEI)[c]	0.10	0.30	0.05	0.21	***
HEI mobility (between HEI)[d]	0.40	0.49	0.42	0.49	Ns
Voluntary mobility (tenured HEI staff)[e]	0.35	0.48	0.24	0.43	***
Forced mobility (nontenured HEI staff)[e]	0.07	0.25	0.26	0.44	***
HEI junior mobility (assistant or temp)	0.21	0.41	0.25	0.43	Ns
HEI senior mobility (associate or above)	0.25	0.43	0.26	0.44	Ns
UK HEI mobility	0.30	0.46			
UK HEI junior mobility	0.17	0.38			
UK HEI senior mobility	0.17	0.38			
EU HEI mobility	0.32	0.47			
EU HEI junior mobility	0.18	0.39			
EU HEI senior mobility	0.18	0.39			
US HEI mobility			0.40	0.49	**[f]
US HEI junior mobility			0.22	0.42	Ns[f]
US HEI senior mobility			0.25	0.43	**[f]
HE career mobility (with promotion)	0.18	0.39	0.16	0.37	Ns
HE career mobility—assistant to associate	0.09	0.29	0.09	0.28	Ns
HE career mobility—associate to full	0.10	0.30	0.09	0.28	Ns
N	292		326		

*** p<0.01, ** p<0.05, * p<0.1.
[a]The same academic can undertake more than one postdoc in two different countries.
[b]Those moving from UK to US and those moving back overlap (the same person in both).
[c]PRO in the UK sample includes mobility to UK Research Councils and European public institutions.
[d]Includes cross-border mobility.
[e]The same academic can be forced and voluntary mobile at different career stages.
[f]Comparing the amount of within US mobility in NIH data to within UK mobility in BBSRC data.

with Commonwealth countries may play an important role here). International job–job mobility between the UK and the US (transatlantic mobility) is important (though it is small in absolute terms) especially for the UK sample with 5% of researchers having previously held a job in the US. Sector job–job mobility involving a move between industry and the public research sector (including higher education institutions (HEI) and public research organizations (PRO)) is small with about 5% of researchers having prior industry experience, in both samples. However, there is an important difference between the UK and US job markets with respect to sector job–job mobility between PRO and HEI, where 10% of UK researchers had a job in a PRO (including UK Research Council and European public research institutions), but only 5% in the US.

About 40% of researchers have changed higher education (HE) employer at least once (HEI mobility) with no significant difference for the two samples. This similarity indicates that policy actions (such as the REF[19]) and incentives for mobility in the UK have made the UK system similar to the US with regard to academic mobility. For mobility within the higher education sector, we can further distinguish between voluntary and forced mobility. The former is defined as a move after an academic is granted a permanent (tenured) academic post, while the latter is a move when occupying a fixed-term academic position. In the UK, assistant professorships are considered permanent positions subject to a three-year probation period. In the US, assistant professorships are tenure-track positions and, thus, not permanent. If an academic moves before achieving associate professor status in the US, this is considered forced mobility. These differences in the academic markets result in significant differences in the number of forced and voluntary moves in the US and the UK samples. Amongst the BBSRC sample, 35% of academics move voluntarily to a different university, while only 7% are forced to move.[20] In the US, 24% change jobs while holding a permanent position, but 26% move while holding a fixed-term position. For comparison, we also look at junior (assistant and temporary jobs) and senior (associate and full professor) mobility and find that there is no significant difference between the two samples, with about 25% of researchers in each group having experienced an academic job change.

Job–job mobility between universities in the same country is more likely amongst US-based academics (40%) than UK-based academics (30%). This is mainly due to the important role of intra-EU mobility (32%) and mobility between the UK and Commonwealth countries, which are especially important for associate and full professors explaining most of the difference between the

---

19. See Moed (2008) for the changes in publications behavior (quantity and quality) encouraged by the Research Assessment Exercise (RAE), the precursor of the REF. See Elton (2000) for more general consequences of the RAE.

20. In the UK, most contracts are permanent and forced mobility is usually observed before academics move to the UK or if they are on rolling teaching contracts.

TABLE 4 Career Mobility by BA/PhD/Postdoc Location

	UK		US	
	Mean	Count	Mean	Count
BA Abroad Postdoc_Abroad	0.49	47	0.19	64
International job–job mobility (cross-border)	0.30	47	0.12	64
BA Local Postdoc_Abroad	0.41	227	0.10	248
International job–job mobility (cross-border)	0.08	227	0.01	248
PhD Abroad Postdoc_Abroad	0.54	46	0.29	35
International job–job mobility (cross-border)	0.22	46	0.20	35
PhD Local Postdoc_Abroad	0.39	239	0.09	279
International job–job mobility (cross-border)	0.11	239	0.01	279
Postdoc Abroad International job–job mobility (cross-border)	0.16	103	0.06	82
Postdoc Local International job–job mobility (cross-border)	0.10	182	0.02	235

UK and the US in HEI senior mobility (HEI junior mobility is not significantly different even at country level).[21]

Finally, for mobility associated with career promotion (promotion to a higher academic rank), there are no significant differences between the two samples. On average, job changes associated with promotion account for about 17% of cases.

4.4 Career Mobility by BA, PhD, and Postdoc Location

In this section, we analyze the career mobility figures in more detail by exploiting differences in location of education (BA and PhD) and postdoc. Table 4 splits the sample according to the location of the BA, PhD, and postdoc and analyzes the subsequent international mobility of the researcher.

Researchers who studied for their BA or PhD outside their current location country are also more likely to have done their postdoc abroad. The correlation between foreign education and later postdoc or job abroad is higher for those located in the UK. For example, as shown in Table 4, 49% of those with a BA outside the UK also did a postdoc outside the UK compared to just 41% of those with a UK undergraduate degree. For the US, these percentages are 19% versus 10%. The correlation between foreign education and subsequent international job–job mobility is even stronger. Scientists who studied abroad are more likely to be internationally mobile; those who obtained their undergraduate degree

21. The difference persists if we control for similar career samples (e.g., only those that are full professors in 2012).

abroad are also more internationally mobile compared with those that did not (30% vs 8% in the UK and 12% vs 1% in the US). The PhD level results are similar, with 22% versus 11% for the UK and 20% versus 1% for the US. The UK sample shows a higher propensity to be internationally mobile respective to the US for both locally and internationally educated researchers. Considering the UK as part of the EU explains part of the international mobility in the UK sample, giving some evidence of a European job market for academics (mobility between continental Europe and the UK). However, even if we discount intra-European mobility, we still see a higher level of internationalization for the UK sample compared to the US for BAs (abroad and local) and local PhDs.

Finally, if we look at postdoc location we observe similar trends; researchers that obtained a postdoc outside one of our two countries of interest are also more job mobile across countries later on, with those finally working in the UK being more internationally mobile compared to those finally working in the US. For higher education and postdoc location and mobility, we find some evidence supporting the view that being mobile during the training period affects the probability of being mobile during the remaining career. This shows a form of path dependence in which mobility in the education steps becomes a predictor of future international doctoral and job–job mobility. This is a possible avenue for future research.

5. MODEL AND RESULTS

In the econometric analysis in this section, we focus our analysis on measuring the relationship between postdoctoral training and publication outcomes, controlling for the quality of the postdoc granting institution, education path, and a variety of other individual and institutional factors. We address three main related research questions based on the unique availability of transatlantic mobility data. Our analysis is performed in three steps. First, we investigate whether academics that work in the US have a performance advantage compared to those working in the UK, and the role of postdoctoral training in this difference. Second, we investigate whether UK academics who did a postdoctoral fellowship in the US have a performance advantage compared to those undertaking a postdoc in the UK. Third, we investigate whether the US is able to retain the best postdocs by estimating the performance of academics in the US and UK that undertook a postdoc in the US. We limit the analysis to papers published from 1991 onwards since the number of researchers already active before 1991 is very small.

5.1 Dependent Variable: Publications

Journal publications were collected from the Medline database using Pub-Harvester (Azoulay, Stellman, & Graff Zivin, 2006).[22] The Medline database includes bibliographical information for articles published in the life sciences and biology. We collected publications for all the academics in our sample.

---

22. See Annex 2 for a discussion of the disambiguation strategy followed.

Those with common name–surname combinations and those with Chinese last names were excluded and publications reliably collected for 512 academics, 244 UK academics and 268 US academics.

To account for journal impact/quality, we matched each publication to the Journal Citation Report (JCR) published annually by Thomson Reuters. The JCR includes fewer journals than Medline and inclusion in that list can be considered a first impact/quality measure. The JCR also includes the journal impact factor (JIF), which measures the average number of citations received by articles published in the focal journal in the previous three years and can serve as a measure of impact/quality for articles published in that journal in the current year, although a controversial one (Bordons, Fernández, & Gómez, 2002). As the JIF of a journal changes over time and journals are constantly added to (or removed from) the JCR, we matched publications to JCRs for each year from 1991 to 2012. For each publication we determine whether it was published in one of the top 5% of science journals (as defined by Thomson Reuters) in that year, thus creating a measure for the number of top impact/quality publications published by each academic in each year.[23] In addition, we calculate the average JIF of all articles published by each academic in each year as a measure for the average impact/quality of their research.

Figure 1 reports the average numbers of publications per academic per year as they appear in Medline, and also the number of publications that appear in JCR and the number of publications in the 95th percentile of journal impact/quality. Figure 1 shows that the average number of publications increased from 2.01 in 1991 to 4.22 in 2012. A similar increase is observed if we consider only publications that appear in JCR (from 1.85 to 3.73). The increase is less pronounced if we consider publications in one of the top science journals. The number is 1.18 in 1991 (representing 58% of publications) and 1.77 in 2012 (representing only 40% of publications).[24] Thus, while the number of publications has more than doubled over the past 20 years, the number of publications in top journals has increased by only 50%. In addition, Figure 1 also reports the average number of publications per academic per year (Medline) weighted by coauthors. The number of coauthors per paper has increased significantly over the 20-year period from 2.54 authors per paper in 1991 to 7.09 authors in 2012, which may explain some of the observed increase in publication numbers. Figure 1 shows that the number of articles divided by the number of coauthors (the coauthor weighted article count) has increased at a much slower rate, from 0.58 in 1991 to 0.72 in 2012, an increase of just 25%.

---

23. The number of articles with an assigned JIF in our sample increased from 4390 in 1991 to 8423 in 2012. The average JIF in JCR increased from 1.085 to 2.053 over the same period. The highest JIF in 1991 was 37.16 and 153.459 in 2012. The JIF cutoff point for the 95th percentile was 3.281 in 1991 and 5.670 in 2012.
24. The average JIF for publications in our dataset increased from 3.21 in 1991 to 4.69 in 2012, an increase of 50%.

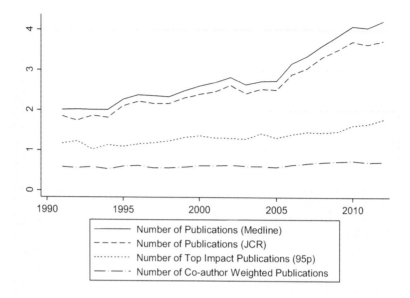

FIGURE 1   Average number of publications per academic per year by impact/quality and by coauthors.

Our data come from two different datasets: BBSRC and NIH. Figure 2 compares the performance of UK and US researchers and shows that the previously observed trend of an increase in publications can be found for researchers in both datasets. The average number of publications per year is slightly lower for researchers in the BBSRC sample, but the difference is not significant. However, academics in the UK publish fewer articles in the top 5% of journals, and articles of lower average impact/quality. This performance gap has been narrowing, with no significant difference between the two samples since 1998. The graphs also show that academics in both the US and the UK have been able to increase the impact/quality of their research and the number of publications in top journals, however, most of this increase happened prior to 2000, with little to no significant increases since.

5.2 Identification Strategy

The descriptive statistics suggest that academics in the US have a performance advantage compared to those in the UK. We therefore want to estimate this performance premium (the difference in publication performance between US and UK researchers) empirically. Since this potential premium may be related to the location of postdoctoral training, we include measures that compare the performance of academics that did their postdoc in the US to those that did their postdoc in the UK or some other country and to those with no postdoc, while controlling for education background and other personal and institutional characteristics.

This simple model does not account for the quality difference in postdoctoral training. Therefore, we include a control that allows us to compare the

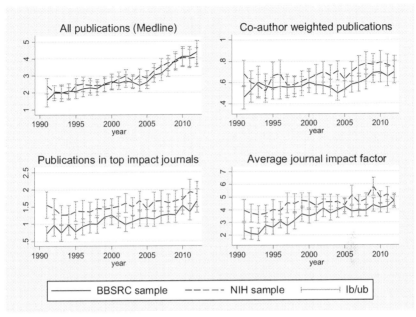

FIGURE 2   Number of publications by dataset.

performance of researchers that did their postdoctoral training in a top biomedi-cal training institution against those that did their postdoctoral training in a less important institution. This allows us to distinguish between the publication pre-mium for a postdoc in the US compared to the UK, and the publication premium that is attributable to institution quality.

This first analysis combines various questions in a heterogeneous sample. As a second and third step, we base our estimation on the difference-in-difference (DD) approach using a subpopulation of our sample. In the second model, we limit our estimation to academics working in the UK who did a postdoc in the US or in the UK. We exclude academics that did their PhD in the US (but were working in the UK) so as not to confound the US postdoc effect with a US PhD effect. This approach is preferable to a regression that includes researchers of all career paths, which does not account for the unobserved heterogeneity of training background. Further, models that include both US and UK researchers do not allow us to check whether researchers with US training also perform bet-ter outside the US. Thus, based on the UK sample, we use a DD identification that allows us to compare the performance of researchers whose postdoctoral training was in the US compared to those that took up a postdoc in the UK. This enables us to investigate whether there is a US postdoc premium also for academics working in the UK academic market. In addition, we consider that a US performance premium might be limited to receiving postdoctoral training at a top US institution. The DD is thus able to tell us whether the US postdoc premium is attributable to institution quality. As a third step, we compare the performance of academics who work in the US with those on similar training paths who work in the UK. We limit the sample to academics who completed their postdoctoral training in the US to account for the unobserved heterogeneity of postdoctoral background. This DD identification also allows us to compare the performance of researchers that did their PhD training in the US with those that did their PhD training elsewhere. The DD thus distinguishes between the publication premium from working in the US (our main variable of interest) and the publication premium attributable to PhD training.

5.3 Postdoc Quality Measure

In order to assess the importance of a US postdoc for future performance, we need to identify those institutions that will provide the greatest prestige or performance benefit, or that are more likely to attract or select the most promising young researchers. We construct a ranking of US universities based on the US National Research Council's assessment of doctorate programs, which is undertaken approximately 10 years. This assessment, available in a more or less comparable manner from 1982 onward, evaluates the quality of US universities by subject area. We limit the ranking measure to doctoral programs in bioscience and biochemistry and identify those programs that were ranked amongst the top 10% in their field for the years 1982, 1993, and 2005. We then generate an indicator variable that takes the value 1 if a postdoc was undertaken in one of the top 10% of universities.[25] Postdocs undertaken before 1985 use the 1982 ranking, those before 1995 use the 1993 ranking, and those after 1995 use the 2005 ranking. Eight universities are ranked in the 90th percentile in all three periods.[26]

We also rank UK universities using a disciplinary research ranking measure based on publication productivity and quality of the institution. We use Web of Science (WoS) publication data on UK universities compiled by Thomson Evidence, for the biomedical sciences for the years 1994 to 2009. We calculate the impact weighted productivity (IWP) of a given department per year (excluding those with an IWP of zero) and identify those in the top 10% as high-quality institutions.[27] Nine institutions appear amongst the top 10% (14 institutions) for all the years. For those undertaking a postdoc prior to 1994, we use the 1994 ranking, and for those undertaking a postdoc after 2009, we use the 2009 ranking. Though this is not a perfect measure, it gives some indication of whether the postdoc was undertaken at a top-quality department.[28]

---

25. In the 1982 sample, we identified 13 top universities. For 1995 and 2005, we identified 15 top universities due to the larger number of evaluated programs.

26. See Table 3A.1 in Annex 3 for a list of universities.

27. See Lawson & Soos (2014) for a detailed explanation of the ranking indicator, and Fernández-Zubieta et al. (Chapter 4) for an application to a sample of UK scientists in natural and engineering sciences.

28. Results are robust if we only consider academics that finished their PhD after 1990, i.e., did their postdoc in the last 20 years for which rankings are available.

Amongst the NIH academics undertaking a postdoc, 114 did a postdoc at one of the top US institutions (48% of those with a US postdoc) and 9 at one of the top UK institutions. Amongst the BBSRC academics, 25 (34% of those with a US postdoc) did a postdoc at a top US university and 119 at a top UK institution (65% of those with a UK postdoc). Eleven BBSRC academics undertook postdocs at a top US and a top UK institution (31% of those with US and UK postdoc).

5.4 Empirical Model

We estimate our baseline model and the DD models as Poisson regressions to account for the count nature of our data (numbers of publications).[29] This leads to an exponential functional form estimation equation for our baseline model:

$$\lambda_{it} = E\left[P_{it} \mid USJob_i, PD_i, X_{it}\right] = \exp\left(\propto USJob_i + \beta PD_i + X'_{it}\gamma\right)$$

where P_{it} is the count variable that represents the publications by academic i in t and is assumed to be Poisson distributed with $\lambda_{it} > 0$. $USJob_i$ is the measure for a job appointment in the US (NIH dataset), $Postdoc_i$ denotes the postdoc experience of the academic, and X_{it} the set of controls for age, gender, PhD country, and institution type, as well as year and career start year (the year of their first job after PhD or after the postdoc for those with postdoc experience) fixed effects.[30] The Poisson model assumes equidispersion, which is often violated in models of publication counts, leading academics to prefer the negative binomial (negbin) model. However, the negbin model is only consistent if the variance term is correctly specified, while Poisson models are consistent with only the mean correctly specified, even if overdispersion is present. The standard errors in the Poisson model can be corrected by applying robust standard errors (Wooldridge, 2002).[31] Standard errors are further clustered at the level of the individual, allowing estimation of a random effects Poisson model.

The number of academics is reduced to 498 due to missing values in some of the explanatory variables; the reduced sample is still comparable between the US and the UK with regard to gender and education mobility of academics; BA and PhD graduation year are different (as in the total sample), but the same within a three-year cohort. There are more full professors in the US compared to the UK sample. In the UK sample, we also have a group of young scientists who were not awarded a grant as PI before 2012 (only Co-I grants). We include a control in the regressions to capture any potentially missing experience effect

---

29. The average journal impact factor is a noninteger value but it follows a Poisson process and is consistent if robust standard errors are specified.

30. Results are robust if we include additional controls, e.g., past job mobility, current country of employment or seniority. These measures raise endogeneity concern, however, and are therefore not included in the models presented here.

31. The consistency of the negbin model is further rejected in the publication impact/quality models. It would be appropriate for the publication count model, which is more skewed, to use negbin, but the results are very similar and since the Poisson estimates are more conservative they are preferred.

of these Co-Is (see Table 3A.2 in Annex 4 for descriptive statistics for all the variables included in the regression).

5.5 Results

The main results are presented in Table 5 and are shown for three different performance measures: (1) the total number of publications, (2) the number of publications in top journals, and (3) the average journal impact factor of all publications. We report the marginal effects. The results we find for the total number of publications (measure 1) are confirmed if we consider only the number of publications in JCR journals or if we weight the number of publications by the number of coauthors.[32]

The results show that generally women produce significantly fewer publications than men and fewer in top journals but that their publications are of equal average impact/quality. The number of publications and their impact/quality increase with age, albeit with diminishing returns.[33] Researchers publish fewer articles, but not articles of lower impact/quality, when employed at private sector firms compared to employment at universities. Those working at research hospitals publish fewer articles in top journals, and of lower average impact/quality, than those working in a university department. Performance does not change when researchers work for public research organizations. We included year and career start year fixed effects, and they are jointly significant. The results are also confirmed if we include an experience (defined as number of years since career start) or a PhD year (year of PhD award) fixed effect in place of the career start year fixed effect.[34]

The US sample dummy is positive and significant in all estimations, showing that, all else being equal, academics working in the US on average produce one publication and 0.9 publications of high impact/quality more than those in the UK, while the average impact/quality of their publications is 1.76 points higher than that of UK-based academics.

The postdoc dummies show that academics that undertook a postdoc do not produce more publications than those without a postdoc and also do not publish more in top impact journals.[35] However, academics with postdoctoral experience publish in journals of higher average impact/quality than those without. The differences between the countries in which the postdoc was held are not significant, meaning that those with a postdoc in the US do not publish more

---

32. Results are available from the authors upon request.
33. As the US and UK promotion systems are different, due to endogeneity concern we do not include a seniority control in our models. However, in robustness checks that include seniority measures we would find that the number of publications and their impact/quality increases with seniority and is highest for full professors. The age effect for impact/quality would become insignificant.
34. Results are available from the authors upon request.
35. Note that our results might underestimate the contribution of foreign PhDs and postdocs as we excluded Chinese names from our sample for technical reasons (see Annex 2).

TABLE 5 Postdoc and Job Effect on Performance—Poisson Estimation on Full Sample

| | Publication Number (Medline) | | Publication Number in Top Journals | | | |
			(95p)		Average Journal Impact Factor	
Female	−0.593** (0.255)	−0.564** (0.255)	−0.286** (0.142)	−0.286** (0.145)	−0.098 (0.287)	−0.156 (0.288)
Age	0.400*** (0.065)	0.397*** (0.063)	0.197*** (0.036)	0.198*** (0.036)	0.200*** (0.071)	0.228*** (0.069)
Age²	−0.004*** (0.001)	−0.004*** (0.001)	−0.002*** (0.000)	−0.002*** (0.000)	−0.002*** (0.001)	−0.003*** (0.001)
US Job	1.018** (0.436)	1.111*** (0.422)	0.908*** (0.231)	0.910*** (0.219)	1.761*** (0.527)	1.646*** (0.514)
US Postdoc	−0.041 (0.246)		0.130 (0.139)		0.713*** (0.267)	
UK Postdoc	0.225 (0.312)		0.183 (0.185)		0.764** (0.332)	
Other Postdoc	−0.196 (0.327)		−0.029 (0.162)		0.606** (0.306)	
Top US Postdoc		−0.101 (0.259)		0.221 (0.147)		0.603** (0.260)
Top UK Postdoc		0.471 (0.289)		0.302* (0.177)		0.482 (0.301)
US PhD	−0.843* (0.483)	−0.763* (0.458)	−0.358* (0.195)	−0.335* (0.186)	−0.458 (0.461)	−0.592 (0.467)
UK PhD	0.072 (0.470)	0.161 (0.448)	0.184 (0.212)	0.196 (0.204)	0.303 (0.500)	0.246 (0.501)
University	Reference					
Firm	−1.072* (0.627)	−1.177* (0.620)	−0.092 (0.286)	−0.140 (0.284)	0.721 (0.578)	0.733 (0.648)
Research Hospital	−0.937 (0.790)	−0.998 (0.801)	−1.360*** (0.483)	−1.265*** (0.473)	−2.508** (1.060)	−2.187** (1.006)
PRO	−0.450 (0.468)	−0.446 (0.483)	−0.446 (0.379)	−0.370 (0.376)	−0.306 (0.756)	−0.151 (0.722)
Co-I Control	0.201 (0.485)	0.200 (0.486)	0.200 (0.242)	0.225 (0.250)	0.003 (0.511)	0.009 (0.546)
N	8768	8768	8768	8768	8768	8768
N_clust	495.000	495.000	495.000	495.000	495.000	495.000
Log-likelihood	−22,543.809	−22,515.894	−15,390.117	−15,352.190	−28,352.604	−28,403.475

Marginal effects are reported; Robust standard errors in parentheses; * p<0.10, ** p<0.05, *** p<0.01; All estimations include year and career start year fixed effects.

than those with a postdoc in the UK once we control for country of employment and other factors.

The quality dummy for the postdoc institution (Top US/Top UK) further allows us to see if those coming from top institutions publish more compared to those from other institutions or those without a postdoc. We find that those with a postdoc in a top UK or US university do not publish more articles than other researchers. Also, despite the large positive coefficient, top UK postdocs do not publish significantly more articles than top US postdocs (test of equality between UK and US top postdoc is only rejected at the 11% significance level). We find, however, that top UK postdocs publish more articles in top impact journals compared to those without a postdoc or a postdoc in a country other than the UK or the US but do not have a significantly higher average impact factor. For the top US postdoc, we find no significant added performance premium in terms of number of publications in either all or top impact journals. The top US postdoc, however, is associated with a higher average JIF of 0.6. This positive correlation remains if we exclude academics without postdoc experience, showing that top US postdocs produce research of higher average impact/quality than those with a postdoc elsewhere.

We also control in our estimations for PhD education and find a negative marginal effect of a US PhD on publication numbers and top publications but not significant on average impact/quality. Most academics with a US PhD remain in the US and, thus, continue to produce more publications than researchers working in the UK. However, they produce fewer publications and fewer top publications than academics trained outside the US that moved to the US for a job or for a postdoc and stayed there to further their careers.

5.6 DD Estimation 1—UK Sample

The baseline model in Table 5 shows that academic performance is higher in the US. It also indicates that those that took up a postdoc in a top US institution perform better in terms of impact/quality than those undertaking a postdoc elsewhere, even when working in the UK. A top UK postdoc is associated with a higher number of top impact/quality publications compared to those without a postdoc, but not with higher average impact/quality. To confirm the robustness of this result, in a second step we analyze whether UK-based academics that undertook a postdoc in the US perform better compared to UK-based academics that did a postdoc in the UK. We limit the analysis to academics whose PhD degree was awarded outside the US in order to measure only the additional performance premium of a US postdoc and not confound it with a potential US PhD correlation. The results are presented in Table 6.

The results show no significant differences between men and women for any of the performance measures. Publication numbers, but not average impact/

TABLE 6 DD Poisson—Postdoc Effect for BBSRC Researchers

	Publication Number (Medline)		Publication Number in Top Journals (95p)		Average Journal Impact Factor	
Female	-0.279 (0.530)	-0.195 (0.540)	-0.061 (0.244)	-0.032 (0.258)	0.260 (0.475)	0.199 (0.498)
Age	0.526*** (0.137)	0.520*** (0.138)	0.284*** (0.068)	0.284*** (0.069)	0.187 (0.128)	0.188 (0.126)
Age^2	-0.004*** (0.001)	-0.004*** (0.001)	-0.003*** (0.001)	-0.003*** (0.001)	-0.002 (0.001)	-0.002* (0.001)
US Postdoc	-0.136 (0.454)		-0.009 (0.252)		0.613* (0.324)	
Top US Postdoc		-0.847 (0.715)		-0.065 (0.377)		1.253*** (0.444)
Top UK Postdoc		0.453 (0.378)		0.226 (0.203)		0.087 (0.354)
University	Reference					
Firm	-1.976*** (0.742)	-2.221*** (0.750)	-0.172 (0.297)	-0.297 (0.294)	0.607 (1.523)	0.682 (1.694)
PRO	-0.136 (0.577)	-0.020 (0.627)	-0.125 (0.359)	-0.086 (0.387)	-0.519 (0.964)	-0.428 (0.973)
Co-I Control	-0.563 (0.602)	-0.451 (0.585)	-0.054 (0.261)	-0.017 (0.259)	0.019 (0.540)	0.131 (0.588)
N	3041	3041	3041	3041	3041	3041
N_clust	178	178	178	178	178	178
Log-likelihood	-7714.395	-7675.299	-4964.614	-4952.198	-8974.079	-8951.882

Marginal effects are reported; Robust standard errors in parentheses; * $p<0.10$, ** $p<0.05$, *** $p<0.01$; All estimations include year and career start year fixed effects. There are no research hospital observations.

quality of the publications, increase with age. We also checked the results including seniority variables, and the results are robust, with age turning insignificant.[36]

For the postdoc measures, we find that academics in the UK with a postdoc at a US institution do not publish more articles than those with a UK postdoc. However, in the model that predicts the average JIF, we find a strong positive result for academics that did a postdoc at a US institution, increasing the average journal impact/quality by 0.6 points. We also compare the performance of those that did their postdoc at a top US or top UK institution to the performance of academics with a postdoc at a lower-quality institution. The results confirm that top UK postdocs do not have a significantly different effect on publication numbers or impact/quality than those at lower-quality institutions. At the same time, we find that academics with a US postdoc publish fewer articles, but that these are of higher average impact/quality. The average JIF of their publications is 1.3 points higher than that of all other academics. Thus, even in a market outside the US, those with a postdoc from a prestigious US university produce research of higher average impact/quality. However, they do not produce more top articles or more publications in general.

5.7   DD Estimation 2—US Postdoc Sample

In the base model in Table 5 we found a performance premium for scientists working in the US, and in the second estimation in Table 6 we found a performance premium for UK researchers with a postdoc in the US. We are further interested in whether the US is able to keep the most talented researchers in the biomedical sciences. As a next step, we therefore reduce the analysis to academics with a postdoc in the US and check whether those staying in the US perform better than those that move to the UK. Table 7 reports the results of the estimation.

We see that women with a US postdoc produce fewer publications and fewer publications in top journals than men with a US postdoc, but the average quality of the publications is equal for men and women. Age has a positive significant effect, with diminishing returns.

Our results show that those US postdocs that continue to work in the US publish more and of higher impact/quality compared to those that move to the UK. However, those that also completed their PhD education in the US publish articles in journals of lower average impact/quality than those that moved to the US from abroad to do their postdoc. We also checked the robustness of these results by dropping the PhD-job interaction variable and the results do not change. The main US job effect remains strong and positive, although with a slightly smaller marginal effect, and the US PhD effect is negative and

---

TABLE 7 DD Poisson—US Job Effect for US Postdocs

	Publication Number (Medline)		Publication Number in Top Journals (95p)		Average Journal Impact Factor	
Female	-1.134*** (0.372)	-1.133*** (0.372)	-0.462* (0.252)	-0.458* (0.251)	-0.136 (0.461)	-0.118 (0.460)
Age	0.391*** (0.089)	0.392*** (0.089)	0.212*** (0.052)	0.216*** (0.053)	0.199* (0.109)	0.205* (0.110)
Age²	-0.005*** (0.001)	-0.005*** (0.001)	-0.003*** (0.001)	-0.003*** (0.001)	-0.003*** (0.001)	-0.003*** (0.001)
US Job	1.171** (0.573)	1.153* (0.589)	0.989*** (0.311)	0.884*** (0.295)	1.771*** (0.623)	1.619*** (0.622)
US PhD	-0.226 (1.029)	-0.227 (1.030)	-0.280 (0.515)	-0.305 (0.488)	0.548 (0.855)	0.517 (0.815)
US PhD*US Job	-1.014 (1.131)	-1.008 (1.136)	-0.398 (0.564)	-0.350 (0.531)	-1.875* (1.021)	-1.793* (0.979)
Top US Postdoc		0.055 (0.281)		0.311* (0.172)		0.517 (0.316)
University	Reference					
Firm	-0.861* (0.460)	-0.857* (0.462)	0.145 (0.339)	0.184 (0.326)	1.588 (1.555)	1.637 (1.603)
Research Hospital	-1.387* (0.840)	-1.364 (0.844)	-1.532*** (0.507)	-1.376*** (0.503)	-1.962 (1.564)	-1.722 (1.510)
PRO	-0.511 (1.133)	-0.499 (1.136)	-0.322 (0.605)	-0.243 (0.617)	-0.432 (1.305)	-0.254 (1.299)
Co-I Control	0.765 (0.688)	0.761 (0.689)	0.679* (0.369)	0.666* (0.370)	0.815 (0.778)	0.813 (0.794)
N	4374	4374	4374	4374	4374	4374
N_clust	253	253	253	253	253	253
Log-likelihood	-10,708.791	-10,708.381	-7640.136	-7614.343	-14,669.239	-14,645.079

Marginal effects are reported; Robust standard errors in parentheses; * p<0.10, ** p<0.05, *** p<0.01; All estimations include year and career start year fixed effects.

significant in all estimations. The second set of models in Table 7 includes a control for whether the US postdoc was completed in a top US institution. While the postdoc quality measure is not related to publication numbers, it is positively correlated with the number of articles in top-quality/impact journals and average journal impact/quality (at 11% significance). These results confirm that PhD education in the US is not correlated to achieving higher publication performance; also, the combination of a PhD, postdoc, and job in the US tends to result in lower impact/quality adjusted performance compared to academics working in the US with a more international career path. To summarize, we find some evidence that the US system is able to retain high-performing academics who completed their PhD degree in another country and went to the US to do their postdoc (especially at top US departments).

6. CONCLUSION

Biomedical science is an important and growing area of academic research, led by the US and the UK, which are able to attract promising researchers from other countries. The field is characterized by a highly internationalized labor force and increasing collaboration between researchers (BIS, 2013; NIH, 2012). This is an ideal setting to study academic labor market characteristics, mobility patterns, and the correlation between international (specifically transatlantic) mobility and research performance across career stages (student, postdoc, untenured, and tenured job levels). In order to carry out this analysis, we constructed the BIOMED-MOB database that includes original individual level data extracted from CVs and semiautomated information on academic performance. This allowed us to trace researchers' movements along their careers, across countries and jobs, while tracking also their academic performance. These unique datasets made it possible to compare the two labor markets in their ability to attract researches at all career stages and to identify the performance premium associated with these different career stages.

The analysis presented in this chapter was based on a sample of 619 US and UK biomedical researchers (327 from the US and 292 from the UK) in the period 1956 to 2012. We found that postdoctoral stays are common among biomedical academics (81%) and that most are located in the US or the UK, although about 20% of researchers working in the UK and about 25% working in the US had undertaken a postdoc in a third country. We found that job changes following the postdoc are common, with about 50% of our sample having changed jobs at least once since their first appointment after the postdoc. We did not find a higher mobility rate for the US sample. In relation to mobility within academia, mobility between universities within the domestic labor market is smaller in the UK than in the US. However, if we take into account international mobility (e.g., EU and Commonwealth mobility), we find a mobility rate similar to that in the US. Also, in terms of mobility for promotion and mobility to and from industry, we found no significant differences between the two samples. Incentives and policy action implemented in the UK during the last 20 years seem to have resulted in a UK academic market for biomedical sciences that is similar to the US market regarding academic mobility.

We observed that publication patterns have changed considerably over the two decades under study, with output increasing more in quantity than impact/ quality and a narrowing of the impact/quality gap between the UK and the US. The number of publications has more than doubled over the period 1991 to 2012, while the number of publications in top journals has increased at a much slower pace (a 50% increase). The number of coauthors per paper has nearly tripled over the 20-year period; if we consider the number of articles per coauthor, then total publication numbers increased by only 25%. Comparing the research performance of academics in both countries, we found that UK-based academics publish less frequently in higher-quality journals (top 5% journals) and have a lower average journal impact factor, although they had been able to reduce this impact/quality gap with US-based academics.

This initial evidence led us to investigate further the degree and source (in terms of career stage) of this performance premium for researchers working in the US. First, we analyzed the effect of US postdoctoral training (compared to a similar training in the UK, in other countries or no postdoctoral training) and its quality, controlling for education background and other personal and institutional characteristics. We confirmed the performance premium for US-based academics in terms of number of publications, publications in top journals, and average journal impact factor. The results for the whole sample (researchers working in both the US and the UK) show that academics with a US or UK postdoc do not publish more than those without this training, but they appear to publish in journals of higher average impact/quality. Postdoctoral training seems more relevant when conducted at a top-quality institution. We found some evidence of a positive correlation between doing postdoctoral training in a top-quality UK institution and publications in top journals and a significant correlation between having top postdoctoral training in the US and subsequent average publication impact/quality JIF. These results are consistent with Long (1978) who found that postdoctoral training is especially important for publication quality. The weak negative results (for total publications and publications in top journals) of PhD training in the US supports the US's ability to attract the best researchers worldwide at postdoctoral level and gives them a research advantage.

We also examined whether this "US postdoctoral training" advantage is transferable geographically and holds for researchers working in the UK. We reduced the heterogeneity of our sample by focusing only on UK-based academics who received their PhD training outside the US, to measure the US postdoctoral effect and perform estimations, by employing a DD-style approach. The results confirmed that US postdoc training is associated with publications of significantly higher average impact/quality later in the academic career in the UK (although lower publication numbers). This premium is higher if the postdoctoral training is undertaken in a top US institution.

We also investigated whether the US was able both to attract the best researchers and give them performance advantages, and to retain the best researchers. We applied the same DD-style approach but focused on academics with a US postdoc to check whether those who stayed in the US perform better than those that leave. The results show that researchers with a US postdoc who stayed in the US gain a performance premium. However, those who did their PhD in the US publish articles of lower average impact/quality than those that move to the US for a postdoc.

Among the control factors, we found a positive correlation between academic rank and our various measures of research output, which is stronger for the US than the UK sample. We also found evidence for the US sample that female researchers show lower productivity in terms of total publications and publications in top journals, but are similar to men with regard to the average impact/quality of publications. For the UK, we found no differences for any of these measures.

Overall, our results provide some support for the view that postdoctoral training is a crucial mechanism for attracting top researchers to the US, that this offers researchers a performance premium in terms of research quality, and that this premium is stronger if the training takes place in a top institution. The performance premium found for researchers that undertook postdoctoral training could be attributable to the selection procedures applied in the US, the resources available, or other institutional and social advantages. We did not have the necessary information and sufficient number of observations to properly test the selection hypothesis. Also, we did not consider the duration of postdoctoral training. This might allow better qualification of our positive results for postdoctoral training in the future, as we would expect a decrease in performance for longer postdoc periods. However, we also cannot say anything about the negative consequences of increasing the duration of postdoctoral training or repeated temporary contracts that also increase in both countries, issues that are heavily discussed in the policy literature.

Finally, the higher performance of US researchers could be attributable to the US university system's ability to attract, select, and retain the best researchers worldwide and to give them the resources and institutional and social advantages to improve their performance. In the setup in this chapter we could not test these reasons. However, it is interesting to note that the UK academic system in biomedicine is highly internationalized (even more so than the US in relation to late career mobility), it shows as much mobility and competitiveness as the US, and it has a promotion path associated with mobility that is similar to the US. Thus, it seems that the UK and US academic labor markets are very similar. Researchers working in the UK of similar age and education to researchers working in the US still underperform compared to their US counterparts. Resources, institutional and social advantages might be reasons for this difference.

In a research world with increasing level of mobility across countries and career stages and countries competing for global talent, this chapter makes it possible to learn more about the individual consequences of internationally mobile researchers, which might help countries to fine-tune their policies, institutions to manage mobile researchers, and researchers to improve their career choices. For example, if our results were to be confirmed, postdoctoral mobility (to top institutions) seems to offer better returns to the individual scientist, the receiving system, and the sending system (if the scientist returns) compared to PhD mobility. Public support (or individual decision) for postdoctoral mobility (or for attracting foreign postdocs) seems to be more justified than support for PhD mobility. The higher level of information at the postdoctoral level allows a better match between foreign researchers and hosting institutions, facilitating the rootedness of foreign researchers in local social networks and culture (as our results on average impact/quality suggest for the US sample) that appears to have a future impact on performance in both the case of a return to the sending country or the case of staying in the hosting country.

ANNEX 1: DATA CONSTRUCTION AND RESPONSE ANALYSIS[37]

US Sample

For the US we use research project grants (R01) awarded by the National Institutes of Health (NIH), the leading funding agency for academic research in biomedicine in the US. NIH grant award data cover grants awarded by the NIH since 1970 and include personal identifiers (IDs) for principal investigators (PIs) since 1985. They also provide information on university and subject affiliation for all funded researchers. R01 grants are assigned to around 230,000 PIs, which include university researchers as well as researchers from NIH institutes and industry. We limited our sample to researchers that received at least one R01 grant during the period 2001–2010 and were working for a university at the time of grant award. We further limited the sample to academics that worked in departments of biology, chemistry, neurology, genetics, or their subfields (at schools of medicine, arts and science, graduate colleges, or schools of engineering) at the time of grant award. This left us with an initial sample of 10,221 PI identifiers.

To collect CVs, we utilized the SiSOB tool (Geuna et al., in press).[38] First, we crawled the personal Web pages of researchers and identified 4037 valid e-mail addresses (representing 40% of the original sample). All researchers were

---

37. The data description and response analysis was also published in Section 5 of Geuna et al. (in press).
38. The SISOB Tool is an open-source Web application used to search, identify, and codify information on the careers of academic scientists identified on the Web. The tool consists of five main items: 1-Crawler, 2-E-mail Extractor, 3-CV and Web Page Extractor, 4-E-mail Survey, and 5-Text Analyzer and Codifier.

surveyed to collect CV and personal information. The survey was conducted in five rounds from October 2013 up to April 2014 and resulted in 169 valid CVs (a response rate of 4%). Second, we crawled the Web for researchers' CVs, a process that resulted in 215 correctly identified CVs. The final set of US CVs consists of 384 entries representing 3.8% of the initial population of 10,221 academics.

To test for nonresponse bias, we first rely on university affiliation as an indicator involving a number of dimensions such as geographic distribution, size, and institutional quality of the two groups. The analysis of institutional distribution revealed a total of 309 universities in the full population and 135 in the respondents' sample (42%), which account for 80% of the most important institutions in the full population. In order to formally address the representativeness of the sample, we used the Wilcoxon Rank Test. As a result, we found a significant match between the two distributions (population and respondents) with a 5% degree of tolerance, suggesting that the sample is not significantly different from the total population. To address additional concerns over sample bias at the individual level, we compare the distribution of subject areas, number of years actively involved in NIH-sponsored research, and number of grants in the full population and the sample population. We perform Kolmogorov–Smirnov tests of the equality of distributions and find that there is no significant difference between the years of grant activity in the respondent sample and those that did not answer (15.93 vs 16.01 years since first grant, $\rho = 0.539$). However, we find some difference in the number of grants (2.7 vs 2.8 grants, $\rho = 0.003$) and in the field distribution ($\rho = 0.035$). As a robustness check, we test the hypothesis excluding the field of chemistry, which has the highest response rates, and no longer find significant field differences ($\rho = 0.177$). Among our respondents, 76% are life scientists and 24% are chemists (compared to only 10% chemists in the original population).

UK Sample

For the UK, we use grants awarded by the Biotechnology and Biological Sciences Research Council (BBSRC), the leading funding agency for academic research and training in nonmedical bioscience in the UK, from 1994 to 2010, and include personal identifiers for 7527 researchers. The database includes both PIs and coinvestigators (Co-I). We limit the sample to those researchers that received at least two grants during the period 1994–2010, resulting in a list of 3615 researcher IDs, which include academics but also researchers working in industry and public research laboratories. In order to gather more thorough and up-to-date information (the most recent grant received by some researchers was in the 1990s) and to identify academics, we cross-referenced these researchers with the 2008 Research

Assessment Exercise (RAE). RAE 2008 includes a comprehensive listing of all research-active staff in all UK universities, for 2007. Amongst the 3615 researchers that received at least two BBSRC grants since 1994, we identified 2426 submitted to RAE 2008 by their university departments. Thus, they could be identified as working at a UK university in 2007. To collect CVs for the BBSRC sample, we first collected e-mail addresses manually and gathered valid e-mail addresses for all 2426 researchers. All researchers were surveyed to ask for their CVs and additional personal information (family situation, nationality). The BBSRC survey consisted of nine rounds, from September 2011 to January 2014, resulting in 296 (12.2%) complete CVs. Then, using the SiSOB tool (Geuna et al., in press) we directly crawled the web for researchers' CVs. This process resulted in 13 additional correctly identified CVs. The final UK database then consists of 309 CVs, corresponding to a response rate of 12.7% from the initial set of 2426 academics.

To test for nonresponse bias, we used the institutional composition of the full population and the sample of respondents based on RAE and BBSRC information. Academics in the full sample population come from 81 universities and respondents from 52 (64%), which account for 80% of the top institutions. Again, we find no difference in population based on universities represented (Wilcoxon Rank Test). We also compare the distribution of the amount of funding received, grant numbers, years actively involved in BBSRC sponsored research, and subject areas by the full and the sample populations (using Kolmogorov–Smirnov tests). We find no significant difference in grant value (£1.82 million vs £1.78 million, $\rho = 0.352$) or in grant numbers (5.2 vs 5.1, $\rho = 0.491$) between the respondent sample and those that did not answer. There is a small difference in years since first grant (12.7 vs 13.3, $\rho = 0.040$) with the respondents sample being slightly younger than nonrespondents. We find no differences in the subject area distribution ($\rho = 0.763$).

ANNEX 2: DISAMBIGUATION STRATEGIES FOR PUBLICATIONS

We searched for individual publications information for the full sample of 619 researchers using the open-source software Publication Harvester, which collects data from the open portal PubMed, a publication search engine for the Medline database. We applied a multisearch method to attribute publication records (articles) to individual researchers, addressing the "author name disambiguation" problem. This mechanism allowed us to semiautomate the search and cleaning of publication records for each researcher; the equivalent manual process is time-consuming and requires other sources of information (e.g., full publication records to improve the cleaning process).

The author name disambiguation problem arises in two ways: an individual researcher may be identified as two or more authors (splitting) and/or several researchers may be identified as a single author (merging) (Milojevic, 2013). Frequently, author names are reported inconsistently across publications and some names are "shared" by different authors.

There are several automated methods for dealing with the disambiguation problem ranging from simple (Newman, 2001) to more advanced methods (Ferreira, Goncalves, & Laender, 2012; Smalheiser & Torvik, 2009; Tang, Fong, Wang, & Zhang, 2012). Simple methods are name based and use only the author's name and initials; advanced methods require additional information (e.g., coauthor names, article titles, subjects, affiliations, citation counts). However, advanced methods also need conceptual and computational efforts that do not necessarily improve accuracy (Milojevic, 2013; Moody, 2004) compared to the simple methods.

We applied a multimethod that involves name-based searchers, uses additional related information (e.g., PhD year) to establish the time span of our search, and considers the name frequency and the size of the dataset to improve accuracy.

We extracted all the publications using an all-initials approach and including PhD year information. This method offers a restrictive framework to avoid merging-ambiguity (same last name that does not belong to the same author). We limited the year of publication based on the year of PhD award, imposing a three-year window before, and 2013 for closing this window. The all initials method might introduce some inconsistencies in author identification (splitting-ambiguity). The same researcher can appear as Smith J. and as Smith J.C. depending on how the name was reported in the paper. Availability of a researcher ID would avoid this issue, but IDs are not implemented completely in PubMed. Although we might lose some publications from the same author (false negatives), we were more concerned about avoiding the merging-ambiguity problem (false positives).

We determined the frequency of the names in our sample in order to identify further merging-ambiguity problems and clean the publication database. We were able to compute root frequencies (names plus first initial, name plus two initials, etc.) by manually downloading the publications from PubMed for the period 1965–2010. The final number of roots appearing at least two times is around 145,000.[39] Publications were reliably collected for 512 researchers after excluding very common roots (higher than five

---

39. We could not retrieve the whole set of publications from 1965 up to 2013 because PubMed does not allow this. Since the propensity to publish is quite high in medical sciences compared to others, we are confident that the 145,000 set of roots is highly representative of the whole set of authors listed in PubMed.

for names with one initial and higher than 19 for names with two initials) and Chinese names for which the disambiguation process did not work. Note that all the initial methods described above can be contaminated if the authors have not correctly reported their full name in their CV. In line with other name-based methods, the hybrid method cannot disambiguate names with the same first and middle initials that may apply to several individuals, and more often affects Asian names (Milojevic, 2013).

The multimethod applied is the result of testing all the name-based approaches (first initial, all initial, and hybrid method (Milojevic, 2013)) and more advanced methods in our database (PubMed). For example, we found that the use of quotation marks, a typical feature of PubMed in order to restrict the publication search, did not work properly with the Publication Harvester software. Once we implemented the script for the automatic search, Publication Harvester treated the Smith J [au] as if it were "Smith J" [au]. This resulted in *closing* instead of *opening* the search. Therefore, we used the *all-initial* method, include CV information to restrict the search and use the frequency of the roots from the hybrid method to clean the publication outputs.

ANNEX 3: TOP-RANKED INSTITUTIONS

TABLE 3A.1 Universities That Remain in the Top 10 Percent Over the Full Sample Period

US
California Institute of Technology
Harvard University
Massachusetts Institute of Technology
Rockefeller University
Stanford University
University of California, Berkeley
University of California San Francisco
Yale University
UK
University of Bristol
University of Cambridge
Imperial College London
King's College London
University College London
University of Oxford
University of Edinburgh
University of Glasgow
University of Manchester

ANNEX 4: DESCRIPTIVE STATISTICS

TABLE 3A.2 Summary Statistics for Regression Variables

	All id = 494				BBSRC id = 238		NIH id = 256	
	Mean	SD	Min	Max	Mean	SD	Mean	SD
Publication number (Medline)	2.94	3.36	0.00	41.00	2.88	3.39	2.99	3.33
Publications in top journal	1.36	2.00	0.00	22.00	1.15	1.75	1.54	2.18
Average JIF	4.14	4.39	0.00	51.30	3.65	3.97	4.57	4.68
Coauthor weighted publication number	0.64	0.72	0.00	7.52	0.59	0.67	0.68	0.76
Publication number (JCR)	2.68	3.12	0.00	37.00	2.62	3.13	2.75	3.12
Female	0.21	0.41	0.00	1.00	0.22	0.41	0.21	0.40
Age	46.54	10.00	26.00	89.00	44.67	8.70	48.19	10.76
US Postdoc	0.50	0.50	0.00	1.00	0.25	0.44	0.72	0.45
UK Postdoc	0.32	0.47	0.00	1.00	0.64	0.48	0.04	0.19
Other Postdoc	0.14	0.34	0.00	1.00	0.20	0.40	0.08	0.27
Top US Postdoc	0.23	0.42	0.00	1.00	0.08	0.27	0.35	0.48
Top UK Postdoc	0.21	0.41	0.00	1.00	0.41	0.49	0.04	0.19
UK PhD	0.43	0.49	0.00	1.00	0.86	0.35	0.05	0.21
US PhD	0.50	0.50	0.00	1.00	0.05	0.22	0.90	0.30
Other PhD	0.07	0.26	0.00	1.00	0.09	0.29	0.05	0.23
Assistant Professor	0.22	0.42	0.00	1.00	0.23	0.42	0.22	0.41
Associate Professor	0.25	0.43	0.00	1.00	0.33	0.47	0.18	0.39
Full Professor	0.49	0.50	0.00	1.00	0.39	0.49	0.58	0.49
Firm	0.01	0.08	0.00	1.00	0.01	0.07	0.01	0.09
Research Hospital	0.00	0.06	0.00	1.00	0.00	0.00	0.01	0.09
PRO	0.02	0.15	0.00	1.00	0.04	0.20	0.01	0.08
University	0.97	0.18	0.00	1.00	0.95	0.21	0.98	0.15
Co-I Control	0.06	0.23	0.00	1.00	0.12	0.32	0.00	0.00

ACKNOWLEDGMENTS

We acknowledge valuable comments from Chiara Franzoni, Richard Freeman, Bhaven Sampat, and Paula Stephan. We thank Jerry Thursby for access to the data of the National Research Council's assessment of doctorate programs in the US. We thank Riccardo Beltrame for his help with building the databases used in this chapter. Financial support from the European Commission (FP7) Project "An Observatorium for Science in Society based in Social Models—SISOB" Contract no. FP7 266588 and the Collegio Carlo Alberto Project "Researcher Mobility and Scientific Performance" is gratefully acknowledged. Ana Fernandez-Zubieta acknowledges financial support from the JAE-Doc "Junta para la Ampliación de Estudios" program that is cofinanced by the Social Structure Funds (SSF).

REFERENCES

Ackers, H. L. (2005). Moving people and knowledge, the mobility of scientists within the European Union. *International Migration, 43,* 99–129.

Adams, J. (1998). Benchmarking international research. *Nature, 396,* 615–618.

Auriol, L., Misu, M., & Freeman, R. (2013). *Careers of doctorate holders: Analysis of labour market and mobility indicators.* STI working paper 2013/4. OECD.

Azoulay, P., Stellman, A., & Graff Zivin, J. (2006). PublicationHarvester: an open-source software tool for science policy research. *Research Policy, 35*(7), 970–974.

Baldi, S. (1995). Prestige determinants of first academic job for new sociology Ph.D.s: 1985–1992. *Sociological Quarterly, 36,* 777–789.

BIS. Business, Innovation and Skills. (2013). *International comparative performance of the UK research base.*

Bordons, M., Fernández, M. T., & Gómez, I. (2002). Advantages and limitations in the use of impact factor measures for the assessment of research performance. *Scientometrics, 53*(2), 195–206.

Borjas, G. (1985). Assimilation, changes in cohort quality, and earnings of immigrants. *Journal of Labor Economics, 4,* 463–489.

Borjas, G., & Bratsberg, B. (1996). Who leaves? The outmigration of the foreign-born. *Review of Economics and Statistics,* 165–176.

Burris, V. (2004). The academics caste system: prestige hierarchies in PhD exchange networks. *American Sociological Review, 69*(2), 239–264.

Chambers, E., Foulon, M., Handfield-Jones, H., Hankin, S., & Michaels, E., III (1998). The war for talent. *The McKinsey Quarterly, 3,* 44–57.

Chiswick, B. (1978). The effect of Americanisation on the earnings of foreign-born men. *Journal of Political Economy, 86,* 897–921.

Corley, E., & Sabharwal, M. (2007). Foreign-born academic scientists and engineers: producing more and getting less than their U.S.-Born peers? *Research in Higher Education, 48*(8), 909–940.

Crane, D. (1972). *The invisible college.* Chicago: University of Chicago Press.

David, P. (1992). Path-dependence in economic processes. In P. David, & C. Antonelli (Eds.), *The invisible hand and the grip of the past: Path dependence in economic processes.* Dordrecht: Kluwer Publishers.

Dustmann, C. (2003). Return migration, wages differentials and the optimal migration duration. *European Economic Review, 47,* 353–367.

Eisenberg, T., & Wells, M. (2000). Inbreeding in law school hiring: assessing the performance of faculty hired from within. *Journal of Legal Studies, 29*(1), 369–388.

Elton, L. (2000). The UK research assessment exercise: unintended consequences. *Higher Education Quarterly, 54*(3), 274–283.

Eurostat. (2012). *Statistics*. http://ec.europa.eu/eurostat/data/database.

FASEB. (2013). *Data compilations*. Available from http://www.faseb.org/Policy-and-Government-Affairs/Data-Compilations.aspx.

Fernández-Zubieta, A., Geuna, A., & Lawson, C. (2015). Mobility and Productivity of Research Scientists. In A. Geuna (Ed.), *Global Mobility of Research Scientists: The Economics of Who Goes Where and Why*. Amsterdam: Elsevier. (Chapter 4).

Ferreira, A. A., Goncalves, M. A., & Laender, A. H. (2012). A brief survey of automatic methods for author name disambiguation. *SIGMOD Record, 41*(2), 15–26.

Franzoni, Ch, Scellato, G., & Stephan, P. (2012). *Foreign-born scientists: Mobility patterns for 16 countries*. NBER Working Paper 18067.

Franzoni, C., Scellato, G., & Stephan, P. (2014). The mover's advantage: the superior performance of migrant scientists. *Economics Letters, 122*(1), 89–93.

Freeman, R. (2006). Does globalization of the scientific/engineering workforce threaten U.S. economic leadership? *Innovation Policy and the Economy, 6*, 123–158.

Gentile, N., Levey, G., Sherman, C., Hough, L. J., Dial, T., & Jolly, P. (1989). *Postdoctoral Research Training of Full-Time Faculty in Departments of Medicine*. Washington, DC, USA: Association of American Medical Colleges.

Geuna, A., Kataishi, R., Toselli, M., Guzmán, E., Lawson, C., Fernández-Zubieta, A., et al. SiSOB data extraction and codification: A tool to analyze scientific careers. Research Policy, in press.

Ghaffarzadegan, N., Hawley, J., & Desai, A. (2013). Research workforce diversity: the case of balancing national versus international postdocs in US Biomedical research. *Systems Research and Behavioural Science, 31*(2), 301–315.

Glanzel, W., Debackere, K., & Meyer, M. (2008). 'Triad' or 'tetrad'? On global changes in a dynamic world. *Scientometrics, 74*, 71–88.

Glover, M., Buxton, M., Guthrie, S., Hanney, S., Pollitt, A., & Grant, J. (2014). Estimating the returns to UK publicly funded cancer-related research in terms of the net value of improved health outcome. *BMC Medicine, 12*, 99.

Graduate Student Survey (GSS). (2013). Accessed July 2014 http://www.nsf.gov/statistics/infbrief/nsf13334/.

Grogger, J., & Hanson, G. H. (2011). Income maximization and the selection and sorting of international migrants. *Journal of Development Economics, 95*(1), 42–57.

Hoare, A. G. (1994). Transferred skills and university excellence?: an exploratory analysis of the geography of mobility of UK academic staff. *Geografiska Annaler. Series B, Human Geography, 76*(3), 143–160.

Horta, H., Veloso, F., & Grediage, R. (2010). Navel gazing: academic inbreeding and scientific productivity. *Management Science, 56*(3), 414–429.

Hunter, R., Oswald, A., & Charlton, B. (2009). The elite brain drain. *The Economic Journal, 119*, 231–251.

Hu, X., & Rousseau, R. (2009). A comparative study of the difference in research performance in biomedical fields among selected Western and Asian countries. *Scientometrics, 81*(2), 475–491.

Institute of International Education. (2012). *International students in the U.S.* http://www.iie.org/opendoors.

Ivancheva, L., & Gourova, E. (2011). Challenges for career and mobility of researchers in Europe. *Science and Public Policy, 38*(3), 185–198.

Jovanovic, B. (1979). Job matching and the theory of turnover. *The Journal of Political Economy*, *87*(5), 972–990.

LaLonde, R., & Topel, R. (1992). The assimilation of immigrants in the U.S. labor market. In G. Borjas, & R. Freeman (Eds.), *Immigration and the workforce* (pp. 67–92). Chicago: NBER, University of Chicago Press.

Lan, X. (2012). Permanent visas and temporary jobs: evidence from postdoctoral participation of foreign PhDs in the United States. *Journal of Policy Analysis and Management, 31*(3), 623–640.

Lawson, C., & Soos, S. (2014). *A thematic mobility measure for econometric analysis*. LEI & BRICK Working Paper 02/2014.

Lee, S. (2004) *Foreign-born scientists in the United States-Do they perform differently than native-born scientists?* Dissertation and Theses: A&I AAT 3155279.

Levey, G. S., Sherman, C. R., Gentile, N. O., Hough, L. J., Dial, T. H., & Jolly, P. (1988). Post-doctoral research training of full-time faculty in academic departments of medicine. *Annals of internal medicine, 109*(5), 414–418.

Long, J. S. (1978). Productivity and academic position in the scientific career. *American Sociological Review, 43*(6), 889–908.

Mahroum, S. (1998). Competing for the highly skilled: Europe in perspective. *Science and Public Policy, 26*(1), 17–25.

Mangematin, V. (2000). PhD job market: professional trajectories and incentives during the PhD. *Research Policy, 29*(6), 741–756.

McGuinnis, R., Allison, P., & Long, S. J. (1982). Postdoctoral training in biosciences: allocation and outcomes. *Social Forces, 60*(3), 701–722.

Meng, Y., & Su, X. (2010). *The impact of postdoc training on academic research productivity: What are the gender differences?* University of Georgia.

Milojevic, S. (2013). Accuracy of simple, initials-based methods for author name disambiguation. *Journal of Informetrics, 7*(4), 767–773.

Moed, H. F. (2008). UK research assessment exercises: informed judgments on research quality or quantity? *Scientometrics, 74*(1), 153–161.

Moody, J. (2004). The structure of a social science collaboration network: disciplinary cohesion from 1963 to 1999. *American Sociological Review, 69*(2), 213–238.

Mortensen, D. (1986). Job search and labor market analysis. In O. Ashenfelter, & R. Layard (Eds.), *Handbook of labour economics* (Vol. 2). Amsterdam: North Holland.

National Institutes of Health (NIH). (2012). *Biomedical research workforce working group report*. http://acd.od.nih.gov/biomedical_research_wgreport.pdf.

National Research Council (NRC). (2012). http://www.nrc.gov/.

Navarro, A., & Rivero, A. (2001). High rate of inbreeding in Spanish universities. *Nature, 410*, 14.

Nerdrum, L., & Sarpebakken, B. (2006). Mobility of foreign searchers in Norway. *Science and Public Policy, 33*, 217–229.

Newman, M. E. J. (2001). The structure of scientific collaboration networks. *Proceedings of the National Academy of Sciences, 98*(2), 404–409.

OECD. (2008). *The global competition for talent: Mobility of the highly skilled*. Directorate for Science Technology and Industry. Paris: OECD.

Oyer, P. (2007). *Ability and employer learning: Evidence from the economist labor market*. NBER Working Papers 12989.

Sastry, T. (2005). *Migration of academic staff to and from the UK. An Analysis of the HESA data*. Higher Education Policy Institute Report.

Smalheiser, N. R., & Torvik, V. I. (2009). Author name disambiguation. In B. Cronin (Ed.), *Annual review of information science and technology* (Vol. 43) (pp. 287–313). Medford, NJ: Information Today.

Steiner, J. F., Lanphear, B. P., Curtis, P., & Vu, K. O. (2002). The training and career paths of fellows in the National Research Service Award (NRSA) Program for Research in Primary Medical Care. *Academic Medicine, 77*(7), 712–718.

Stephan, P. E. (2012). *How economics shapes science.* Cambridge: Harvard University Press.

Stephan, P. E., & Levin, S. G. (1992). *Striking the mother lode in science: The importance of age, place, and time.* USA: Oxford University Press.

Stephan, P., & Levin, S. (2007). Foreign scholars in U.S. Science: contributions and costs. In R. Ehrenberg, & P. Stephan (Eds.), *Science and the university.* Wisconsin: University of Wisconsin Press.

Stephan, P., & Ma, J. (2005). The increased frequency and duration of the postdoctoral career stage. *American Economic Review Papers and Proceedings, 95,* 71–75.

Su, X. (2011). Postdoctoral training, departmental prestige and scientists' research productivity. *The Journal of Technology Transfer, 36,* 275–291.

Tang, J., Fong, A. C. M., Wang, B., & Zhang, J. (2012). A unified probabilistic framework for name disambiguation in digital library. *IEEE Transactions on Knowledge and Data Engineering, 24*(6), 975–987.

Thorn, K., & Holm-Nielsen, L. B. (2008). International mobility of researchers and scientists policy options for turning a drain into a gain. In *The international mobility of talent: Types, causes, and development impact* (pp. 145–167).

Universities UK. (2007). *Statement of recommended practice: Accounting for further and higher education.* http://www.universitiesuk.ac.uk/highereducation/Documents/2007/SORP.pdf.

Webster, B. (2005). International presence and impact of the UK biomedical research, 1989–2000. *Aslib Proceedings: New Information Perspectives, 57*(1), 22–47.

Webster, B. M., Lewison, G., & Rowlands, I. (2003). *Mapping the landscape II: Biomedical research in the UK, 1989–2002.* London: City University.

Weinberg, B. A. (2009). An assessment of British science over the 20th century. *The Economic Journal, 119,* 252–269.

Wooldridge, J. (2002). *Econometric analysis of cross section and panel data.* MIT Press.

Wu, R. (2004). Making an impact. *Nature, 428,* 206–207.

Ziman, J. (1991). Public understanding of science. *Science, Technology, & Human Values, 16*(1), 99–105.

Zumeta, W. (1985). *Extending the educational ladder: The changing. Quality and value of postdoctoral Study.* Lexington MA: Heath/Lexington Books.

Chapter 4

△ This study is also
individual - level
△ method ✓

Mobility and Productivity of Research Scientists[1]

Ana Fernández-Zubieta[1], Aldo Geuna[2,3], Cornelia Lawson[2,3,4]

[1]*Institute for Advanced Social Studies – Spanish Council for Scientific Research, Campo Santo de los Mártires, Córdoba, Spain;* [2]*Department of Economics and Statistics Cognetti De Martiis, Università di Torino, Turin, Italy;* [3]*BRICK, Collegio Carlo Alberto, Moncalieri, Turin, Italy;* [4]*School of Sociology and Social Policy, University of Nottingham, Nottingham, UK*

Chapter Outline

1. INTRODUCTION

Researcher mobility between institutions, disciplines, sectors, and countries is increasingly being encouraged at policy level (EC 2001, 2006, 2012; OECD 2000) as an instrument to improve the performance of the research system by facilitating knowledge and technology transfer and to increase productivity. The assumed positive effects of researcher mobility are related to the embedded nature of knowledge (Griliches, 1973; Granovetter, 1985). Mobility allows researchers to spread and increase their human (Becker, 1962, 1964; Nelson & Phelps, 1966; Schultz, 1961, 1990) and social capital (Bourdieu, 1986; Burt,

---

1. Some of the material presented in this chapter is also discussed in Fernández-Zubieta, Geuna, & Lawson (2015).

105

assumption :
mobility
+ ↓
productivity

1997; Coleman, 1988). This transfer and augmentation of human and social capital can have positive effects on researchers' performance, patterns of collaboration, and career development. This perspective thus assumes that both the research system and the individual researcher benefit from mobility. However, to date there is scant evidence on researcher mobility and its consequences (Franzoni, Scellato, & Stephan, 2012; Musselin, 2004; Teichler 1996).

Changes to the research system require researchers to be able to adapt to new institutions, sectors, and work roles. They also require institutions to properly manage mobile researchers and their careers. Researchers moving across sectors, or moving as a result of career advancement, can facilitate the knowledge and technology transfer process and gain access to knowledge, equipment, and networks that could improve their performance. We propose a framework to analyze the individual effects of researcher mobility on research performance, based on a job-matching approach (Jovanovic, 1979; Mortensen, 1986) adapted for academics that emphasizes research and reputation factors. Drawing on the idea that academic performance is driven by the availability of capital—both human and social—and peer effects (Azoulay, Zivin, & Wang, 2010; Waldinger, 2012; Weinberg, 2007), we hypothesize different short- and medium-term effects of mobility on research performance. We test our predictions with a sample of 171 mobile and nonmobile UK academic researchers in science and engineering for which we collected information on employment patterns and publishing activities over their entire career up to 2005, covering a period from 1957 to 2005. We find no evidence that mobility per se boosts the scientific productivity of researchers; what matters is the destination. Mobility to a lower-ranked university is accompanied by a decrease in the number of publications, while mobility to a higher-ranked university is associated with a positive increase in productivity but no quality effect. In both cases we find strong evidence of short-term negative effects. Intersector mobility, i.e., mobility from industry to academia, does not affect publication rates, making researchers with a background in industry as productive as their purely academic peers.

destination
↓ +
productivity

2. THE EFFECT OF RESEARCHER MOBILITY ON RESEARCHER PRODUCTIVITY

Starting from the traditional analytical model of scientific productivity (Cole, 1979; Levin & Stephan, 1991), we study scientific productivity (sp) as a function of individual characteristics, environmental specificities, and mobility events.

The impact of a job change (M) on scientific productivity (sp) is affected by the researcher's reasons for the move. For example, job mobility may have a positive impact on research productivity only if the researcher finds better conditions for pursuing her research endeavor in the new job location—in other words, if she moves to a new job in order to increase her research performance. Thus, a researcher moves to a new job if the value V_{t+1} of her utility function is higher than the value V_t before the move at time t. This may be due to traditional job search-related factors (e.g., wages, search efforts, mobility cost) and/or because of an expected better research and reputation environment (r).

Only if the job change is driven by research and reputation-related motives (r) can we expect a positive impact on performance. Hence, we do not expect all types of job mobility to be associated with increased research productivity.

Following from the above, we consider the following function for scientific productivity:

$$sp = f(M(r), pt, pf, h) \qquad (1)$$

where M is the mobility event, pt is individual academic characteristics such as career rank, pf is individual personal characteristics such as gender, and h is institution, field, country, and time-specific environmental characteristics affecting scientific productivity (e.g., the greater tendency to publish and cite in medicine than in economics) for which we need to control.

Although we expect mobility driven by research and reputational factors to result in better performance, there are accompanying mobility costs that negatively affect research productivity. The time needed to learn new tasks and administrative procedures in the new institution means that the mobile researcher will have less time to devote to research activities (Groysberg, 2008; Shaw, 1987). In addition, expected and real adjustments costs can differ, which can have a negative impact on postmobility productivity. Therefore, it is reasonable to expect a period of decreased productivity after the job change regardless of the reasons for the move. The length of the adjustment period and the intensity of the reduced productivity will depend on the specific adjustment costs.

To summarize, a job change will be associated with a positive effect on researchers' productivity only if it is motivated by research and reputational factors, and we should expect a decrease in productivity in the short term due to adjustment costs. Below we discuss how this plays out for two types of mobility observed in academia: social mobility and intersector mobility.[2]

2.1 Social Mobility: A Move to a Higher-Ranked University

The search and match model predicts that researchers with high-potential productivity will move from a lower-quality department or university to a higher-quality department or university (upward mobility), which provides a better research and reputation environment to realize their research potential.[3] A job move to a higher-quality department provides access to better equipment (Martin-Rovet, 2003) and a research group where the positive peer (Weinberg, 2007)[4] and network effects are likely to increase the researcher's performance. In addition, mobile researchers can continue to benefit from

---

2. Chapter 1 of this book discusses various other possible mobility types.
3. Oyer (2007) shows that highly productive researchers tend to be concentrated in highly ranked departments.
4. However, Kim, Morse, and Zingales (2009) find that peer effects have decreased since 1990 (see also Ding, Levin, Stephan, & Winkler, 2009).

their previous networks, which are carried into the new environment (Azoulay, Zivin, & Sampat, 2012; Waldinger, 2012), creating extended networks and possibilities for recombination, learning, collaboration, and productivity. Also, the science and technology human capital theory (Bozeman & Rogers, 2002) predicts that researchers acquire human and social capital through mobility and supports the expected positive effect of mobility on productivity. Thus, job-matching approach and human and social capital arguments can be combined to support the positive effects of upward job mobility. A job move to a higher-quality/reputation institution could lead to increased medium-to long-term performance following an initial short period of decreased performance due to adjustments costs.

2.2 Intersector Mobility: Job Move from Industry to Academia

Early analyses of intersector mobility (Hagstrom, 1965; Kornhauser, 1962; Krohn, 1961; Marcson, 1960) show that differences in reward systems in different sectors can influence both the costs of job mobility and the mobile researcher's performance. The adaptation costs related to intersector job changes are expected to be higher than within sector mobility. Good matches for intersector job changes are also less likely since access to information about the new job is more difficult. Job mobility to a firm could direct the researcher's work to more applied research, product development or non-research tasks and discourage publications. Different priorities could negatively affect future scientific performance (Cotgrove & Box, 1970) due to decreased accumulation of publishable knowledge. However, experience in industry could positively affect the performance of researchers returning to academia. Dietz & Bozeman (2005) analyze this side of the relationship and consider the productivity of researchers that have spent time in industry. They find a positive effect on patent productivity of years spent outside academia. Thus, while researchers involved in intersector job changes may suffer some adaptation costs, they may also benefit from presumed higher human capital acquired during their time in industry, and they may patent or publish more in the medium term.

Figure 1 summarizes the expected job mobility effects on academic performance across mobility types. In what follows, we test these expectations empirically.

Job mobility		Social mobility (Upward mobility)	Intersector mobility
Short term	Medium term	Medium term	
(-)	(+) / (-)	(+)	(-) / (+)

FIGURE 1 Job mobility effects across mobility types.

3. EMPIRICAL ANALYSIS

3.1 Data

The empirical study is based on a sample of 171 research-active academics working at 53 UK universities, in four scientific fields: chemistry; physics; computer science; and mechanical, aeronautical, and manufacturing engineering in 2005.[5] We code career information taken from curricula vitae (CVs) in order to construct comprehensive profiles for the 171 researchers, spanning their careers from PhD award to 2005, resulting in a panel for the period 1957–2005. Researchers' CVs include unique information on career paths and the timing and nature of job transitions. This information was complemented with publication and citation data collected from the Web of Science (WoS).[6]

The three-step promotion system and race for positions in the most prestigious institutions (Hoare, 1994) make the UK system more competitive than other academic systems in Europe. There is no obligation to move after PhD completion; however, mobility barriers are very low and mobility is usually rewarded, making the UK academic labor market very fluid. This makes the UK a suitable setting to test our approach. In the UK, the minimum tenure-track positions in academia are lecturer, followed by senior lecturer, reader, and professor. Since the early 1990s, in parallel with the traditional teaching and research academic career ladder, a research-only career[7] within the university system has developed, financed by soft money. Academics in the UK are usually hired on permanent contracts, which in the case of lecturer appointments or research fellowships[8] are subject to a three-year probation period. Thus, job mobility in our sample is likely to be voluntary, i.e., based on researchers leaving a permanent position for reasons other than termination of contract.

Our sample consists of researchers aged 29–77 who were research active in 2005. The mean age of the sample is 49 in 2005. The first researcher joins our sample in 1957 and the last in 2003. Accordingly, the career years recorded in our sample range from 3 to 49, with an average observation period of 20 years. In our sample of 171 UK academics, 145 (85%) started out as lecturers or research fellows; 22 researchers (13%) took up a first position in industry, and 2 began their careers in senior academic positions. For another two researchers, the first

---

5. The sample is based on a 2004 survey of academic researchers awarded a grant from the Engineering and Physical Sciences Research Council (EPSRC) at least once between 1999 and 2003, who therefore can be considered research active. CVs were collected for a subsample of survey respondents. See Crespi et al. (2011) for a detailed description of the database.

6. Using data collected from CVs combined with data from the ISI, WoS improved the accuracy of our data since it avoids mismatches arising from common names and changes in researchers' institutional affiliations.

7. There are three types of research positions: research fellow, senior research fellow, and research professor. This career path has resulted in a greatly increased number of short-term contracts at research fellow level.

8. We consider the position of research fellow as tenure-track equivalent to lecturer only if it persists for at least five years, indicating a long-term relationship with the university equivalent to a probation period.

position was not evident from their CVs. The mean starting age is 28.6 with a minimum of 22 years and a maximum of 38 years.[9] The mean PhD age is slightly lower at 27.2 years. Among our researchers sample, 45.2% took up their first permanent position immediately after PhD award, while 48.8% embarked on a postdoc; 6% of the researchers in our sample started their work careers during or before studying for their PhD degree; 109 researchers (64%) changed jobs at least once during their career. In total, we have 159 job changes, with 31 academics changing positions twice during their career, 8 academics changing three times, and 1 researcher moving four times. The mean number of years in one job is 10.

Although we consider only researchers that worked at UK universities in 2005, this includes researchers from outside the UK and researchers with an industry background. Along their careers, 28 researchers changed jobs between industry and academia, and 20 researchers moved internationally. Fifty researchers (29%) were born and raised outside the UK, primarily in Europe (33 researchers). Researchers often move from their home country to take up a first permanent post; for 52 researchers the first permanent position is outside their country of birth, which includes 11 UK-born researchers that took up a permanent position abroad. Nevertheless, the majority of researchers find a position in their country of birth (the median distance between first permanent job and place of birth is 176 miles).

Between 1982 and 2005, the academics in our sample produced an average of 4.45 publications per year. Eighty-eight researchers (59%) published their first article during their PhD study or postdoctoral period and before their first permanent position. The average number of publications per researcher per year increased from an average of 4.08 in 1982 to 5.05 in 2005 (Figure 2) with a similar increase in publication quality. Quality is measured as the number of WoS citations to a publication in the first five years after publication. Quality-adjusted publication numbers increased from 46 in 1982 to 74 in 2005, which could be due to life cycle, year, or mobility effects, which this chapter attempts to measure.

3.2 Mobility and Reputation: Social Mobility

In Section 2 of this chapter, we stressed the importance of research and reputation factors for explaining the academic labor market. Access to resources and an improved research environment are incentives for mobility and are fundamental to an analysis of the impact of mobility on scientific productivity. In the period analyzed in this chapter, wages play a smaller role in the UK academic labor market, in particular because of the high level of standardization in UK academic salary scales.[10] Therefore, we assume that mobility is driven primarily

---

9. Researchers joining the sample at an older age may have had pre-PhD experience in academia or industry; however, this is not recorded in our data.
10. Starting in 2004 (following the higher education pay framework), universities paid higher wages and offered higher incentive payments to higher-reputation and more successful researchers.

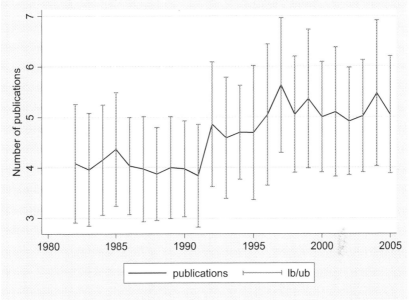

FIGURE 2   Average publication numbers.

by reputation factors and classify job changes according to a move to a higher or a lower quality/reputation institution.

To measure university prestige, we build an original indicator of the university's disciplinary research ranking, based on publication productivity and quality. We use WoS publication data on UK higher education institutions (HEI) compiled by *Thomson Evidence*, in two main subject categories (natural sciences and engineering sciences) for the years 1982–2005.[11] Our data include information on researchers in chemistry, physics (natural sciences), computer science, and mechanical engineering (technical sciences). We calculate our research-ranking indicator as percentile ranks (*PR*) based on the underlying distribution of impact-weighted productivity of a given department, per year, normalized linearly. Thus, we measure the contribution of the particular HEI to the production of the UK sector relative to the highest contributor.[12]

This measure of research reputation for a 23-year panel can be constructed only for UK universities. Thus, an econometric analysis making use of the ranking excludes mobility from companies (28 researchers), and those that are internationally mobile (8 researchers), leaving a sample of 108 researchers mobile within the UK.[13]

---

11. *Thomson Evidence* cleans UK address information found in WoS (taking account of university mergers) and completes missing records.
12. See Fernández-Zubieta, Geuna, & Lawson (2015) for technical details on the ranking indicator.
13. We had to exclude a further 19 researchers due to incomplete information on year of promotion.

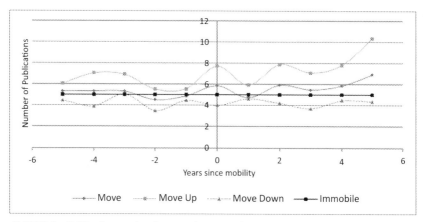

FIGURE 3   Publication numbers in years since move for academics working at UK universities.

Researchers in this reduced sample worked at 52 different UK institutions between 1982 and 2005, and 48 were involved in 58 moves between UK universities. According to the percentile ranking, among the 52 UK universities in the sample, 47 are in the top 50% and 17 are in the top 10% in the engineering and science disciplines.

We define upward mobility as a move to a department ranked at least five percentile points higher than the previous department, in the year preceding the move (before the focal academic joined the new department), and downward mobility as a move to a department ranked at least five percentile points lower than the previous department. In our sample, between 1982 and 2005, 21 academics were involved in 22 moves to more prestigious institutions, and 19 researchers were involved in 19 moves to less prestigious institutions.[14]

Figure 3 shows the mean number of publications for the five years prior to and following the move. We plot the graph for: the immobile sample, for all moves between UK universities, for upward mobility, and for downward mobility. We assume a one-year lag between the research and its publication. Thus, articles published in the year of the move (year zero) refer to research undertaken in the previous institutions. The disruption caused by the mobility event results in a decline in the publication pipeline, followed by decreased publication numbers in year 1 after the move. Figure 3 confirms the one-year lag between a move and publication. This may be a reflection of the mobility and adjustment costs, which likely result in decreased research efficiency in year t. However, from year 2 onwards, the number of publications increases. In the case of downward mobility, publication rates do not improve. On average, a mobile researcher making a downward move performs worse than a nonmobile researcher.

---

14. We observed 15 lateral moves, i.e., moves between universities of equal or similar ranking. These are not analyzed separately here.

An upward mobile researcher even in the years prior to the move produces a higher number of publications than a downward mobile or nonmobile researcher. Hence, academics moving to higher-quality institutions are already performing above the average before the move, while academics moving to less prestigious universities are showing below-average performance. The difference between the two groups increases further in the years following the move. The graph in Figure 3 is consistent with the results in Allison & Long (1990) regarding the positive effects of department quality on productivity, but in contrast to their results, our results show that the upward mobile group starts out with higher productivity than the downward mobile group, which supports our job-match hypothesis.

3.3 Econometric Specification

We use count data models to estimate the effect of mobility on publications, since numbers of publications and citations are positive count values. The data are characterized by overdispersion, which we account for by using pooled negative binomial models that take the form:

$$E\left(sp'_{it} | M_{it}, X_{it}, c_i\right) = \exp\left\{\beta_1 M_{it} + \beta_2 X_{it} + c_i + \tau_t + \upsilon_{it}\right\} \qquad (2)$$

where sp'_{it} is the count variable representing scientific productivity as either number of publications (Pub_{it}) or number of citations to these publications in the first five years following publication ($Cit5YR_{it}$) of researcher i in year t. M_{it} is the mobility measure, X_{it} is a set of explanatory variables including the researcher's personal and academic characteristics (pf, pt), and institution and field effects (h); c_i is an individual time-invariant unobserved effect that includes ability and attitude, τ_t is the time-fixed effect, and υ_{it} other time-variant unobserved effects.

To measure the performance difference between the pre- and the postmobility periods, we assume a lasting career effect of mobility on publication outcomes and record mobility as a one-time shift by defining $PostMob_{it} = 1$ for all the years following the first move (or the first upward/downward move). Since the effect of mobility may vary, and different short- and medium- to long-term effects can be envisaged, we introduce an indicator variable (Mob_{it}), which takes the value 1 in the year of the move, and include its lags in the regression. To investigate the effect of short-term postmobility research performance, we consider lags of three years after job transition.

The advantage of estimating pooled models is that they relax the strict exogeneity assumption of the fixed-effects model. However, pooled models do not control for unobserved individual heterogeneity (c_i). In our case, these unobserved effects might be the individual researcher's specific skills, which are positively correlated with the right-hand-side variables such as mobility, leading to a potential endogeneity problem. In the presence of unobserved individual heterogeneity (c_i), the estimated coefficient of the mobility variables will be upward biased. This problem can be addressed if presample information on the dependent variable is available. Specifically, Blundell, Griffith, & Van Reenen (1995) and Blundell, Griffith, & Windmeijer (2002) suggest a solution that controls for individual heterogeneity (c_i) by specifying the academic's average productivity before entering the sample, i.e., by using presample information on publications and citations. The presample mean of the dependent variable is a consistent estimator of the unobserved individual effect (Blundell et al. 1995, 2002) if it mostly corresponds to the academic's intrinsic ability and motivation, both factors that are not directly observable but that may affect scientific productivity. Blundell et al. (2002) use Monte Carlo simulations to show that the estimator remains consistent in the presence of unobserved heterogeneity and predetermined regressors—as is the case in our estimation. Blundell and colleagues show also that the efficiency of the estimator increases with longer presample observation periods. We measure the average number of publications (or citations) published since the start of the PhD and before the academic enters the sample (before appointment to first position or before 1982), resulting in presample observation periods of at least 3 and up to 21 years with a mean of 4.6 years (median of 4 years).

Theory suggests further that research activity is subject to dynamic feedback (Dasgupta & David, 1994), i.e., heterogeneous dynamic effects, because each researcher's performance is driven by cumulative unobserved factors (v_{it}), such as learning, family, and health, which are not controlled for through fixed effects. Blundell et al. (1995, 2002) argue that it is important to consider continuous sample-period dynamics when modeling research outcomes. This knowledge stock changes over time, and while it increases with experience as a by-product of research, it decreases at a rate of δ as the quality of this knowledge decreases over time. Thus, to proxy for dynamic feedback within the sample period, we calculate the depreciated stock of publications (or citations) produced during the observation period. We assume that knowledge depreciates at a constant rate of 10%,[15] hence the sample period feedback measure is defined as:

$$sp'\,stock_{it} = sp'_{it-1} + (1 - \delta)\,sp'\,stock_{it-1} \qquad (3)$$

The presample value and the stock variable are included in our baseline estimations resulting in a linear feedback model. This dual approach helps to address the problem of endogeneity that arises from correlated individual effects and feedback from the dependent variable.

3.4 Variables

Our primary objective is to measure the effect of job mobility on research productivity. The main dependent variables in our specifications are number of publications in year t (PUB_{it}) and number of citations received by the researcher's published work in the five years after publication ($CIT5YR_{it}$).

The main explanatory variables in the regression refer to the mobility event. To measure the potential performance difference between pre- and postmobility periods, we introduce two dummies that measure the mobility event: (1) $PostMob_{it}$,

---

15. Depreciation rates of 15% and 30% return similar results.

which switches from zero to one in the year of first mobility, clearly indicating the pre- and postmobility periods and (2) Mob_{it}, which takes the value 1 only in the year of the move, indicating a one-time shock. Since our main focus is on mobility between UK universities, we run additional models for moves between UK universities ($PostUNIMob_{it}$, $UNIMob_{it}$) that exclude all researchers with international mobility experience.

We argued above that mobility is affected by the reputation of the sending and receiving institutions. Therefore, we use additional measures for mobility that consider the nature of transition: (1) *Upward Mobility* ($PostUP_{it}$, UP_{it}) defining a move to a higher-ranked university and (2) *Downward mobility* ($PostDOWN_{it}$, $DOWN_{it}$) defining a move to a less prestigious university.

To address the issue of industry experience with regard to mobility as discussed above, we run an additional regression that considers mobility from industry ($PostIndmob_{it}$ $Indmob_{it}$) and measures a transition from industry back to academia.

As controls we include the academic's age (AGE_{it}) to account for potential life cycle effects (Levin & Stephan, 1991) and gender ($FEMALE_i$). We control also for the researcher's academic rank. The UK university system has some minimum requirements for consideration for promotion. Thus, less-senior academics should have a greater incentive to publish, while professors, because of their access to research assistance and funding, may achieve higher publication rates. We consider three levels of seniority in our analysis: lecturer or research fellow before first promotion ($RANK1_{it-1}$), senior position or rank after first promotion ($RANK2_{it-1}$), and professorship ($RANK3_{it-1}$). We also include an indicator for postdoctoral research experience ($POSTDOC_i$). To account for the researcher's commercial orientation (Crespi, D'Este, Fontana, & Geuna, 2011), we include patent stock ($PATENT_{it-1}$), which counts the number of patents filed in previous years. To account for any potential department effects related to access to resources and networks, we include the university's rank in $t-1$ as defined in Section 3.2 ($UniRanking_{it-1}$), in the set of regressions that consider only UK institutions. We can also expect a "London" effect due to proximity to funding bodies and networks that might positively affect research output ($London_{it-1}$). We include subject dummies to control for discipline effects and year dummies to control for time effects. A summary of the main variables used in the regressions is provided in Table 1, while Table 2 presents the descriptive statistics.

TABLE 1 Dimensions and Variables of Mobility

Job-to-Job Mobility (Change of Employer)	Intersector Mobility	Social Mobility (Change in Social Position)
$PostMob_{it}$	$Indmob_{it}$	Upward Mob
Mob_{it}	$PostIndmob_{it-1}$	$PostUP_{it}$
$PostUNIMob_{it}$		Downward Mob
$UNIMob_{it}$		$PostDOWN_{it}$

TABLE 2 Definition and Summary Statistics of Variables Used in the Regression 1982–2005

Variables	Definition	Full Sample of 2367 Observations		HE Sample of 1850 Observations		Reduced Sample of UK HE of 1579 Observations	
		Mean	SD	Mean	SD	Mean	SD
Dependent Variable							
PUB_{it}	Number of publications in t	4.77	6.31	5.19	6.80	5.52	7.24
$CIT5YR_{it}$	Number of citations in t to $t+5$ to publications in t	63.33	100.94	70.78	108.24	75.37	113.55
Mobility Variable							
$PostMOB_{it}$	Moved at least once between HEI before t	0.40	0.49	0.33	0.47		
MOB_{it}	Moved between HEI in t	0.05	0.21	0.04	0.20		
$PostINDMOB_{it}$	Moved at least once from industry to HEI before t	0.13	0.33				
$INDMOB_{it}$	Moved from industry to HEI in t	0.01	0.10				
$PostUNIMOB_{it}$	Moved at least once between UK HEI before t					0.27	0.44
$UNIMOB_{it}$	Moved between UK HEI in t					0.03	0.18
$PostUP_{it}$	Moved upward at least once before t					0.10	0.30
UP_{it}	Moved upward in t					0.01	0.11
$PostDOWN_{it}$	Moved downward at least once before t					0.12	0.33
$DOWN_{it}$	Moved downward in t					0.01	0.11

Variable	Description	Mean	SD	Mean	SD	Mean	SD
Feedback Measures							
Presample average$_i$ (PUB)		0.62	0.65	0.70	0.67	0.76	0.66
Stock$_{it-1}$ (PUB)		25.58	33.07	27.65	35.34	29.36	37.49
Presample average$_i$ (CIT)		8.50	13.22	9.50	14.39	10.22	14.12
Stock$_{it-1}$ (CIT)		323.68	481.42	358.12	517.91	376.34	544.55
Control Variables							
AGE$_{it}$	Age in t	43.27	10.15	43.46	10.34	43.58	10.46
FEMALE$_i$	Dummy = 1 if female	0.11	0.31	0.11	0.31	0.10	0.31
FIRM$_{it-1}$	Working in Industry in $t-1$	0.09	0.29				
RANK1$_{it-1}$	Lecturer or Research Fellow in $t-1$	0.28	0.45	0.33	0.47	0.33	0.47
RANK2$_{it-1}$	Senior position in $t-1$	0.33	0.47	0.33	0.47	0.35	0.48
RANK3$_{it-1}$	Professor in $t-1$	0.30	0.46	0.34	0.47	0.32	0.47
POSTDOC$_i$	Dummy = 1 if postdoc before first position	0.44	0.50	0.50	0.50	0.53	0.50
PATENT$_{it-1}$	Stock of patents up to $t-1$	1.03	3.25	0.95	3.11	1.11	3.34
UNIRANKING$_{it-1}$	Percentile ranks (PR) of UK HEI in $t-1$	0.14	0.34	0.13	0.33	0.31	0.32
LONDON$_{it-1}$	Dummy = 1 if working in London in $t-1$					0.12	0.32
CHEMISTRY$_i$	Chemistry	0.39	0.49	0.47	0.50	0.51	0.50
PHYSICS$_i$	Physics	0.34	0.48	0.30	0.46	0.29	0.45
COMPUTER$_i$	Computer Science	0.13	0.33	0.11	0.32	0.09	0.29
MECHANICAL$_i$	Mechanical Engineering	0.14	0.35	0.12	0.33	0.11	0.31

4. RESULTS

We estimate pooled negative binomial regressions. Standard errors are clustered at the individual level and robust to heteroscedasticity and serial correlation. Table 3 shows the results for all (including international) mobility between universities (columns 1–4) and the results for mobility between UK universities (excluding internationally mobile academics; columns 5–8).

To address the problem of endogeneity arising from unobserved effects and reverse causality, we use the linear feedback model (Blundell et al., 2002) by including in our models the presample mean and dynamic feedback measure (stock). Both measures are significant and positive in the publication equation (Table 3, columns 1 and 2), while only the measure for dynamic stock remains significant across the citation count equations (columns 3 and 4). Implementation of a "quasi-fixed" effect measured by the preperiod mean of the dependent variables and their moving stock, which accounts for dynamic effects, allows us to proxy for researcher's ability and avoids confusing ex ante conditions with ex post events. Thus, the feedback model reflects the stock of knowledge that is available ex ante, and the effect of mobility can be expected to be net of these ex ante effects.

4.1 Job-to-Job Mobility

In Table 3 columns 1–4, which show the results for all (including international) mobility between higher education institutions, the number of observations is 1850 in column 1, reducing to 1673 in column 2 due to longer lags that require a minimum of four observation years, i.e., consider only academics whose careers began before 2002.

Column 1 shows publication performance changes after the mobility event. The mobility variable is positive but insignificant, indicating that academics do not perform significantly better after mobility.[16] Column 2, which presents the yearly effects of the mobility shock, shows some evidence of a short-term albeit insignificant negative effect. The results are similar for citations-weighted output (columns 3 and 4).

We can conclude that the results for the general mobility measures provide weak support for our expectation of an initial negative effect on research performance. We observe negative signs in the first few years following mobility,

---

16. As robustness checks we also analyzed the difference in research performance between mobile and nonmobile researchers to investigate whether mobile researchers have a performance premium compared to nonmobile researchers, along the whole of their careers. The mobility dummy is positive but insignificant indicating that mobile academics do not perform better relative to the group of nonmobile researchers. If we exclude postmobility observations of mobile academics, an estimator that corresponds to a premobility indicator and shows whether researchers were more productive before the move, we still find a positive but insignificant effect.

TABLE 3 Effect of Mobility between Higher Education Institutions (HEI) on Publication Performance

	Mobility between HEI				Mobility between UK-HEI			
	(1)	(2)	(3)	(4)	(5)	(6)	(7)	(8)
Variables	PUB	PUB	CIT5YR	CIT5YR	PUB	PUB	CIT5YR	CIT5YR
Presample average (PUB/CIT)	0.115**	0.120**	0.005*	0.002	0.109*	0.117*	0.004	0.002
	(0.054)	(0.056)	(0.003)	(0.003)	(0.061)	(0.063)	(0.003)	(0.003)
Stock (PUB/CIT)	0.013***	0.013***	0.001***	0.001***	0.013***	0.013***	0.001***	0.001***
	(0.002)	(0.002)	(0.000)	(0.000)	(0.002)	(0.002)	(0.000)	(0.000)
$PostMob_{it}/PostUnimob_{it}$	0.088	0.073	0.105	0.104	0.114	0.130	0.126	0.133
	(0.069)	(0.069)	(0.096)	(0.092)	(0.086)	(0.087)	(0.111)	(0.109)
L. Mob_{it}/L.$UniMob_{it}$		-0.159		-0.011		-0.220*		0.012
		(0.097)		(0.154)		(0.115)		(0.196)
L2. Mob_{it}/L2.$UniMob_{it}$		0.009		0.050		-0.075		-0.012
		(0.089)		(0.124)		(0.093)		(0.138)
L3. Mob_{it}/L3.$UniMob_{it}$		-0.094		-0.185		-0.146		-0.155
		(0.107)		(0.141)		(0.122)		(0.167)
AGE_{it}	0.039	0.016	0.083*	0.069	0.036	0.006	0.089*	0.080
	(0.029)	(0.032)	(0.045)	(0.053)	(0.031)	(0.033)	(0.047)	(0.054)
AGE_{it} 2	-0.000	-0.000	-0.001**	-0.001	-0.000	-0.000	-0.001**	-0.001*
	(0.000)	(0.000)	(0.000)	(0.001)	(0.000)	(0.000)	(0.000)	(0.001)
$FEMALE_i$	0.146	0.004	0.067	-0.122	0.192	0.020	0.150	-0.092
	(0.135)	(0.096)	(0.135)	(0.134)	(0.157)	(0.113)	(0.171)	(0.166)
Reference: $RANK1_{it-1}$								
$RANK2_{it-1}$	0.089	0.078	-0.086	-0.061	0.106	0.094	-0.036	-0.020
	(0.076)	(0.073)	(0.131)	(0.130)	(0.084)	(0.081)	(0.142)	(0.143)
$RANK3_{it-1}$	0.070	0.062	-0.101	-0.083	0.144	0.136	0.002	-0.009
	(0.107)	(0.106)	(0.163)	(0.163)	(0.130)	(0.125)	(0.184)	(0.187)
$POSTDOC_i$	-0.133	-0.071	-0.017	0.059	-0.186*	-0.108	-0.017	0.092
	(0.090)	(0.082)	(0.110)	(0.109)	(0.103)	(0.092)	(0.125)	(0.124)
$PATENT_{it-1}$	-0.003	-0.001	-0.002	-0.002	-0.003	-0.000	-0.004	-0.004
	(0.007)	(0.007)	(0.010)	(0.009)	(0.008)	(0.007)	(0.013)	(0.011)

Continued

TABLE 3 Effect of Mobility between Higher Education Institutions (HEI) on Publication Performance

Variables	Mobility between HEI				Mobility between UK-HEI			
	(1) PUB	(2) PUB	(3) CIT5YR	(4) CIT5YR	(5) PUB	(6) PUB	(7) CIT5YR	(8) CIT5YR
$UniRanking_{t-1}$					0.053	0.079	0.311**	0.287*
					(0.107)	(0.113)	(0.144)	(0.158)
$LONDON_{t-1}$	−0.112	−0.062	−0.221	−0.211	−0.074	−0.057	−0.193	−0.225
	(0.117)	(0.116)	(0.164)	(0.160)	(0.141)	(0.133)	(0.199)	(0.189)
Reference: $CHEMISTRY_i$								
$PHYSICS_i$	−0.075	−0.083	−0.127	−0.140	−0.063	−0.074	−0.157	−0.173
	(0.082)	(0.077)	(0.119)	(0.123)	(0.088)	(0.084)	(0.133)	(0.139)
$COMPUTER_i$	−0.953***	−0.839***	−1.742***	−1.732***	−1.133***	−0.961***	−1.860***	−1.797***
	(0.154)	(0.138)	(0.233)	(0.235)	(0.197)	(0.179)	(0.292)	(0.298)
$MECHANICAL_i$	−0.601***	−0.556***	−1.240***	−1.247***	−0.640***	−0.582***	−1.320***	−1.331***
	(0.172)	(0.161)	(0.221)	(0.210)	(0.215)	(0.202)	(0.255)	(0.235)
Constant	0.642	1.173	2.258**	2.556**	0.798	1.453*	2.086**	2.235*
	(0.670)	(0.750)	(0.999)	(1.208)	(0.711)	(0.768)	(1.053)	(1.239)
lnalpha	−1.208***	−1.366***	0.392***	0.305***	−1.174***	−1.337***	0.362***	0.273***
Log likelihood	−4436.187	−4062.195	−8847.143	−8113.580	−3855.741	−3523.254	−7651.487	−6999.140
Observations	1850	1673	1850	1673	1579	1424	1579	1424
Clusters	124	122	124	122	108	106	108	106

Robust clustered standard errors in parentheses; Year fixed effects in all models; ***p < 0.01, **p < 0.05, *p < 0.1.

but these effects remain insignificant. We also find no support for the positive impact of mobility on scientific performance.

To introduce our ranking measure, *PR*, which takes account of the university department quality, we consider only mobility between UK universities (Table 3, columns 5–8). We include researchers who were born abroad but have moved only within the UK, but exclude all researchers that moved internationally since it is not possible to produce a 23-year field-specific ranking that includes non-UK organizations. The number of observations reduces to 1579 in column 5 and 1424 in column 6.

Column 5 shows how publication performance changes after the mobility event. The mobility variable is positive, indicating that mobile academics perform better than nonmobile academics after mobility but that the effect is insignificant. In column 6, which presents the effects of the mobility shock, the postmobility variable remains insignificant. As in column 2, there are indications of a weakly significant negative short-term effect of mobility. The results are similar but not significant for the citation-weighted output (columns 7 and 8). Overall, these results show that mobile academics do not outperform nonmobile academics and provide weak support for our hypothesis of an initial negative effect following mobility.

4.2 Social Mobility

In Table 4, the mobility effect is conditioned by the nature of the job transition. Column 1 measures the effect of upward mobility on publication numbers. The effect is positive and significant at an 85% confidence. A detailed look at the short-term effects (column 2) shows that scientific output decreases in the short term, but that in the medium term we can expect a nonnegative effect indicated by the strong positive coefficient of *PostUp*.

The estimations for citations confirm the short-term negative effect of upward mobility and the expectation of a nonnegative effect in later years, but the coefficients are insignificant. The university ranking control variable is positive in column 3, which considers citation outputs for all researchers. This indicates that although not all researchers that are upward mobile produce better-quality research (as indicated by the insignificant coefficient of $PostUP_{it}$), researchers in more prestigious departments do produce more-visible research. Therefore, upward mobile researchers will benefit from this additional prestige effect, potentially outperforming their peers in their previous department (since belonging to a higher-ranked department is associated with a higher number of citations).

Table 4 columns 5–8 report the results for downward mobility (*DOWN*). They show that downward mobile researchers have lower publication productivity than their nonmobile peers or colleagues who moved to a higher-ranked institution. This effect persists after isolating the short-term effect in column 6. The negative signs are confirmed for the quality-adjusted

TABLE 4 Effect of Upward and Downward Mobility between UK Higher Education Institutions (HEI) on Publication Performance

	(1)	(2)	(3)	(4)	(5)	(6)	(7)	(8)
	UP	UP	UP	UP	DOWN	DOWN	DOWN	DOWN
Variables	PUB	PUB	CIT5YR	CIT5YR	PUB	PUB	CIT5YR	CIT5YR
Presample average (PUB/CIT)	0.130** (0.062)	0.135** (0.064)	0.004* (0.003)	0.002 (0.003)	0.128** (0.057)	0.141** (0.060)	0.005* (0.003)	0.003 (0.003)
Stock (PUB/CIT)	0.013*** (0.002)	0.012*** (0.002)	0.001*** (0.000)	0.001*** (0.000)	0.013*** (0.002)	0.012*** (0.002)	0.001*** (0.000)	0.001*** (0.000)
$PostUP_{it}/PostDOWN_{it}$	0.213 (0.135)	0.278** (0.127)	0.011 (0.172)	0.070 (0.161)	-0.173* (0.096)	-0.240** (0.097)	-0.061 (0.144)	-0.215 (0.149)
L. UP_{it}/L. $DOWN_{it}$		-0.384** (0.174)		-0.067 (0.314)		0.270 (0.189)		0.711** (0.332)
L2. UP_{it}/L2. $DOWN_{it}$		-0.246 (0.184)		-0.272 (0.225)		0.116 (0.146)		0.166 (0.235)
L3. UP_{it}/L3. $DOWN_{it}$		-0.442** (0.190)		-0.312 (0.261)		-0.057 (0.160)		0.214 (0.272)
AGE_{it}	0.036 (0.031)	0.010 (0.031)	0.088* (0.047)	0.076 (0.053)	0.037 (0.032)	0.013 (0.034)	0.088* (0.047)	0.088* (0.052)
AGE_{it} 2	-0.001 (0.000)	-0.000 (0.000)	-0.001** (0.000)	-0.001* (0.001)	-0.001 (0.000)	-0.000 (0.000)	-0.001** (0.000)	-0.001** (0.001)
$FEMALE_i$	0.218 (0.155)	0.044 (0.113)	0.151 (0.168)	-0.084 (0.164)	0.187 (0.154)	0.010 (0.113)	0.148 (0.166)	-0.091 (0.164)
Reference: $RANK1_{it-1}$								
$RANK2_{it-1}$	0.121 (0.082)	0.094 (0.079)	-0.001 (0.136)	0.008 (0.141)	0.155* (0.086)	0.127 (0.084)	0.007 (0.141)	0.019 (0.145)
$RANK3_{it-1}$	0.186 (0.128)	0.157 (0.123)	0.033 (0.182)	0.019 (0.185)	0.210 (0.134)	0.171 (0.128)	0.042 (0.187)	0.022 (0.192)

	(1)	(2)	(3)	(4)	(5)	(6)	(7)	(8)
$POSTDOC_i$	-0.190*	-0.111	-0.009	0.100	-0.180*	-0.099	-0.010	0.103
	(0.103)	(0.091)	(0.127)	(0.126)	(0.103)	(0.090)	(0.128)	(0.127)
$PATENT_{it-1}$	-0.001	0.001	-0.004	-0.004	-0.002	0.002	-0.003	-0.002
	(0.009)	(0.008)	(0.013)	(0.012)	(0.010)	(0.009)	(0.014)	(0.012)
$UniRanking_{it-1}$	0.016	0.047	0.296**	0.275*	0.026	0.046	0.288**	0.270*
	(0.097)	(0.104)	(0.144)	(0.159)	(0.109)	(0.115)	(0.147)	(0.163)
$LONDON_{it-1}$	-0.106	-0.086	-0.166	-0.196	-0.035	-0.031	-0.161	-0.231
	(0.138)	(0.130)	(0.197)	(0.186)	(0.141)	(0.133)	(0.193)	(0.184)
Reference: $CHEMISTRY_i$								
$PHYSICS_i$	-0.055	-0.063	-0.163	-0.178	-0.087	-0.100	-0.166	-0.193
	(0.086)	(0.081)	(0.132)	(0.138)	(0.089)	(0.086)	(0.131)	(0.138)
$COMPUTER_i$	-1.123***	-0.952***	-1.893***	-1.827***	-1.162***	-1.009***	-1.903***	-1.877***
	(0.196)	(0.178)	(0.286)	(0.291)	(0.189)	(0.172)	(0.285)	(0.296)
$MECHANICAL_i$	-0.632***	-0.580***	-1.297***	-1.316***	-0.651***	-0.604***	-1.295***	-1.325***
	(0.215)	(0.198)	(0.258)	(0.258)	(0.222)	(0.205)	(0.259)	(0.234)
Constant	0.791	1.375*	2.125**	2.326*	0.791	1.301*	2.129**	2.046*
	(0.707)	(0.734)	(1.053)	(1.217)	(0.734)	(0.787)	(1.056)	(1.200)
lnalpha	-1.181***	-1.355***	0.364***	0.274***	-1.178***	-1.342***	0.363***	0.271***
Log likelihood	-3853.608	-3518.873	-7652.747	-6999.892	-3854.932	-3520.293	-7652.574	-6997.226
Observations	1579	1424	1579	1424	1579	1424	1579	1424
Clusters	108	106	108	106	108	106	108	106

Robust clustered standard errors in parentheses; Year fixed effects in all models; ***p < 0.01, **p < 0.05, *p < 0.1.
Note: The results hold if we include upward and downward mobility in the same regression model. Results are also robust if we exclude other mobile researchers and compare upward (downward) mobility only to immobile peers.

publication measure (columns 7 and 8).[17] Interestingly, in contrast to the case of upward mobility, for downward mobile researchers we find a positive short-term effect of mobility in both the publications and the citations equations. The effect is strongly significant for citation-weighted output, suggesting that academics benefit from a delayed positive effect of their publication pipeline, which diminishes quickly. Thus, the results for downward mobility are generally associated with reduced productivity, possibly due to reduced resources. For the majority (all but four) of researchers who moved to a lower-ranked university, the job change involved a promotion and, thus, potentially more resources. However, the negative effect indicates that lower-ranked institutions do not offer better packages that might compensate for loss of institutional prestige and departmental colleagues.

For the department quality measure (*UniRanking*), we find an additional positive effect for citations. This indicates that researchers moving to a lower-quality institution but joining a department of recognized high quality may perform better than their counterparts who move to a low-quality department.

To summarize, we find no evidence for an overall positive effect of mobility, but we find that the mobility effect is conditioned by the nature of the job transition. The econometric analysis provides some evidence supporting a positive effect of upward mobility and some evidence of a negative effect of downward mobility. We also found evidence that academic job mobility is most often associated with a short-term decrease in research performance especially in the case of upward mobile researchers.

4.3 Intersector Mobility

Table 5 reports the results for mobility from industry to academia. The regressions include all researchers including those that moved between universities. Columns 1 and 2 include all observations, and columns 3 and 4 include only those observations years when the researcher is working in academia. The number of observations is 2367 in column 1 and 2151 in column 3.

We find no significant effect of mobility from industry (*PostIndMob*) on research productivity. Researchers that join academia from industry (*IndMob*) publish significantly less than their peers during the first two years after the move (column 2). This initial negative effect turns positive in year 3, although the effect is insignificant. Thus, while industry researchers may suffer some adaptation costs for a readjustment period related to joining academia, they benefit from increased human capital acquired during their time in industry, and in the medium term publish as much as researchers that never move out of

---

17. For both upward and downward mobility, we consider a different quality weighted variable based on the total number of citations received before April 2013 (date of data download) by each year's papers. Thus, we allow for longer (at least 8 years and up to 31 years) time periods of citation accumulation. Results are confirmed with stronger significance for the positive impact of upward mobility.

TABLE 5 Effect of Industry to Higher Education Institutions Mobility on Publication Performance

Variables	(1) NBREG PUB	(2) NBREG PUB	(3) NBREG PUB	(4) NBREG PUB	(5) NBREG CIT5YR	(6) NBREG CIT5YR	(7) NBREG CIT5YR	(8) NBREG CIT5YR
Presample average (PUB/CIT)	0.125***	0.133**	0.123**	0.129**	0.007**	0.004	0.005**	0.003
	(0.047)	(0.052)	(0.049)	(0.053)	(0.003)	(0.004)	(0.003)	(0.003)
Stock (PUB/CIT)	0.014***	0.014***	0.014***	0.013***	0.001***	0.001***	0.001***	0.001***
	(0.002)	(0.002)	(0.002)	(0.002)	(0.000)	(0.000)	(0.000)	(0.000)
$PostIndMob_{it}$	−0.058	−0.021	−0.050	−0.000	−0.015	0.047	0.027	0.109
	(0.099)	(0.104)	(0.104)	(0.109)	(0.149)	(0.157)	(0.152)	(0.163)
L. $IndMob_{it}$		−0.593***		−0.650***		−0.518		−0.597
		(0.221)		(0.222)		(0.381)		(0.394)
L2. $IndMob_{it}$		−0.266		−0.311*		−0.071		−0.160
		(0.164)		(0.163)		(0.265)		(0.268)
L3. $IndMob_{it}$		0.240		0.203		0.022		−0.070
		(0.182)		(0.174)		(0.301)		(0.272)
AGE_{it}	0.058**	0.039	0.051*	0.027	0.074	0.071	0.089**	0.067
	(0.028)	(0.030)	(0.028)	(0.030)	(0.046)	(0.052)	(0.043)	(0.050)
AGE_{it} 2	−0.001**	−0.000	−0.001**	−0.000	−0.001*	−0.001	−0.001***	−0.001*
	(0.000)	(0.000)	(0.000)	(0.000)	(0.000)	(0.001)	(0.000)	(0.001)
$FEMALE_i$	0.045	−0.086	0.110	−0.020	−0.074	−0.250	−0.009	−0.172
	(0.124)	(0.099)	(0.126)	(0.099)	(0.152)	(0.161)	(0.147)	(0.158)
Reference: $RANK1_{it-1}$	$FIRM_{it-1}$	$FIRM_{it-1}$	$RANK1_{it-1}$	$RANK1_{it-1}$	$FIRM_{it-1}$	$FIRM_{it-1}$	$RANK1_{it-1}$	$RANK1_{it-1}$
$RANK1_{it-1}$	0.339**	0.342**			0.435*	0.469*		
	(0.160)	(0.157)			(0.245)	(0.245)		

Continued

TABLE 5 Effect of Industry to Higher Education Institutions Mobility on Publication Performance—cont'd

Variables	(1) NBREG PUB	(2) NBREG PUB	(3) NBREG PUB	(4) NBREG PUB	(5) NBREG CIT5YR	(6) NBREG CIT5YR	(7) NBREG CIT5YR	(8) NBREG CIT5YR
$RANK2_{it-1}$	0.407***	0.401***	0.092	0.081	0.344	0.387*	−0.095	−0.067
	(0.146)	(0.147)	(0.077)	(0.073)	(0.227)	(0.228)	(0.127)	(0.128)
$RANK3_{it-1}$	0.334**	0.321*	0.045	0.032	0.360	0.396	−0.062	−0.029
	(0.165)	(0.165)	(0.104)	(0.103)	(0.256)	(0.259)	(0.158)	(0.159)
$POSTDOC_i$	−0.112	−0.057	−0.117	−0.065	−0.036	0.042	−0.041	0.030
	(0.079)	(0.072)	(0.081)	(0.074)	(0.105)	(0.107)	(0.106)	(0.107)
$PATENT_{it-1}$	−0.013	−0.010	−0.007	−0.004	−0.020	−0.019	−0.009	−0.007
	(0.011)	(0.010)	(0.008)	(0.007)	(0.019)	(0.019)	(0.011)	(0.010)
$LONDON_{it-1}$	−0.081	−0.041	−0.071	−0.032	−0.180	−0.170	−0.171	−0.162
	(0.103)	(0.103)	(0.103)	(0.103)	(0.129)	(0.127)	(0.130)	(0.127)
Reference: $CHEMISTRY_i$								
$PHYSICS_i$	−0.079	−0.078	−0.081	−0.082	−0.093	−0.090	−0.144	−0.145
	(0.076)	(0.071)	(0.077)	(0.071)	(0.110)	(0.112)	(0.107)	(0.109)
$COMPUTER_i$	−1.016***	−0.911***	−0.956***	−0.855***	−1.846***	−1.830***	−1.813***	−1.782***
	(0.149)	(0.132)	(0.152)	(0.137)	(0.201)	(0.202)	(0.207)	(0.208)
$MECHANICAL_i$	−0.499***	−0.469***	−0.499***	−0.464***	−1.089***	−1.116***	−1.172***	−1.175***
	(0.152)	(0.143)	(0.147)	(0.139)	(0.203)	(0.195)	(0.194)	(0.187)
Constant	−0.191	0.247	0.343	0.869	1.890*	1.944	2.123**	2.617**
	(0.675)	(0.697)	(0.644)	(0.712)	(1.098)	(1.207)	(0.969)	(1.143)
lnalpha	−1.108***	−1.251***	−1.146***	−1.292***	0.524***	0.443***	0.446***	0.368***
log likelihood	−5533.131	−5109.331	−5121.162	−4735.606	−10,931.544	−10,116.790	−10,142.350	−9401.899
Observations	2367	2161	2151	1970	2367	2161	2151	1970
Clusters	150	148	149	147	150	148	149	147

Robust clustered standard errors in parentheses; Year fixed effects in all models; ***$p < 0.01$, **$p < 0.05$, *$p < 0.1$.
Note: Results are robust if we also include mobility between universities to this model.

academia. The results are confirmed in columns 3 and 4, which exclude observations during the years spent in industry. The results are similar for citation
counts (columns 5–8). We find an initial negative effect that may turn positive
in later years; however, the effects remain insignificant. Thus, we find evidence
that researchers who move to academia from industry do not produce lower-
quality publications compared to pure academic scientists.

4.4 Control Variables

The coefficients of the nonmobility control variables vary slightly across the
different mobility measures and lags. We report their results in column 5, which
controls also for university ranking. Age is not significantly correlated with
publications but has an inverted U-shaped effect on the quality-adjusted number of publications. Thus, while the number of publications does not change
significantly over the life cycle, the quality of publications increases in the first
few years of the researcher's career and then declines after around the age of 40.
We do not find a significant gender effect, which is in line with Crespi et al.'s
(2011) findings for the same sample of researchers. Patent stock is negative but
insignificant in all the estimations, confirming Crespi et al. (2011).

We find also that a postdoctoral appointment, or other temporary research
contract after completing the PhD, does not improve future publication numbers
or citation counts. Instead, we observe a negative effect, which is significant for
publication number. This negative effect may be due in part to job insecurity
and a fragmented career path associated with postdoctoral appointments and
temporary contracts (Stephan, 2012). This negative effect seems to persist and
hold for later career stages.

The effect of mobility could be mediated by the academic position, and
promotion may result in other types of benefits that directly affect performance.
According to the rank indicators in the regression, seniority does not affect
publication outcomes significantly (see Table 3). Senior academic staff are not
expected to publish more than researchers in the category *RANK1*.

University ranking (*PR*) has no significant effect on publication numbers.
However, we find a strong positive sign for the quality-adjusted measure. Thus,
researchers in the most prestigious institutions may not produce more but may
produce better quality publications and achieve more visibility than their peers
in lower-ranked institutions.

Finally, we find strong differences across disciplines; researchers in
chemistry and physics publish significantly more, and are more frequently cited
than colleagues in other fields, with computer science researchers producing the
smallest number of publications and receiving the lowest number of citations.

5. CONCLUSIONS

We approach the study of mobility by assuming that in order to properly analyze the effect of mobility in the current research system it is necessary to

consider different types of mobility events, and short- and medium- to long-term return opportunities, and not just to consider mobility as a one-time, one-way process.

The theoretical framework based on the job-matching approach for academics emphasizes research and reputation aspects and allowed us to formulate different expectations regarding the short- and medium-term effects of the job mobility of permanent academic staff on their productivity across different mobility types—social and intersectoral.

We applied our framework to a sample of 171 UK academic researchers in the period 1957–2005. Based on this sample, which should not be biased toward mobility, we found a high level of job mobility: two-thirds of researchers changed jobs at least once, and one-third were involved in two job moves. Analysis of the difference in performance between mobile and nonmobile researchers showed a positive although insignificant overall effect of mobility, and a negative weakly significant short-term effect. When considering mobility to a better, or a worse, department than the department of origin, we found that mobility to a higher-ranked university has a weakly positive impact on publication output but not citations, while downward mobility tends to decrease the researcher's overall research performance. We found evidence of decreased productivity in the years after a job change, probably or most likely due to adjustment costs for all types of job changes with the exception of downward mobility. Downward mobile researchers may benefit from their preexisting publication pipeline on joining the new department, resulting in a short-term positive effect. However, their performance drops significantly in later years. Thus, hiring researchers from top departments might be a short-term strategy for lower-ranked departments to improve their visibility, with negative medium- to long-term productivity payoffs for mobile researchers. These results partially confirm the findings in Allison & Long (1990), which find a publication increase associated with a move to a higher-ranked department and a performance decrease associated with a downward move.

The analysis of intersector mobility shows that the performance of researchers that moved to academia from industry does not differ significantly from that of purely academic researchers. Researchers coming from industry suffer short-term mobility costs, but they appear to adapt quickly in terms of research performance. However, we need to take into account that the industry experience of most of the researchers in our sample was in large company laboratories that would have supported their research activity. While Dietz & Bozeman (2005) find a positive effect of industry experience on patent counts, in the case of publication counts we found no effect of industry experience. Finally, we found evidence that temporary research positions, in our case either postdoc positions or short-term research fellow contracts, which have increased in frequency in recent years (Stephan, 2012), have a long-term negative effect on research performance, which perhaps should be of concern to policy makers and academia.

These results indicate that policies encouraging the mobility of researchers should be refined to take account of different mobility events and short- and long-term consequences. Mobility per se appears not to have clear positive effects on the scientific productivity of the researchers. On the contrary, it has clear short-term negative effects probably associated with mobility costs. Job mobility to a higher-quality department increases publication performance. This could indicate that policies encouraging mobility might unintentionally exacerbate the dynamics of an unequal individual and institutional distribution of scientific performance that favors the current winners. The negative effects of downward mobility on academic performance suggest the need for additional institutional measures to ensure the high performance of individual researchers who move to lower-quality departments to avoid that mobility decisions resulting in individual and institutional quality mismatches.

ACKNOWLEDGMENTS

We thank Sotaro Shibayama for helpful comments when drafting this chapter. Thanks also to Daniel Lopez Gonzales and Manuel Toselli for their contributions to the creation of the database. Financial support from the European Commission (FP7) Project "An Observatorium for Science in Society based in Social Models—SISOB" Contract no.: FP7 266588 and the Collegio Carlo Alberto Project "Researcher Mobility and Scientific Performance" are gratefully acknowledged. Ana Fernández-Zubieta also acknowledges financial support from the JAE-Doc "Junta para la Ampliación de Estudios" program, which is cofinanced by the Social Structure Funds.

REFERENCES

Allison, P. D., & Long, J. S. (1990). Departmental effects on scientific productivity. *American Sociological Review, 55*(4), 469–478.

Azoulay, P., Zivin, J. S. G., & Sampat, B. N. (2012). The diffusion of scientific knowledge across time and space: evidence from professional transitions for the superstars of medicine. In J. Lerner & S. Stern (Eds.), *The rate and direction of inventive activity revisited* (pp. 107–160). Chicago: University of Chicago Press.

Azoulay, P., Zivin, J. S. G., & Wang, J. (2010). Superstar extinction. *The Quarterly Journal of Economics, 125*(2), 549–589.

Becker, G. S. (1962). Investment in human beings. *Journal of Political Economy, 70*, 9–49.

Becker, G. S. (1964). *Human capital. A theoretical and empirical analysis, special reference to education.* New York: National Bureau of Economic Research.

Blundell, R., Griffith, R., & Van Reenen, J. (1995). Dynamic count data models of technological innovation. *Economic Journal, 105*(429), 333–344.

Blundell, R., Griffith, R., & Windmeijer, F. (2002). Individual effects and dynamics in count data models. *Journal of Econometrics, 108*, 113–131.

Bourdieu, P. (1986). The forms of social capital. In J. G. Richardson (Ed.), *Handbook of theory and research for the sociology of education* (pp. 241–258). New York: Greenwood.

Bozeman, B., & Rogers, J. D. (2002). A churn model of scientific knowledge value: Internet researchers as a knowledge value collective. *Research Policy, 31*, 769–794.

Burt, R. S. (1997). A note on social capital and network content. *Social Networks, 19*, 355–373.

Cole, S. (1979). Age and scientific performance. *American Journal of Sociology, 84*, 958–977.

Coleman, J. C. (1988). Social capital in the creation human capital. *American Journal of Sociology, 94*, 95–120.

Cotgrove, S., & Box, S. (1970). *Science, industry and society*. London: George Allen and Unwin.

Crespi, G., D'Este, P., Fontana, R., & Geuna, A. (2011). The impact of academic patenting on university research and its transfer. *Research Policy, 40*, 55–86.

Dasgupta, P., & David, P. A. (1994). Toward a new economics of science. *Research Policy, 23*(5), 487–521.

Dietz, J. S., & Bozeman, B. (2005). Academic careers, patents, and productivity: industry experience as scientific and technical human capital. *Research Policy, 34*, 349–367.

Ding, W. W., Levin, S. G., Stephan, P. E., & Winkler, A. E. (2009). *The impact of information technology on scientists' productivity, quality and collaboration patterns*. Harvard, MA: National Bureau of Economic Research. NBER Working Paper 15285.

European Commission. (2001). *High-level expert group on improving mobility of researchers*. Luxembourg: Office for Official Publications of the European Communities.

European Commission. (2006). *Mobility of researchers between academia and industry*. Luxembourg: Office for Official Publications of the European Communities.

European Commission. (2012). *Excellence, equality and entrepreneurialism: Building sustainable research careers in the European Research Area*. Luxembourg: Publications Office of the European Union.

Fernández-Zubieta, A., Geuna, A., & Lawson, C. (2015). Productivity pay-offs from academic mobility: Should I stay or should I go?, Industrial and Corporate Change, forthcoming.

Franzoni, C., Scellato, G., & Stephan, P. (2012). Foreign-born scientists: mobility patterns for 16 countries. *Nature Biotechnology, 30*(12), 1250–1253.

Granovetter, M. S. (1985). Economic action and social structure: the problem of embeddedness. *American Journal of Sociology, 91*, 481–510.

Griliches, Z. (1973). Research expenditures and growth accounting. In B. R. Williams (Ed.), *Science and technology in economic growth* (pp. 59–95). London: Macmillan.

Groysberg, B. (2008). How star women build portable skills. *Harvard Business Review, 86*(2), 74–81.

Hagstrom, W. O. (1965). *The scientific community*. New York: Basic Books.

Hoare, A. G. (1994). Transferred skills and university excellence? An exploratory analysis of the geography of mobility of UK academic staff. *Geografiska Annaler. Series B, Human Geography, 76*(3), 143–160.

Jovanovic, B. (1979). Job matching and the theory of turnover. *Journal of Political Economy, 87*(5), 972–990.

Kim, E. H., Morse, A., & Zingales, L. (2009). Are elite universities losing their competitive edge. *Journal of Financial Economics, 93*, 353–381.

Kornhauser, W. (1962). *Scientists in industry: Conflict and accommodation*. Berkeley, CA: University of California Press.

Krohn, R. C. (1961). The institutional location of the scientist and his scientific values. *IRE Transactions on Engineering Management, 8*, 133–138.

Levin, S. G., & Stephan, P. E. (1991). Research productivity over the life cycle: evidence for academic scientists. *American Economic Review, 81*, 114–132.

Marcson, S. (1960). *The scientist in American industry*. Princeton, NJ: Princeton University Press.

Martin-Rovet, D. (2003). *Opportunities for outstanding young scientists in Europe to create an independent research team*. Strasbourg: European Science Foundation.

Mortensen, D. (1986). Job search and labor market analysis. In O. Ashenfelter & R. Layard (Eds.), *Handbook of labour economics* (Vol. 2) (pp. 849–919). Amsterdam: North Holland.

Musselin, C. (2004). Towards a European academic labour market? Some lessons drawn from empirical studies on academic mobility. *Higher Education, 48*, 55–78.

Nelson, R., & Phelps, E. (1966). Investment in humans, technological diffusion and economic growth. *American Economic Review, 61*, 69–75.

Organisation for Economic Cooperation and Development (OECD). (2000). *Mobilising human resources for innovation.* Paris: OECD.

Oyer, P. (2007). Is there an insider advantage in getting tenure? *American Economic Review, 97*(2), 501–505.

Schultz, T. (1961). Investment in human capital. *The American Economic Review, 51*(1), 1–17.

Schultz, T. (1990). *Restoring economic equilibrium: Human capital in the modernizing economy.* Oxford: Backwell.

Shaw, K. (1987). Occupational change, employer change, and the transferability of skills. *Southern Economic Journal, 53*(3), 702–718.

Stephan, P. (2012). *How economics shapes science.* Cambridge, MA: Harvard University Press.

Teichler, U. (1996). Research on academic mobility and international cooperation in higher education: an agenda for the future. In P. Blumenthal, et al. (Ed.), *Academic mobility in a changing world Higher education policy* (Vol. 29) (pp. 338–358). London: Jessica Kingsley Publishers.

Waldinger, F. (2012). Peer effects in science - evidence from the dismissal of scientists in Nazi Germany. *Review of Economic Studies, 79*, 838–861.

Weinberg, B. A. (2007). *Geography and innovation: Evidence from Nobel laureate physicists.* mimeo: Ohio State University.

Chapter 5

Who Leaves and Who Stays? Evidence on Immigrant Selection from the Collapse of Soviet Science

Ina Ganguli
University of Massachusetts, Amherst, MA, USA

Chapter Outline

1. INTRODUCTION

Many countries design immigration policies to attract the "best and the brightest" individuals to cross their borders, with the understanding that highly skilled immigrants positively contribute to innovation, productivity, and economic growth. Evidence suggests that immigrant scientists and engineers are indeed often the best and the brightest as compared to natives (Hunt, 2013; for the US). Moreover, many of the top, "highly cited" scientists in the world are immigrants; they were born in developing countries, but did not remain there to do their research (Hunter, Oswald, & Charlton, 2009; Weinberg, 2010).

While there is growing evidence of how immigrant scientists compare to natives in destination countries in terms of research productivity and other performance measures, we still know very little about how immigrants compare to individuals in their home countries *who do not emigrate*. Who leaves and who stays behind? Is it the best and the brightest among the scientists in the source country who emigrate? Such differences in terms of skills and other observable characteristics between immigrants and those who chose not to emigrate are referred to as immigrant selection.

There has been considerable attention in the economics literature on immigrant selection, and the literature has pointed to the fact that immigrants are not a random subsample of the population in the home country. Understanding how emigrants, and particularly how their skills, differ from those who stay behind helps provide insights into the factors underlying the decision of individuals to emigrate and the extent of "brain drain," which is important for policy makers in the source country. It can also help understand immigrants' trajectories after they arrive in destination countries and how their arrival can impact natives.

While there has been great interest in immigrant selection generally, there has been very little analysis of immigrant selection among scientists. It is typically difficult to examine selection empirically, since one must be able to observe scientists and their characteristics *before* they make the decision to emigrate. Because of the difficulty in obtaining this information, much of the existing research on the mobility and selection of scientists has used samples of several hundred scientists who have emigrated or is comprised of individuals in a few fields of science.

This chapter draws upon the end of the Soviet Union and the subsequent emigration of scientists westward to provide new estimates of immigrant selection and to contribute to a greater understanding of the factors underlying the emigration decision. Before its end in 1991, the USSR had a large scientific community and devoted a considerable amount of funding to science. It was, however, relatively "closed" to contact with researchers outside of the Eastern bloc. Scientists were rarely able to travel and were legally barred from emigrating. When the Soviet Union collapsed, almost suddenly there were opportunities for scientists to meet Western scientists, to travel, and to emigrate. Many scientists chose to move abroad to the United States, Israel, or Europe to continue their careers, and opportunities for collaboration between former Soviet and Western scientists increased greatly.

The collapse of the Soviet science system provides a useful setting to study immigrant selection for several reasons. First, there were a large number of immigrants whose location, research output, and other characteristics can be measured before they emigrated using information culled from publications. Second, since the system was relatively closed to emigration before 1991, it is possible to compare the group of individuals who later emigrated to the full population of scientists in the home country. In most cases, it is not possible to observe a system in which no one is able to emigrate, so that the entire pool of potential emigrants is observable.

In this chapter, I first provide some background about science in the Soviet Union and the changes that accompanied the end of the USSR. I then discuss a conceptual framework for considering emigration decision facing Soviet scientists and how this may affect selection of emigrants. For the empirical analysis, I use a large unique dataset of over 15,000 Russian scientists across many fields of science who were publishing in the top Soviet journals just before the end of the USSR. I match them to their publications and other characteristics using the Thomson Reuters Web of Science (WoS) database, which provides a rich set of variables that allows me to measure immigrant selection.

The results show that on a number of observable characteristics, emigrant scientists look very different from those who stayed at home. The emigrants tended to be men, were younger, and were selected from the upper part of the productivity distribution as measured by papers published during the 10 years before the end of the USSR. Emigrants were much more likely to have a foreign coauthor during Soviet times and to have published in a non-Russian journal. There are also large differences by field, with fewer emigrants coming from the field of chemistry and more from physics. I also found that the most skilled left early in the transition period and were more likely to emigrate to the US compared to European countries. The results are consistent with the predictions from the conceptual framework that positive selection increases with migration costs and the wage premium.

I conclude by discussing how these results relate to the predicted nature of selection based on a model of the emigration decision for scientists, some caveats to interpreting the results based on the Soviet setting, and how the results might generalize to other contexts.

2. BACKGROUND

According to Soviet science scholars, the most notable characteristics of the Soviet system were "its bigness and its high degree of centralization" (Graham & Dezhina, 2008). The Soviet Union was on par with the West in terms of the science and engineering labor force. For example, in 1988, the USSR/Eastern Europe had an estimated 26.6% of the world's scientists and engineers, while North America had 25.4% and Western Europe had 16.7%. In the 1970s, the USSR/Eastern Europe and North America were also even on R&D expenditures with each having about one-third of the world's total (Salomon, Sagasti, & Sachs-Jeantet, 1994).

Soviet science was highly centralized and "departmentalized" (Saltykov, 1997). Every research group was under the control or a ministry of agency that controlled its research agenda and resources. Scientists were distributed among institutes of the Academy of Sciences, universities, as well as in industrial and military facilities. The focus of the analysis in this chapter is scientists publishing in the top scientific journals, and these scientists would primarily have been working in institutes of the Academy of Sciences. Individuals teaching only in universities would not have been publishing, due to the separation of teaching and research in the Soviet system, and researchers from industrial and military facilities would have likely not published their work.

While the USSR had a large scientific community, it was very "closed" to contact with researchers outside of the Eastern bloc. Scientists were rarely able to travel abroad, although there was substantial contact with scientists in other communist countries. In terms of access to journals and existing knowledge, scientists had access to the many Soviet journals and were also able to order reprints from Western journals from Moscow. However, there was usually a lag in receiving reprints and often the reprints were censored. Graham & Dezhina (2008) and Saltykov (1997) each describes some of the other features of Soviet science in further detail, including political restrictions that included secrecy, discrimination against ethnic groups, and suppression of certain scientific fields for ideological reasons.

When the Soviet Union collapsed in 1991, there were dramatic drops in funding for science and the wages of scientists. The average salaries of scientists were 10–20% higher than the average wage during Soviet times, but dropped to 65% of the average wage in 1992, and then grew to 80% by 1996 (Saltykov, 1997). However, based on interviews conducted with scientists in former Soviet republics about this period, many scientists said they did not receive their salaries at all for some periods in 1990s or received only a small share of their salary, although this varied by region.[1] Another significant challenge was the deteriorating research conditions, primarily due to the skyrocketing prices of electricity, heat, and water in 1992. Larger cities, especially Moscow, tended to have better conditions and more resources, but only marginally so, and there was considerable variation.

Despite this bleak picture, the end of the USSR also brought about many freedoms for scientists, including greater mobility and contact with the Western world, as well as alternative career options in the private sector. Many scientists chose to move abroad to the United States, Israel, or Europe to continue their careers. Others remained at home and sought opportunities to continue their research, in spite of the economic instability. Some, meanwhile, left science completely and pursued other career options. By 1993, Russian government estimates of the decrease in researchers in the Academy of Science as a share of 1991 levels were 6.5%, 31% in industrial science and technology, and 35.2% in higher education institutions (Graham & Dezhina, 2008).

It has been difficult to estimate the number of scientists who emigrated, but Graham & Dezhina (2008) cite conservative estimates of 7000 researchers leaving Russia from 1993 to 1996, while they note that less conservative estimates are much higher at 30,000–40,000 researchers emigrating during the same time period. Gokhberg & Nekipelova (2002) use data from the Ministry of Internal Affairs (MVD) and the State Committee on Statistics (Goskomstat) and estimate approximately 20,000 individuals working in the "Science and Scientific Services" sector emigrated during the 1990s, although many of these individuals would not have been research scientists. In 1994, the Minister of Science, Higher Education and Technology Policy, Boris Saltykov, stated that over 4500 scientists had left in 1992 alone (Kneen, 1995) and later wrote in 1997 that between 11,000 and 12,000 scientists and engineers had emigrated

---

1. Interviews conducted with scientists in Estonia, Tajikistan, and Ukraine in 2009, and Azerbaijan and Georgia in 2010.

from Russia in the previous 5–6 years, with an equally large number working abroad on temporary contracts (Saltykov, 1997).

During the 1990s, the Russian government took measures to reform the science sector in response to the changing environment. According to Saltykov (1995), as early as 1992, the Russian government emphasized a policy of "openness to the scientific community and a pragmatic approach to international scientific collaboration" when negotiating with foreign scientific organizations and governments. Graham & Dezhina (2008) describe the many changes in the science sector in the early 1990s, noting that the goal was to "preserve science in a crisis period." Some of the changes during this period included introducing support for selected programs and scientists, which led to competition for resources; the creation of government science foundations; the passage of intellectual property laws; bringing together research and teaching; and laws providing additional pay for earned qualifications and for young scientists. Indeed in some research organizations, the Russian government took active measures to try to retain young researchers, such as by providing stable financing and obtaining new equipment.

Moreover, in the 1990s, there were many foreign grant programs, most aimed at fostering exchanges and international collaboration between Russian and Western collaborators. Perhaps the most well-known and earliest assistance program for scientists after the end of the USSR was the International Science Foundation (ISF), which was initiated by George Soros. The ISF provided $500 individual grants to more than 26,000 Soviet scientists in 1993. As Ganguli (unpublished manuscript-a) shows, these grants had large and long-lasting impacts on helping scientists remain in the science sector.

While funding from the Russian government and Western programs like the ISF continued to support scientists and increased possibilities for foreign exchanges, many challenges made science and international collaboration difficult during the 1990s. Challenges facing scientists included political instability, organizational turnover that made long-term funding agreements difficult to implement, difficulty transferring funds due to the underdeveloped banking system, high taxation and customs duties, lack of effective intellectual property rights, poor infrastructure, lack of a shared language (both linguistic and cultural), and external regulations (OECD, 1994). Thus, emigration was sometimes seen as the only option to continue to do science. Many challenges persist today, such as poor infrastructure and the burden of bureaucracy, and efforts to revitalize science by promoting research and innovation at institutions of higher education are considered a priority in the continuing reform of the science and technology sector (Ganguli, unpublished manuscript-b; Gokhberg, Kuznetsova, & Zaichenko, 2009).

The collapse of the Soviet system and the exodus of scientists to the West undeniably impacted the production of scientific knowledge. Figure 1 shows the total number of publications in the Thomson Reuters WoS database with an address in the former USSR. There is a notable drop in publications after the

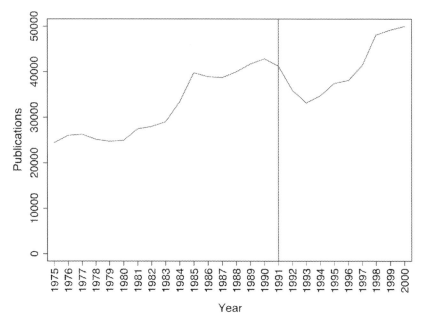

FIGURE 1 Total publications in (former) USSR countries, 1975–2000. *Notes: This figure shows the trend in the total number of publications with an address in the (former) USSR in the Thomson Reuters Web of Science database. The vertical line indicates the end of the USSR in 1991.*

end of the USSR in 1991. However, it is not clear whether the "brain drain" was completely destructive for Russian science. Kneen (1995) describes Saltykov's perspective in the early 1990s: "In September 1992, Saltykov remarked that the spontaneous loss of scientific personnel was not a wholly negative phenomenon. He suggested that those able scientists who had gone abroad might subsequently return...The loss of the untalented, he observed, would not harm science."

3. THE MIGRATION DECISION

To understand the nature of immigrant selection being tested in this chapter, Section I has briefly discussed some factors underlying Soviet scientists' decision to emigrate and how they are related to the type of selection among immigrants we may observe. In a typical economic model of the migration decision, immigrants self-select into the country that gives them the highest expected income (see Borjas, 1999). Income at home and abroad is a function of skill and is net of migration costs (direct or other costs, such as psychic costs of leaving behind family). It does not generally include other factors (e.g., influence of personal networks), apart from their role in increasing/decreasing migration costs. In the Borjas framework, which is derived from Roy's (1951) Model of Self-selection in Occupational Choice, the relative returns to skills at home versus abroad are the salient factor.

In this framework, we can describe the nature of selection as positive, negative, or intermediate based on what part of the home country wage distribution immigrants would fall in compared to non-emigrants *had they not emigrated*. If the returns to skill are higher in the destination country, the model predicts positive selection. This means that *had they not emigrated*, emigrants would have higher wages than non-emigrants. The high-skill workers want to leave a home country with a compressed wage distribution, since it essentially places a "tax" on their earnings, while it insures the earnings of lower-skill workers. On the other hand, the model predicts negative selection of immigrants when the returns to skill are lower in the destination country, which means emigrants would have lower wages than non-emigrants *had they not emigrated*.

It is important to note that in this framework, the comparisons are usually between the low skilled and high skilled, while in this case all the individuals are essentially highly skilled. Hunter et al. (2009) show that also for the most highly skilled, in their case elite scientists, if the cost of mobility and the wage premium are both positive, we would expect the return from migrating to be the largest for those with the highest ability, as the return from moving is greatest for them.

Based on this framework, we would expect former Soviet scientists who emigrated in the 1990s to be positively selected. Given that the returns to skill were likely higher in Western countries than in the post-Soviet states in the 1990s, then it would be the most highly skilled who would have chosen to emigrate. Moreover, we would expect the emigrants going to the US to be more positively selected than those going to Europe, where wages are more compressed.

In this setting, there is likely variation in levels of skill among scientists given the large size of the Soviet scientific sector and the competition among Russian scientists to get academic jobs abroad during this time, which would likely mean the returns to skill would be even higher abroad for the most highly skilled. As described in Ganguli (2015), it was difficult for Russian émigré scientists to find jobs abroad during the 1990s. A *Science* article from this time mentions the dire situation: "Many have been trying to support their families with menial jobs—taxi driving, dog walking, doorkeeping…" (Holden, 1990). Those who could find jobs in science sometimes initially worked as lab technicians. Thus, even though they had high levels of education and publication records, it is only those with the highest levels of skills, which can be proxied for by publications, who we would expect to benefit from the higher wages abroad.

It is useful to discuss some further salient factors facing Soviet scientists in the 1990s and how they relate to existing evidence on immigrant selection. First, one assumption of the Borjas-type model is that skills gained in home countries are also productive in the destination countries. The lack of transferability of education and the types of skills gained under the communist-style education systems could affect this assumption, which Drinkwater, Eade, & Garapich (2009) suggest may have affected immigrant outcomes in Western Europe.

As Docquier & Rapoport (2012) discuss, as the earnings of workers abroad depends on the transferability of human capital, it is not surprising that workers trained primarily in the home country have lower earnings in the destination country. They note that this makes it more profitable to migrate as a student. Even those who already finished their advanced degrees could still gain additional training or gain additional skills, but this would be more likely for younger scientists. For the Soviet case, this would imply that the scientists who emigrated may have been younger, as they would still have an opportunity to retrain or gain additional experience after they emigrated.

Another important factor is the role of networks. Beine, Docquier, & Özden (2011) show that larger diaspora networks are associated with greater migration and lower education levels of migrants on average in the destination country. Given the lack of information and minimal contact with the Western world during Soviet times, we would expect scientists with connections to diaspora abroad or other global networks may have been more likely to emigrate. A larger network would thus reduce migration costs by lowering the information barriers or even by lowering migration costs directly (e.g., a travel grant).

Moreover, in the case of scientists we would expect larger networks would be associated with a higher skill level among scientists who emigrated. First, for scientists, being near other scientists is important for productivity, as existing knowledge and ideas are key inputs into the knowledge production function, so access to larger networks through which knowledge is diffused should be associated with greater skill. As Zucker & Darby (2006) show empirically for the US, star scientists—or those scientists with the highest skills and ability—tend to move from places with few peers in their discipline to places with many, which leads to a concentration of star scientists over time. They also find that foreign scientists tend to return to their home country when there is a significant level of strength in their field, again suggesting that if networks are present, we may expect higher skills among scientists who move.

Finally, one characteristic of the Soviet science system was a relatively large share of female scientists compared to other countries. From the immigration literature, it is not clear whether female Soviet scientists would have been more or less likely to emigrate than male. Some studies have suggested that skilled women have higher propensities to emigrate than skilled men, one reason being that by migrating, women can avoid gender discrimination in a labor market. However, using data on immigrants in the OECD, Docquier, Marfouk, Salomone, & Sekkat (2012)'s empirical evidence shows it is not likely the case that skilled women migrate more. Evidence from the general gender gap literature has also shown that women tend to be more risk averse than men (see discussion in Bertrand, 2011). Since emigrating could be considered a risky choice given the associated uncertainty with moving to a new environment, perhaps women would be less likely to make this decision. Anecdotal evidence based on interviews conducted with Soviet scientists suggests that family responsibilities may have led to fewer women emigrating since it was easier for men to initially emigrate by themselves and bring their families later, but women may have not seen this as an option. It is also important to note that other factors may be correlated with gender, such as productivity and scientific field, are also likely associated with a higher or lower likelihood of migration.

In summary, this discussion of a conceptual framework for considering the type of immigrant selection among scientists in the post-Soviet context suggests that immigrants should have been the most highly skilled (or most productive during the Soviet period), younger, have had larger global networks, and tended to be men.

4. DATA

For the analysis, I used a panel dataset of Soviet scientists and their publications before and after the end of the Soviet Union. I first identified a sample of scientists who were "doing science" in Russia around the time of the Soviet collapse. I used publication data from the Thomson Reuters WoS[2] database to create a sample of Russian scientists who were actively doing scientific research before and after the end of the Soviet Union in 1991.

To do this, I identified the top Soviet and Russian language journals in the WoS and extracted names of all authors publishing in these journals between 1986 and 1994. The WoS database includes over 100 top journals of the former USSR and Russian language journals. It included many of the top Soviet journals by the 1970s (and subsequently Russian journals). Ganguli (unpublished manuscript-a) provides a full description of the preparation of the publication data, including information on transliteration and name matching and assigning scientific fields.

Next, I identified the subset of authors who had at least two articles between 1980 and 1990 with an address that included a city in the former Russian Republic of the USSR. I dropped any individuals with a foreign address before 1990 and individuals with an address in a different Soviet republic. I further restricted to authors who "stayed in science" and I could identify their location, meaning they published at least one article after the end of the USSR through 2005. I then matched each scientist to his or her publications and affiliations, which resulted in a scientist-year-level dataset.

Using the affiliation information from the address fields, I coded the location of each scientist in the sample by year. This allowed me to assign a country

---

2. Web of Science® prepared by THOMSON REUTERS®, Inc. (Thomson®), Philadelphia, Pennsylvania, USA: © Copyright THOMSON REUTERS® 2010. All rights reserved.

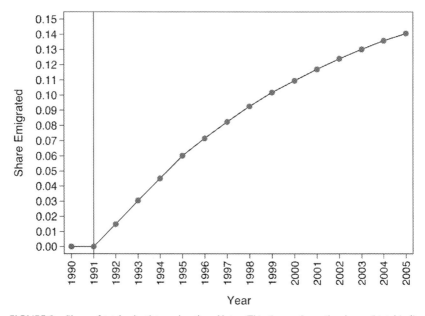

FIGURE 2   Share of total scientists emigrating. *Notes: This figure shows the share of total individuals with a foreign affiliation. After an individual has a foreign affiliation, he is thereafter considered an emigrant. The vertical line indicates the end of the USSR in 1991.*

(and a city) to each scientist for each year and to identify which individuals emigrated from Russia.[3] Almost half the emigrants in the sample went to the United States, and then the top destinations are Germany and other countries in Western Europe. Figure 2 shows the share of scientists in the sample emigrating (with a non-Russian address) after 1991. The share emigrating increases over time, although the slope begins to decline around 1997. By 2005, 14% of the sample were emigrants.

Note that I do not account for return migrants—once I observed that an individual was outside of Russia, they are thereafter coded as an emigrant.[4]

---

3. For years in which I do not observe a scientist's affiliation information, I impute the country based on previous year. If a scientist has multiple affiliations, he/she is coded as an emigrant as long as one affiliation is foreign. Since address information is not available for all publications in the WoS, there may be cases where I cannot assign a location to a scientist at all, and in these cases the scientist is dropped from the sample. This is problematic if the missing addresses are restricted to the post-Soviet period, so that some migrants are misclassified as non-migrants since I cannot observe their foreign addresses from the publication affiliation fields. However, I checked a random subsample of 50 scientists among the non-migrant sample for CV information online to see if I could find whether they did indeed emigrate. While CV information is not available online for most of these individuals, it does not appear that I have miscoded migrants as non-migrants based on this analysis.

4. During the time period studied, temporary migration was common, and my emigration measure includes these individuals.

I also assigned a Russian city to each individual based on information for articles published prior to 1991. To reduce the likelihood of false matches due to name ambiguity, I excluded any individual with more than two cities assigned to them from 1980 to 1990.

The final panel dataset includes publication, location, and citation information for each scientist from the year they first enter the WoS database through 2008. I limit the sample to 1980–2005 for most of the analysis to ensure that a large share of the scientists is in the sample for the majority of years.

Using the location information, I can split the sample into *emigrants* (scientists who emigrated after the end of the USSR in 1991) and *non-emigrants* (scientists who stayed in Russia but did not emigrate[5]). Due to the reliance on reprint author addresses and researcher addresses to assign scientists to each of these groups, which are far from complete in the WoS database, it is likely that I have miscoded individuals who may have emigrated.

Some additional information on scientist-level characteristics that I extract from the publication data include:

- *Gender*: Since I cannot observe an individual's first name in the WoS publications, I must rely on the last name. I assign a gender based on whether the last name ends in "-va," "-na," or "-ya," which typically indicate that the individual is a woman among Slavic last names.[6]
- *Year of First Publication*: This is the year of the first publication by a scientist among all their publications appearing in the WoS database. This can be used as a proxy for career age.
- *Number of publications from 1980 to 1990*: This is a key measure of productivity during Soviet times and allows me to see where in the pre-1991 productivity distribution emigrants fall. I create deciles based on this measure by field and assign each scientist to a decile to indicate his place in the field-specific distribution.
- *Number of citations for articles published 1980–1990*: This is a measure of how many citations are in the publications by 2008.
- *Non-USSR coauthor before 1990*: This is an indicator for any articles published in a given year with a coauthor from a country outside of the USSR.
- *Non-Russian journal before 1990*: This is an indicator for any articles published in a given year in a non-Russian language journal, as denoted in the ISI.

Table 1 provides summary statistics for the full sample of Russian scientists extracted from the WoS database who met the criteria described above, which

---

5. Since I can only observe a scientist's location through affiliation information on a publication, this means that I can only include individuals in my sample who continued to publish in the 1990s or stayed in science.
6. This approach likely leads to error in this variable, as some last names that do not end in "a" may also be women.

TABLE 1 Summary Statistics for Full Russian Scientist Sample (Means)

	Mean	Std. Dev.
Female	0.194	0.395
Year of first publication	1971.106	8.893
No. pubs 1980–1990	18.378	16.267
No. cites 1980–1990	86.700	214.292
Non-USSR coau. pre-1990	0.180	0.384
Non-Russian journal pre-1990	0.626	0.484
Ave. no. coau. 1980–1990	3.575	1.513
Scientific Field		
Astronomy	0.020	0.139
Chemistry	0.300	0.458
Earth sciences	0.082	0.274
Life sciences	0.240	0.427
Mathematics	0.048	0.214
Mechanics	0.003	0.057
Physics	0.307	0.461
City		
Moscow (pre-1990)	0.537	0.499
St Petersburg (pre-1990)	0.134	0.341
Observations	15,607	

Notes: Summary statistics are based on scientist-level data constructed using publication data from the Thomson Reuters Web of Science database.

includes 15,607 scientists. About 20% of the sample is women. The average year of the first publication was 1971. If we assume individuals published their first article around the age of 28, then the emigrants would have been about 46 years old on average by the time of the Soviet collapse while non-emigrants would have been about 49. Most of the scientists were located in Moscow (53.7%). About 13% of the sample had a coauthor outside of the USSR before 1990. The largest shares of scientists were publishing in the fields of chemistry (30%), the life sciences (24%), and physics (30.7%). Only 4.8% were publishing primarily in mathematics journals. In terms of publications, on average individuals in the sample published about 18.4 articles appearing in WoS from 1980 to 1990, and they received about 86.7 citations for these publications by 2008.

5. ANALYSIS OF IMMIGRANT SELECTION

To provide estimates of immigrant selection, I first provided simple comparisons of the means of available observables pre-1990 and time-invariant characteristics of emigrants and non-emigrants. Table 2 shows the mean characteristics of the groups and the third column shows the differences with the results of t-tests for the equality of means. Clearly, emigrants and non-emigrants look very different not only in terms of productivity measures (publications and citations) but also in their fields and global networks during Soviet times.

TABLE 2 Characteristics of Emigrants versus Non-emigrants (Means)

	Didn't Migrate	Migrated	Difference
Female	0.21	0.07	0.139**
Year of first publication	1970.81	1973.61	−2.805**
No. pubs 1980–1990	18.03	21.33	−3.305**
No. cites 1980–1990	71.59	213.43	−141.846**
Non-USSR coau. pre-1990	0.16	0.31	−0.147**
Non-Russian journal pre-1990	0.60	0.81	−0.209**
Ave. no. coau. 1980–1990	3.61	3.27	0.339**
Scientific Field			
Astronomy	0.02	0.03	−0.007
Chemistry	0.32	0.14	0.175**
Earth sciences	0.08	0.05	0.030**
Life sciences	0.24	0.21	0.033*
Mathematics	0.04	0.07	−0.029**
Mechanics	0.00	0.01	−0.005**
Physics	0.29	0.48	−0.196**
City			
Moscow pre-1990	0.53	0.59	−0.059**
St Petersburg pre-1990	0.13	0.15	−0.018+
Distribution 1980–1990 Publications (By Field)			
Decile 1	0.06	0.02	0.031**
Decile 2	0.10	0.07	0.027**
Decile 3	0.08	0.06	0.015+
Decile 4	0.12	0.09	0.025*
Decile 5	0.12	0.11	0.002
Decile 6	0.10	0.09	0.010
Decile 7	0.11	0.11	0.002
Decile 8	0.11	0.13	−0.017+
Decile 9	0.11	0.16	−0.051**
Decile 10	0.11	0.15	−0.045**
Observations	13,944	1663	

Notes: Summary statistics are based on scientist-level data constructed using publication data from the Thomson Reuters Web of Science database. Stars indicate the results of t-tests for the equality of means. +$p<0.10$, *$p<0.05$, **$p<0.01$.

First, emigrants were much more likely to be men than women. Over 20% of the non-migrants were women, while only 7% of the emigrants were women. This suggests that when considering whether to emigrate or not, women likely faced different costs of migration than men did, perhaps due to family related considerations as anecdotal evidence suggests.

Second, emigrants tended to be younger, with the average year of the first publication in 1973 versus 1970 for non-emigrants. Again, if we assume individuals published their first article around the age of 28, then the emigrants would have been about 46 years old on average by the time of the Soviet collapse while non-emigrants would have been about 49.

Third, emigrants were much more likely to have connections outside of the former Soviet Union. They were almost 15 percentage points more likely to have a foreign coauthor during Soviet times and over 20 percentage points more likely to have published in a non-Russian journal. However, they tended to have fewer coauthors on the papers they published, about one-third fewer on average.

Notably, there appear to be large differences by field, with fewer emigrants coming from chemistry (32% of all non-emigrants versus 14% of all emigrants coming from chemistry) and more from physics (29% vs 48%). Recall that physics made up approximately 30% of the overall sample; since almost half of the emigrants were physicists (or primarily publishing in physics journals), this shows that the emigrants were disproportionately coming from this field. These differences likely reflect the strength of fields, as Turkevich (1965) noted in the 1960s, "Chemistry has been a weak area in the Soviet scientific scene…Physics, on the other hand, is a strong area."

Another significant difference is from which cities the emigrants were leaving. We saw earlier that over half of the scientists in the sample were from Moscow, but a slightly greater share of emigrants were from Moscow (close to 60%). A slightly larger share also came from Leningrad (now St Petersburg).

Lastly, the decile measures reflect the significant differences in the skill distribution of emigrants and non-emigrants, if we consider their 1980–1990 publications as measure of skill. Most of the differences are at the bottom and the top of the distribution: emigrants are less likely to have been in the bottom four deciles and are more likely to be in the top three. The means of number of publications and number of citations to articles published from 1980 to 1990[7] also show that emigrants on average appear to be more productive than the non-emigrants.

These productivity differences can also be seen in Figures 3 and 4. Figure 3 shows the average number of publications published in each year for emigrants and non-emigrants from 1975 to 1991, when the Soviet Union ended. Clearly, the scientists in each group started at a similar level, but by 1991, the individuals who subsequently emigrated had about 0.7 publications more on average. Figure 4 contains the distribution of 1980–1990 publications for the two groups, which shows that the individuals who later emigrated tended to have more publications.

Table 3 shows results from ordinary least squares (OLS) regressions predicting whether a scientist has emigrated by 2005 conditional on these observable characteristics. Since the outcome variable is dichotomous, it is a linear probability model, so the coefficients can be interpreted as probabilities. While Table 2

---

7. There are several reasons why emigrants' Soviet-era work may be cited more than non-emigrants. One reason is the difference in their productivity during the Soviet period, as reflected by the differences in average number of publications. However, there are other possible channels as well. Some of the difference in citations is due to the diffusion of knowledge by emigrants, since as Ganguli (2015) shows, emigrants' Soviet-era work was cited by US authors more than non-emigrants' work after they moved.

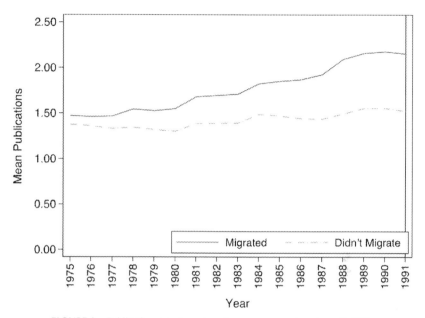

FIGURE 3 Publications trends: emigrants versus non-emigrants, until 1991.

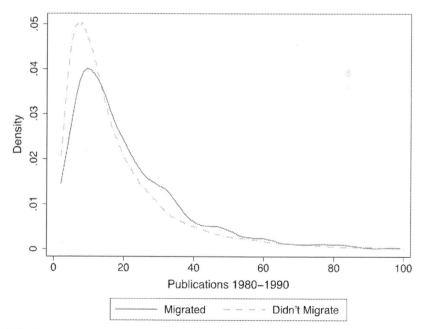

FIGURE 4 Distribution of publications, 1980–1990. *Notes: This is a kernel density estimate of the publications of each scientist from 1980 to 1990.*

TABLE 3 Regressions Predicting Emigration

	(1)	(2)	(3)
No. pubs 1980–1990	0.000*		
	(0.000)		
No. cites 1980–1990	0.000**		
	(0.000)		
Female	−0.044**		−0.043**
	(0.005)		(0.005)
Year of first publication	0.005**		0.006**
	(0.000)		(0.000)
Non-USSR coau. pre-1990	0.068**		0.090**
	(0.008)		(0.008)
Ave. no. coau. 1980–1990	−0.016**		−0.019**
	(0.002)		(0.002)
Moscow pre-1990	0.035**		0.035**
	(0.005)		(0.005)
St Petersburg pre-1990	0.031**		0.029**
	(0.008)		(0.008)
Distribution 1980–1990 Publications (By Field)			
Decile 2		0.029**	0.031**
		(0.010)	(0.011)
Decile 3		0.038**	0.048**
		(0.011)	(0.011)
Decile 4		0.035**	0.063**
		(0.010)	(0.010)
Decile 5		0.055**	0.079**
		(0.011)	(0.011)
Decile 6		0.046**	0.078**
		(0.011)	(0.011)
Decile 7		0.054**	0.090**
		(0.011)	(0.011)
Decile 8		0.071**	0.106**
		(0.011)	(0.011)
Decile 9		0.098**	0.136**
		(0.011)	(0.012)
Decile 10		0.095**	0.137**
		(0.011)	(0.012)
Constant	−9.440**	0.050**	−11.160**
	(0.610)	(0.008)	(0.633)
R2	0.095	0.008	0.076
No. of Obs.	15,166	15,607	15,166

Notes: Estimated with ordinary least squares (OLS). Robust standard errors in parentheses. Observations are at the scientist level and include scientific field dummies in (1) and (3). The difference in the samples is because (2) does not include the city dummies, and it was not possible to assign a Russian city to each scientist in the sample. $^+p<0.10$, $^*p<0.05$, $^{**}p<0.01$.

showed the mean differences between migrants and non-migrants for individual factors, the regression results allow me to estimate differences between migrants and non-migrants while holding the other factors constant. For example, the regression allows me to examine whether women were more or less likely to emigrate after accounting for the number of publications an individual published from 1980 to 1990.

Column 1 of Table 3 includes the aggregate productivity variables from the Soviet period (1980–1990 publications and citations to those publications) rather than the decile dummies, which I include next. The coefficients on the productivity variables are very small, but they are positive, indicating that on average, emigrants were more productive in terms of Soviet period publications. Column 2 includes dummies for the deciles of 1980–1990 publications without any other control variables. The coefficients on the decile dummies show that relative to the omitted decile dummy (the bottom 10%), emigrants are more likely to come from the higher parts of the productivity distribution, and the probability tends to increase as we move up the distribution.

In Column 3, I include the decile measures as well as the other control variables. After controlling for other factors, the results show that emigrants were 4% less likely to be female and they were slightly younger (i.e., the year of the first publication was later). The results also show that they were more likely to have a more global network, as they were 9% more likely to have coauthored with a non-USSR scientist during Soviet times. They also tended to have published with a smaller number of coauthors on their Soviet period publications. They were also more likely to come from Moscow or Leningrad. Finally, the results show that after controlling for these other factors, emigrants were much more likely to come from the upper deciles of the productivity distribution (measured by 1980–1990 publications and within fields).

Table 4 shows results for OLS regressions predicting whether a scientist has emigrated separately by time period (early or late in the 1990s) and by destination country (USA or Western European countries of England, France, or Germany). In columns 1 and 2, I compare the characteristics of individuals who emigrated early in the transition period (1992–1997) versus later (1998–2002). The relative magnitudes of the coefficients suggest that there are differences by time of emigration. The results show that those who emigrated 1992–1997 were less likely to be female, younger, more likely to have foreign coauthors, more likely to be from Moscow and St Petersburg, and more likely to be from the upper part of the productivity distribution, so they were even more positively selected. Since the costs of migration and the expected returns abroad were likely highest during the early transition period, the results are consistent with the framework regarding the migration decision—when the wage premium and costs are highest, we observe the most able emigrating.

Columns 3 and 4 are the results for emigration to the US versus Western Europe (England, Germany, or France). This comparison is useful because we would expect both lower migration costs and a lower return to skills in Europe than in the US. This would suggest that selection should be more positive in the US compared to European destination countries. The results confirm that this is the case, with emigrants to the US more likely to be from the upper parts of the publication distribution.

TABLE 4 Regressions Predicting Emigration: Time Period and Destination Country

| | Time Period | | Destination Country | |
| | 1992–1997 | 1998–2002 | USA | W. Europe |
	(1)	(2)	(3)	(4)
Female	−0.027**	−0.010**	−0.024**	−0.006**
	(0.004)	(0.003)	(0.003)	(0.002)
Year of first	0.004**	0.001**	0.002**	0.001**
publication	(0.000)	(0.000)	(0.000)	(0.000)
Non-USSR coau.	0.078**	0.009*	0.032**	0.017**
pre-1990	(0.007)	(0.004)	(0.005)	(0.004)
Ave. no. coau.	−0.015**	−0.003**	−0.005**	−0.004**
1980–1990	(0.001)	(0.001)	(0.001)	(0.001)
Moscow	0.026**	0.008**	0.014**	0.011**
pre-1990	(0.004)	(0.003)	(0.004)	(0.002)
St Petersburg	0.020**	0.008⁺	0.009	0.010**
pre-1990	(0.007)	(0.004)	(0.005)	(0.004)
Distribution 1980–1990 Publications (By Field)				
Decile 2	0.017*	0.014*	0.009	0.005
	(0.008)	(0.006)	(0.007)	(0.004)
Decile 3	0.031**	0.012⁺	0.018*	0.012*
	(0.009)	(0.006)	(0.008)	(0.005)
Decile 4	0.045**	0.012*	0.024**	0.011*
	(0.008)	(0.005)	(0.008)	(0.004)
Decile 5	0.050**	0.027**	0.023**	0.018**
	(0.008)	(0.006)	(0.008)	(0.005)
Decile 6	0.055**	0.020**	0.023**	0.016**
	(0.009)	(0.006)	(0.008)	(0.005)
Decile 7	0.069**	0.018**	0.026**	0.017**
	(0.009)	(0.006)	(0.008)	(0.005)
Decile 8	0.074**	0.026**	0.037**	0.018**
	(0.009)	(0.006)	(0.008)	(0.005)
Decile 9	0.102**	0.029**	0.045**	0.025**
	(0.010)	(0.006)	(0.008)	(0.005)
Decile 10	0.099**	0.034**	0.046**	0.021**
	(0.010)	(0.007)	(0.009)	(0.005)
Constant	−8.033**	−2.504**	−4.727**	−2.684**
	(0.533)	(0.334)	(0.438)	(0.303)
R2	0.066	0.011	0.024	0.021
No. of Obs.	15,166	15,166	15,166	15,166

Notes: Estimated with ordinary least squares (OLS). Robust standard errors in parentheses. Observations are at the scientist level and include scientific field dummies. The dependent variables are as follows: (1) migrated from 1992 to 1997; (2) migrated from 1998 to 2002; (3) migrated to US; (4) migrated to England, France, or Germany. ⁺$p<0.10$, *$p<0.05$, **$p<0.01$.

Table 4 highlights the role that migration costs play in migration decisions. For example, immigrants to Western Europe are more likely to be from St Petersburg. This is consistent with the migration costs being much lower from St Petersburg to Europe than to the US, as St Petersburg is close both geographically and culturally to Europe. Moreover, both groups of regressions in Table 4 show that women likely face greater migration costs, as they were more likely to have emigrated early in the transition period and to the United States, also after controlling for productivity differences, which is consistent with qualitative evidence suggesting that it may be that family factors play a larger role for women that make migration more costly.

6. DISCUSSION

In this chapter, I used the context of the end of the Soviet Union and the subsequent exodus of scientists to the West to provide new estimates of immigrant selection and to contribute to a greater understanding of the factors underlying the emigration decision. While there has been considerable attention in the economics literature on immigrant selection, and the literature has pointed to the fact that immigrants are not a random subsample of the population in the home country, empirical evidence on how immigrants compare to others in the home country in terms of skills and other observable characteristics is still sparse. Moreover, there has been very little analysis of immigrant selection among scientists. This is primarily because it is difficult to examine immigrant selection empirically, since one must be able to observe scientists and their characteristics before they make the decision to emigrate and as well as the full home country population.

The results of my analysis show that on a number of observable characteristics, emigrant scientists look very different from those who stay at home. Using publications during the Soviet period as a measure of skill and productivity, the results show that Soviet scientist emigrants were positively selected, as they came from the upper part of the productivity distribution as measured by papers published during the 10 years before the end of the USSR. The emigrants also tended to be men, were slightly younger, and had larger global networks. There are also large differences by field, with fewer emigrants coming from chemistry and many more from physics.

In terms of the model of the migration decision discussed in Section 3, the results are consistent with the predictions, in that the most skilled scientists left, as the return to skill was higher in the West than in Russia in the 1990s. Even though wages were low across the board for scientists in the 1990s as discussed in Section 2, the lower skilled may have still found that remaining in Russia would provide more stable earnings than going abroad. Moreover, the most skilled left early in the transition period and left for the US, which is consistent with the predictions that the extent of positive selection increases with migration costs and the wage premium.

However, interpreting publications during Soviet times as a measure of skill must be done with caution. It is not necessarily the case that individuals who were able to publish the most during Soviet times were the most *scientifically skilled*, so that the measures of where individuals fall in the "productivity" distribution may be measuring something unobserved that is correlated with being successful in being able to publish during the Soviet period. For example, it may be that those who were able to publish were better able to access resources or information, which would likely have also been useful for emigration (as these "skills" would effectively lower migration costs).

As discussed in the conceptual framework section, we would have also predicted the younger scientists to emigrate, as they would have been more able to retrain or otherwise gain new skills abroad, given that the transferability of the Soviet-style education may have been low in many cases. It was also discussed that having a global network would have reduced migration costs, leading those with foreign contacts to be more likely to emigrate, which we also observed with the foreign coauthor variable.

While the results suggest that the most productive and younger scientists left Russia, which points to a "brain drain," a closer examination is needed to understand what impact their emigration had on Russian science. A growing literature on the role of immigrants in knowledge diffusion shows that immigrants can transfer knowledge back to the home country that can be especially valuable as an input for invention (Agrawal et al., 2011; Kerr, 2008), and it is also possible that the departure of the most highly skilled Soviet scientists had measurable benefits for Russian science through such knowledge diffusion.

Economic theory also suggests that the immigration of Soviet scientists may have benefited the US researchers through knowledge spillovers, and we would expect these impacts to be largest if immigrants are more positively selected. However, evidence to date from Borjas & Doran (2012) shows that the arrival of Soviet mathematicians in the US tended to have negative productivity effects on natives. However, immigrants do seem to potentially be a channel through which knowledge is diffused to natives, as Ganguli (2015) shows that Soviet scientists did play an important role in diffusing Soviet scientific knowledge to US scientists during the 1990s.

The analysis presented here suggests that the nature of immigrant selection can also provide a greater understanding about immigrants' research trajectories. The results show that it was the "best and the brightest" from Russia who arrived in the US, and this suggests that immigrants may outperform natives in research productivity. For example, Gaulé & Piacentini (2013) show that Chinese students who leave for the US to do their training in chemistry departments outperform most American students, likely because they are positively selected from the distribution of Chinese students.

While these results on selection among immigrant scientists are based on experience from the end of the Soviet Union, we can imagine that many of the conditions facing these scientists in the 1990s relating to low earnings, access to resources and global networks are also relevant in many developing country settings. Thus, we might expect a similar story of self-selection among scientists in these other contexts where there are large science and engineering labor forces, but data is lacking that allows us to accurately measure how emigrants compare to the home country population of scientists, in countries such as China and India, which are the focus of many discussions of international scientific mobility today.

ACKNOWLEDGMENTS

I appreciate comments from Richard Freeman, George Borjas, Asim Khwaja, Pierre Azoulay, Alberto Abadie, Ricardo Hausmann, Supreet Kaur, Julia Lane, and Paul David. I appreciate data assistance from Raviv Murciano-Goroff and programming guidance from Cesar Hidalgo. I gratefully acknowledge funding and support from the Center for International Development, the Davis Center for Russian and Eurasian Studies, and the Institute for Quantitative Social Science at Harvard University, and the Harvard Labor and Worklife Program.

REFERENCES

Agrawal, A., Kapur, D., McHale, J., & Oettl, A. (2011). Brain drain or brain bank? The impact of skilled emigration on poor-country innovation. *Journal of Urban Economics*, 69(1), 43–55.

Beine, M., Docquier, F., & Özden, Ç. (2011). Diasporas. *Journal of Development Economics*, 95(1), 30–41.

Bertrand, M. (2011). New perspectives on gender. *Handbook of Labor Economics*, 4, 1543–1590.

Borjas, G. (1999). The economic analysis of immigration. *Handbook of Labor Economics*, 3, 1697–1760.

Borjas, G. J., & Doran, K. B. (2012). The collapse of the Soviet Union and the productivity of American mathematicians. *The Quarterly Journal of Economics*, 127(3), 1143–1203.

Docquier, F., Marfouk, A., Salomone, S., & Sekkat, K. (2012). Are skilled women more migratory than skilled men? *World Development*, 40(2), 251–265.

Docquier, F., & Rapoport, H. (2012). Globalization, brain drain, and development. *Journal of Economic Literature*, 50(3), 681–730.

Drinkwater, S., Eade, J., & Garapich, M. (2009). Poles apart? EU enlargement and the labour market outcomes of immigrants in the United Kingdom. *International Migration*, 47(1), 161–190.

Ganguli, I. *Saving soviet science: The impact of grants when government R&D funding disappears.* Harvard University, unpublished manuscript-a.

Ganguli, I. *Location and scientific productivity: Evidence from the soviet brain drain.* Harvard University, unpublished manuscript-b.

Ganguli, I. (2015). Immigration & ideas: what did Russian scientists "bring" to the US? *Journal of Labor Economics*, 33(3).

Gaulé, P., & Piacentini, M. (2013). Chinese graduate students and US scientific productivity. *Review of Economics and Statistics*, 95(2), 698–701.

Gokhberg, L., & Nekipelova, E. (2002). International migration of scientists and engineers in Russia. In *International mobility of the highly skilled* (pp. 177–187). OECD.

Gokhberg, L., Kuznetsova, T., & Zaichenko, S. (2009). Towards a new role of universities in Russia: prospects and limitations. *Science and Public Policy*, 36(2), 121–126.

Graham, L. R., & Dezhina, I. (2008). *Science in the new Russia: Crisis, aid, reform*. Indiana University Press.

Holden, Constance. (1990). No American dream for Soviet emigres. *Science*, 248(4959), 1068.

Hunt, J. (2013). *Are immigrants the best and brightest US engineers?* National Bureau of economic research working paper No. w18696.

Hunter, R. S., Oswald, A. J., & Charlton, B. G. (2009). The elite brain drain. *Economic Journal*, *119*, F231–F251.

Kerr, W. (2008). Ethnic scientific communities and international technology diffusion. *The Review of Economics and Statistics*, *90*(3), 518–537.

Kneen, P. (1995). Science in shock: Russian science policy in transition. *Europe-Asia Studies*, *47*(2), 281–303.

OECD. (1994). *Science, Technology, and Innovation Policies*. Federation of Russia. Paris: Organisation for Economic Co-operation and Development (OECD).

Roy, A. D. (1951). Some thoughts on the distribution of earnings. *Oxford economic papers*, *3*(2), 135–146.

Salomon, J. J., Sagasti, F. R., & Sachs-Jeantet, C. (Eds.). (1994). *The uncertain quest: Science, technology and development*. New York and Paris: United Nations University Press.

Saltykov, B. (1995). New Russian problems of international scientific collaboration. In V. Koptyug, & J. Klerkx (Eds.), *Science policy: New mechanisms for scientific collaboration between east and west* (pp. 3–8). Dordrecht: Kluwer Academic Publishers.

Saltykov, B. G. (1997). The reform of Russian science. *Nature*, *388*(6637), 16–18.

Turkevich, J. (1965). Soviet science appraised. *Foreign Affairs*, *44*, 489.

Weinberg, B. (2010). Developing science: scientific performance and brain drains in the developing world. *Journal of Development Economics*.

Zucker, L. G., & Darby, M. R. (2006). *Movement of star scientists and engineers and high-tech firm entry*. National Bureau of economic research working paper No. w12172.

Chapter 6

China's "Great Leap Forward" in Science and Engineering

Richard B. Freeman, Wei Huang

Harvard University and NBER, Cambridge, MA, USA

Chapter Outline

The Cultural Revolution (1966–1976) devastated science and engineering (S&E) education and research in China. It led to the closing of China's national entrance exam, which had for hundreds of years been the pathway for students to enter colleges and universities. Universities admitted no new undergraduate students from 1966 through 1969 and admitted no new graduate students through 1977. In 1970 China had only 47,000 undergraduate students and essentially no graduate students (Li, 2010, Table 8.1). Recovering from the Cultural Revolution in the 1970s and 1980s, enrollments in 4-year programs increased to 2.1 million in 1990 (Li, 2010, Table 8.2), whereas enrollments in all programs, including more vocationally oriented less than bachelor's programs, reached 3.8 million (Table 1). Still, China's share of world enrollments (5.6%) fell short its one-fifth (31%) of the world's 1990 population.[1] With few S&E graduates, China had fewer research scientists and engineers than did some countries with a tenth of China's population,

---

1. Statistics about the Population Growth in China, 2001–2011, World Bank, July 2012. Retrieved 10 April 2013. http://www.statista.com/statistics/270129/population-growth-in-china/

TABLE 1 Enrollments (in Millions) and Shares of Enrollment in Tertiary Education, by Area of the World, 1970–2010

Area	1970	1990	2010
Worldwide	29.4	67.6	177.6
Developing countries	16.0 (54%)	41.0 (61%)	136.5 (76%)
China	<0.1 (0%)	3.8 (6%)	30 (17%)
India	2.5 (9%)	5 (7%)	20.7 (12%)
United States	8.5 (29%)	13.7 (20%)	20.4 (11%)
Other advanced countries	4.9 (17%)	12.9 (19%)	23.7 (13%)

Notes: Data source is UNESCO, Institute for Statistics, on line files, 2010, from Tables 15, 20A.

whereas China-based researchers contributed fewer papers to international science journals than China-born researchers outside the country.[2]

The great leap forward in S&E that gives this chapter its title was concentrated in the two decades of the 1990s and 2000s. In this short span of time China leaped from bit player in global S&E to become the world's largest source of S&E graduates, second largest spender on research and development (R&D), and second largest producer of scientific papers, in both cases behind the United States. The number of patents in China increased so rapidly as to make China the number 1 country in patents (WIPO, 2014).[3] The number of China addresses on US Patent and Trademark Office patents increased enough to move China from a negligible producer of US patents to seventh among non-US countries with US patents. As a latecomer to modern S&E, China trailed the United States and other advanced countries in the quality of its universities and research but was improving both through the mid-2010s.

This chapter analyzes China's great leap forward in S&E. It presents evidence that China's leap benefited greatly from the country's positive response to global opportunities to educate overseas many of its best and brightest and from the deep educational and research links it developed with the United States. China first permitted students to self-finance overseas study and for scientific specialists to undertake cross-country research; then the country awarded fellowships for research students and researchers to study or work overseas, while encouraging

---

2. Some scholars argue that the parts of Chinese science that fit with the goals of the government fared reasonably well during the Maoist period (Wei & Brock, 2013), but there is no gainsaying that the drops in admission to undergraduate and graduate S&E programs, banishment of professors and other researchers to the rural parts of the country, and the absence of scientific papers wrecked the bulk of China's research community.

3. Incentives linking pay to number of patents have produced a patent system with many short single-claim patents that are not readily comparable to patents in the United States, European Union, and Japan. That China is number one in World Intellectual Property Organization patent data does not mean that it is top of the world in patenting. The number of China addresses on US, European Union, and Japanese patents has increased but place China far from the top countries in patenting.

Chinese universities to hire faculty from abroad and to undertake international research collaborations and seek multinational transfers of knowledge.[4] Global mobility of people and ideas allowed China to reach the scientific and technological frontier much faster than if it had gone down a more parochial path.

This chapter has three parts. Section 1 examines the increase in domestic university enrollments and in students studying overseas that turned China into the number 1 source country for scientists and engineers worldwide. Section 2 documents the growth of R&D spending, production of scientific papers, and international research collaborations that improved the quality of Chinese science. Section 3 makes the case that the close links that developed between China and the United States in education and research constitute a "special relationship" that augurs well for research in both countries and throughout the world.

1. CHINA BECOMES A HIGHER EDUCATION POWERHOUSE

1.1 Increase of Domestic Higher Education

Table 1 places China's leap forward in university enrollments in the context of the longer-run increase in the share of tertiary enrollments in developing countries from the 1970s to the 2010s. Convinced that the development of human capital and adaption of modern technology was critical to economic growth, many developing countries invested in higher education in the last two to three decades of the twentieth century, producing a continuous increase in developing countries' share of global tertiary enrollments.[5] China's leap forward—an eightfold increase in enrollments that moved it from 6% of world enrollments in tertiary education to 17%—was exceptional, even in the context of the worldwide expansion of higher education.[6] The only comparable expansion was in much smaller Korea, which invested so much in education and research from the 1980s onward that it became the number 1 country in the proportion of young people attending college and university and in the proportion of gross domestic product spent on R&D.[7] Another hugely populous country, India, expanded higher education more slowly but still enrolled 21 million students in 2010. In 2010 one in three college students in the world was from China or India.

Behind the huge increase in enrollments in developing countries were national investments in new colleges and universities, the expansion of existing institutions, and upgrades of lower-level institutions into colleges or universities granting

---

4. The role of multinational transfer of knowledge is important in China's application of modern technology to the economy but raises diverse issues that go beyond the scope of our analysis: industrial secrecy, use of patents, Chinese purchase of high-tech companies in advanced countries, and the like.
5. The increase in enrollments in developing countries (16 to 137 million) is 81% of the total increase.
6. The absolute increase was from 3.8 million in 1990 to 30 million in 2010.
7. Freeman (2015).

TABLE 2 Number of Bachelor's, Master's, and PhDs Graduating in China (Total and S&E), by Year

	Bachelor's		Master's		PhDs	
Year	Total	S&E	Total	S&E	Total	S&E
2012	3,038,473	1,258,643	434,742	191,048	51,713	27,652
2011	2,796,229	1,163,643	379,705	165,450	50,289	27,584
2010	2,590,535	1,082,271	334,613	145,266	48,987	27,066
2009	2,455,359	1,028,129	322,615	145,380	48,658	26,956
2008	2,256,783	956,214	301,066	138,441	43,759	24,229
2007	1,995,944	861,834	270,375	127,357	41,464	22,530
2006	1,726,674	770,441	219,655	104,282	36,247	19,371
2005	1,465,786	680,301	162,051	80,084	27,677	14,885
2004	1,196,290	576,627	127,331	61,042	23,446	12,572
2003	929,598	454,946	92,241	44,279	18,806	10,278
2002	655,763	324,550	66,203	31,884	14,638	8060
2001	567,839	283,080	54,700	25,715	12,867	7647
2000	495,624	262,119	47,565	25,421	11,004	7019
1999	440,935	237,705	44,189	25,119	10,320	6450
1998	404,666	222,103	38,051	22,443	8957	5711
1997	381,647	214,552	39,114	22,729	7319	4803
1996	347,194	199,754	34,026	20,613	5430	3564
1995	325,484	186,873	27,123	17,591	4641	3091
1994	310,291	178,380	24,181	15,443	3723	2481
1993	298,959	142,536	25,167	16,263	2940	2054
1992	–	–	23,015	–	2528	1769
1991	323,434	156,461	29,193	18,672	2610	1727
1990	307,865	148,886	31,505	20,303	2457	1626
1989	308,930	153,032	32,890	21,169	2046	1,890
1988	279,791	137,065	34,732	–	1538	–
1987	252,973	121,802	20,307	13,629	464	350
1986	227,764	109,101	15,221	9704	284	228

Notes: Data source is Ministry of Education of People's Republic of China and Educational Statistics Yearbook of China. The bachelors here are those with normal courses and do not account those with short-cycle courses.

baccalaureate degrees (e.g. International Association of Universities, see http://www.iau-aiu.net/). In the case of China, Li (2010) reported that the number of higher education institutions in China more than doubled from the mid-1970s to the mid-1980s, which allowed the country to increase the proportion of students admitted to college after taking the national entrance exam from single digits to 48% in 1999.[8] Looking at developing countries, many of whom barely had any universities, the increase in the number of universities around the world was more strongly associated with changes in enrollments than any other single factor.

Table 2 shows that the huge expansion of enrollments produced a commensurately large increase in students obtaining bachelor's, master's, and PhD degrees in China in the 1990s and 2000s. From 1990 to 2010, the number of

8. See Tables 8.1 and 8.2 and p. 273 in the work by Li (2010).

bachelor's graduates increased tenfold, from 307,865 to 3,038,473. The difference between the 3 million graduates and the 30 million enrollments noted in Table 1 might suggest that China suffered from high university drop out during its enrollment spurt. With 4–5 years normally spent to earn a bachelor's degree, 30 million enrollments could be expected to produce approximately 6–7 million graduates.[9] But the divergence reflects something very different: the fact that nearly half of enrolled students take 2- to 3-year degree programs with greater occupational training and less academic content than traditional baccalaureates.

The data for postbaccalaureate degrees in Table 2 show that the number of students receiving master's and doctorate degrees increased more rapidly than those receiving bachelor's degrees. Master's degrees increased nearly 15-fold from 1990 to 2010. Doctorate degrees increased nearly 20-fold. Comparing S&E PhDs in China and the United States, in 1990 just 5–7% as many S&E PhDs graduated in China as in the United States,[10] whereas in 2010 about the same numbers of S&E PhDs graduated in China as in the United States.[11] Moreover, because many Chinese citizens earn PhDs in advanced countries, China's contribution to the world's supply of new S&E specialists was even greater.

All of these developments reflected both the policies of the Chinese government to expand higher education and the desire of young Chinese students to invest in additional years of schooling, in part because of the high returns to education in China's new market economy.

There are three caveats to China's leap forward in world higher education. First, the huge number of enrollments and degrees results from China's large population more than from exceptionally high rates of college-going relative to the population. With a population roughly four times that of the United States, China would have as many students/graduates as the United States with a students/graduates-to-population ratio about one-fourth that of the

---

9. Estimated as about one-fourth to one-fifth of the 30 million.

10. See Table 5 in "Doctorate Recipients from United States Universities: Summary Report 2000" (available from http://www.nsf.gov/statistics/doctorates/pdf/sed2000.pdf; p. 36) for US PhDs by field in 1990. Subtracting humanities, education, and professional from the total gives 23,228. Footnote 12 in the National Science Board Science and Engineering Indicators 2004, Foreign Doctoral Degree Recipients estimates that 1069 S&E doctoral degrees were granted to Chinese students within Chinese universities in 1990 (http://www.nsf.gov/statistics/seind04/c2/c2s4.htm). The 7% figure divides the number in Table 2 by the 23,228 from the United States. The 5% uses the smaller National Science Foundation estimate for China.

11. China–US comparisons vary with how one treats Hong Kong and social/behavioral sciences. With Hong Kong counted as part of China, China produces more S&E PhDs than the United States when excluding social/behavioral sciences but fewer when including social/behavioral sciences. Science and Engineering Indicator (2014) (Appendix Table 2-39, http://www.nsf.gov/statistics/seind14/content/chapter-2/at02-39.pdf) reports 32,649 US S&E PhDs inclusive of the social/behavioral sciences and 24,559 excluding them, and 31,410 China PhDs inclusive of social/behavioral sciences and 29,039 excluding them. This exceeds the 27,066 in Table 2, which covers mainland universities and seems to exclude social sciences. All told, these data show that China graduates from 10% to 18% more natural science and engineering PhDs than the United States, whereas it graduates 3.8% fewer in all S&E.

TABLE 3 Rating of Universities in China, the United States, the United Kingdom, Germany, and Japan, 2003–2014

Measure	China	United States	United Kingdom	Germany	Japan
No. of universities in top 500					
2014	32	146	38	39	19
2003	9	157			
No. of universities in top 200					
2014	6	77	20	13	8
2003	0	86			
No. of universities in top 100					
2014	0	52	8	4	3
2003	0	53	9	5	5
Rank/name of top university					
2014	101–150, Peking, Tsinghua, Shanghai Jiao Tong	1, Harvard	5, Cambridge	49, Heidelberg	21, Tokyo
2003	201–250, Tsinghua	1, Harvard	5, Cambridge	49, Munich	19, Tokyo

Notes: Data source is Shanghai Jiao Tong University, Academic Ranking of Work Universities.

United States.[12] Given China's large rural population and relatively low quality of education for people with rural hukou, the country would have to invest substantially in elementary and secondary school to increase the proportion of young people in tertiary education much beyond 2010 levels.

The second caveat is that the quality of China's college and university system lags behind that of higher educational systems in the United States and other advanced countries. Table 3 demonstrates this with statistics on the global rank

---

12. Taking a broader age group, the Organisation for Economic Co-operation and Development (OECD) estimates that the 2010 ratio of people who attained at least a tertiary education to people aged 25–34 years was 8% in China compared to 42% in the United States, 38% for the OECD average, and a world high of 65% for Korea (OECD, 2012, Chart A1.1). The China figures are for people aged 25–34 years. Because the OECD does not make clear the relevant age group it has chosen, the above comparison is based on the assumption that the relevant group is the number of people at a single age between 25 and 34, assuming a flat distribution of people within the age category. The figures reported in the Scorecard (2012) for China are a decimal point off. At the PhD level, the ratio of graduates to people in the relevant age group was about 0.25% for China (STI Performance of China, Annex, p. 4) compared with 1.6% for the United States and 1.5% for the OECD (OECD, 2011, Figure 2.1.1).

of universities in China from Shanghai Jiao Tong University's Academic Ranking of World Universities in 2003 (the first year of its report) and 2014 compared with the rank of universities in the United States, United Kingdom, Germany, and Japan. In 2003 just 10 Chinese universities were among the top 500 universities in the world.[13] None were in the top 100 or 200. The leading university was Peking in the 251–300 grouping. The next decade's improvement still left China's universities far behind the world's best. In 2014, 32 Chinese universities were in the top 500, 6 were in the top 200, and 3 in the 101–150 grouping, but none had reached the top 100.[14]

The improved rating of China's universities did not occur by happenstance. The government spent considerable sums on a diverse set of number-designated funding programs to improve the quality of the university system and create a few world-class academic centers: the 211 project to support the top 100 universities; the 985 project to transform the 40 top universities to world-class status; the 863 program to fund R&D of technology; and the 973 project to fund basic research.[15] Aware of the quality gap between top universities in China and in more advanced economies, Chinese students and researchers have sought to compensate for their country's lagging quality by going abroad to learn from the best in foreign countries.

1.2 Going Out: More International Students and Visiting Researchers

The globalization of higher education was characterized by an exceptionally rapid growth in the number of international students. From 1975 through 1990 the number of international students doubled from 0.6 million to 1.2 million. The number then increased 3.8-fold to 4.5 million in 2012. China was a latecomer in sending students overseas. In 1978 China's Ministry of Education asked the central government to send more students abroad, but the numbers were minuscule—barely 2000 students in the 5 years between 1978 and 1982—of whom 16% were graduate students and 9% undergraduate students, with the vast majority being visiting researchers. The government selected students for overseas study on the basis of its goals rather than the students' career plans.[16]

---

13. The Shanghai Academic Ranking of World Universities uses six objective indicators to rank world universities: the number of alumni and staff winning Nobel Prizes and Fields Medals, the number of highly cited researchers selected by Thomson Reuters, the number of articles published in the journals of *Nature* and *Science*, the number of articles indexed in Science or Social Sciences Citation Index, and the per capita performance of a university. On the basis of these statistics, it ranks the top 100 universities and groups the rest into categories with 50 each. Other well-known rating systems give roughly comparable ratings, with some idiosyncrasy; the London Times ranking, for example, places British universities higher in its rankings than does the Shanghai rating.
14. For an assessment of China's higher education system, see OECD (2009).
15. See Li (2010) Section 8.4.
16. The State Board of Education's "The temporal policies about the students studying abroad and going back" emphasized the main channel of students to go abroad is being sent by the government.

Few Chinese had the funds to self-finance study abroad, and those that did needed administrative department approval of their studies.

The flow of Chinese international students increased in the 1980s, with the United States being the favored destination. The Chinese government maintained the policy of allowing international students and researchers to study outside the country even after the 1989 Tiananmen incident, which led many overseas students to seek permanent immigrant status in the United States.[17] This loss of talent would almost surely have caused many countries to stop the flow of students overseas, but China went in the other direction.[18] In 1993 the Communist Party Central Committee endorsed overseas education with the slogan "Support Going, Encourage Back, Go and Back Free."[19] The number of Chinese studying overseas increased moderately through 2000, then accelerated as the State Board of Education simplified procedures for self-financed students to study abroad.[20] In 2005 the Ministry of Education announced that it would "select the highest talent student in China and send them abroad to the best universities/institutes and follow the best advisers." In 2007 it joined with the Ministry of Finance to set up the "national high-level university researchers program" to subsidize more students and visiting researchers.

Figure 1 shows the ensuing increase in the number of Chinese international students from the late 1990s through 2014, with a break after 2001 due to the US State Department rejecting more visa applicants than in the past and making it difficult for international students to travel outside the United States—all in response to the 9/11 terrorist destruction of the World Trade Center. The increased flow of Chinese students to Australia in the early 2000s suggests that some Chinese students went to Australia instead of the United States. In 2005/2006 the number of Chinese students going to the United States increased massively as the State Department reformed the student visa program (National Academies, 2005). This change in policy may have reduced the number of Chinese students going to Australia, as shown in the Figure 1.

---

17. The United States, in particular, offered Chinese students an opportunity to remain in the country, first through administrative decree and then in 2002 with the Chinese Student Protection Act that targeted permanent residence for Chinese students in the United States. An estimated 54,000 persons gained green cards and presumably citizenship thereafter.

18. We can only speculate on the possible reasons the government continued its international student policies. One likely reason the government was so favorable to top Chinese students studying overseas was recognition that it was necessary for them to reach their potential as scholars, consistent with China's historic cultural respect for scholarship. Another likely reason was the need for up-to-date scientific and technological expertise available only from overseas experts. The government also likely was influenced by the desire of top officials and wealthy businesspeople to give their children best education world has to offer.

19. Central Committee of Communist Party, "The decisions about constructing the socialism market economy system."

20. It canceled the qualification check procedure and the "training fees" charges for going abroad and set up a "Chinese Government Award for Outstanding Self-Financed Student Abroad."

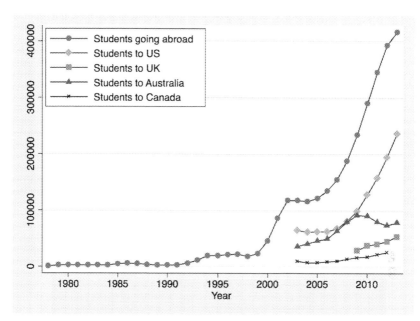

FIGURE 1 The increase in Chinese international students in the 2000s. *Notes: Data are not available for all countries in all years. Data for students going abroad is from* www.eol.cn, *whose data source is Ministry of Education of the People's Republic of China. Data for US students are open-door data. Data for UK students is from the Higher Education Statistics Agency* (https://www.hesa.ac.uk/). *Data for Canada is from the Canadian Government Department of Immigration. Data for Australia is from Australian Government Department of Immigration and Border Protection. Data for the United Kingdom, Canada, and Australia are collected by* www.eol.cn.

With so many students overseas, the Central Committee's tenth Five Year Plan (2000) declared that the government would expand policies to attract and hire overseas Chinese talent and to encourage international students to come back. In 2003 the Personnel department declared that it wanted the talent coming back "to innovate and register new companies that served the nation." (Li 2010, Section 8.7) describes a host of programs that offered high salaries and opportunities for returning researchers: Changjiang Scholarship fellowships, various province-level fellowships; distinguished young scholar awards, and the joint Research Fund for Overseas Chinese Young Scholars to do part of their work at a Chinese institute. In addition, China sought to attract foreign-born talent to lead research activities in China, in particular through the 1000 Talents Program.[21]

Table 4 documents the concentration of Chinese students overseas in the United States. Indicative of the preference of Chinese students for the United States, the US share of Chinese overseas students far exceed the US share of international students from outside China. Between 2007 and 2012, the Chinese

---

21. Mara Hvistendahl. (October 2014). *Science.*

TABLE 4 Growing Mainland China–US Special Relation in International Education

Year	Students Going Abroad (per 10,000)	Students Going to the United States (per 10,000)	Proportion Going to the United States	Proportion of Mainland Chinese among International Students in the United States
2005	14.24	6.3	0.44	–
2006	14.71	6.7	0.46	–
2007	16.64	8.1	0.49	11.6
2008	17.94	9.7	0.54	13.0
2009	22.32	12.1	0.54	14.6
2010	28.47	15.8	0.55	18.5
2011	33.97	19.4	0.57	21.8
2012	39.96	23.6	0.59	25.4
2013	41.39	–	–	28.7

Notes: Data source for first three columns is Ministry of Education of the PRC and the data are collected by www.eol.cn. The last column is from open door data (http://www.iie.org/Research-and-Publications/Open-Doors).

international students going to the United States increased from an already high 44% to 59%. With more Chinese enrolling in US colleges and universities, China's proportion of US international students grew from 12% (in 2007) to 29% (in 2012), exceeding China's share of all international students. In 2013 the 236,000 students from China to the United States was over twice the number from the second largest supplier, India (Institute of International Education 2014).

Furthering the link between China and the United States, a larger proportion of Chinese earning PhDs in the United States remain there than graduates from any other country. An analysis of the social security numbers of foreign-born students by Finn (2014) shows that 86% of Chinese PhD graduates of 2006 worked in the United States 5 years later, the highest rate of staying from a sizable country. His data show further that the rate at which Chinese PhDs stay in the United States drops by about two percentage points a year, so that on the order of 75% would remain in the United States 10 years after gaining their PhD.[22] National Science Foundation data on the postgraduate plans of foreign-born PhD graduates tells a similar story. In 2000–2003, 92.5% of new S&E doctorate graduates from China planned to stay in the United States—a figure above those for all countries, including India, where relatively many PhDs planned to remain in the United States. From 2000 to 2003 to 2008 to 2011, however, the proportion of Chinese planning to stay fell to 85.6% (NSB, 2014, Appendix Table 3-22).

---

22. Consistent with this, data for graduates of 2001 (Finn, 2014, Figures 2 and 3) show modest declines in stay rates for cohorts of foreign-born PhDs of all nationalities.

Does China benefit or lose from having so many international students working in the United States or in other foreign countries upon completion of their studies? The early "brain drain" literature worried that developing countries suffered from the immigration of highly educated workers, but more recent analyses stress the value of information flows from people working overseas back to their country of birth that can speed up economic development.[23] Whether the benefits from having researchers overseas dominate the initial brain drain concerns about the reduced supply of researchers in the home country is not known. Given the huge increase in the supply of S&E PhDs in China, it is at least plausible that the value of information flows exceeds the loss of supply because of international students remaining in the United States and other advanced countries.

2. CHINA BECOMES A RESEARCH GIANT

2.1 China's Emerging S&E Research

China massively increased its R&D expenditures and demand for researchers in the 1990s and 2000s. In 1990 China spent negligible amounts on R&D. Two decades later, China's research spending surpassed that of all of the major R&D spending countries save the United States (Figure 2). While China spent less on R&D than the European Union, the ratio of R&D spending to GDP in China jumped from 0.76 in 1999 to 1.84 in 2011, nearly the same ratio as the European Union. Extrapolating the trends in R&D spending of China, the European Union, and the United States in 2014, the Organisation for Economic Co-operation and Development expected that China would surpass the European Union in total R&D in 2014–2015 and surpass the United States in 2019.[24]

The increased supply of professionals with doctorates and other scientists and engineers, expansion of higher education, and increase in R&D spending set the stage for a huge increase in the key measurable outputs from scientific research, academic papers, and citations to those papers.[25] Panel A of Table 5 shows the quantity of scientific papers in the United States, Japan, Germany, United Kingdom, and China in 1990, 2000, and 2012. China jumped from being a minor producer of papers to become a major producer between 1990 and 2012. Its share of world papers tripled from 3.3% in 2000 to 13.7% in 2012. The contrast of China's rising position in the production of papers with Japan's

---

23. Docquier and Rapoport (2012) provide a valuable overview of how this literature has changed.

24. Data can be found at http://www.oecd.org/newsroom/china-headed-to-overtake-eu-us-in-science-technology-spending.htm.

25. In China, as in other countries, the vast majority of papers have UNIV or COLL in their addresses, whereas few have addresses of firms. Tabulating addresses in China, we found that 70.1% are universities (which are defined as names that include "UNIV" or "COLL"), whereas 23.3% are institutes (which are defined as names that include "INST" or "ACAD," usually the Chinese Academy of Sciences or Social Sciences). Therefore, in China, over 93% of the papers are from universities or institutes (the above-mentioned two have little overlap).

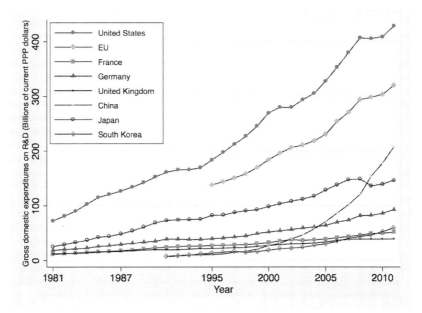

FIGURE 2 Gross expenditures on research and development (R&D) by country and area, 1981–2011. EU, European Union; PPP, purchasing power parity. *Notes: The figure is from Science and Engineering Indicator (2014). The data source is Organization for Economic Co-operation and Development Main Science and Technology Indicators (2013/1). Data are not available for all countries in all years.*

declining position is striking. In 2000 China had one-third as many papers as Japan, but in 2010 China had twice as many papers as Japan.

What about the quality of Chinese science? The most widely used metric for measuring the quality of scientific output is the citations that a paper garners. Because citations are influenced by the social norms of citations in different fields and by the network links among scientists, as well as by the "innate quality" of the science itself, citations are an imperfect measure of the scientific contribution of a paper (Adler, Ewing, & Taylor, 2009). Because scientists in a given area are more likely to cite papers written by people in the same locale, papers with a country address from a major science-producing country such as the United States generally receive more citations than papers from countries with smaller scientific communities, even if the papers include comparable scientific content.[26] These problems notwithstanding, citations remain the most widely used indicator of the scientific contribution of a paper. A paper cited by more scientists has greater value than one of comparable quality cited by fewer scientists.

To examine the position of China in citations, panel B of Table 5 records the share of the top 1% cited papers with addresses for China and other leading

26. NSB, *Science and engineering indicator 2014*, Table 5-26.

TABLE 5 Quantity and Quality of Papers by Country Addresses, 1990–2012

Panel A: Quantity of Papers

	Papers (n)			Share of World Papers (%)		
	1990	2000	2012	1990	2000	2012
World	508,795	619,680	852,110	100	100	100
United States	191,559	212,781	262,266	32.5	34.3	30.8
China	6,285	20,900	116,633	1.2	3.3	13.7
United Kingdom	39,069	59,855	71,156	7.7	9.7	8.4
Germany	32,295	55,648	70,533	6.3	9	8.3
Japan	38,570	61,343	55,316	7.6	9.9	6.5

Panel B: Quality of Papers

	Share of Top 1%		Relative Share (Share of Top 1%/Share of All Papers)	
	2002	2012	2002	2012
United States	57	46.4	1.8	1.7
European Union	28.2	29.8	0.8	0.9
China	0.3	5.8	0.1	0.4
Japan	5	4	0.6	0.6

Notes: Data source are NSB, Science and Engineering Indicators 2004, Table 5-35 and NSB, Science and Engineering Indicators 2014, Tables 5-41 and 5-57.

producers of scientific papers. The table also reports the ratio of China's share of the top 1% of cited papers to its share of all papers. This ratio exceeds 1 when a country has a higher share of the top 1% papers than of all papers and falls short of 1 in the opposite situation. It is a rough indicator of the average quality of papers. By these metrics, China lags behind the lead countries in the quality of its scientific output. In 2002, China had a negligible absolute share and modest relative share of the top 1% of papers. Both statistics increase through 2012, however, with China moving ahead of Japan in its share of top 1% papers. Still, China fell far short of reaching the position of the United States and European Union in top cited papers. It is easier to leap forward in the quantity than in the quality of research activity.

2.2 More International Collaborations

Science has increasingly moved from individual researchers to teams of researchers, as evidenced by a continuous upward trend in the number of authors per paper (Adams, Black, Clemmons, & Stephan, 2005; Wuchty, Jones, & Uzzi, 2007). Scientific research also has increasingly become international, with the proportion of papers with coauthors from different countries trending upward even more rapidly (Adams, 2013; National Science Board, 2014).

While the number of authors per paper increased in China as in other countries, Table 6 shows that China diverged from the trend in increased internationalization of papers. The ratio of articles with two or more international addresses relative to all in-country articles (shown in the column "Share of Country S&E Articles Internationally Coauthored") increased worldwide save for China. China's increase in articles was fueled by papers written by within-country collaborations,[27] presumably because the massive growth of researchers in China made it relatively easy for Chinese scientists to find coauthors in their own country.[28]

Turning to the countries with which Chinese researchers collaborated, the column "Country's Share of China's international collaborations" records the ratio of papers with at least one address from China and at least one from the specified country relative to the total number of Chinese international collaborations. The large and increasing share for the United States, China's biggest collaborator by far, is striking. In 2012, the United States accounted for 47.5% of China's international collaborations.

The column labeled "China's share of Country's International Collaborations" shows that the growth of Chinese papers was so large that China's share

---

27. The higher share of internationally coauthored papers for individual countries than for the world in Table 6 is because the tabulations count an international paper with coauthors from two countries as a single paper at the world level but as two international papers at the country level, with one for each country.
28. The same pattern is observed in Korea, which also has zoomed forward in the number of researchers, the amount of research spending, and the number of papers written (Freeman, 2015).

TABLE 6 Share of Articles Internationally Co-authored and Country Shares of Collaborations

	Share of Articles Internationally Co-authored (%)		Country's Share of China's International Collaboration (%)		China's Share of Country's International Collaboration (%)	
	1997	2012	1997	2012	1997	2012
World	15.7	24.9	–	–	4.1	16.1
China	25.7	26.7	–	–	–	–
United States	19.3	34.7	35.1	47.5	3.2	16.2
Japan	16.4	30.0	8.2	8.8	3.4	18.1
Germany	35.5	55.5	11.0	8.1	2.3	7.0
United Kingdom	31.0	55.1	11.1	9.5	2.4	8.2

Notes: Data are tabulated from Science and Engineering Indicators 2014, Tables 5-41 and 5-56.

of international papers increased nearly fourfold, from 4.1% in 1997 to 16% in 2012. China became the United States' number one international collaborator, surpassing the United Kingdom, Canada, and Germany in the numbers of co-addressed papers.

2.3 It Matters: Associations with Scientific Quality

To understand how international collaborations affect the quality of China's scientific papers, we regressed the impact factor of the journal that published a paper[29] and citations to a paper 5 years after it was published to various measures of international collaborations. Table 7 records the estimated regression coefficients and standard errors linking impact factors and citations to dummy variable measures for whether the first author and/or last author of a paper had a Chinese name (1) or had a non-Chinese name (0). To identify Chinese-named authors we use William Kerr's name–ethnicity matching program (Kerr, 2008; Kerr & Lincoln, 2010), which assigns an ethnic identity to authors based on the distribution of names by ethnicity.[30] The identification hinges on the fact that last names such as Zhang are likely to be Chinese, names like Johnson are likely to be Anglo-American, names like Singh are likely to be Indian, and so on.

The sample for these regressions is the papers that appeared in the PubMed database for life and medical sciences. We use this sample rather than the Web of

29. The impact factor of the journal of publication has problems as a measure of quality, as noted by European Association of Science Editors (2007).

30. The program divides ethnicity into nine categories: Chinese (CHN), Anglo-Saxon/English (ENG), European (EUR), Indian/Hindi/South Asian (HIN), Hispanic/Filipino (HIS), Japanese (JAP), Korean (KOR), Russian (RUS), and Vietnamese (VNM).

TABLE 7 Impact Factors and Five Year Citation Rates for Papers Written by Chinese Authors with International Connections, Based on PubMed Data

Sample	Non-China-Based Papers		China-Based Papers with All Chinese Authors		China-Addressed Papers	
Variables	Impact factor	Five-year citations	Impact factor	Five-year citations	Impact factor	Five-year citations
Surname Ethnicity of First and Last Authors (Reference Group is Anglo-Saxon)						
First author Chinese	0.276***	2.216***				
	(0.00730)	(0.0602)				
Last author Chinese	0.191***	2.189***				
	(0.00950)	(0.0783)				
Overseas Experience (Reference Group is Authors with No Oversea Experience)						
US			0.689***	1.852***		
			(0.0698)	(0.371)		
Other country			0.671***	1.770***		
			(0.0591)	(0.288)		
English journal			0.602***	0.743***		
			(0.0297)	(0.221)		
Collaboration or Country Where the Paper is Produced (Reference Group is China Only)						
China-only US collaboration					0.598***	1.967***
					(0.0251)	(0.177)
China-only other collaboration					0.263***	0.799***
					(0.0282)	(0.199)
China–US and other collaboration					0.717***	4.312***
					(0.0447)	(0.315)
Observations	5,884,586	5,884,586	51,802	51,802	118,837	118,837
R^2	0.388	0.168	0.405	0.265	0.421	0.208

Note: Covariates controlled for in all columns include indicators of number of authors, number of addresses, number of references, language of paper, countries, publication years, and fields. Standard errors are in parentheses.

Science sample of all papers because it allows us to use the algorithm by Torvik & Smalheiser (2009) for differentiating same-named people, which is important in some comparisons. Because we are interested in the relationship between China and the United States, we restrict the sample to the papers with any address in the United States or China. Because the life and medical sciences publish the most papers of any scientific fields, our analysis treats a large sample. To compare likes with likes, we included an array of covariates, listed at the bottom of the table: the number of authors, number of addresses, and number of references—all of which are positively associated with impact factors and citations; as well as dummy variables for language of the paper (most are in English), for the country addresses, for the year of the paper, and for the field of the journal of publication.

The column "Non-China-based papers with Chinese-named authors" records the estimated relation between having first or last Chinese names and both the impact factor of the journal in which a paper appeared and 5-year forward citations for papers with all addresses in the United States, and thus relate to the research contribution of Chinese researchers usually working in advanced countries. The surname ethnicities are divided into four categories: Anglo-Saxon, Chinese, other Asian, and other non-Anglo-Saxon. The reference group is Anglo-Saxon authors and the coefficients on other Asian and other non-Anglo-Saxon are not reported. The coefficients for Chinese-named authors are positive for both the impact factor and citation regressions, indicating that the papers with first or last author having Chinese surnames gain greater attention and are more likely to be published in high-impact journals than papers by other papers. One likely reason for this is positive selectivity of Chinese researchers working in the United States and other overseas destinations. Chinese international students and visiting researchers to the United States and elsewhere are often the best and brightest from China, whereas the non-Chinese researchers to which the regression compares them include people with a wider range of research skills. Note, however, that the coefficients on Chinese-named last authors are positive but have a smaller magnitude, especially for impact factor. Because last authors are often the senior authors who have the connections or reputation to best place a paper in more prestigious journals, the smaller effect on impact factors may come from the older generation of Chinese researchers having weak connections in placing papers.

The column "Overseas experience of Chinese authors on China-based papers" distinguish Chinese authors working in China by whether they had published a previous paper based on overseas research, which we define as a paper with no address in China. This definition assures us that the researcher worked outside of China on the earlier paper. It is a conservative estimate of research and publication experience outside China, since an author located in China could have worked outside China with someone in China, and thus have research experience outside China that we would not capture. This measurement error should downward bias our estimated coefficients on the overseas experience variable. Even so, the regressions show that past overseas publication experience in the United States (defined as a paper with all addresses in the United States) or elsewhere (other papers with no China addresses) by China-based authors are associated with higher impact factors and citations. We report the coefficients of the English-language dummy to show the huge value of publishing in English-language journals, which invariably have higher impact factors than other journals and are associated with more citations.

One likely reason for the estimated positive coefficients on the overseas experience variables is that the Chinese researchers learned valuable skills from international experience, ranging from better research techniques to gaining insight into the latest scientific ideas, which often depend on tacit knowledge from the leading researchers who developed them. Another likely reason is that working overseas created connections that increase the likelihood that international journals accept someone's papers and of generating citations from overseas researchers. It is also possible that the positive effect of overseas experience may reflect the positive selection of researchers who published papers while working overseas.

Finally, the column "Overseas collaboration on China-addressed papers" examines the relation between papers based on collaborations of China-based scientists with scientists in the United States or in other countries and the impact factors and forward citations to their papers. The sample for these calculations is limited to papers in PubMed with at least one address in China. Because papers written in China have, on average, lower impact factors and citations than those written in the United States and other major research-producing locations, we expect that collaborations between researchers in China and researchers in advanced countries raises the impact factor and the number of citations of collaborative papers relative to papers written solely in China. The estimated coefficients confirm this expectation. The regressions also show that collaborating with US-based scientists has larger positive effects on impact factors and citations than does collaborating with scientists in other countries. This result fits with the fact that US-based papers average higher impact factors and citations than papers from most other countries. The estimates in the last line of the column "China–US & other collaboration" shows that papers with US and other country collaborations have the largest impact factors and citations. The scientific input that goes into multicountry papers is often greater than that of smaller collaborations, in part because of the use of special equipment, such as huge telescopes, or special research facilities, like the CERN Hadron collider, or involvement in large clinical trials. A paper with authors from many counties is also likely to gain greater attention by tapping into networks of researchers in more countries.

3. CONCLUSION

China's leap forward in science and engineering in the 1990s and 2000s is one of the defining events in modern intellectual history and as important to the future of the world as China's extraordinary economic growth. With hundreds of thousands of Chinese researchers contributing to the advance of scientific knowledge, and millions of Chinese engineers and scientists working to apply modern scientific technology to the production of goods and services, the frontier of useful knowledge will almost surely advance more rapidly than if China had remained a scientific backwater.

Our analysis shows that this achievement was accomplished not only by China's decision to rebuild itself from the disaster of the Cultural Revolution and Mao Zedong's "great leap forward" in the 1960s but also by China accessing to the global higher education and research system, particularly through a "special relation" in education and research with the United States, the world's leading scientific power (Freeman & Huang, 2014). The special relation took the form of international student flows, where the United States is the main destination of China's overseas students; China is the single largest source of international students in the United States. The high rate at which Chinese PhDs from US universities remain in the United States, together with immigrant scientists and engineers, creates a sizable share of researchers with US addresses; to each country being the major partner of the other in international collaborations on scientific papers; and to the higher impact factor of journals of publication and numbers of citations of papers with Chinese addresses from US and other foreign collaborations. Much more can be done to explore the special relation between China and the United States and China's education and research link to other countries, as well. Analysis of the extent to which collaborations develop between faculty advisers and their PhD students and/or among students in the same university or laboratory; the extent to which people of Chinese ethnicity in the United States (or other foreign addresses) disproportionately collaborate with researchers in China and whether any such pattern holds for people of other ethnicity (which we would expect to be the case); and the contribution of Chinese government support for international students and research visits on scientific outcomes are natural follow-ups of the findings in this paper. More broadly, all of our results regarding the relation between the United States and China could be fruitfully expanded to include other countries.

Ideally, the China–US collaboration in the education of scientists and engineers and in research will spur the development and spread of knowledge in ways that benefit not only the Chinese and American people but also people around the world and that strengthens the cooperative relations between the two countries. Globalization of knowledge may not be the "one ring that rules them all," which Freeman (2014, pp. 11–43) hypothesized, but it is surely a necessary ring for the world to overcome its problems and to improve lives everywhere. We look forward to China's increasing contribution to the global world of knowledge production. In research, perhaps more than anywhere else, the emerging China needs the world, and the world needs an emerging China. 崛起的中国需要世界，世界需要一个崛起的中国。

REFERENCES

Adams, James D. (2013). Collaborations: the fourth age of research. *Nature*, *497*(7451), 557–560.

Adams, James D., Grant C. Black, J. Roger Clemmons, and Paula E. Stephan (2005). "Scientific teams and institutional collaborations: evidence from US universities, 1981–1999." *Research Policy*, 34(3), 259–285.

Adler, Robert, Ewing, John, & Taylor, Peter (2009). Citation statistics. *Statistical Science*, *24*(1), 1.

Docquier, F., & Rapoport, H. (2012). Globalization, brain drain, and development. *Journal of Economic Literature*, 681–730.

European Association of Science Editors. (2007). *The EASE statement on inappropriate use of impact factors*. Available at http://www.ease.org.uk/sites/default/files/ease_statement_ifs_final.pdf.

Finn, M. G. (2014). *Stay rates of foreign doctorate recipients from US universities, 2011*. National Center for Science and Engineering Statistics of the National Science Foundation. Available at http://orise.orau.gov/files/sep/stay-rates-foreign-doctorate-recipients-2011.pdf.

Freeman, Richard B. (2014). *"One ring to rule them all? Globalization of knowledge and knowledge creation" Nordic economic policy review: Globalization, labour market institutions and wage structures, number 1, 2013*. Available at NBER Working Paper 19301 http://www.nber.org/papers/w19301.

Freeman, Richard B. (2015). *Knowledge, knowledge, my economy for knowledge*. Korea Development Institute.

Freeman, Richard B., & Huang, Wei (2014). In *"Research collaborations between Chinese and US scientists and engineers: A new special relationship?" Presented at AEA meeting, January 5, 2014 Philadelphia*.

Hvistendahl, M. (2014). China tries to kick its salt habit. *Science*, *345*(6202), 1268–1269.

Kerr, William R. (2008). Ethnic scientific communities and international technology diffusion. *The Review of Economics and Statistics*, *90*(3), 518–537.

Kerr, William R., & Lincoln, William F. (2010). The supply side of innovation: H-1B visa reforms and U.S. ethnic invention. *Journal of Labor Economics* University of Chicago Press, *28*(3), 473–508, 07.

Li, Haizheng. (2010). Higher education in China: Complement or competition to US universities? In *American universities in a global market* (pp. 269–304). University of Chicago Press.

The National Academies. (May 2005). Committee on Science, Engineering, and Public Policy. *Policy Implications of International Graduate Students and Postdoctoral Scholars in the United States, Washington, DC*.

National Science Board (NSB). (2014). *Science and engineering indicators 2014*. Arlington, VA: National Science Foundation (NSB 14–01).

OECD. (2009). *Review of tertiary education in China*.

OECD. (2011). *Education at a Glance 2011: OECD Indicators*. OECD Publishing. http://dx.doi.org/10.1787/eag-2011-en.

OECD. (2012). *Education at a Glance 2012: OECD Indicators*. OECD Publishing. http://dx.doi.org/10.1787/eag-2012-en.

Torvik, Vetle I., & Smalheiser, Neil R. (2009). Author name disambiguation in MEDLINE. *ACM Transactions on Knowledge Discovery from Data (TKDD)*, *3*(3), 11.

UNESCO, Institute for statistics, on line files, 2010.

Wei, Chunjuan Nancy, & Brock, Darryl E. (Eds.). (2013). *Mr. Science and chairman Mao's cultural revolution: Science and technology in modern China*. Rowman & Littlefield.

WIPO. (2014). World Intellectual Property Indicators. *Economics & Statistics Series*. http://www.wipo.int/edocs/pubdocs/en/wipo_pub_941_2014.pdf.

Wuchty, Stephan, Jones, Benjamin F., & Uzzi, Brian (May 18, 2007). The increasing dominance of teams in production of knowledge. *Science*, *316*(5827), 1036–1039.

FURTHER READING

Australia, Department of Immigration and Border Protection.

Bound John, Sarah Turner, & Patrick Walsh (March 2009). *Internationalization of US doctorate education* (NBER Working Paper 14792). http://www.nber.org/papers/w14792.

Cao, C. (2004). *China's scientific elite*. Routledge.

Cao Cong & Denis Simon. (2007). *China's emerging technological edge*. Cambridge University Press.

Gomory, Ralph E., & William J. Baumol. (2001). *Global trade and conflicting national interests*. Cambridge, MA: MIT Press.

International Mathematical Union. (2008). *Joint IMU/ICIAM/IMS—Committee on quantitative assessment of research citation statistics*. Available at http://www.mathunion.org/fileadmin/IMU/Report/CitationStatistics.pdf.

OECD, M. (2008). *OECD reviews of innovation policy: China. Chapter 6 human resource for science and technology and innovation in China*. Paris: OECD Publishing.

OECD. (2013). *Science and technology scoreboard*.

OECD. (2014). *Education at a glance 2014: OECD indicators*. Paris: OECD Publishing, http://dx.doi.org/10.1787/eag-2014-en.

People's Republic of China, Ministry of Education, Educational Statistics Year book of China, various editions.

Science, technology and innovation (STI) performance of China D9: Final report annex http://eeas.europa.eu/delegations/china/documents/eu_china/research_innovation/4_innovation/sti_china_study_annex.pdf.

Springut Micah, Stephen Schlaikjer, & David Chen. (2011). *China's program for science and technology modernization: Implications for American competitiveness: Prepared for the US-China economic and security review commission*. CENTRA Technology.

Websites Referenced in Paper

http://en.wikipedia.org/wiki/World_population.

http://en.wikipedia.org/wiki/Demographics_of_China.

http://www.oecd.org/newsroom/china-headed-to-overtake-eu-us-in-science-technology-spending.htm.

http://www.nsf.gov/statistics/doctorates/pdf/sed2000.pdf.

http://www.nsf.gov/statistics/seind04/c2/c2s4.htm.

www.eol.cn.

http://www.iie.org/Research-and-Publications/Open-Doors.

Chapter 7

factors → mobility of researchers

Which Factors Influence the International Mobility of Research Scientists?

Silvia Appelt[1], Brigitte van Beuzekom[1], Fernando Galindo-Rueda[1,3], Roberto de Pinho[2]

[1]Economic Analysis and Statistics Division, Directorate for Science, Technology and Innovation, Organisation for Economic Co-operation and Development (OECD), Paris, France; [2]Science, Technology and Innovation Indicators Unit, Ministry of Science, Technology and Innovation, Brazil; [3]IZA, Institute for the Study of Labour

Chapter Outline

1. INTRODUCTION

It is widely held that mobile talent contributes to the creation and diffusion of knowledge, particularly tacit knowledge as it is often shared through direct personal interactions (OECD, 2001, 2008, 2010). The international mobility of skilled human resources can play an important role in driving scientific progress not only at the level of a given country but also on a global basis. Highly skilled individuals exhibit particular mobility patterns whose implications have warranted attention by researchers and policy makers alike. It is, for example, known that the share of foreign born among doctorate holders is higher than for other tertiary level graduates (Carrington & Detragiache, 1998; Docquier & Marfouk, 2006; OECD, 2008). Figures from the OECD/UNESCO/Eurostat study on the careers of doctorate holders[1] reveal that in 2009, an average of 14% of national citizens with a doctoral degree had been internationally mobile in the previous 10 years (Auriol, Misu, & Freeman, 2013), confirming earlier findings reported in Auriol (2010).

Factors such as relative wage premia, career advancement and research opportunities, research facilities, the opportunity to work with significant peers and in prestigious institutions, and increased autonomy and freedom to debate and carry out research are considered to be strong drivers of mobility among the highly skilled.[2] These factors come into play alongside migration policy settings as well as family and personal factors (OECD, 2010). The globalization of the education and research systems associated with policies aimed at attracting talent appears to have contributed to the international mobility of the very highly skilled. Global competition for talent operates at the level of institutions and firms, and governments also play an active role through a number of policies.

From the perspective of organizations investing in knowledge embedded in people, a potential downside of mobility is the risk that the period over which benefits can be accrued may be too short to make the investment worthwhile. As a result, the discussion on international mobility of skilled labor has often been framed as a competitive process in which individual countries or organizations strive to attract or retain talent. However, while highly relevant, this perspective underplays the broader significance of knowledge flows in a global science and innovation system, ignoring in large part the role of offsetting flows and the scope for specialization and mutual gains arising from mobility. For example, returning professionals can make the knowledge that they have acquired available to their home country and can also maintain networks abroad that facilitate continuing knowledge exchange and collaboration.

Most countries have in place a range of policies focused on assisting and encouraging the mobility of scientists or highly skilled individuals more generally, with policies that range from economic incentives to encourage inflows, immigration-oriented assistance, procedures for recognizing foreign qualifications, and support for research abroad (OECD, 2008). There is generally more support for inflows of researchers and other highly skilled than for outflows, perhaps because countries judge outward mobility to be already adequate or because they

---

1. For further information on indicators on the careers of doctorate holders, see www.oecd.org/sti/cdh.
2. The study on the Careers of Doctorate Holders indicates that academic motivations are the main self-reported drivers of past and planned international mobility decisions. Subject to constraints, researchers appear to use international mobility as a mechanism to gain personal access to leading researchers, centers of expertise, and networks that enable them to progress in their research careers.

are reluctant to encourage it in light of the aforementioned arguments (OECD, 2014). The Organisation for Economic Co-operation and Development (OECD) Innovation Strategy of 2010 stated that policies on mobility should aim to support knowledge flows and the creation of enduring linkages and networks across countries, enabling movement on a short-term or circular basis (OECD, 2010). Several national agencies and even nonprofit organizations provide support for academic sabbaticals abroad and to host visiting researchers from overseas.[3]

This chapter investigates the potential drivers of the mobility of a population of particularly high relevance to policy makers using a new measure of international scientist mobility. A recently developed indicator for the OECD Science, Technology and Industry Scoreboard 2013 tracks changes in the affiliation of scientific authors publishing in scholarly journals over the period 1996–2011 (OECD, 2013a). Changes in authors' institutional affiliations, as reported on publications, are not always related to actual changes in scientists' location but can serve as a reasonably good proxy measure of mobility. A significant advantage is that the use of publication records provides a more comprehensive coverage across all countries in a way that is not subject to the gaps in survey coverage that can be found in related international analyses of scientist mobility.

This chapter seeks to explore which economic, cultural and scientific factors, and linkages between origin and destination countries help explain the observed, aggregate international scientist mobility patterns over the 1996–2011 period. Using bibliometric data to capture scientist mobility independent of patenting activity, it sets out to provide further evidence on a number of topical questions:

- Which model best describes the international scientist mobility network—a net flow, brain-drain picture, or a more complex brain circulation pattern?
- How does scientist mobility behave relative to scientific collaboration?
- Which aspects of absorptive capacity (e.g., R&D intensity of host and sending country) matter as a factor for driving scientist flows? Is mobility sensitive to variables under policy control?

The remainder of this chapter is structured as follows: Section 2 reviews the literature on the mobility of scientists as a specific group among the population of highly skilled individuals. Section 3 sets out the analytical framework, describing the empirical approach and research questions addressed by the empirical study. Highlighting the observed patterns of scientist mobility, Section 4 describes the construction of the analytical database and defines the variables employed in the regression analysis. Section 5 presents the econometric results. Section 6 concludes with some suggestions for further research.

---

3. The so-called "sandwich" PhD grants programs available from Brazil's main funding agencies could be seen as a concrete example of such policies. The PhD candidate begins and finishes her PhD studies at a Brazilian institution with up to a one-year-long period abroad, seeking the benefits of mobility while requiring the return and maintaining strong ties with the original home institutions. http://www.cienciasemfronteiras.gov.br/web/csf-eng/home.

2. REVIEW OF THE LITERATURE

The body of empirical work on the incidence, causes, and impacts of mobility among the highly skilled, and among scientists in particular, has drawn on various types of data sources. These include targeted surveys (Auriol, 2010; Auriol et al., 2013; Franzoni, Scellato, & Stephan, 2012; Gibson & McKenzie, 2013; Scellato, Franzoni, & Stephan, 2012; Trippl, 2013), general surveys, and censuses as typically used for migration (Docquier & Rapoport, 2009, 2012), repositories of curricula vitae (Bozeman & Corley, 2004; Cañibano, Otamende, & Solís, 2011; Dietz, Chompalov, Bozeman, O'Neil Lane, & Park, 2000; Jonkers & Tijssen, 2008), or a combination thereof (Hunter, Oswald, & Charlton, 2009). In addition to these sources, published documents subject to some form of expert validation, as in the case of scientific publications subject to peer review and patent applications subject to examination (Trajtenberg, 2005 and other references cited below), can also provide a basis for tracking the mobility of disambiguated authors and inventors, respectively.

Scientific publication records not only help measure international scientific collaboration through coauthorship patterns (Abramo, D'Angelo, & Solazzi, 2012; Luukkonen, Tijssen, Persson, & Siversten, 1993; Narin, Stevens, & Whitlow, 1991; Science Europe and Elsevier, 2013; Wagner, 2005; Wagner & Leydesdorff, 2005; Yoshikane & Kagura, 2004), but can also inform the analysis of scientist mobility (Conchi & Michels, 2014; Elsevier, 2011, 2013; Laudel, 2003; Moed, Aisati, & Plume, 2013; Pierson & Cotegrave, 2000; Science Europe and Elsevier, 2013), alone or in combination with other data sources (Baruffaldi & Landoni, 2012; Jonkers & Cruz-Castro, 2013). Bibliometrics-based work on scientist mobility further seeks to shed light on the incidence and consequences of brain circulation. The focus may be on a defined group of scientists in a country such as those who are doctorate holders (Pierson & Cotegrave, 2000), those in a specific scientific domain (Laudel, 2003), or the whole population of scientists in a specific set of countries (Conchi & Michels, 2014; Moed et al., 2013; Science Europe and Elsevier, 2013; Weinberg, 2011). International scientist collaboration tends to occur more frequently than international scientist migration (Science Europe and Elsevier, 2013). The increase in scientific collaboration is well documented, but it is not clear whether scientist mobility is outpacing collaboration or failing to keep up with it. Compared to other population groups, the relative magnitude of skilled migration has increased over time (Docquier & Rapoport, 2009, 2012; UN-DESA and OECD, 2013). Despite their potentially far-reaching implications for international knowledge creation and diffusion, empirical evidence about the drivers and impact of scientist mobility remains scarce.

The findings of empirical work on inventor mobility (Breschi & Lissoni, 2009; Breschi, Lissoni, & Tarasconi, 2014; Hoisl, 2007; Miguélez & Fink, 2013; Miguélez & Moreno, 2013; Trajtenberg, 2005; Trajtenberg, Shiff, & Melamed, 2006) may provide some first indication of which factors potentially influence international scientist mobility patterns, as there may be a nonnegligible degree of overlap between the populations of patenting inventors and publishing scientists. Inventor mobility studies highlight the role of inventor productivity as well as geographical, social, and technological distance between origin and destination country in shaping their international mobility patterns. Mobility is generally found to be positively associated with inventor productivity as proxied, for example, by the education level of the inventor and the use of external sources of knowledge such as university research or scientific literature (Hoisl, 2007).

Geographic proximity between regions is also found to encourage inventor mobility (Miguélez & Moreno, 2013). Economic (e.g., transportation costs) and social factors such as cultural and linguistic similarities and personal linkages may explain this phenomenon, in particular as coinvention networks and interpersonal formal ties of inventors (Breschi & Lissoni, 2009) tend to be regional in nature. Mobility of researchers provides a principal way of knowledge diffusion, facilitating access to localized knowledge spillovers (Audretsch & Feldman, 1996, 2004; Jaffe, Trajtenberg, & Henderson, 1993) or to a leading international scientific collaboration network. While mobility can induce scientific collaboration, new or existing collaboration ties may also drive mobility decisions, that is, the link between mobility and collaboration is likely to run in both directions. Furthermore, the same set of factors may impact mobility and collaboration decisions in a similar fashion. The technological proximity of regional scientific undertakings, for instance, proves to encourage both mobility and collaboration (Miguélez & Moreno, 2013).[4]

3. A FRAMEWORK FOR ANALYZING THE DETERMINANTS OF SCIENTIST MOBILITY FLOWS

This chapter adopts an empirical gravity model of international flows to describe and analyze new aggregate, bilateral data on international scientist mobility. The gravity framework has been applied to several types of models in the social sciences, in particular in dealing with trade and foreign direct investment (Baldwin & Taglioni, 2006; Bergstrand, 1985; De Groot, Linders, Rietveld, & Subramanian, 2004; Jansen & Piermartini, 2009; Kleinert & Toubal, 2010; Linders & De Groot, 2006; Neumayer, 2011; Rose, 2007; Zwinkels & Beugelsdijk, 2010) and in the analysis of migration (Clark, Hatton, & Williamson, 2007; Karemera, Iwuagwu Oguledo, Davis, 2000; Mayda, 2010). It has also been used more recently by Miguélez & Moreno (2013) and Fink, Miguélez, & Raffo (2013) in the study of inventor mobility. Gravity models predict bilateral flows based on the attributes of origin and destination economies for the phenomenon

[Handwritten margin notes: "mobility ↓ collaboration / but this collaboration does not restrict to... but it doesn't specify researchers (domestic or expat...)"]

---

4. Miguélez & Moreno (2013) measure technological similarity as the uncentered correlation between regional vectors of technological patent classes (Jaffe, 1986).

under investigation, and measures of the distance between the two economies that can bear upon the costs and incentives for flows to arise. Empirical gravity models can be consistent with theoretical models of constrained utility—maximizing migration choices.[5]

The model ultimately can be simplified into a regression framework in which the log of flows of scientists from country (i) to country (j), namely y_{ij}, can be written as a function of characteristics of the origin and destination country, m_i and w_j, respectively, as well as a number of measures of the link between origin country (i) and destination country (j), including measures of proximity z_{ij} and other bilateral linkages x_{ij}, and allowing for an error term ε_{ij}:

$$\ln y_{ij} = \alpha \ln x_{ij} + \beta \ln z_{ij} + \theta m_i + \pi w_j + \varepsilon_{ij}$$

Since it is impossible to identify and capture the full range of attributes of origin (m_i) and destination (w_j) locations that may be relevant for the phenomenon of mobility, it is a common approach in the literature to apply fixed effect estimation methods that control for unobserved, potentially correlated, and systematic features related to both origin (u_i) and destination country (v_j). Because the available measure of scientist mobility used in this chapter is time invariant—it reflects the aggregated affiliation flows of a highly specific population over an extended period of time—the identification stems from the cross-sectional variation in destinations (origins) for each origin (destination) economy:

$$\ln y_{ij} = \alpha \ln x_{ij} + \beta \ln z_{ij} + u_i + v_j + \varepsilon_{ij}$$

The empirical analysis proceeds in a staged approach. It starts with a basic model that accounts for a set of standard variables employed in empirical gravity models such as geographical, cultural, and economic proximity, to which further explanatory variables are subsequently added:

- **Model 1** controls for the effect of geographical distance, the existence of a common border, common official language, trade services flows. It also seeks to estimate how scientific dissimilarity and collaboration, international tertiary student and migrant stocks affect the patterns of bilateral scientist mobility over the 1996–2011 period.
- **Model 2** accounts for two distinct categories of service trade flows as well as indicators for travel visa restrictions to provide evidence on the effect of knowledge intensive services and visa policies on bilateral scientist mobility and collaboration over the period 1996–2011.

---

5. Gravity models are regularly used to impute missing bilateral flows in trade and migration databases. This can pose problems in further analysis if no account is made for potential data construction endogeneity. This problem does not apply to our analysis as our dependent variable has been created entirely separate from the explanatory variables.

The distinction between distance (dissimilarity) variables z_{ij} and those that capture the linkages between origin and destination countries x_{ij} reflects the fact that distance-related measures z_{ij} are by construction symmetric ($z_{ij}=z_{ji}$), whereas "oriented flow" variables such as trade or migration are asymmetric. This is relevant for the identification of a number of potential effects in this empirical model of bilateral scientist mobility.

- **Model 3** explores the effect of the counterflows of international students and migrants to shed light on the magnitude and nature of international brain circulation. For example, we are interested in understanding whether the flow of students (migrants) from (j) to (i) has a different impact on scientist flows from (i) to (j), relative to student (migrant) flows from (i) to (j). The following specification is estimated, where the coefficients α and γ would not be separately identified if $x_{ij}=x_{ji}$.

$$\ln y_{ij} = \alpha \ln x_{ij} + \gamma \ln x_{ji} + u_i + v_j + \varepsilon_{ij}.$$

- **Model 4** accounts for changes in the relative scientific and economic conditions between origin and destination country alongside changes in scientist collaboration, international student, and migrant stocks to explore the effect of convergence in science and economic factors that may influence scientists' mobility decisions.

Another approach to control for unobserved heterogeneity is to explore only the variation within each set of country pairs (dyads). Thus, if we take model 3 as reference, the difference in log flows applying within dyad $<i,j>$ is as follows:

$$\ln y_{ij} - \ln y_{ji} = (\alpha - \gamma)(\ln x_{ij} - \ln x_{ji}) + (u_i - v_i + v_j - u_j) + (\varepsilon_{ij} - \varepsilon_{ji}).$$

- **Model 5** implements this approach, which identifies $\alpha - \beta$ under some basic conditions by means of a dyad fixed-effects regression. This not only accounts for unobserved heterogeneity concerning the bond between a given pair of countries but also helps infer the dominant influencing factor in the presence of feedback effects (i.e., whether $\alpha > \gamma$ or $\alpha < \gamma$). The following specification is estimated:

$$\ln y_{ij} = \psi \ln x_{ij} + \mu \ln w_j + \varphi_{<i,j>} + \varepsilon'_{ij},$$

where the dyad fixed effect is defined such that: $\varphi_{<i,j>} = \varphi_{<j,i>}$ and $\psi = \alpha - \gamma$, reflecting the net effect.

In this case, symmetric variables are not identified. Furthermore, identification of additional, idiosyncratic origin and destination fixed effects cannot be completed for both origin and destination countries at the same time. It is, however, possible to identify the role of either origin or destination country features (μ).

This exploratory analysis seeks to document some new and policy-relevant relationships between scientist mobility and a number of fundamental science-related and socioeconomic variables. The estimated relationships may not necessarily reflect causal effects. Clearly, a number of variables such as scientist collaboration, international student and migrant stocks are likely to be endogenous, being possibly influenced by scientist mobility or common unobserved underlying factors. Our econometric analysis is based on aggregate data on scientist mobility and its potential drivers.[6] It relies on cross-sectional variation in data and thus indicates average effects over the reference period. Future work may be able to explore natural experiments within our sample.

The empirical models presented in this chapter are implemented in a negative binominal regression framework to account for zero flows in the dependent variable. We verify the robustness of econometric results to the choice of estimator and specification. Some robustness checks are implemented on the logged regressors by instead applying the log transformation to one plus the relevant variable when the zeroes are genuine, rather than missing observations. To avoid overstating the precision of our estimates and take into account the correlation within dyads, standard errors are clustered by dyad.

4. DATA SOURCES

The analysis of international scientist mobility relies on multiple data sources, including bilateral scientist mobility, collaboration, international student stock, proximity, travel visa policy, R&D intensity, and economic data. This section describes the construction of the analytical database and variables used in the regression analysis.

4.1 Bilateral International Scientist Flows

Bilateral scientist flows have been derived by the OECD using bibliometric data on publications published between 1996 and 2011. Authors of peer-reviewed publications indexed in Elsevier's Scopus Custom Data (OECD licensed version of May 2012) are identified by a unique author ID assigned by Elsevier. Episodes of international mobility and general mobility profiles can be inferred from authors with at least two publications over the reference period, based on the sequence of changes in institutional affiliation revealed in

---

6. Sufficiently broad time windows are required to observe at least two publication events and a potential change in affiliation. As a result, the scope for confining the analysis to shorter time-spans is rather limited.

those publications. Bibliometric indicators can provide a complementary picture of scientist mobility at global level. First developed by Elsevier (2011), they are experimental and require careful interpretation (Moed et al., 2013, 2014).[7] Implied mobility records are less accurate for less prolific authors and for those who move from and into roles for which disclosure in scholarly journals is not the norm, as is often the case of researchers working in industry or researchers in some domains using books as the main scholarly communication vehicle.

We chose to base our analysis on authors with at least two publications over the reference period 1996–2011, rather than restrict the analysis to the most prolific authors, in order to obtain the largest possible sample and minimize the impact of publication bias restricting the analysis to the most productive authors. The bilateral mobility indicators used in this analysis are solely based on the very first and very last reported publication for each individual author. They can be consulted online.[8] This means that a scientist moving from country (i) to country (j) and then from (j) to (k), as implied by her affiliation record, would only count toward the calculation of flows from (i) to (k), thus netting out interim mobility flows. In previous, separate work, the OECD has developed indicators that tease out more detailed mobility patterns that reflect, for example, returning individuals, but not on a bilateral basis.[9]

The choice of reference period and observation windows can also have an impact on the derived indicators. Reported institutional affiliations may indicate the status at the time of publishing and may not reflect where the research took place but do reflect some form of "intellectual presence." A practical challenge faced in identifying mobility through affiliations is the apparently increasing incidence of multiple affiliations. In line with other related works using this source, publication-author records with affiliations in multiple countries were

---

7. A number of studies lend some qualified support to the use of these data for tracking mobility. Laudel (2003) and Conchi & Michels (2014) compared scientist mobility records derived from bibliometric data with those derived from alternative data sources, including CV and self-reported data from scientist surveys. Moed et al. (2014) evaluate the potential and limitations of the bibliometric approach in terms of author profile accuracy and interpretation, looking at the coherence between related statistics and scientist mobility as implied in Scopus publication records for authors in 17 countries. The authors conclude that the bibliometric approach is promising but that its outcomes should be interpreted with care and ideally combined with complementary data sources such as scientist surveys or CV data.

8. A simplified version of the bilateral flow indicators are publicly available from the interactive charts published alongside the 2013 OECD Science, Technology and Industry Scoreboard (OECD, 2013a), using the Tableau® software application. http://www.oecd.org/sti/scoreboard-2013-interactive-charts.htm. The dynamic chart sits under "Researchers on the move," with the heading "Bilateral flows."

9. These related indicators are available on the same link, under the heading "Mobility and impacts."

removed from the database on which the mobility indicator was calculated, as the seemingly least harmful option.[10]

Failure to assign author identification numbers (IDs) consistently over time can also distort mobility estimates by understating mobility when an individual has multiple IDs or overstating it for individuals with common names that are not correctly disambiguated.[11] Changes in academic status from a PhD to a postdoc position or from associate to full professorship cannot be identified based on the information available. The same limitation applies to information about the nationality of mobile scientists. No attempt has been made to classify the institution to which the scientist is affiliated according to institutional sectors, but evidence available elsewhere points to most records coming from individuals affiliated with academic institutions, followed by government and health, with only a minority from the private/business sector.[12]

A significant pitfall of the Scopus version used (May 2012) concerns indexing gaps in the early 2000s, immediately before the launch of Scopus in November 2004. For this period, Scopus performed a range of backfill activities and material already present in the databases that fed into other Elsevier systems. For years 2001–2003, two such databases, namely EMBASE and Compendex, did not capture complete article data. In a number of cases only the first author's identity and affiliation were captured.[13] Visual inspection of the data shows a short-lived increase in the share of single-author publications over that same period that is consistent with the lack of coauthor profiles for a significant subset of the population. Using simple interpolation assumptions, the number of documents with missing noncorresponding authors could be as large as 25% of the total number of documents indexed. Because missing authors in one document can be picked up in other articles published in the same year, the severity of this problem will be less pronounced. Indeed, looking at the number of unique authors over time, the author coverage gap appears to be on the order of 10% or less, still significant but much less pronounced.[14] Overall, this implies that mobility records for individuals who are not first authors will be incomplete through this short spell, but only provided that their first or last publication goes missing as a result of this coverage gap. This may bias downward

---

10. Approaches for dealing with the multiple affiliation phenomenon would require additional assumptions that cannot be tested with the data at hand. Alternatively, the implied observed "mobility" from a move from (*i*) to (*j*) when (*i*) is retained as affiliation could have been dealt with by weighting such flow as 0.5 as opposed to a full count, but in the interest of simplicity this approach was not pursued at this stage.

11. A nonprofit global initiative—the open researcher and contributor ID (ORCID)—seeks to deal with this problem by assigning unique identifiers linkable to an individual's research output. Elsevier's Scopus database, used in this study, is linking its data to ORCID IDs. http://orcid.org.

12. See for example: http://www.scimagoir.com/index.php.

13. Personal communication between one of the authors and Elsevier staff.

14. Diagnostics are available from the authors upon request.

the measurement of bilateral flows, particularly understating flows from and to countries that are less likely to host first-in-line authors who in some fields tend to be the leading and first-listed authors. The direction of this bias and its potential implications for the analysis cannot be easily gauged without further investigation. Scopus has been undertaking further efforts to address the indexing gap, and it is hoped that future versions of the database will allow for a more accurate analysis.

Despite their many limitations, the experimental indicators on mobility enable a highly relevant and unique perspective on the size and direction of bilateral research scientist flows. The top nine international bilateral flows (Figure 1) as measured by the sum of bilateral flows between two countries (total bilateral flows) involve exchanges featuring the United States. While the total inflow exceeds the outflow, more scientists who start by publishing in the United States move to affiliations in China and Korea than vice versa, the respective net flows from the United States (outflow minus inflow) to China and Korea as percentage of bilateral flows amounting to 3.4% and 23.7%, respectively. German-based researchers moving to Swiss affiliations account for the largest flow between non-English speaking countries. Table 7A.1 in the Annex contains a list with the top 10 source countries for the United States, United Kingdom, and Germany as top destination countries. The United Kingdom is the second most connected economy in terms of mobile scientists. These statistics do not account for the mobility of individuals before their first publication, for example, as students. As a result, many of these flows may represent foreign nationals returning to their home countries.

Although leading research economies tend to attract more scientific authors from abroad to offset outward flows, flows within each pair tend to be of a similar order of magnitude in both directions, suggesting

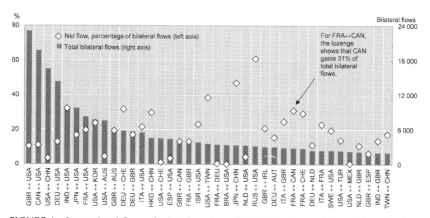

FIGURE 1   International flows of scientific authors, 1996–2011. Largest bilateral flows, by first and last affiliation. *Source: OECD (2013),* OECD Science, Technology and Industry Scoreboard 2013, *based on OECD calculations applied to Scopus Custom Data, Elsevier, version 5.2012.* http://dx.doi.org/10.1787/888932891511.

the existence of complex patterns of knowledge circulation representing the mobility of individuals at different stages of their careers, from students to established professors. The implied international mobility network of scientists (Figure 2) also displays a number of interesting patterns that reveal affinities between different economies based on linguistic, historical, as well as political and cultural linkages. The recent GlobSci survey study by Franzoni et al. (2012) for some specific fields of science, provides some confirmatory evidence for these descriptive findings. A high share of foreign-raised scientists study and work in a number of

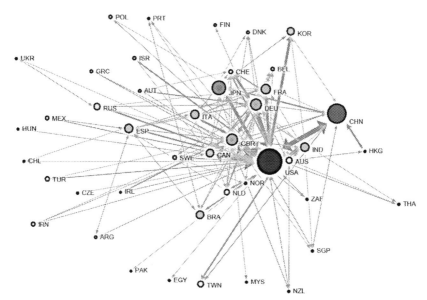

FIGURE 2   International mobility network of scientific authors, 1996–2011. Counts of bilateral flows, by first and last affiliation. Note: The position of selected economies (nodes) is determined by the number of bilateral flows of publishing scientific authors from 1996 to 2011. A visualization algorithm has been applied to the international mobility network to represent the linkages in a two-dimensional layout where distances reflect the combined strength of mobility forces between economies.[15] Bubble sizes are proportional to the number of scientific authors who stay in the economy. The thickness of the arrows joining the nodes represents the number of moves between each pair. A difference in the size of the arrow tip within each pair denotes a marked difference in the volume of flows in each direction. *Source: OECD (2013),* OECD Science, Technology and Industry Scoreboard 2013, *based on OECD calculations applied to Scopus Custom Data, Elsevier, version 5.2012.*

---

15. The algorithm simulates a system of forces defined on an input graph and outputs a locally minimum energy configuration. Nodes resemble mass points repelling each other and the edges simulate springs with attracting forces. The algorithm tries to minimize the energy of this physical system of mass particles. The result has been visualized using the Kamada–Kawai (Kamada & Kawai, 1989) force algorithm and has been implemented using the Sci^2 tool (Sci^2 Team, 2009).

countries. The survey also shows that many economies, not only the United States, rely strongly on foreign talent. By contrast, there are some economies—including India, Italy, Japan, Brazil, and Spain—where foreign scientists and engineers are extremely rare.

Some of these countries exhibit average mobility rates according to the new OECD indicator, thus suggesting that many of those mobile researchers are returning former students or academics. Consistent with the OECD bibliometric results, this survey also finds considerable variation in migration patterns across economies. Swiss and Indian scientists are the most mobile; those from the United States the least. The survey also documents that, as is the case in the Careers of Doctorate Holders (CDH) study, for virtually all the core countries studied, the United States is the dominant destination country.

4.2 Scientific Collaboration

Mobility can be an important conduit to expand collaboration networks, but it can also be an outcome of mobility episodes. International scientific collaboration is a proven mechanism for promoting excellence in scientific research. Scientists collaborate across borders for a variety of reasons: to bring together the most talented and qualified individuals; to pool intellectual, technological, and financial resources; and to effectively address scientific questions that transcend geographical and political boundaries. Evidence presented in the 2013 Science, Technology and Industry Scoreboard (Annex: Figures 7B.1 and 7B.2) shows that economies with higher international collaboration rates tend to have higher average citation rates and top-cited publications are more likely to involve scientific collaboration across institutions (especially international) than "average" publications. International collaboration appears to allow economies to attain higher citation impact rates than they would otherwise achieve.

The collaboration indicator measures the total number (whole counts) of coauthored documents between pairs of countries as calculated based on Scopus Custom Data, Elsevier, version of April 2014, for the 1996–2011 period, through an update of the version reported in OECD (2013a).[16] The analysis relies on the average number of collaborations over the period, while averages are also calculated at the three-year subperiods at the beginning and end of the reference period to investigate whether scientist flows are related to changes in collaboration. As expected, the scientific collaboration and mobility networks documented in this publication show a high degree of similarity. This chapter investigates the extent to which different factors influence these networks in a comparable or distinctive fashion.

---

16. For the aggregate analysis, the indicator is computed on the entire available population. The population is thus not constrained to match the same population from which the mobility indicator is computed, as would be required for an analysis at the individual microlevel.

4.3 International and Foreign Students (Tertiary Level)

According to Freeman (2010), the international mobility of students is one way through which the globalization of scientific and engineering talent proceeds. We look at the distribution of tertiary-level international (mobile) students and foreign (noncitizen) students by destination and source country and by year, as a potential predictor of scientist flows. If highly skilled individuals tend to move in the same direction, the student flows from (i) to (j) should strongly correlate with scientist flows in the same direction. Conversely, student flows from (j) to (i) can contribute to the stock of future scientists in (i) with a potential interest in returning to country (j) (and the attributes required to do so, such as language, etc.). This provides a potential basis for testing competing hypotheses regarding the nature of international knowledge flows through people. The number of students enrolled refers to the count of tertiary-level[17] students studying in the reference period. Because time series before 2004 are only available for foreign (noncitizen) students, we combine for analytical purposes such data with more recent data on international (mobile) students, which better capture student mobility.[18] Data are only available for 40 reporting "destination" countries, while the number of countries of origin exceeds 200. The United States is the top destination location for international students between 1996 and 2011.

4.4 Degree of Proximity

4.4.1 Scientific Proximity and Distance

Science proximity is defined as the Pearson correlation of the vector of the scientific output for each country aggregated by the 28 two-digit All Science Journals Classification (ASJC) categories. Scientific output is measured by total number of indexed documents from publicly available SCImago (2007) data for the 1996–2012 period. This follows a similar approach to framework adopted

---

17. A better approximation could be potentially achieved by looking only at PhD-level students.
18. Each student enrolled in the education programs covered by the corresponding category is counted only once. National data collection systems permitting, the statistics reflect the number of students enrolled at the beginning of the school/academic year. Students are classified as foreign students (noncitizens) if they are not citizens of the country in which the data are collected. While pragmatic and operational, this classification is deemed inappropriate by the OECD and other international bodies for capturing student mobility because of differing national policies regarding the naturalization of immigrants. Countries that have lower propensity to grant permanent residence to its immigrant populations are likely to report second-generation immigrants as foreign students. Therefore, for student mobility and bilateral comparisons, interpretations of data based on the concept of foreign students should be made with caution. Students are classified as international students if they left their country of origin and moved to another country for the purpose of study. Depending on country-specific immigration legislation, mobility arrangements, and data availability, international students may be defined as students who are not permanent or usual residents of their country of study or alternatively as students who obtained their prior education in a different country, including another EU country.

by Miguélez & Moreno (2013) to measure technological similarity. Scientific dissimilarity or distance is then obtained by subtracting scientific proximity from one.

4.4.2 Geographic and Linguistic Distance

Data on contiguity, physical distance, and commonly spoken (official) languages were obtained from the CEPII distance database (Mayer & Zignago, 2011). These variables are commonly employed in gravity models of bilateral trade and foreign direct investment flows, reflecting dyadic migration costs and strength of bilateral linkages. Whereas contiguity indicates the presence of a common border between the bilateral counterparts, physical distance between the two countries reflects the bilateral distance between the largest cities of countries within a dyad (based on their latitude and longitude), using the cities' shares in the total population (in 2004) as weights to obtain a more nuanced measure of bilateral distance. These data also provide two indicators of language commonality, one indicating whether two countries have the same official primary language, the other specifying whether one language is spoken by at least 9% of the population in both countries.

4.4.3 Economic Proximity: Service Trade Flows

The analysis focuses on service trade flows as opposed to general trade flows comprising goods in order to avoid potential distortions caused by raw materials, fuel, and other commodities that are unrelated to knowledge circulation. Service trade data were kindly provided by the OECD Directorate for Trade and Agriculture based on an internal working version of the OECD Trade in Services[19] database used as input for the OECD/WTO TiVA database. Different categories of services trade can be distinguished according to the 2002 Extended Balance of Payments Services classification (EBOPS, 2002). We thus explore the role of trade in more knowledge-intensive services such as computer and information services and other business services with respect to scientist flows and collaboration over 1996–2011.

4.5 Policy Levers

Migration policies can help shape international migration flows, their magnitude, direction, and nature. Migration policies related to the skills of migrant populations tend to be nonbilateral in nature, that is, they are not specific to a given pair of countries.[20] Given the lack of systematic data on national policies that may directly or indirectly influence migration

---

19. http://www.oecd-ilibrary.org/trade/data/oecd-statistics-on-international-trade-in-services/trade-in-services-by-partner-country_data-00274-en?isPartOf=/content/datacollection/tis-data-en.
20. For information on trends about international migration flows and policies, see OECD (2013b).

decisions, there is currently only little evidence on how migration, skills-based or other policies[21] in sending and receiving countries affect international migration. Czaika & de Haas (2014) find that travel visa policies significantly decrease bilateral inflow and outflow dynamics in the general population.[22] Data on tourist visa policies provide first insights into how traveling restrictions affect bilateral migration flows, notwithstanding the fact that tourist visa policies differ from those for skilled professionals in terms of eligibility requirements, scope, and time limit. Nevertheless, travel visa restrictions may reduce the probability of scientist mobility and collaboration across two countries where either bilateral or unilateral visa restrictions are in place, impeding personal contacts across borders by raising the cost of travel.

4.5.1 Travel Visa Restrictions

The analysis draws on data on bilateral and unilateral visa restrictions from the November 2004 edition of the International Civil Aviation Association's Travel Information Manual (IATA, 2004) as collected by Neumayer (2011). The manual provides authoritative information on existing visa restrictions. Data are available for 205 countries, that is, 41,820 country pairs. Visa restrictions are a fairly common phenomenon. Only about 17% of those country pairs are entirely free of such restrictions. As the measure of unilateral visa restrictions solely states whether one of the two countries imposes visa restrictions on the other country, but not vice versa, it is not possible to identify the direction of restrictions within a given dyad. As both visa restriction measures are symmetric, visa restriction effects cannot be identified in a dyad fixed-effects regression context.

4.6 Bilateral Migration Trends

Scientist flows between countries are at least to some extent related to the bilateral migration flows within dyads. Data on bilateral migration stocks from the World Bank Global Bilateral Migration Database were used to control for the general migration pattern between two countries. The database provides a comprehensive picture of bilateral migrant stocks for the period 1960–2000, covering 226 economies across the five continents based on decennial census

---

21. For example, Moretti & Wilson (2014) estimate that the state-based provision of subsidies for biotech employers in the United States over the period 1990–2010 encourages the mobility of star biotech scientists to the state providing the incentive. Cervantes & Goldsetin (2008) point to the role of labor and product market regulations, entrepreneurship, education, and immigration policies in shaping high-skilled migration in OECD regions.

22. At the time of submitting this draft, the Determinants of International Migration (DEMIG) project at the University of Oxford was in the process of compiling new migration and policy databases to provide evidence on the impact of sending and receiving countries' migration policies on international migration. http://www.imi.ox.ac.uk/pdfs/projects/demig/briefing.

information. General bilateral migration data reveal that the global migrant stock increased from 92 to 165 million between 1960 and 2000. The United States remains the most important migrant destination in the world, home to one-fifth of the world's migrants and the top destination for migrants from no less than 60 sending countries. As the empirical analysis of scientist flows covers the time period 1996–2011[23], variables denoting the migrant stocks for 1990 and 2000 were included in the regressions.

4.7 Research Resources and Economic Factors

4.7.1 R&D Intensity

R&D efforts by countries may shape bilateral scientist mobility and collaboration flows as the highly skilled seek new opportunities to work with peers in other economies dedicating substantial resources to scientific research. Data on gross domestic expenditures on R&D (GERD) as a percentage of gross domestic product (GDP) were obtained from the OECD Main Science and Technology Indicators and the UNESCO Institute for Statistics (UIS) R&D databases. We have extracted this indicator for 152 countries to investigate the degree to which scientist mobility and collaboration between two countries are related to the R&D intensity in the receiving (or sending) country and differences in the relative R&D intensity ratio of origin versus destination country over time.

4.7.2 Economic Development

Economic factors are also likely to play a major role in driving observed mobility patterns. Evidence from the OECD/UNESCO/Eurostat study on the Careers of Doctorate Holders (CDH) shows that median gross annual earnings, converted in purchasing power parities (PPPs), vary greatly across economies, ranging from 18,306 US dollar (USD) PPPs in the Russian Federation to 93,000 USD in the United States. Doctorate holders are least well paid in Central and Eastern European countries (with the exception of Slovenia), while the highest median gross annual earnings are found in the United States and the Netherlands. Although with a different target population, a study conducted by the European Commission in 2007 (EC, 2007) also notes a large variation in the remuneration of researchers across countries. While it captures the immediate years after the onset of the global financial crisis, our work deals with the entire 1996–2011 period as the object of analysis, thus capturing a general trend. For some countries, this general trend may have recently switched in the opposite direction, for example,

---

23. The OECD migration databases provide tables with recent annual series on migration flows and stocks in OECD countries from the 1990s onward as well as comprehensive and comparative information on a broad range of demographic and labor market characteristics of immigrants living in OECD countries (http://www.oecd.org/els/mig/oecdmigrationdatabases.htm).

as a result of deteriorating economic conditions or fiscal consolidation policies reducing public funding of science and technology in specific countries.[24]

The analysis includes information on the income and population size of countries to account for the economic well-being as well as basic demographic developments in origin and destination economies. Data on annual population size and GDP per capita (in constant USD 2005 million) over 1996–2011 were extracted for 252 countries from the World Development Indicators Database. The indicator of total population denotes the number of residents regardless of legal status or citizenship (except for refugees not permanently settled in the country of asylum, who are generally considered part of the population of their country of origin). As a measure of the convergence of dyad countries in terms of economic performance, we compute the difference in the relative GDP per capita ratio of origin versus destination country at the end of the reference period (2009–2011 average) and the onset of the observation period (1996–1998 average), thus minimizing the effect of annual fluctuations in economic performance in the analysis.

The previous sources are combined into an analytical dataset. Some analyses are confined to a reduced sample for which data on all required variables are available. Lack of information on some bilateral trade flows is the factor that accounts for the largest reduction in sample size. Also, analyses investigating the relationship between scientist mobility and international student stocks are by construction limited to a small set of destination countries for which foreign students were recorded. Summary statistics, reporting on the number of countries and dyads for which relevant data are available, and an overview of the definition and data sources of the variables used in this analysis are provided in the Annex (Tables 7C.1 and 7C.2). Whenever possible, we document the impact of using different samples as additional controls are introduced in some specifications to show that differences between original and retained samples do not by themselves account for the observed results.

5. EMPIRICAL RESULTS

The estimates displayed in Table 1 show results from negative binomial regressions of the number of scientist flows on a set of distance measures and linkage variables as well as origin and destination fixed effects.[25] Geographic, cultural, economic, and scientific distance measures relate to the indicator of bilateral scientist flows in the expected way (column 1). For example, countries or economies with similar specialization profiles tend to exhibit higher flows between them, all else being equal. Column 2 shows that there are no major systematic

---

24. A general picture of migration in the aftermath of the economic crisis is available in Arslan et al. (2014).

25. The results do not appear to be particularly sensitive to the choice of estimator. Reestimating the main specifications in Tables 2–4 using the fixed effects estimator we obtain results that are very similar in a qualitative and quantitative basis. Results are available from the authors upon request.

TABLE 1 International Scientist Flows, 1996–2011. Negative Binomial Regression with Fixed Effects (FE)

Number of Scientist Flows ($i{\to}j$)	(1)	(2)	(3)	(4)	(5)	(6)
Contiguity ($i{\to}j$) (0/1)	0.303 (0.153)*	0.010 (0.145)	−0.149 (0.100)	−0.033 (0.068)	−0.193 (0.109)	−0.043 (0.072)
Log (geographical distance ($i{\to}j$))	−0.535 (0.044)**	−0.322 (0.060)**	−0.061 (0.043)	0.133 (0.039)**	−0.114 (0.044)*	0.103 (0.036)**
Common official language ($i{\to}j$) (0/1)	0.923 (0.126)**	0.776 (0.136)**	0.275 (0.112)*	0.139 (0.087)	0.342 (0.109)**	0.164 (0.087)
Common language ($i{\to}j$) (0/1)	0.608 (0.114)**	0.582 (0.120)**	0.336 (0.100)**	0.198 (0.072)**	0.340 (0.098)**	0.197 (0.071)**
Log (service exports) ($i{\to}j$)	0.336 (0.033)**	0.467 (0.049)**	0.204 (0.036)**	0.086 (0.031)**	0.223 (0.035)**	0.086 (0.029)**
Scientific dissimilarity ($i{\to}j$)	−12.390 (1.839)**	−10.965 (2.722)**	−5.215 (2.383)*	3.388 (1.945)	−3.684 (2.221)	3.175 (1.792)
Log (migrants1990 ($i{\to}j$))			0.069 (0.012)**	0.034 (0.010)**		
Log (international students ($i{\to}j$))			0.369 (0.019)**	0.160 (0.017)**		
Log (collaborations ($i{\to}j$))				0.968 (0.034)**		
Log (1 + migrants1990 ($i{\to}j$))					0.061 (0.011)**	0.038 (0.008)**
Log (1 + International students ($i{\to}j$))					0.346 (0.019)**	0.156 (0.016)**
Log (1 + Collaborations ($i{\to}j$))						0.979 (0.033)**
Origin economy FE	yes	yes	yes	yes	yes	yes
Destination economy FE	yes	yes	yes	yes	yes	yes
Chi2 statistic	14,874.4	12,409.3	20,178.1	34,461.0	19,995.4	33,791.9
Log-likelihood	−16,509.0	−8689.0	−8270.0	−7790.0	−9278.0	−8762.0
Number of observations	8010	2583	2583	2583	3310	3310
Number of dyad clusters	4005	2058	2058	2058	2603	2603
<Complete dyads>	4005	525	525	525	707	707
<One-way-only dyads>	0	1533	1533	1533	1896	1896

Note: *p<0.05; **p<0.01; heteroscedasticity-robust standard errors clustered by dyad.

differences between the full sample and the restricted sample for which additional information on migration and international students are available.[26] In our bilateral scientist mobility database, data may be available for both countries in the dyad (complete dyad) or only one ordered pair (one-way-only dyad). As the estimation sample is restricted to observations with available data, the share of one-way dyads in the estimation sample tends to increase, as shown in the bottom panel.

Column 3 introduces migration-related variables, separating overall migration stocks in 1990 (predating the reference period) and the average stock of tertiary-level international students over the reference period. Both variables are statistically significant and have the expected sign. As one could hypothesize, the student "migration" variable exhibits a stronger relationship with scientist flows than general migration. After controlling for the number of scientific collaborations, it is possible to note that the elasticity between collaborations and scientist flows is close to one. The significance of several proximity variables vanishes (e.g., common official language) or even gets turned around (e.g., geographical distance and scientific dissimilarity) once the scientific collaboration variable (columns 4 and 6) is added to the regression, suggesting that collaborations and mobility are codetermined (endogenous). In this paper, we do not try to estimate the structural relationship between these two variables and the potential direction of causation between them. Additional specification checks are reported in columns 5 and 6—accounting for zeroes in the migration, international student and collaboration variables that confirm the robustness of these results.

Although highly correlated (correlation=0.93), collaboration and mobility linkages exhibit some noteworthy differences. Mobility flows are more concentrated than collaborations—the Gini index for the distribution of mobility flows is 0.91 against 0.87 for collaboration. On average, the main mobility partner accounts for 46% of all bilateral flows, while the comparable figure for collaboration stands at 38%, with medians at 37% and 26%, respectively. Inspecting individual countries, there is no single country with an output of more than 1100 publications in 2010 where mobility is less concentrated than collaboration: neither there is one where the top partner in scientific collaborations accounts for a bigger share than the top mobility partner in mobility.[27]

Table 2 investigates in more detail the factors that contribute to explaining observed mobility (a) and collaboration patterns (b). Column 2a introduces

---

26. The model specification in columns 1 and 2 is identical and applied to data sets of different sizes to gauge the mere effect of a sample size reduction. In column 2, the model is applied to a sample where migration information is available for at least one of the two countries in the dyad (see column 3).

27. This pattern may be due in part to the use of whole counts for collaborations that may involve more than two countries, while a mobility episode is constrained to be between a given pair of countries.

TABLE 2 Comparing International Scientist Flows and Collaborations, 1996–2011. Negative Binomial Regression with Fixed Effects (FE)

	Number of Scientist Flows ($i{\to}j$)			Number of Scientist Collaborations ($i{\leftrightarrow}j$)		
	(1a)	(2a)	(3a)	(1b)	(2b)	(3b)
Contiguity ($i{\leftrightarrow}j$) (0/1)	−0.149 (0.100)	−0.135 (0.101)	−0.155 (0.098)	−0.113 (0.062)	−0.116 (0.062)	−0.120 (0.056)*
Log (geographical distance ($i{\leftrightarrow}j$))	−0.061 (0.043)	−0.052 (0.044)	−0.074 (0.043)	−0.228 (0.025)**	−0.230 (0.025)**	−0.236 (0.024)**
Common official language ($i{\leftrightarrow}j$) (0/1)	0.276 (0.112)*	0.284 (0.112)*	0.274 (0.113)*	0.170 (0.071)*	0.169 (0.071)*	0.162 (0.071)*
Common language ($i{\leftrightarrow}j$) (0/1)	0.336 (0.100)**	0.341 (0.100)**	0.337 (0.101)**	0.127 (0.061)*	0.127 (0.061)*	0.130 (0.062)*
Scientific dissimilarity ($i{\leftrightarrow}j$)	−5.204 (2.384)*	−5.225 (2.385)*	−4.520 (2.431)	−9.586 (1.305)**	−9.572 (1.309)**	−8.790 (1.366)**
Log (migrants1990 ($i{\to}j$))	0.069 (0.012)**	0.070 (0.012)**	0.067 (0.013)**	0.038 (0.007)**	0.038 (0.007)**	0.036 (0.007)**
Log (international students ($i{\to}j$))	0.370 (0.019)**	0.368 (0.019)**	0.364 (0.019)**	0.199 (0.011)**	0.199 (0.011)**	0.191 (0.010)**
Log (service exports ($i{\to}j$))	0.203 (0.036)**	0.159 (0.051)**	0.195 (0.036)**	0.092 (0.018)**	0.105 (0.025)**	0.086 (0.018)**
Log (computer/info service exports ($i{\leftrightarrow}j$))		0.033 (0.019)			−0.002 (0.012)	
Log (other business services export) ($i{\to}j$)		0.016 (0.033)			−0.013 (0.019)	
Bilateral visa restrictions ($i{\leftrightarrow}j$) (0/1)			−0.345 (0.137)*			−0.504 (0.109)**
Unilateral visa restrictions ($i{\to}j$) (0/1)			−0.081 (0.061)			−0.144 (0.039)**
Origin economy FE	yes	yes	yes	yes	yes	yes
Destination economy FE	yes	yes	yes	yes	yes	yes
Chi2 statistic	20,218.2	20,519.6	20,379.8	58,563.9	58,604.7	60,785.5
Log-likelihood	−8272	−8270	−8265	−10,582	−10,582	−10,540
Number of observations	2603	2603	2603	2603	2603	2603
Number of dyad clusters	2078	2078	2078	2078	2078	2078
\<Complete dyads\>	525	525	525	525	525	525
\<One-way-only dyads\>	1553	1553	1553	1553	1553	1553

Note: *p<0.05; **p<0.01; heteroscedasticity-robust standard errors clustered by dyad.

more detailed information on specific, knowledge-intensive categories of service trade. The incremental effect of this type of trade in services is positive but not statistically significant at the 5% level. It is interesting to see that no such effect is found in the case of collaborations (column 2b). Columns 3a and 3b explore the impact of visa restrictions, which turn out to have statistically significant negative effects on both scientist flows and collaborations. In the case of bilateral restrictions, collaborations can decrease by as much as 50%. This higher impact on collaboration may be due to the fact that short visits to build up and support the collaboration are more sensitive to the baseline tourist visa restrictions that underpin the indicator, while longer spells that result in affiliation changes may require other types of visas that are not captured in the indicator.

The larger effect of bilateral restrictions is also a plausible result, but it must be noted that there can be attenuation bias impacting on the unilateral visa variable because it has been constructed to equal one regardless of the direction in which the unilateral visa applies, and zero otherwise. Future analysis should aim to reconstruct this indicator to account for this asymmetry and complement it with additional information about the types of skill-related visa requirements that most likely apply to the mobility episodes captured by our indicator. While collaboration may occur on a remote basis, interactions may only be enabled by short-term visits for which a normal visa can be more relevant. In contrast, common language and distance appear to have a stronger impact on mobility than collaboration. This may relate to the higher emotional, travel, and opportunity costs associated with the move to a distant country with no common official language.

A third set of analytical results is available in Table 3, documenting the statistical association between flows that operate in opposite directions within a dyad. The research question in this case has to do with the way in which scientist flows interact with other population flows. For example, a potential driver of mobility from country (i) to country (j) is the stock of population in country (j) with personal ties to country (i), for example, by virtue of permanent residence or nationality. Such stocks depend in turn on flows from country (j) to country (i) built up over time. If that is the case, we can be considering a more developed notion of brain circulation that goes beyond the specific group of publishing scientists. We focus in particular on the role of tertiary international students—a rather imperfect proxy for flows of advanced degree and PhD students. We attempt to control for other confounding factors by comparing the impact of such flows with those for a broader population group as implied by the stock of migrants at the beginning of the period. The results indicate a very significant elasticity of scientist flows to student flows in the opposite direction. This elasticity is of similar magnitude (10%) to the elasticity found in the same direction of the flow. In contrast, for the general stock of migrant population, we do not find evidence for such an effect. We interpret this as evidence of a significant brain circulation effect.

TABLE 3 The Role of Population Counterflows in Explaining Scientist Flows, 1996–2011. Negative Binomial Regression with Fixed Effects (FE)

Number of Scientist Flows (i→j)	(1)	(2)	(3)	(4)	(5)
Contiguity (i→j) (0/1)	-0.033 (0.058)	-0.012 (0.062)	-0.014 (0.062)	-0.019 (0.061)	-0.109 (0.084)
Log (geographical distance (i→j))	0.133 (0.035)**	0.227 (0.036)**	0.227 (0.036)**	0.232 (0.035)**	0.078 (0.039)
Common official language (i→j) (0/1)	0.139 (0.078)	0.218 (0.089)*	0.216 (0.090)*	0.194 (0.089)*	0.268 (0.106)*
Common language (i→j) (0/1)	0.198 (0.066)**	0.083 (0.062)	0.085 (0.062)	0.078 (0.060)	0.149 (0.083)
Log (service exports) (i→j)	0.086 (0.029)**	0.108 (0.033)**	0.107 (0.034)**	0.094 (0.034)*	0.193 (0.037)**
Scientific dissimilarity (i→j)	3.388 (1.880)	1.162 (4.905)	1.316 (5.037)	-0.682 (5.020)	-23.740 (6.530)**
Log (collaborations (i→j))	0.968 (0.033)**	1.210 (0.061)**	1.207 (0.062)**	1.103 (0.061)**	0.039 (0.021)
Log (migrants1990 (i→j))	0.034 (0.009)**	0.043 (0.013)**	0.040 (0.016)**	0.033 (0.016)*	0.248 (0.024)**
Log (international students (i→j))	0.160 (0.017)**	0.126 (0.024)**	0.124 (0.023)**	0.116 (0.022)**	-0.003 (0.019)
Log (migrants1990 (j→i))				-0.005 (0.016)	
Log (international students) (j→i)			0.008 (0.016)	0.092 (0.018)**	0.224 (0.022)**
Origin economy FE	yes	yes	yes	yes	yes
Destination economy FE	yes	yes	yes	yes	yes
Chi2 statistic	40,834	25,753	25,870	27,506	17,595
Log-likelihood	-7790	-4343	-4343	-4326	-4521
Number of observations	2583	1050	1050	1050	1050
Number of dyad clusters	2058	525	525	525	525
<Complete dyads>	525	525	525	525	525
<One-way-only dyads>	1533	0	0	0	0

Note: *p<0.05; **p<0.01; heteroscedasticity-robust standard errors. Standard errors are not clustered by dyad to ensure the full rank of the covariance matrix and computation of Chi2 statistics. Heteroscedasticity-robust standard errors clustered by dyad do not vary significantly from those reported. Results are available from the authors upon request.

This is a plausible explanation for the observation that there are often more scientists "moving" from highly developed countries to emergent and developing economies than otherwise.

An additional, complementary hypothesis is considered in Table 4. This further set of results provides a test of the role of convergence across countries on a number of indicators that may reflect on the relative attractiveness as residence locations for scientists. The results indicate that a reduction in the relative R&D intensity and GDP per capita gap between countries (i) and (j)—for example, country (i) moving from having a tenth of country (j)'s GDP per capita to half— is associated with a lower level of scientist flows from (i) to (j). The effect of convergence in R&D intensity is only statistically significant once the level of collaboration is controlled for. While the cross-sectional correlation with collaboration is very strong over the period, we observe, however, no such relationship between changes in collaboration over 1996–2011 and the level of bilateral scientist flows in that period.

To complete the presentation of empirical results, Table 5 reports the analysis of mobility focusing on the variation in scientist mobility flows within country dyads, which restricts the set of dependent variables to non-symmetric and destination (or sending) country-specific variables. The results are consistent with previous findings, in particular the negative coefficient associated with international student flows, in contrast to the positive coefficient found for overall migration. The mobility of students in a given direction has predictive power on the observed mobility of scientists in the opposite direction, thus lending support to the knowledge circulation paradigm. It is likely that this result reflects how flows from one country to another may be partly driven by the subset of students originally coming from the latter and returning to their homes to continue their careers. These results are robust to the inclusion of further controls on the characteristics of destination countries.

This evidence on the brain circulation paradigm is consistent with separate OECD analysis on the same underlying data. Such work shows not only a significant degree of temporary mobility in the form of scientists returning to their original country of affiliation but also a remarkable difference in the status of the journals that mobile scientists publish in relative to those who are not observed to be internationally mobile (OECD, 2013a). Mobile scientists publish in journals with higher citation impact rankings. Interestingly, that work also shows, for a majority of countries, a large similarity in the status of journals across different types of mobile scientists, that is, inflows, outflows, and returnees. Returnees contribute significantly to raising the average publishing profile for the near totality of countries. Our analysis here confirms the view that brain circulation is a complex and multidirectional phenomenon, particularly linked and most likely drawing upon flows of tertiary-level students in the opposite direction.

TABLE 4 International Scientist Flows and Other Changes Over the Period 1996–2011. Negative Binomial Regression with Fixed Effects

Number of scientist flows ($i{\rightarrow}j$)	(1)	(2)	(3)	(4)	(5)
Log (service exports ($i{\rightarrow}j$))	0.179 (0.043)**	0.198 (0.043)**	0.174 (0.038)**	0.056 (0.030)	0.049 (0.030)
Scientific dissimilarity ($i{\rightarrow}j$)	−5.367 (2.716)*	−8.291 (2.706)**	−9.310 (3.612)**	0.797 (2.522)	2.740 (2.495)
Log (migrants1990 ($i{\rightarrow}j$))	0.070 (0.015)**	0.070 (0.015)**	0.029 (0.014)*	0.024 (0.011)*	0.034 (0.013)**
Log (international students ($i{\rightarrow}j$))	0.331 (0.025)**	0.325 (0.026)**	0.398 (0.028)**	0.118 (0.021)**	0.118 (0.021)**
Change in relative R&D intensity ratio ($i{\rightarrow}j$)	0.077 (0.076)	0.087 (0.075)	−0.065 (0.099)	−0.213 (0.065)**	−0.224 (0.065)**
Change in relative GDP per capita ratio ($i{\rightarrow}j$)		−0.386 (0.123)**	−0.505 (0.125)**	−0.529 (0.090)**	−0.488 (0.087)**
Log (change in intl. student stock ($i{\rightarrow}j$))			−0.040 (0.023)	0.017 (0.018)	0.008 (0.017)
Log (collaborations ($i{\rightarrow}j$))				1.080 (0.045)**	1.084 (0.045)**
Log (change in collaboration ($i{\rightarrow}j$))				−0.042 (0.038)	−0.052 (0.038)
Log (change in migrant stock ($i{\rightarrow}j$))					0.021 (0.013)
Origin economy FE	yes	yes	yes	yes	yes
Destination economy FE	yes	yes	yes	yes	yes
Chi2 statistic	14,748.2	14,925.9	13,771.0	29,658.9	29,697.5
Log-likelihood	−5153	−5048	−3867	−3582	−3512
Number of observations	1384	1358	953	937	918
Number of dyad clusters	1048	1022	761	745	729
<Complete dyads>	336	336	192	192	189
<One-way-only dyads>	712	686	569	553	540

Note: *$p < 0.05$; **$p < 0.01$; heteroscedasticity-robust standard errors clustered by dyad. Other symmetric controls not reported include contiguity dummy, geographical distance, and common language.

TABLE 5 Scientist Flows Within "Country Pairs" or Dyads, 1996–2011

| | OLS | | Negative Binomial Regression | | |
| | Log (Scientist Flows (i→j)) | | Counts of Scientist Flows (i→j) | | |
	(1)	(2)	(3)	(4)	(5)[a]
Log (migrants1990 (i→j))	0.072 (0.021)**	0.058 (0.023)*	0.075 (0.009)**	0.073 (0.010)**	0.076[a] (0.009)**
Log (international students (i→j))	−0.021 (0.023)	−0.035 (0.025)	−0.028 (0.010)**	−0.021 (0.010)*	−0.029[a] (0.010)**
Log (service exports (i→j))	0.085 (0.066)	0.094 (0.056)	0.068 (0.028)*	0.079 (0.023)**	0.068 (0.028)*
Log (GDP per capita (j))		0.277 (0.087)**		0.202 (0.034)**	
Log (GERD/GDP(j))		−0.226 (0.064)**		−0.236 (0.024)**	
Log (population (j))		−0.066 (0.022)**		−0.071 (0.009)**	
Dyad fixed effect <i,j>	yes	yes	yes	yes	yes
F-statistic/Chi2 statistic	5.2	8.9	4,474,713	14,075,168	4,609,496
R-squared/log-likelihood	0.94	0.95	−3986	−3875	−3985
Number of observations	966	966	1050	1050	1050
Number of dyad clusters	483	483	525	525	525
<Complete dyads>	483	483	525	525	525
<One-way-only dyads>	0	0	0	0	0

Notes: Fixed effect regressions for each dyad <i,j>. *p<0.05; **p<0.01; F- and R-squared statistics and heteroscedasticity-robust standard errors clustered by dyad are reported for the OLS regression. Chi2- and log-likelihood statistics and robust-standard errors are reported for the negative binomial regression. Standard errors are not clustered by dyad to ensure the full rank of the covariance matrix and computation of Chi2 statistics. Heteroscedasticity-robust standard errors clustered by dyad do not vary significantly from those reported. Results are available from the authors upon request.
[a]As a robustness check, specification (5) uses Log (1 + Migration1990 (i→j)) and Log (1 + International students (i→j)) instead of the simple log transformation.

6. CONCLUSIONS AND FURTHER REMARKS

The research presented in this chapter provides an initial, exploratory contribution to the analysis of the factors that drive the international mobility of research scientists. The findings from this work lend support to a knowledge or brain circulation perspective of scientist flows rather than a more traditional view of brain gain/brain drain in which some countries win at the expense of others' loss of high potential individuals. Scientist mobility appears to occur in the context of a wider, more complex network of mobile, highly educated and skilled individuals that provides the basis for training and collaboration. We have found that mobility flows are statistically related to policy-related variables such as bilateral and unilateral travel visa restrictions and to changing economic and research conditions, with evidence that convergence between countries is associated with increased mobility toward the countries that are catching up, at least in relative terms.

The implications of this work can be far reaching but need to be considered in the context of the broader evidence on mobility and high-skilled migration. Policy makers need to evaluate which are the policies that make most effective use of complex international networks and mobility opportunities that individuals appear to be increasingly willing to use. They should also be aware of the potential reversibility of some of the observed flows if the conditions change, for example, if the R&D catching-up process comes to a halt and the conditions or expectations that first attracted scientists cease to apply.

There are several possible avenues for future research. Firstly, it is important to go beyond the analysis of aggregate mobility patterns to explore in more detail mobility episodes at the micro (scientist) level. This is a necessary step in order to understand whether mobility has a genuine impact on scientific collaboration and the productivity of researchers (e.g., as measured by citations) or whether it is the more collaborative and productive researchers that are more likely to identify mobility opportunities. This is also necessary for understanding how mobile researchers contribute to national and global scientific performance. Micro-based analysis should also help provide improved evidence on the dynamic processes that result in individual scientists being matched to positions and the efficiency of this largely global and unique marketplace.

The study of scientist mobility also requires paying more attention to specific science policies that bear on mobility. In that respect, there are potential avenues to begin exploring, for example, what bilateral collaboration and mobility agreements for scientists are in place, and what level of resources are dedicated to promote the overseas training of students and scientists as well as to open up inbound flows. Our analysis has used a very crude estimate of visa restrictions as applicable to tourists, which can provide cover for short-term stays and collaborations. The regimes that govern the granting of student and work visas can be more instrumental for shaping more lasting flows. Other policy aspects such as the recognition of foreign tertiary degrees, the administrative burdens involved in applying for positions, and the openness of the process to outsiders can clearly matter and shape mobility patterns.

Pursuing further research in this area requires a conscious effort to build up accurate databases that trace policy changes over time.

It is equally important to work on developing new tools and instruments to trace mobility of the highly skilled. This chapter has used a rather new application of bibliometric data to trace scientist mobility, but this approach is limited to those researchers who keep publishing in scholarly journals. Flows to business or other activities where publishing is not the norm can bias the overall picture. Excess emphasis on a given, easy-to-measure populations such as publishing scientists may obscure the relevance for policy of flows into other sectors and types of STI activity that do not necessarily entail scholarly publishing.

Other complementary statistical approaches can be brought in to complement the picture presented in this work and may be further integrated in the future. For example, the motivations underpinning mobility decisions or informal linkages with home institutions can be gauged from targeted, linked surveys. This information can be useful for policy makers wishing to design outward mobility incentives that generate real benefits to the domestic economy. Developing the tools and the analysis for better understanding the nature and impact of knowledge flows through people is part of the agenda of the OECD and its measurement work on science, technology, and innovation.

REFERENCES

Abramo, G., D'Angelo, C. A., & Solazzi, M. (2012). A bibliometric tool to assess the regional dimension of university-industry research collaborations. *Scientometrics*, *91*, 955–975.

Arslan, C., Dumont, J.-C., Kone, Z., Moullan, Y., Özden, C., Parons, C., et al. (2014). *A new profile of migrants in the aftermath of the recent economic crisis*. OECD Social, Employment and Migration Working Papers, No. 160. OECD Publishing. http://dx.doi.org/10.1787/5jxt2t3nnjr5-en.

Audretsch, D. B., & Feldman, M. P. (1996). R&D spillovers and the geography of innovation and production. *American Economic Review*, *86*, 630–640.

Audretsch, D. B., & Feldman, M. P. (2004). Knowledge spillovers and the geography of innovation. In V. Henderson, & J. Thisse (Eds.), *Handbook of urban and regional economics* (Vol. 4) Elsevier, Amsterdam, pp. 2713–2739.

Auriol, L. (2010). *Careers of doctorate holders: Employment and mobility patterns*. OECD Science, Technology and Industry Working Papers, 2010/04. OECD Publishing. http://dx.doi.org/10.1787/5kmh8phxvvf5-en.

Auriol, L., Misu, M., & Freeman, R. A. (2013). *Careers of doctorate holders: Analysis of labour market and mobility indicators*. OECD Science, Technology and Industry Working Paper, 2013/04. OECD Publishing. http://dx.doi.org/10.1787/5k43nxgs289w-en.

Baldwin, R., & Taglioni, D. (2006). *Gravity for dummies and dummies for gravity equations*. Working Paper 12516. Cambridge, MA: National Bureau of Economic Research.

Baruffaldi, S. H., & Landoni, P. (2012). Return mobility and scientific productivity of researchers working abroad: the role of home country linkages. *Research Policy*, *41*, 1655–1665.

Bergstrand, J. H. (1985). The gravity equation in international trade: some microeconomic foundations and empirical evidence. *The Review of Economics and Statistics*, *67*(3), 474–481.

Bozeman, B., & Corley, E. (2004). Scientists' collaboration strategies: implications for scientific and technical human capital. *Research Policy*, *33*, 599–616.

Breschi, S., & Lissoni, F. (2009). Mobility of skilled workers and co-invention networks: an anatomy of localized knowledge flows. *Journal of Economic Geography, 9*, 439–468.

Breschi, S., Lissoni, F., & Tarasconi, G. (January 2014). *Inventor data for research on migration and innovation: A survey and a pilot* WIPO Economic Research Working Paper No. 17.

Cañibano, C., Otamende, F. J., & Solís, F. (2011). International temporary mobility of researchers: a cross-discipline study. *Scientometrics, 89*, 653–666.

Carrington, W., & Detragiache, E. (1998). *How big is the brain drain?* IMF Working Paper 98. Washington, DC: International Monetary Fund.

Cervantes, M., & Goldsetin, A. (2008). Talent mobility in the global economy: Europe as a destination. In A. Solimano (Ed.), *The international mobility of talent: Types, causes, and development impact*. Oxford University Press.

Clark, X., Hatton, T. J., & Williamson, J. G. (2007). Explaining U.S. immigration 1971–1998. *Review of Economics and Statistics, 89*(2), 359–373.

Conchi, S., & Michels, C. (2014). *Scientific mobility – An analysis of Germany, Austria, France and Great Britain*. Fraunhofer ISI Discussion Papers Innovation Systems and Policy Analysis No. 41, Karlsruhe. http://www.isi.fraunhofer.de/isi-wAssets/docs/p/de/diskpap_innosysteme_policyanalyse/discussionpaper_41_2014.pdf.

Czaika, M., & de Haas, H. (April 2014). *The effect of visa policies on international migration dynamics*. DEMIG project paper 18. http://www.imi.ox.ac.uk/pdfs/wp/wp-89-2014.pdf.

De Groot, H. L. F., Linders, G. J., Rietveld, P., & Subramanian, U. (2004). The institutional determinants of bilateral trade patterns. *Kyklos, 58*, 103–124.

Dietz, J., Chompalov, I., Bozeman, B., O'Neil Lane, E., & Park, J. (2000). Using curriculum vita to study the career paths of scientists and engineers: an exploratory assessment. *Scientometrics, 49*, 419–442.

Docquier, F., & Marfouk, A. (2006). International migration by educational attainment, 1990–2000. In C. Özden & M. Schiff (Eds.), *International migration, remittances and the brain drain*. New York: Palgrave Macmillan.

Docquier, F., & Rapoport, H. (2009). Documenting the brain drain of "la crème de la crème" three case-studies on international migration at the upper tail of the education distribution. *Journal of Economics and Statistics, 229*, 617–705.

Docquier, F., & Rapoport, H. (2012). Globalization, brain drain and development. *Journal of Economic Literature, 50*, 681–730.

EBOPS. (2002). *Extended Balance of Payments Services Classification*. Accessed from http://unstats.un.org/unsd/tradekb/Knowledgebase/EBOPS-2002.

Elsevier. (2011). *International comparative performance of the UK research base: 2011*. Report commissioned by the UK Department for Business, Innovation and Skills. http://www.elsevier.com/__data/assets/pdf_file/0020/171830/11-p123-international-comparative-performance-uk-research-base-2011.pdf.

Elsevier. (2013). *International comparative performance of the UK research base: 2013*. Report commissioned by the UK Department for Business, Innovation and Skills. https://www.gov.uk/government/uploads/system/uploads/attachment_data/file/263729/bis-13-1297-international-comparative-performance-of-the-UK-research-base-2013.pdf.

European Commission. (2007). *Remuneration of researchers in the public and private sectors by CARSA*. European Commission.

Fink, C., Miguélez, E., & Raffo, J. (2013). *The global race for inventors* forthcoming as a WIPO Economic Research Working Paper.

Franzoni, C., Scellato, G., & Stephan, P. (2012). Foreign born scientists: mobility patterns for sixteen countries. *Nature Biotechnology, 30*(12), 1250–1253. Accessed from www.nber.org/workinggroups/ipe/ipe_researchproject.html.

Freeman, R. (2010). Globalization of scientific and engineering talent: international mobility of students, workers, and ideas and the world economy. *Economics of Innovation and New Technology, 19,* 393–406.

Gibson, J., & McKenzie, D. (2013). *Scientific mobility and knowledge networks in high emigration countries: Evidence from the Pacific.* Discussion Paper No 05/13, Center for Research and Analysis of Migration, Department of Economics, University College London. http://www.cream-migration.org/publ_uploads/CDP_05_13.pdf.

Hoisl, K. (2007). Tracing mobile inventors – the causality between inventor mobility and inventor productivity. *Research Policy, 36,* 619–636.

Hunter, R. S., Oswald, A. J., & Charlton, B. G. (2009). The elite brain drain. *Economic Journal, 119,* 231–251.

IATA. (2004). *Travel information manual.* Badhoevedorp: International Air Transport Association.

Jaffe, A. B. (1986). Technological opportunity and spillovers of R&D: evidence from firms patents, profits and market value. *American Economic Review, 76,* 984–1001.

Jaffe, A. B., Trajtenberg, M., & Henderson, R. (1993). Geographic localisation of knowledge spillovers as evidenced by patent citations. *Quarterly Journal of Economics, 108,* 577–598.

Jansen, M., & Piermartini, R. (2009). Temporary migration and bilateral trade flows. *World Economy, 32,* 735–753.

Jonkers, K., & Cruz-Castro, L. (2013). Research upon return: the effect of international mobility on scientific ties, production and impact. *Research Policy, 42,* 1366–1377.

Jonkers, K., & Tijssen, R. (2008). Chinese researchers returning home: impacts of international mobility on research collaboration and scientific productivity. *Scientometrics, 77,* 309–333.

Kamada, T., & Kawai, S. (1989). An algorithm for drawing general undirected graphs. *Information Processing Letters, 31,* 7–15.

Karemera, D., Iwuagwu Oguledo, V., & Davis, B. (2000). A gravity model analysis of international migration to North America. *Applied Economics, 32,* 1745–1755.

Kleinert, J., & Toubal, F. (2010). Gravity for FDI. *Review of International Economics, 18,* 1–13.

Laudel, G. (2003). Studying the brain drain: can bibliometric methods help? *Scientometrics, 57,* 215–237.

Linders, G. J., & De Groot, H. L. F. (2006). *Estimation of the gravity equation in the presence of zero flows.* Tinbergen Institute Discussion Paper 2006-072/3. Amsterdam and Rotterdam: Tinbergen Institute.

Luukkonen, T., Tijssen, R. J. W., Persson, O., & Siversten, G. (1993). The measurement of international scientific collaboration. *Scientometrics, 28,* 15–36.

Mayda, A. M. (2010). International migrations: a panel data analysis of the determinants of bilateral flows. *Journal of Population Economics, 23*(4), 1249–1274.

Mayer, T., & Zignago, S. (2011). *Notes on CEPII's distances measures (GeoDist).* CEPII Working Paper 2011-25.

Miguélez, E., & Fink, C. (2013). *Measuring the international mobility of inventors: A new database.* WIPO Working Paper No. 8. Accessed from http://www.wipo.int/export/sites/www/econ_stat/en/economics/pdf/wp8.pdf.

Miguélez, E., & Moreno, R. (2013). *Do labour mobility and technological collaborations foster geographical knowledge diuffsion? The case of European regions.* Research Institute of Applied Economics Working Paper, 2013/14 University of Barcelona. Accessed from www.ub.edu/irea/working_papers/2013/201314.pdf.

Moed, H. F., Aisati, M., & Plume, A. (2013). Studying scientific migration in scopus. *Scientometrics, 94*(3), 929–942.

Moed, H., & Halevi, G. (2014). A bibliometric approach to tracking international scientific migration. *Scientometrics, 101,* 1987–2001.

Moretti, E., & Wilson, D. J. (2014). State incentives for innovation, star scientists and jobs: evidence from biotech. *Journal of Urban Economics*, *79*, 20–38.

Narin, F., Stevens, K., & Whitlow, E. S. (1991). Scientific co-operation in Europe and the citation of multinationally authored papers. *Scientometrics*, *21*, 313–323.

Neumayer, E. (2006). Unequal access to foreign spaces: how states use visa restrictions to regulate mobility in a globalised world. *Transactions of the British Institute of Geographers*, *31*, 72–84.

Neumayer, E. (2011). On the detrimental impact of visa restrictions on bilateral trade and foreign direct investment. *Applied Geography*, *31*(3), 901–907.

OECD. (2001). *International mobility of the highly skilled*. OECD Publishing. http://dx.doi.org/10.1787/9789264196087-en.

OECD. (2008). *The global competition for talent: Mobility of the highly skilled*. Paris: OECD.

OECD. (2010). *The OECD innovation strategy: Getting a head start on tomorrow*. Paris: OECD.

OECD. (2013a). *OECD science, technology and industry scoreboard 2013*. OECD Publishing. www.oecd.org/sti/scoreboard.htm.

OECD. (2013b). *OECD international migration outlook 2013*. OECD Publishing. http://dx.doi.org/10.1787/migr_outlook-2013-en.

OECD. (2014). *OECD science, technology and industry outlook 2014*. OECD Publishing.

Pierson, A. S., & Cotegrave, P. (2004). Citation figures suggest that the UK brain drain is a genuine problem. *Nature*, *407*, 13.

Rose, A. K. (2007). The foreign service and foreign trade: embassies as export promotion. *World Economy*, *30*, 22–38.

Scellato, G., Franzoni, C., & Stephan, P. (2012). *Mobile scientists and international networks* NBER Working Paper 18613. Cambridge, USA.

Sci² Team. (2009). *Science of Science (Sci²) Tool*. Indiana University and SciTech Strategies. http://sci2.cns.iu.edu.

Science Europe and Elsevier. (2013). *Comparative benchmarking of European and US research collaboration and researcher mobility*. A report prepared in collaboration between Science Europe and Elsevier's SciVal Analytics. http://www.elsevier.com/__data/assets/pdf_file/0010/171793/Comparative-Benchmarking-of-European-and-US-Research-Collaboration-and-Researcher-Mobility_sept2013.pdf.

SCImago. (2007). *SJR – SCImago Journal & Country Rank*. Retrieved June, 2014, from http://www.scimagojr.com.

Trajtenberg, M. (2005). Recombinant ideas: the mobility of inventors and the productivity of research. In *Proceedings of the CEPR conference, Munich, May 26–28, 2005*.

Trajtenberg, M., Shiff, G., & Melamed, R. (2006). *The "names game": Harnessing inventors' patent data for economic research* NBER Working Paper No. 12479, Cambridge, MA.

Trippl, M. (2013). Scientific mobility and knowledge transfer at the interregional and intraregional level. *Regional Studies*, *47*, 1653–1667.

UN-DESA and OECD. (2013). *World migration in figures*. A joint contribution by UN-DESA and the OECD to the United Nations High-Level Dialogue on Migration and Development, 3–4 October 2013. http://www.oecd.org/els/mig/World-Migration-in-Figures.pdf.

Wagner, C. S. (2005). Six case studies of international collaboration in science. *Scientometrics*, *62*, 3–26.

Wagner, C. S., & Leydesdorff, L. (2005). Network structure, self-organization, and the growth of international collaboration in science. *Research Policy*, *34*, 1608–1618.

Weinberg, B. A. (2011). Developing science: scientific performance and brain drains in the developing world. *Journal of Development Economics*, *95*, 95–104.

Yoshikane, F., & Kagura, K. (2004). Comparative analysis of coauthorship networks of different domains: the growth and change of networks. *Scientometrics*, *60*, 433–444.

Zwinkels, R. C. J., & Beugelsdijk, S. (2010). Gravity equations: workhorse or Trojan horse in explaining trade and FDI patterns across time and space? *International Business Review*, *19*, 102–115.

ANNEX

TABLE 7A.1 International Scientist Flows to the Three Countries with Highest Number of Inflows, 1996–2011

Top 10 Source Countries

#	USA Source Country	Scientist Flow	%Total	GBR Source Country	Scientist Flow	%Total	DEU Source Country	Scientist Flow	%Total
1	GBR	12,739	13	USA	10,323	28	USA	6210	24
2	CAN	10,932	11	DEU	3283	9	GBR	2330	9
3	DEU	8042	8	AUS	2455	7	CHE	1979	8
4	CHN	7978	8	FRA	2212	6	FRA	1726	7
5	IND	6550	6	CAN	1829	5	AUT	1265	5
6	JPN	5668	6	ITA	1764	5	ITA	1090	4
7	FRA	4913	5	NLD	1199	3	NLD	1060	4
8	AUS	3596	4	IRL	1192	3	RUS	1049	4
9	ITA	3331	3	IND	1142	3	CAN	614	2
10	KOR	2942	3	ESP	991	3	ESP	592	2
Total		101,463	66		37,491	70		25,839	69

Source: OECD calculations applied to Scopus Custom Data, Elsevier, version 5.2012, http://www.oecd.org/sti/scoreboard-2013-interactive-charts.htm#researchers (Bilateral flows option). The corresponding charts for other countries, as well as outflows, can be obtained from the same source.

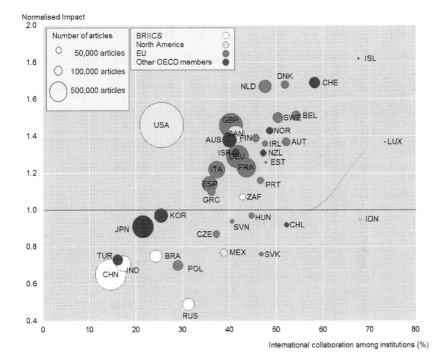

FIGURE 7B.1 The impact of scientific production and the extent of international scientific collaboration, 2003–2011. Notes: The normalized impact is derived as the ratio between the average number of citations received by the documents published by authors affiliated with an institution in a given economy and the world average of citations, over the same time period, by document type and subject area. The values show the relationship of the unit's average impact to the world average of 1, that is, a score of 0.8 means the unit cited is 20% less than average. The international institutional collaboration indicator is based on the proportion of documents involving institutional affiliations with other countries, as a proportion of documents attributed to authors with an affiliation in the reference economy. Single-authored documents with multiple affiliations across boundaries can therefore count as institutional international collaboration. *Source: OECD (2013a), OECD and SCImago Research Group (CSIC), Compendium of Bibliometric Science Indicators 2014, based on Scopus Custom Data, Elsevier, May 2013.* http://dx.doi.org/10.1787/888932890314.

FIGURE 7B.2 The quality of scientific production and international collaboration, 2003–2011, as a percentage of scientific publications. Notes: As an indicator of research excellence, the "top-cited publications" are the 10% most cited papers in each scientific field. Estimates are based on whole counts of documents by authors affiliated with institutions in each economy. Top-cited ("excellence") publications attributed to a given economy are defined as having a domestic leading author when the document's corresponding author is affiliated with a domestic institution. Collaboration is defined at institutional level. A scientific document is deemed to involve collaboration if there are multiple institutions in the list of affiliations reported by a single or multiple authors. *Source: OECD (2013a). OECD and SCImago Research Group (CSIC), Compendium of Bibliometric Science Indicators 2014, based on Scopus Custom Data, Elsevier, May 2013.* http://dx.doi.org/10.1787/888932891606.

TABLE 7C.1 Summary Statistics

Variable	Source Countries	Destination Countries	Dyads (Complete)	Dyads (Total)	N	Mean	Median	Min	Max	SD
Scientist flows (i→j)	253	253	31,864	31,864	63,728	6.65	0.00	0.00	12,739.00	135.73
Collaborations (i→j)	253	253	31,864	31,864	63,728	13.26	0.00	0.00	12,125.13	184.05
Log (collaborations (i→j))	248	248	12,817	12,817	25,634	-0.21	-0.69	-2.77	9.40	2.33
Change in collaboration (i→j)	218	218	4957	4957	9914	1.70	1.63	-4.49	6.12	1.11
Log (international students (i→j))	210	39	608	2865	5729	3.01	2.93	-1.61	11.55	2.57
Change in international student stock (i→j)	193	24	236	1416	2832	1.07	0.93	-4.32	7.28	1.27
Scientific dissimilarity (i→j)	236	236	27,730	27,730	55,460	0.08	0.06	0.00	0.51	0.07
Contiguity (i→j) (0/1)	221	221	24,306	24,306	48,612	0.01	0.00	0.00	1.00	0.11
Log (geographical distance (i→j))	221	221	24,306	24,306	48,612	8.83	9.00	4.11	9.89	0.76
Common official language (i→j) (0/1)	221	221	24,306	24,306	48,612	0.17	0.00	0.00	1.00	0.38
Common language (i→j) (0/1)	221	221	24,306	24,306	48,612	0.17	0.00	0.00	1.00	0.37
Bilateral visa restrictions (i→j) (0/1)	193	191	18,145	18,336	36,672	0.48	0.00	0.00	1.00	0.50
Unilateral visa restrictions (i→j) (0/1)	193	191	18,145	18,336	36,672	0.35	0.00	0.00	1.00	0.48
Log (migrants1990 (i→j))	226	225	6909	10,866	21,731	3.75	3.14	0.00	15.47	2.85
Change in migrant stock (i→j)	226	225	6159	10,001	20,001	0.35	0.19	-7.24	8.28	1.21
Log (service exports (i→j))	91	91	4095	4095	8190	2.92	2.88	-5.42	10.64	2.33
Log (computer/info services exports (i→j))	91	91	4095	4095	8190	-2.53	-2.52	-16.03	8.05	3.71
Log (other business services exports (i→j))	91	91	4095	4095	8190	0.57	0.56	-9.20	9.72	2.81
Log (GERD/GDP (j))	131	131	8514	16,500	32,999	-0.96	-0.87	-3.78	1.42	1.21
Change in relative R&D intensity ratio (i→j)	68	68	2192	2192	4384	0.42	0.00	-42.56	55.74	3.98
Log (population (j))	210	210	21,945	26,453	52,906	15.14	15.50	9.17	20.98	2.31
Log (GDP per capita (j))	198	198	19,503	24,941	49,882	8.14	8.03	4.93	11.75	1.65
Change in relative GDP per capita gap ratio (i→j)	180	180	16,110	16,110	32,220	-0.83	0.00	-583.00	285.03	13.20

Notes: As information on dyad linkages is available only on an aggregate basis for the time period 1996–2011, linkages related to country reformations (e.g., breakup of former Yugoslavia) cannot be identified separately and are dropped as within-country linkages from the analysis. This concerns overall 28 country-pair linkages, resulting in overall 63,728 country-pair observations. The column "Dyads (complete)" denotes the number of dyads in case of which data are available for both countries in the dyad.
Source: OECD calculations based on linked data on bilateral scientist mobility flows (Scopus Custom Data, Elsevier, version 5.2012).

TABLE 7C.2 Summary Description of Variables Used in the Regression Analysis

Variable	Definition	Source
Scientist flows $(i \rightarrow j)$	Number of publication authors reporting an affiliation based in country/economy (i) at the outset of their publication spell and an affiliation in (j) in their latest recorded publication between 1996 and 2011.	OECD analysis, based on Elsevier custom Scopus® database.
Collaborations $(i \leftrightarrow j)$	Average yearly number of scientific collaborations (whole counts) implied by publication coauthorship within the $(i \leftrightarrow j)$ dyad between 1996 and 2011.	
Change in collaboration $(i \leftrightarrow j)$	Ratio of collaborations $(i \leftrightarrow j)$ averaged over 2009–2011 to collaborations $(i \leftrightarrow j)$ averaged over 1996–1998.	
International students $(i \rightarrow j)$	Number of international students from country (i) residing in country (j) averaged over 1996–2011. International student status is based on nonresidency. Where not available on that basis, data based on foreign citizenship.	OECD Education Database, UNESCO-OECD-Eurostat (UOE) data collection on education statistics (Bilateral stock of international students)
Change in international student stock $(i \rightarrow j)$	Ratio of international students $(i \rightarrow j)$ averaged over 2009–2011 to international students $(i \rightarrow j)$ averaged over 1996–1998.	
Scientific dissimilarity $(i \leftrightarrow j)$	Defined as 1 minus similarity measure of scientific publication patterns, based on the Pearson correlation of vectors of published documents by the All Science Journal Classification (ASJC) categories.	Own calculations, based on data published by SCImago (2007).
Contiguity $(i \leftrightarrow j)$ (0/1)	Dummy variable = 1 if economies (i) and (j) share a common border, else zero.	CEPII distance database (Mayer & Zignago, 2011)
Geographical distance $(i \leftrightarrow j)$	Population-weighted distance between country (i) and (j) in km. Bilateral distances between the largest cities of country (i) and (j) are weighted by their shares in the total population of country (i) and (j), respectively.	
Common official language $(i \leftrightarrow j)$ (0/1)	Dummy variable = 1 if countries (i) and (j) share common official primary language, else zero.	
Common language $(i \leftrightarrow j)$ (0/1)	Dummy variable = 1 if a language is spoken by at least 9% of the population in both country (i) and (j), else zero.	
Bilateral visa restrictions $(i \leftrightarrow j)$ (0/1)	Dummy variable = 1 if bilateral visa restrictions are in place between countries (i) and (j) as of November 2004, else zero.	Neumayer (2006, 2011), based on November 2004 edition of IATA's Information Manual
Unilateral visa restrictions $(i \rightarrow j)$ (0/1)	Dummy variable = 1 if unilateral visa restrictions are in place between countries (i) and (j) as of November 2004, else zero.	

Variable	Description	Source
Migrants1990 ($i{\rightarrow}j$)	Number of migrants from economy (i) reported in economy (j) as of 1990.	World Bank Global Bilateral Migration Database (Bilateral migrant stocks)
Change in migrant stock ($i{\rightarrow}j$)	Ratio of stock of migrants ($i{\rightarrow}j$) in 2000 to stock of migrants ($i{\rightarrow}j$) in 1990.	
Service exports ($i{\rightarrow}j$)	Service exports from country (i) to country (j) in constant USD 2005 million averaged over 1996–2011.	OECD Trade in Services Database (EBOPS (2002): Extended Balance of Payments Services classification)
Computer/info services exports ($i{\rightarrow}j$)	Computer and information services exports (EBOPS class: 6) from country (i) to country (j) in constant USD2005 million averaged over 1996–2011.	
Other business services exports ($i{\rightarrow}j$)	Other business services exports (EBOPS class: 7) from country (i) to country (j) in constant USD2005 million averaged over 1996–2011.	
GERD/GDP (j)	Gross domestic expenditures on R&D (GERD) as percentage of gross domestic product (GDP)	UNESCO (UIS) database; OECD MSTI Main Science and Technology Indicators data base
Change in relative R&D intensity ratio ($i{\rightarrow}j$)	Average relative GERD/GDP ratio over 2009–2011 (GERD/GDP of country (i) over GERD/GDP of country (j)) minus average relative GERD/GDP ratio over1996–1998.	
Population (j)	Population of country (j) averaged over 1996–2011.	World Development Indicators Database World Bank
GDP per capita (j)	GDP per capita in constant USD 2005 million averaged over 1996–2011.	
Change in relative GDP per capita ratio ($i{\rightarrow}j$)	Average relative GDP per capita ratio over 2009–2011 (GDP per capita of country (i) over GDP per capita of country (j)) minus average relative GDP per capita ratio over1996–1998.	

.

Chapter 8

Destinations of Mobile European Researchers: Europe versus the United States

Reinhilde Veugelers[1,2,3], Linda Van Bouwel[1]
[1]*Faculty of Business and Economics, KU Leuven, Leuven, Belgium;* [2]*Bruegel, Brussels, Belgium;*
[3]*CEPR, London, UK*

Chapter Outline

1. INTRODUCTION

Many world regions, including newly emerging markets like China, have raised their ambitions to become knowledge-based economies. To realize these ambitions, the search for scientifically skilled talent has become global. In its EU2020 Strategy and its Innovation Union Flagship, Europe identifies the supply of scientific talent as a potential bottleneck for its innovation-based growth strategy. To this end, it recognizes the importance of not only increasing investment in higher education but also attracting and retaining talent in Europe during their research careers.

The European Union's (EU's) policy to establish an integrated research area aims at improving the mobility of researchers inside the EU. Policy initiatives provide funding to researchers for intra-EU mobility (e.g., Marie Curie fellowships). The pattern of intra-EU mobility of researchers shows a gradual increase (Lowell, 2007; Parey & Waldinger, 2011).

Global Mobility of Research Scientists.

A much more sensitive issue in the global competition for talent is the extra-EU mobility of researchers, particularly the mobility flows to the United States. To what extent does Europe lose its scientific talent to the United States? How does improved intra-EU mobility affect extra-EU mobility? The perspectives on this issue are clouded by a lack of good data. Not only do we know very little about the size of the flows of researchers between the European Union and the United States, we also know little about the motivations and impediments underpinning mobility decisions for extra-EU mobility compared with intra-EU mobility.

This chapter contributes to our understanding of the factors that drive intra-EU and EU–US mobility of researchers after receiving their PhD. Using unique survey data on internationally mobile European PhD holders, we compare the researchers who are mobile within Europe and researchers who choose to become mobile to the United States. In particular we look at a mix of differences in personal and home country characteristics, as well as different profiles of subjectively perceived drivers and impediments for international mobility. Our two major findings are (1) "post-PhD" mobility to the United States is driven by career motivations to a larger extent than intra-EU mobility and (2) prior intra-EU mobility experience as PhD students motivates researchers to remain mobile within the EU more than to the US after receiving their PhD.

The remainder of the chapter is organized as follows: Section 2 reviews the existing literature on the motivations and influencing factors that drive mobility. Section 3 sets out our conceptual framework and research questions; Section 4 presents data, while Section 5 presents the results, both descriptive and econometric. Section 6 provides a conclusion.

2. A REVIEW OF THE EVIDENCE ON MOTIVATIONS AFFECTING THE INTERNATIONAL MOBILITY OF RESEARCHERS

Although it is widely recognized that human capital mobility is instrumental in the development and dissemination of new ideas and technologies (Goldin, Cameron, & Balarajan, 2011), there is still a lack of comprehensive data and analysis on international mobility of the highly skilled workforce and of researchers in particular. Data on the size and direction of migration flows of researchers is an important first step in understanding international researcher mobility. For a review of this, see Stephan (2012). In addition, studying the factors that drive the decision of researchers to be mobile is also important. This section reviews the existing evidence and analysis on the factors influencing researcher mobility. This may differ at various stages of the research career, as pre-and postdoctoral students, tenured and nontenured professors in academe, and researchers in industry.

We start with the factors and motivations that drive student mobility. Although obtaining a degree in an industrialized country is often a first step in permanent migration into that country (Borjas, 2002; Tremblay, 2001), other specific factors —beyond the "classic" migration factors such as geographic and cultural distance, differences in economic conditions, and income differentials—affect student mobility (Agarwal & Winkler, 1985; Bessey, 2007; Cummings, 1984; McMahon, 1992). Many students go abroad in search of a higher-quality education than they could obtain at home (Alberts & Hazen, 2005; Van Bouwel & Veugelers, 2014).

Fewer studies address the motivations and factors influencing the mobility of researchers after receiving their PhD. Rindicate (2008) surveyed academic researchers in eight European countries on their international mobility and what factors they perceived as barriers to mobility. They found that 46% of their sample had been mobile and another 35% were interested in becoming mobile in the future. A broad array of factors were perceived as inhibitors to mobility: lack of funding for mobility, salary concerns, lack of open recruitment, misalignment in social security benefits, personal relationships, and practical things such as concerns about accommodation and health insurance. Researchers who had not yet been internationally mobile expressed most concern about the lack of recognition of mobility for career progression and the lack of funding for mobility (Rindicate, 2008). A study carried out in the context of the seventh Framework Program on European Careers for Researchers in eight European countries asked respondents about, among other things, their experience with and motives for international mobility. Of the researchers included in the study, 59% indicated having participated in an international mobility program in the past. The researchers indicated that the possibility for future career development, working on an interesting research topic, and participation in a collaborative research project were among the most important motives for mobility, whereas the reputation of the host institution also plays a significant role. Major obstacles for mobility are family and other personal connections, as well as the complex administration of relocation and lack of support from the home institution (Ivancheva & Gourova, 2011). De Grip, Fouarge, & Sauermann (2009) studied the factors that influence European science and engineering graduates in becoming internationally mobile right after their studies and 5 years later. They found that a strong research and development sector is a key attractive factor of destination countries, and previous experience with mobility is a strong predictor of future mobility, especially intra-EU mobility.

Other authors confirmed that student mobility indeed increases the probability of future labor mobility. King & Ruiz-Gelices (2003) surveyed UK students who spent a year abroad during their undergraduate studies as well as a control group of their classmates who did not; they found that the mobile group was significantly more likely to indicate interest in working abroad later, particularly in the country where the exchange year was spent. Dreher & Poutvaara (2006) examined the impact of student flows to the United States upon subsequent migration there and found that student mobility is a significant predictor of migration. Within Europe, Parey & Waldinger (2011) studied the effect of the introduction of the ERASMUS program in Germany on international labor market mobility later in life and found a significant link: Studying abroad increases by 15–20% an individual's probability of working abroad. This suggests that the ERASMUS program is an effective policy instrument to stimulate international labor market mobility within Europe.

3. CONCEPTUAL FRAMEWORK AND RESEARCH QUESTIONS

Most variables included in models of international mobility can be thought of as increasing or decreasing the benefits or costs of moving to a particular destination. Within a human capital formation perspective, mobility can be considered an investment-in-human-capital decision: A researcher will become internationally mobile if the net benefits of such a move, discounted over time, exceed the costs (Ehrenberg & Smith, 2011). The higher the costs to mobility, for example, to more distant locations, the higher the benefits need to be to compensate. In short, researcher j will become mobile if the present value of the net benefits, expressed as

$$\sum_{t=1}^{T} \frac{Bjkl_t}{(1+i)^t} - Cjkl$$

is positive. The benefits and costs of mobility are influenced by characteristics of researcher j, her source country k, and the destination country l she chooses, with $Bjkl_t$ being the net benefit of mobility for researcher j from country k to the destination country l in time period t, $Cjkl$ the mobility costs incurred at the beginning of the move, i the discount factor, and T the number of periods over which the researcher j incurs benefits.

With this framework in mind, we address two main research questions. First, how do the personal characteristics, benefits, and costs of mobility for intra-EU-mobile researchers differ from researchers mobile to the United States? Do particular characteristics or motivations increase the likelihood of choosing the United States as a destination over another European country? For policy makers, understanding why researchers choose a particular destination is important for policy design. If researchers mobile to the United States indicate that this is primarily because of financial motivations (meaning the benefits of US mobility exceed those of EU mobility in that respect), then funding for research and researchers' salaries in Europe need to be addressed; if, by contrast, a concern with administrative barriers is hindering intra-EU mobility (which can be interpreted as the costs of intra-EU mobility exceeding those of mobility to the United States), then removing these should be the primary policy goal.

Second, does previous degree-mobility experience within the EU affect the likelihood of remaining mobile within the EU compared with becoming mobile to the United States? In other words, does intra-EU student mobility alters the cost–benefit analysis of post-PhD intra-EU mobility compared with mobility to the United States? Are the effects of motivations and influencing factors for mobility different for researchers with degree-mobility experience? As discussed in the literature review, student mobility is often a precursor for subsequent mobility. We examine whether this is also the case in our data, specifically whether intra-EU degree mobility makes students more likely to remain mobile within the EU after receiving a PhD compared with going to the United States. Intra-EU degree-mobile students acquire essential language and cultural skills and establish networks that make further intra-EU mobility less costly for them. In addition, degree mobility could trigger a learning process that alters students' motivations for mobility or their perceptions of impeding factors. By contrast, intra-EU degree mobility could also serve as a stepping stone for mobility to the United States if the intra-EU degree mobility increased the researcher's human capital, making the mobility event to the United States more beneficial. Obtaining a degree from a more prestigious university during the intra-EU student mobility event could become an intermediate step to postdoctoral mobility to the United States.

4. DATA: THE MORE SURVEY

This analysis is based on data from the extra-EU MORE survey. Appendix 1 describes the MORE survey in more detail. The sample of MORE data we use contains researchers (1) holding a PhD, (2) who are EU-born, and (3) who have post-PhD mobility experience within Europe or to the United States.[1,2] We retained only those researchers who obtained their PhD in Europe, whether in their birth country or in another European country. Immobile researchers and those European researchers with a PhD degree from the United States are not included because these researchers were addressed in the MORE survey with a different questionnaire. There are 998 researchers in this subsample, 582 of which are mobile to the United States and 416 who are mobile within Europe.

Figure 1 illustrates the breakdown of our sample into the various mobility groups. The number of respondents in each group and subgroup is included.

The major drawback of this sample is that it is not representative of the population of EU researchers because nonmobile researchers are not covered by the sample and because the MORE survey specifically targeted EU–US mobile researchers, which means this group is probably overrepresented in our sample relative to the

---

1. A small number of researchers are mobile to other countries, such as Australia, but these are omitted from the analysis. Canada was originally considered together with the US as one destination, North America, but after cleaning no European researchers mobile to Canada remained in the sample.
2. A mobility experience is defined in the MORE survey as being at least 3 months. Unfortunately we could not analyze any differences in the duration of the mobility event beyond this 3 months cut-off.

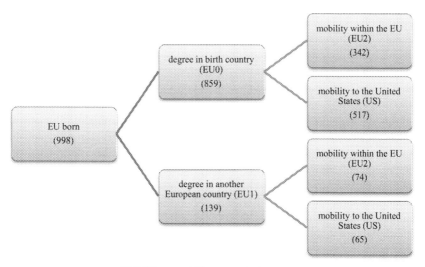

FIGURE 1 Mobility groups in the sample.

population of mobile EU-born researchers.[3] Because there are no comprehensive data sets that track the population of EU-born researchers, we have no way to correct our sample for this bias. The nonrepresentativeness of our sample affects the alternative-specific constants in our models but not necessarily the estimates for the determinants of mobility destination outcomes (Train, 2002). Nevertheless, results should be interpreted with caution, especially the descriptive statistics, which are not corrected for the bias toward EU–US mobile researchers, and should thus not be taken as representative of the population of mobile European researchers.

Table 1 lists the major degree countries in Europe where the respondents in our sample obtained their PhD. Italy is the largest source country of mobile researchers, with 190 individuals in the sample. Germany, Spain, and the United Kingdom make up the rest of the top four, with 136, 127, and 119 researchers, respectively.

Table 2 shows the major destination countries in North America and Europe. The United States is by far the most popular destination of post-PhD mobility. After the United States, the United Kingdom is the most popular destination country, receiving 89 researchers from our sample. Germany, France, and the Netherlands complete the top five of the most frequent destination countries.

The source and destination countries reveal interesting information about mobility patterns but say little about particular links between specific countries. Table 3 presents the major degree country–destination country dyads and includes the relative share of the degree country in a destination country's inflow of researchers. For example, the United Kingdom may attract 10% of all researchers in the sample but 20% of all Italians; this means that

---

3. Another implication of the US–EU focus of the MORE survey is that when researchers have multiple mobility events, only the US–EU mobility event is being surveyed.

TABLE 1 Major PhD Degree Countries

PhD Degree Country	Frequency	Percentage
Italy	190	0.19
Germany	136	0.14
Spain	127	0.13
United Kingdom	119	0.12
France	65	0.07
The Netherlands	48	0.05
Austria	33	0.03
Sweden	31	0.03
Belgium	30	0.03
Others	219	0.22

TABLE 2 Major Destination Countries for Post-PhD Mobility

Major Destination Country	Frequency	Percentage
United States	582	0.58
United Kingdom	89	0.09
Germany	60	0.06
France	58	0.06
The Netherlands	32	0.03
Spain	32	0.03
Switzerland	25	0.03
Italy	22	0.02
Others	98	0.10

TABLE 3 Major PhD Degree Country–Post-PhD Mobility Destination Country Dyads

Degree Country	Destination Country	Frequency	Percentage	Relative Share
Italy	United States	96	9.62	0.87
	United Kingdom	20	2	1.18
	Spain	14	1.4	2.30
	Germany	14	1.4	1.23
	France	13	1.3	1.18
Germany	United States	84	8.42	1.06
	United Kingdom	12	1.2	0.99
United Kingdom	United States	83	8.32	1.20
Spain	United States	83	8.32	1.12
	United Kingdom	12	1.2	1.06
France	United States	38	3.81	1.00
The Netherlands	United States	29	2.91	1.04
Austria	United States	24	2.4	1.25
Belgium	United States	21	2.1	1.20
Sweden	United States	19	1.9	1.05
Denmark	United States	18	1.8	1.06
Switzerland	United States	17	1.7	1.01
Finland	United States	14	1.4	0.86
Poland	United States	11	1.1	0.86

the share of Italians in the UK's inflow is twice as high as expected and suggests that Italians have a specific preference for the United Kingdom (or the United Kingdom has a preference for incoming Italian researchers). A relative share above 1 indicates that the inflow from a particular country is larger than expected given the average inflow into the destination country. The relative share is calculated only for mobility flows of at least 10 individuals.

The flow of Italians to Spain is 2.3 times larger than expected given Spain's average attractiveness. This special link may be due to proximity and similarities in language and culture. Certain degree countries also have relatively larger flows to the United States, such as Austria, Belgium, and the United Kingdom. Other countries send relatively fewer researchers to the United States, including Italy, Poland, and Finland. For Italy, this is partly explained by a disproportionate preference for mobility within Europe, to the United Kingdom, Germany, France, and Spain in particular.

5. RESULTS

5.1 Mobility Statistics

We first present some descriptive statistics on the post-PhD mobility patterns in the sample. In line with our data description above, we defined four groups: researchers who obtain their PhD degree in their birth country and become intra-EU mobile (EU0–EU2) or mobile to the United States (EU0–US) and researchers who obtain their PhD degree in another European country and are mobile within Europe (EU1–EU2) or to the United States (EU1–US). Table 4 illustrates how the 998 researchers in our mobile sample are divided among these four groups.

Looking at the total sample of post-PhD mobile EU researchers, the majority (58.3%, $n = 582$ researchers) are mobile to the United States, whereas only 41.7% are mobile within the EU. Looking only at the group of researchers who obtained their degree from another EU country, however, the likelihood of being mobile within the EU is significantly higher (53.2%) compared with their peers with a degree from their birth country (39.8%). A Pearson chi-square test confirmed that degree mobility and intra-EU mobility are indeed related. The data thus confirm that intra-EU PhD mobility enhances intra-EU mobility

TABLE 4 Composition of the Sample By Mobility Group

| | Degree Country | | |
	EU0 (Birth Country)	EU1 (Other EU)	Total
Intra-EU mobility	342 (39.81)	74 (53.2)	416 (41.7)
Mobility to the United States	517 (60.19)	65 (46.8)	582 (58.3)
Total	**859 (100)**	**139 (100)**	**998 (100)**

compared to US mobility at later stages of the research career. For EU researchers who obtained their PhD in another EU country, the EU becomes a more attractive destination than the United States for post-PhD mobility compared with non-PhD mobile researchers.

5.2 Descriptive Statistics on Factors Influencing Mobility

The MORE survey contains information on three sets of factors influencing the mobility decision: personal characteristics, stated motivations, and perceived barriers. We compare these factors across the four mobility groups and report t tests comparing the degree mobility groups (EU0 vs EU1) and comparing intra-EU mobility with US-mobility within degree mobility groups.

A first set of variables include the personal characteristics of researchers: sex, age, marital status, number of children, and type of employer (academic vs industry). Most personal characteristics influence the costs of mobility; researchers who are married or cohabiting often need to take the preferences of their spouse into account in their mobility decision. For example, several types of temporary visas in the United States allow researchers to bring dependents but do not automatically grant them a work permit, whereas within the EU there is no such work permit restriction for mobile EU nationals. Children also increase mobility costs, bringing considerations of school quality and availability of accommodation into the equation. Age influences the period over which the benefits of mobility can be enjoyed: Younger researchers can enjoy the benefits of mobility over a longer time period than their older colleagues. In academe, mobility often is expected of researchers and brings more career benefits, and the labor market for academic researchers tends to be more international.

Table 5 compares these characteristics for the four mobility groups. Among the total sample, 73% of respondents are male, 80% are married, and 64% have children. The average respondent is a little more than 44 years old. Few significant differences arise across the different mobility groups, with the exception of age and employer. Researchers with a PhD degree obtained in another European country are significantly younger and less likely to currently be working for an academic employer compared with researchers with a degree from their birth country. Compared with researchers with a degree from their birth country who are intra-EU mobile after their PhD, researchers who are mobile to the United States are significantly older as well as more likely to be working for an academic employer.

The second set of variables of interest is the researcher's motivations for mobility. The survey asked researchers to score seven motivations on a scale ranging from not important at all (1) to extremely important (5):

1. Personal education and/or research agenda (i.e., the content and direction of the respondent's research)
2. Career progression goals (the possibility for the respondent's career as a researcher to evolve further)

TABLE 5 Personal Characteristics by Mobility Groups

Mobility Categories	Male	Age	Married/ Cohabiting	Children	Academic Employer
EU0	0.74	44.93	0.81	0.64	0.76
EU0–EU2	0.75	43.75	0.8	0.65	0.73
EU0–US	0.73	45.72[a]	0.82	0.64	0.79[a]
EU1	0.68	41.71[b]	0.75[b]	0.64	0.68[b]
EU1–EU2	0.68	42.37	0.78	0.68	0.64
EU1–US	0.66	40.97	0.72	0.60	0.74
Total	**0.73**	**44.48**	**0.80**	**0.64**	**0.75**

[a] t tests comparing intra-EU and US mobility statistically significant (below 5%).
[b] t tests comparing an EU0 degree with an EU1 degree statistically significant (below 5%).

3. Getting access to the facilities or equipment necessary for the respondent's research
4. The prospect of working with leading experts ("star scientists") in the respondent's field of research at (or close to) the respondent's new employer
5. Personal/family factors
6. Personal interest in the culture of the country
7. Salary and other financial incentives

A principal component analysis checked whether these motivations could be regrouped into a smaller number of factors. The individual motivations are grouped into three composite motivations: career motivations, comprised of the first four motivations; personal motivations, including the next two; and financial motivations (Table 6).

Career-motivated or financially motivated researchers value more professional benefits from mobility than researchers who move for personal or family reasons. Researchers who care more about career advancement or financial rewards should be attracted more to destinations that offer better opportunities to realize these ambitions. If the mobility costs would be higher to move to a more distant US destination, we could expect larger scores for the effect of US-destined mobility on motivations to compensate for these higher mobility costs.

Career-related motivations are the most important motivations for mobility for all groups, dominating financial motivations as well as personal motivations. This suggests that the expectation of furthering one's career goals or improving access to resources that can help to achieve this seem to be the most important factor to explain migration flows. Comparing the motivations between EU- and US-mobile groups reveals that researchers mobile to the United States report significantly higher career motivations, regardless of where they obtained their PhD. Researchers with PhD mobility experience are more likely to be motivated by financial reasons, regardless of their destination, compared with researchers

TABLE 6 Motivations by Mobility Groups

Mobility Categories	Mean Score		
	Career Motivations	Personal Motivations	Financial Motivations
EU0	3.87	2.48	2.63
EU0–EU2	3.71	2.43	2.65
EU0–US	3.97[a]	2.52	2.62
EU1	3.81	2.47	3.02[b]
EU1–EU2	3.55	2.48	2.89
EU1–US	4.12[a]	2.51	3.2
Total	**3.86**	**2.49**	**2.69**

[a] t tests comparing intra-EU and US mobility statistically significant (below 5%).
[b] t tests comparing an EU0 degree with an EU1 degree statistically significant (below 5%).

with a PhD from their home country. The other motivations are not significantly different across groups. Surprisingly, salary motivations are not significantly higher for US-mobile researchers, although in Europe the perception seems to be that low salaries and a lack of flexibility in terms of wage offers is a significant handicap in attracting and retaining talented researchers.

A third group of explanatory variables covers external factors influencing the decision to become mobile. The survey asked respondents to score eight external influencing factors on a scale from 1 to 5. These external influencing factors capture possible impediments to move. They are:

1. Immigration regulations (e.g., immigration law, labor permission law, law of residence permission)
2. Pension and social care provisions in the destination country
3. Obtaining funding for research
4. Potential loss of contacts with the respondent's professional network at the location where he or she previously worked
5. Work permission for partner (and other family members)
6. Availability of adequate schools for children
7. Quality and cost of accommodation
8. Language

The external influencing factors were regrouped into a few composite factors (Table 7): regulatory factors, which include factors 1 and 2, and personal factors, including factors 5, 6, and 7. The remaining influencing factors are included individually.

The external factors influence the cost side of the mobility decision. Researchers who report greater concern about these factors may experience higher impediments to mobility than researchers who report weaker concerns.

TABLE 7 External Influencing Factors by Mobility Groups

Mobility Categories	Mean Score				
	Regulatory Factors	Funding	Loss of Contacts	Personal Factors	Language
EU0	1.75	2.82	2.08	2.1	2.76
EU0–EU2	1.75	2.85	2.06	2	2.5
EU0–US	1.75	2.8	2.1	2.16[a]	2.93[a]
EU1	1.91[b]	2.97	2.18	2.13	2.57[b]
EU1–EU2	1.92	2.72	2.22	2.05	2.28
EU1–US	1.91	3.29[a]	2.12	2.26	2.91[a]
Total	**1.77**	**2.84**	**2.1**	**2.1**	**2.73**

[a] t tests comparing intra-EU and US mobility statistically significant (below 5%).
[b] t tests comparing an EU0 degree with an EU1 degree statistically significant (below 5%).

Given that our sample consists of only mobile researchers, we expect that most researchers will, on average, indicate that external influencing factors were not very important in their mobility decision. What might be more revealing is any difference among the various influences factors, as well as any differences between the EU and the US mobile researchers.

In general, obtaining research funding is the most important external factor influencing mobility, closely followed by language, whereas regulatory factors are the least important. Note, however, that all external influencing factors are rated, on average, as unimportant with scores below 3. Researchers who obtained their PhD in another EU country and move to the United States (EU1–US) are more likely to attach importance to obtaining funding for their own research compared with their peers who remain mobile within the EU. Researchers mobile from their birth country to the United States (EU0–US) rank personal factors higher as an impediment. Language receives a larger weight as an impediment in the mobility decision of US-mobile researchers, regardless of PhD mobility.

5.3 Regression Analysis

To analyze the impact of individual factors associated with intra-EU and US mobility, controlling for other influencing factors, we use econometric analysis. We use a logit model with the probability to become mobile to the United States relative to the EU as our dependent variable. The main explanatory variables of interest are the motivations for mobility and impediments (external influencing factors). Another pivotal explanatory variable is a dummy variable for researchers who have obtained their degree in a European country other than their birth country. This allows testing whether mobility during the PhD influences the postdoctoral mobility destination. To test further the influence of predoctoral mobility, we perform a split logit analysis with separate regressions for PhD-mobile and non-PhD-mobile researchers. The results of the logit analysis are reported in Table 8. The split logit results are reported in Table 9. Before discussing the results, it is important to stress that the results should not be interpreted as suggesting causality but merely as establishing associations.

TABLE 8 Logit Model for Mobility to the United States

Variables	Mobility to United States	
	(1)	(2)
Male	−0.212 (0.165)	−0.210 (0.168)
Age (years)	0.002,57 (0.0155)	0.006,96 (0.0159)
Cohort 10–19	−0.0631 (0.214)	−0.0250 (0.220)
Cohort 20–29	−0.0464 (0.354)	−0.0551 (0.361)
Cohort 30–49	0.727 (0.489)	0.827* (0.501)
Industry	0.0851 (0.399)	0.0209 (0.412)
Degree in other EU country	−0.387* (0.225)	−0.363 (0.230)
Career motivations	0.582*** (0.0999)	
Education/research agenda		0.002,95 (0.0793)
Career progression goals		0.336*** (0.0778)
Access to facilities		0.0191 (0.0641)
Star scientists		0.273*** (0.0736)
Personal motivations	−0.0178 (0.0849)	0.0322 (0.0875)
Money motivations	−0.0100 (0.0648)	−0.004,99 (0.0679)
Regulatory influencing factors	−0.169* (0.0995)	
Pension/social care provision		−0.481*** (0.110)
Immigration regulations		0.285*** (0.106)
Research funding	−0.120** (0.0594)	−0.117* (0.0607)
Loss of contacts	−0.0883 (0.0725)	−0.0864 (0.0744)
Personal influencing factors	0.193** (0.0898)	
Work permission partner		0.0782 (0.0761)
Adequate schools		0.116 (0.0806)
Accommodation		−0.0458 (0.0880)
Language	0.358*** (0.0652)	0.341*** (0.0666)
Exact sciences	0.122 (0.268)	−0.0397 (0.278)
Life sciences	0.387 (0.336)	0.249 (0.344)
Social sciences	−0.176 (0.284)	−0.302 (0.294)
Mediterranean	−0.428** (0.195)	−0.410** (0.200)
Anglo-Saxon Europe	0.725** (0.321)	0.709** (0.327)
Scandinavia	−0.290 (0.253)	−0.323 (0.260)
Central and Eastern Europe	−0.655* (0.348)	−0.622* (0.354)
Relative impact of degree country publication	0.430 (0.580)	0.369 (0.592)
Constant	−2.575** (1.007)	−2.835*** (1.038)
Observations	998	998
Pseudo R^2	0.1047	0.1310

Standard errors are in parenthesis; *** $p<0.01$, ** $p<0.05$, * $p<0.1$. Values outside parenthesis indicate estimated coefficients.

TABLE 9 Logit Models for Mobility to the United States: EU Degree versus Home-Country Degree

Variables	Mobility to United States	
	EU0	EU1
1 if Male	−0.235 (0.182)	−0.290 (0.480)
Age (years)	0.008,10 (0.0167)	−0.0322 (0.0537)
Cohort 10–19	−0.0952 (0.232)	0.337 (0.704)
Cohort 20–29	−0.0590 (0.378)	−1.381 (1.577)
Cohort 30–49	0.654 (0.524)	0.469 (1.824)
Industry	0.253 (0.472)	−0.536 (0.968)
Career motivations	0.562*** (0.110)	0.657** (0.306)
Personal motivations	0.007,63 (0.0932)	−0.195 (0.242)
Money motivations	−0.0109 (0.0717)	0.191 (0.190)
Regulatory influencing factors	−0.150 (0.110)	−0.424 (0.292)
Research funding	−0.182*** (0.0645)	0.180 (0.197)
Loss of contacts	−0.0331 (0.0791)	−0.567** (0.234)
Personal influencing factors	0.177* (0.0992)	0.500* (0.272)
Language	0.370*** (0.0717)	0.317 (0.196)
Exact sciences	0.0732 (0.294)	−0.186 (0.825)
Life sciences	0.508 (0.366)	−1.112 (1.143)
Social sciences	−0.148 (0.313)	−1.082 (0.829)
Mediterranean	−0.743*** (0.239)	−0.122 (0.526)
Anglo-Saxon Europe	0.756** (0.340)	1.958 (1.245)
Scandinavia	−0.310 (0.266)	0.360 (1.087)
Central and Eastern Europe	−1.686*** (0.511)	0.139 (0.589)
Relative impact of degree country publication	−1.183 (0.794)	3.368** (1.654)
Constant	−1.032 (1.225)	−4.697 (3.126)
Observations	859	139
Pseudo R^2	0.1051	0.2190

Standard errors are in parenthesis; *** $p<0.01$, ** $p<0.05$, * $p<0.1$. Values outside parenthesis indicate estimated coefficients.

As control variables we included sex, age, whether the current job is in industry or academe, research field, the region of birth in Europe, and a research quality indicator of the degree country.[4]

Researchers are divided into cohorts based on when they obtained their PhD degree. Because the time span covered by the survey is rather wide, we aggregated the cohort effects into three 10-year windows for researchers who obtained their PhD

---

4. Marital status and children are not included in the regressions because these were reported at the time of the survey as opposed to the time of mobility. Inclusion of marital status and children does not affect the results reported.

less than 10 years ago, between 10 and 20 years ago, and between 20 and 30 years ago. A fourth cohort dummy is included for researchers who obtained their PhD more than 30 years ago. The most recent cohort serves as the base group. Ten-year cohort windows may be too wide to capture all the events and short-term trends that affect researchers' mobility outcomes. They should, however, capture broad trends such as the progress in European integration and long-term evolutions in the general working conditions of researchers in the United States and Europe.

Research field fixed effects are included to capture specifics in the four broad fields of researchers' PhD degrees: the exact sciences, life sciences, social sciences, and humanities (the base group). Opportunities, motives, impediments, and expectations of mobility may differ across disciplines. Mobility is often a necessity in certain fields of exact sciences, such as particle physics or astronomy, to be able to access certain specialized equipment that is only present in a few countries. By contrast, possibilities for and expectations of mobility may be fewer in the humanities when research is more strongly embedded in local culture.

Fixed effects for the birth regions within Europe are included, that is, Scandinavia, the Mediterranean countries, central and eastern European countries, and the Anglo-Saxon countries (Ireland and the United Kingdom). Western Europe serves as the base region. Researchers from different birth regions in Europe face different possibilities for and constraints on mobility. We also included an indicator for the strength of the research environment. This indicator is included at the level of the degree country, measuring the relative impact of the degree country's publications.[5] Researchers who obtained a degree in a country with strong research performance probably enjoyed a higher-quality graduate education and may have more opportunities and benefit more from international mobility to the United States than researchers with a degree from a country with a weaker scientific performance, all else being equal.

The econometric results show that mobile researchers do not seem to differ significantly across destination in their personal characteristics: neither sex, nor age, nor cohort, nor a current job in industry are significantly related to an increased probability of mobility to either destination. Replacing the cohort dummies with a single, continuous variable measuring time since degree (results not reported) reveals that researchers who graduated more recently are more likely to be mobile within the EU, which suggests that intra-EU mobility has been on the rise in recent years.

Researchers who obtained their PhD degree in a European country other than their birth country are significantly less likely to be mobile to the United States. The marginal effect of being intra-EU degree mobile for the average male, western European researcher in the exact sciences and from the most

---

5. This measure is computed as the share of the degree country's citations in total world citations, divided by the share of the degree country's publications, divided by total world publications. The relative impact intends to capture whether the average publication in the degree country receives more or fewer citations than the average world publication.

recent cohort is a 9% decrease in the probability of being mobile to the United States after receiving a PhD compared with being intra-EU mobile. This confirms, as also found in the descriptive statistics, that degree mobility within Europe creates a precedent for follow-up intra-EU mobility as a researcher.

The econometric results further confirm the importance of career motivations for mobility to the United States: Researchers who indicate that career motivations were important in their decision to become mobile are more likely to be mobile to the United States than within the EU. For an average researcher, the marginal effect of a one-unit increase in career motivations is a 13% increase in the probability of becoming mobile to the United States. This could be because stronger career motivations are needed to offset the potentially larger cost of mobility to the United States. It could also reflect that the United States is considered to be a better destination than the EU for researchers who want to advance their career and further their research agenda. The other two motivation components, personal and financial, were not significantly different between the two mobility groups.

Replacing the composite career motivations variable with its constituent individual motivations (column 2) suggests that career progression goals and the prospects of working with leading experts ("star scientists") in their field are the significant motivations that direct researchers toward the United States rather than to another EU country. Star scientists are indeed more concentrated in the United States (Laudel, 2003). Researchers who are motivated by the prospect of working with them are primarily oriented toward the United States. With respect to career progression goals, compared with the United States, there is still relatively substantial heterogeneity in Europe in terms of internal governance and typical career progression (Haeck & Verboven, 2013), which could hinder mobility within Europe.

Concerns about obtaining funding make researchers significantly less likely to choose the United States rather than the EU as destination for post-PhD mobility: A one-unit increase in concern about funding reduces by 3% the probability of going to the United States. This suggests that the initiatives taken by the EU and its member states to make enough funding available for mobility may have reduced the impediments for mobility within Europe, diverting mobility away from the United States.

Regulatory impeding factors make researchers less likely to choose the United States rather than the EU as a destination for post-PhD mobility: A one-unit increase in concerns about regulatory factors decreases by 4% the probability of mobility to the United States for an average researcher. This suggests that the initiatives taken by the EU and its member states to reduce administrative barriers to mobility have helped to stimulate mobility within Europe, diverting mobility away from the United States. This holds for pension and social care regulations in particular (column 2). The more researchers are concerned with pensions and social care provisions, the less likely they are to be mobile to the United States. By contrast, the more weight researchers give to immigration regulations, the more likely they are to be mobile to the United States.

Personal impeding factors make researchers more likely to become mobile to the United States. Apparently, researchers find moving their families to the

United States easier than moving within Europe.[6] Language significantly negatively contributes to choosing an intra-EU destination compared with choosing the United States.

Field fixed effects were not significant, but some of the regional fixed effects were. Researchers from Anglo-Saxon countries are more likely to be mobile to the United States than to another EU country. By contrast, researchers from the Mediterranean and from central and eastern Europe are less likely to become mobile to the United States compared with being mobile within the EU. Cultural differences or differences in scientific profile with the United States might be bigger from the perspective of these regions. Our measure for the scientific quality of the researcher's degree country positively affects the choice for the United States rather than intra-EU as a destination. After controlling for regional fixed effects, however, this effect is not significant.

Although we found that PhD mobility significantly changed the destination of post-PhD mobility in favor of the EU, a Chow test indicated that PhD-mobile and non-PhD-mobile researchers do not have jointly significantly different effects from motivations, impediments, and other factors influencing mobility. Wald tests for separate groups of explanatory variables also indicate no significant differences between these two groups: Neither the personal characteristics, the motivations, nor the impeding factors are jointly significantly different for these two groups. However, this does not preclude certain individual factors from differing between PhD-mobile and non-PhD-mobile researchers. To investigate further the difference between those researchers who obtained their PhD degree in another European country versus in their birth country, we ran an econometric analysis on the split sample. This allowed us to check in more detail which personal characteristics, motivations, and external influencing factors affect the destination choice differently for both subgroups. Results are reported in Table 9.

The importance of career motivations to move to the United States rather than within the EU holds for both groups, as do the personal influencing factors. The importance of access to funding, favoring the EU rather than the United States as a destination, is significant only for the group of researchers with a PhD from their birth country. This might suggest that it is access to national funding in particular that crowds out mobility to the United States.

Potential loss of contacts is a significant factor for choosing the EU rather than the United States as a destination among those with a PhD from another EU country. This is consistent with network effects, which builds path dependency. Researchers who are mobile as students have made efforts to build a network in their host country and are more fearful of losing these new contacts if they move too far away.[7]

---

6. Surprisingly, none of the components of personal influencing factors were individually significant. A Wald test confirmed that work permission for the spouse, adequate schools, and accommodation are not jointly significant.

7. An interaction term between EU-degree mobility and funding in the full sample was significantly different from zero at the 5% level and from the potential loss of contacts at the 10% level (results are not reported here).

Language is a factor increasing the probability of choosing the United States rather than another EU country as a destination only for researchers with a degree from their home country, whereas language is not a significant factor in destination choice for researchers with a degree from another EU country. This suggests that mobility experience within Europe reduces the impeding effect of language on mobility.[8]

The lower probability for researchers from central and eastern Europe and from the Mediterranean to move to the United States rather than within the EU holds only for the researchers who obtained their PhD in their birth country. By contrast, for degree-mobile researchers, there are no significant regional effects. This suggests that for researchers from central and eastern Europe and the Mediterranean, degree mobility within Europe could be a stepping stone to later mobility to the United States.

For researchers who obtained their PhD degree elsewhere in Europe, the relative research strength of the PhD degree country matters for the destination choice of post-PhD mobility: The higher the research strength of the PhD degree country, as measured by the more citations its publications attract, on average, the higher the odds that this researcher will be mobile to the United States rather than to another EU country. This implies that although intra-EU degree mobility seems to divert mobility from the United States to the EU in later stages of the research career, this diversion away from the United States is mitigated when the PhD degree is obtained in a country with a strong science environment.[9]

6. CONCLUSION

Using a sample of 998 European-born researchers who obtained their PhD in Europe, we studied the differences in personal characteristics, motivations, and external impeding factors between researchers who are internationally mobile within Europe after receiving their PhD or internationally mobile to the United States. We found that career motivations are more strongly related to post-PhD mobility to the United States than within the EU. This suggests that the United States is still perceived as a strong destination country for advancing one's research career. Researchers with previous experience with mobility within Europe as PhD students are, however, more likely to remain internationally mobile within Europe after receiving their PhD. These researchers have a different perception of impeding factors, in particular the potential loss of contacts and access to funding. Among our set of determining

---

8. These results are, however, not very strong. An interaction term between EU-degree mobility and language in the full sample was not significantly different from zero.

9. In the full sample model, the interaction between the EU–PhD dummy and the relative impact of the degree country's publications was also positive and significant at the 5% level (results are not reported here).

factors, financial motivations were not significant in determining the location choice for postdoctoral mobility, whereas language barriers continue to hinder intra-EU mobility. Finally, intra-EU degree mobility seems to operate as a stepping stone for later mobility to the United States: Researchers who leave their birth country, particularly those from central and eastern Europe and the Mediterranean, to obtain their PhD in a European country with strong scientific performance are more likely to become mobile to the United States later in their career.

This analysis suffers from several drawbacks. First, although knowing how certain factors relate to mobile researchers' destination outcomes is interesting, we cannot answer the logically preceding question: What factors are related to a researcher's choice of whether to become internationally mobile in the first place? To answer this question, the survey should have been organized to allow us to compare the nonmobile respondents in the sample with the mobile respondents.

A related drawback of the survey is that it is not always clear how respondents interpreted certain questions. For example, in the set of external influencing factors, respondents were asked to evaluate to what extent language was an important factor in their decision to become mobile. This question asks respondents to assess the weight of language in the mobility decision, but whether language enters the consideration positively (i.e., "I became mobile to improve my language skills" or "I chose the United States because I already speak English") or negatively ("I perceive overcoming language barriers as a cost of mobility") is not clear ex ante. The ambivalence of whether certain factors positively or negatively affect the mobility decision limits the scope of interpretation of our results. Future versions of the survey might benefit from asking respondents to indicate whether a particular factor was considered a benefit or a cost in addition to asking them to indicate the weight of that particular factor in the overall decision.

Finally, a few key variables that might influence mobility outcomes were not or only partially controlled for. One aspect is researchers' ability: Researchers with high ability can be expected to have more opportunities to become mobile if their visibility and reputation aids them in getting international job offers or invitations for extended research stays. An interesting research question that we cannot answer is whether ability is related to researchers' destination choices. For example, are the most talented researchers more likely to become mobile to the United States rather than within the EU, as is suggested by the "elite brain drain" literature (Hunter, Oswald, & Charlton, 2009; Laudel, 2003)? Another line of research that would be interesting to explore further is the distinction between shorter and longer or permanent mobility decisions.

In conclusion, there are still many aspects of mobility, and of researcher mobility in particular, that remain underexplored or for which the evidence is inconclusive. To further our understanding of the factors that drive researchers to become mobile, indicators should continue to be improved, and further extensive data collection is needed.

APPENDIX 1: THE MORE SURVEY AND OUR SAMPLE

The analysis is based on survey data from the extra-EU MORE survey, part of a group of surveys carried out in the context of a study on mobility patterns and career paths of EU researchers.[10] In the MORE survey, mobility is defined as a minimum 3-month stay in a country different from the country where the highest degree was obtained. The target group for the extra-EU MORE survey are researchers who obtained their highest degree in the EU and who worked in the United States for a minimum of 3 months. There are three additional target groups: researchers who obtained their highest degree in the United States and who worked in the EU for a minimum of 3 months, researchers who have been mobile but who do not belong to the previous two groups, and researchers who have not been internationally mobile.

The main sampling method of the survey was a web-based search.[11] The sampling method allowed the construction of a relatively large group of respondents, but the sampling method also has drawbacks. The major drawback is a lack of information on the representativeness of the sample relative to the underlying population. The survey sample cannot be corrected for possible biases that distort its representativeness. The findings drawn from these data therefore cannot be generalized to the whole population and are valid only for this particular sample. Despite these caveats, given the scarcity of data on EU researchers and particularly on mobility, this sample provides an interesting source of information for analysis.

The survey was initially sent to 93,183 e-mail addresses. Of these, 22,206 people viewed the e-mail and 5572 responded (6% of the total invited and 25% of those who viewed the e-mail), of whom 4571 respondents fully completed the questionnaire. An additional 1393 fully completed surveys were received from nonpanel individuals, adding up to a total of 5964 fully completed questionnaires. After sorting through responses, a total of 5544 responses remained. This sample was used for the MORE report for the European Commission (MORE, 2010).

---

10. This study was carried out by IDEA Consult in consortium with NIFU Step, WIFO, Logotech, and the University of Manchester for the European Commission in 2009–2010.

11. The search identified html pages or PDF files that match a few key words that identify an academic curriculum vitae and likely mobility between the United States and the European Union. The resulting list of e-mail addresses was the primary direct sampling source. Indirect sampling methods also were used, including publishing the survey on LinkedIn and forwarding it to the Euraxess community, the EU Centers of Excellence in the United States, and the coordinators of the ATLANTIS Program on EU–US Cooperation in Higher Education and Vocational Training.

We have no data available to assess the extent to which this sample is biased toward EU–US mobility. As a small check, we compared the researchers in our sample who are currently residing in Belgium with the Belgian sample of the Careers of Doctorate Holders survey (CDH) carried out in several Organisation for Economic Co-operation and Development countries in 2006 in cooperation with the Organisation for Economic Co-operation and Development, Eurostat, and UNESCO Institute of Statistics.[12] The CDH sample includes only PhD holders currently working in Belgium and does not take into account researchers who moved abroad permanently or who have not yet returned. This biases the mobility rates in CDH downward. The comparison reveals that our sample picks up four times as much "career mobility" (i.e., mobility after the highest degree is obtained) as the CDH sample, and this mobility is more likely to be geared toward North America: 52% of career mobility goes toward the United States in our sample versus 12% in the CDH sample. This indicates that the MORE sample is strongly biased toward EU–US mobility. The true population mobility rates are likely to lie somewhere between the MORE estimate and the CDH estimate. Because we have no good information to correct for the bias, we hope that the nonrepresentativeness of our sample affects the alternative-specific constants in our econometric analysis but not necessarily the estimates for the determinants of mobility destination outcomes (Train, 2002). Nevertheless, results should be interpreted with caution, especially the descriptive statistics.

The survey itself consists of two parts. The first addresses all mobility groups and asks about researchers' personal and family situation, education and training, current employment as a researcher, and experience with mobility. The second part asks respondents about their views on mobility, including personal motivations for mobility, external influencing factors for the decision to become mobile, and the effects of mobility they experienced. The second part differs by target group. Although the questions to the immobile group were designed to be "mirror questions" to those for the mobile group, a different wording was used, which may have caused a different interpretation by mobile and nonmobile respondents.[13] This implies we cannot use the data to compare mobile researchers with nonmobile researchers. We can, however, address the question of whether the effects of mobility differ among researchers who are mobile to different destinations.

---

12. We are grateful to the Belgian Federal Science Policy Office for allowing us access to the data.
13. For example, one of the questions in the EU–US-mobile group is, To what extent were the following aspects important as factors motivating you to become mobile to the US? The mirror question for the nonmobile group is, To what extent were the following aspects important as factors dissuading you from becoming mobile? Aspects such as family considerations may be given little weight by the first group if they became mobile *despite* family considerations, even if family considerations received a lot of weight in the overall mobility decision, and vice versa for the nonmobile group.

ACKNOWLEDGMENT

The chapter has benefited from the comments of two anonymous referees, Dirk Czarnitzki, Otto Toivanen, Elissavet Lykogianni, and the participants of the ENID STI Conference (Rome, September 2011) and the TEMPO Conference (Vienna, November 2011).

REFERENCES

Agarwal, V. B., & Winkler, D. R. (1985). Foreign demand for United States higher education: a study of developing countries in the eastern Hemisphere. *Economic Development and Cultural Change, 33*(3), 623–644.

Alberts, H. C., & Hazen, H. D. (2005). "There are always two voices…": International students' intentions to stay in the United States or to return to their home countries'. *International Migration, 43*(3), 131–145.

Bessey, D. (2007). *International student migration to Germany.* Swiss Leading House working paper no.6.

Borjas, G. J. (2002). *An evaluation of the foreign student program,* working paper RWP02-026.

Cummings, W. K. (1984). Going overseas for higher education: the Asian experience. *Comparative Education Review, 28*(2), 241–257.

De Grip, A., Fouarge, D., & Sauermann, J. (2009). *What affects international migration of European science and engineering graduates?* IZA discussion paper no. 4268.

Dreher, A., & Poutvaara, P. (2006), *Student flows and migration: an empirical analysis,* KOF-Arbeitspapiere/Working Papers No. 142, July, Zurich.

Ehrenberg, R. G., & Smith, R. S. (2011). *Modern labor economics: Theory and public policy (11th ed.).* Boston: Pearson.

Goldin, I., Cameron, G., & Balarajan, M. (2011). *Exceptional people: How migration shaped our world and will define our future.* Princeton University Press.

Haeck, C., & Verboven, F. (2013). The internal economics of a university: evidence from personnel data. *Journal of Labor Economics, 30*(3), 591–626.

Hunter, R. S., Oswald, A. J., & Charlton, B. G. (2009). The elite brain drain. *Research Policy, 36*(5), 619–636.

IDEA Consult. (2008). *Evidence on the main factors inhibiting mobility and career development of researchers,* Rindicate report for EC.

Ivancheva, L., & Gourova, E. (2011). Challenges for career and mobility of researchers in Europe. *Science and Public Policy, 38*(3), 185–198.

King, R., & Ruiz-Gelices, E. (2003). International student migration and the European "Year Abroad": effects on European identity and subsequent migration behaviour. *International Journal of Population Geography, 9*(3), 229–252.

Laudel, G. (2003). Studying the brain drain: can bibliometric methods help? *Scientometrics, 57*(2), 215–237.

Lowell, L. B. (2007). *Trends in international migration flows and stocks, 1975–2007,* OECD Social, Employment and Migration Working Papers (58).

McMahon, M. E. (1992). Higher education in a world market. An historical look at the global context of international study. *Higher Education, 24*(4), 465–482.

MORE. (2010). *Study on mobility patterns and career paths of EU researchers, final technical report 3: Extra-EU mobility pilot study, Report prepared for the European Commission.* Research Directorate-General, EU.

Parey, M., & Waldinger, F. (2011). Studying abroad and the effect on international labor market mobility: evidence from the introduction of ERASMUS. *The Economic Journal*, *121*(551), 194–222.

Stephan, P. E. (2012). *How economics shapes science*. Harvard University Press.

Train, K. E. (2002). *Discrete choice models with simulation*. Cambridge University Press.

Tremblay, K. (2001). Student mobility between and towards OECD countries in 2001: a comparative analysis. In *International mobility of the highly skilled* (pp. 39–67). Paris: OECD.

Van Bouwel, L., & Veugelers, R. (2014). An "elite" brain drain: are foreign top PhDs in the US less likely to return home? In S. Uebelmesser & M. Gerard (Eds.), Cross border mobility of students & researchers, Cambridge: MIT Press, pp. 57–81.

Chapter 9

Appointment, Promotion, and Mobility of Bioscience Researchers in Japan

Cornelia Lawson[1,2,3], Sotaro Shibayama[4]

[1]*Department of Economics and Statistics Cognetti De Martiis, Università di Torino, Turin, Italy;* [2]*BRICK, Collegio Carlo Alberto, Moncalieri, Turin, Italy;* [3]*School of Sociology and Social Policy, University of Nottingham, Nottingham, UK;* [4]*Research Center for Advanced Science and Technology, University of Tokyo, Meguro-ku, Tokyo, Japan*

Chapter Outline

1. INTRODUCTION

The study of the determinants of scientific productivity has been a major focus in the economics of science, but the analysis of career and mobility has received less attention, perhaps because both are assumed to be closely linked to productivity (Allison & Long, 1990; Long, Allison, & McGinnis, 1993). However, while one would assume that promotion and hiring decisions are made on the basis of merit, there is no conclusive evidence confirming that this is the case. Instead, in many countries merit is not the only driver behind promotion decisions; seniority and sex are equally if not more important (e.g., Long et al., 1993). Similarly, hiring can rely heavily on prestige effects, favoring graduates of top institutions (Crane, 1965, 1970), and, to a concerning extent, inbreeding, that is, the hiring of graduates from the same institution (Burris, 2004; Hargens & Farr, 1973; Horta, Veloso, & Grediaga, 2010).

In this context the mobility of researchers has received increasing support from policymakers around the world. Enhanced transparency in hiring decisions and the movement of university staff between universities and to firms is viewed as crucial for the advancement of knowledge (MEXT, 2003a; OECD, 2000, 2008), and localism and inbreeding are considered inhibitors of scientific advancement and innovation (MEXT, 2003b; OECD, 2008). However, academic careers were (and mostly still are) characterized by stability, long-term employment relationships (tenure), and a rigid structure of hierarchy (Pezzoni, Sterzi, & Lissoni, 2012). Career steps are well defined, and requirements for advancement are outlined in internal guidelines, which usually emphasize merit and seniority (time in rank). In most of Europe as well as Japan mobility during later career stages is further discouraged by life-long contracts and the importance of local scholarly networks in increasing one's chances to be hired and promoted (Cruz & Sanz, 2010; Horta, Sato, & Yonezawa, 2011; Pezzoni et al., 2012). Voluntary and forced employment breaks or job changes may harm these local links and may therefore not be pursued. Nonmobile careers could thus be considered a consequence of early permanent positions.[1]

Using a unique data set of 370 bioscience professors in Japan that covers their whole careers, this chapter evaluates the role of PhD prestige and mobility for careers in the Japanese context. In Japan, inbreeding—that is, employment at the same institution from which one graduated—has been observed to be institutionalized, representing practices "to [en]sure organizational stability and institutional identity" (Horta et al., 2011, p. 1). The university system is highly hierarchical, dominated by a few old universities, a structure that is reinforced by an alma mater–based form of patronage for graduates of one's university, which further endorses inbreeding. Japan also traditionally exhibited high levels of job security for even junior academics, though this is currently undergoing reform in an attempt to increase mobility. By looking at whether institutional prestige, localism, and mobility enable access to elite institutions and quicker promotion, we can draw some conclusions regarding the proposed reforms.

---

1. Changes in promotion patterns occurring in recent years are, however, important to note. The linear career progress from PhD to professor is no longer straightforward, with more part-time and short-term contracts (Stephan, 2012; Stephan & Ma, 2005). Alternative work arrangements are commonly established in universities, and postdoctoral appointments become more common.

Moreover, in our analysis we find some differences in the effect of prestige, mobility, and merit at different career stages.

The remainder of this chapter is structured as follows: In Section 2 we review the literature on mobility and promotion. Section 3 gives background information on the Japanese labor market and educational system, and Section 4 introduces the data. Section 5 discusses the empirical strategy and presents the results, and Section 6 discusses these results and provides a conclusion.

2. LITERATURE REVIEW

It is generally assumed that academics' career progression corresponds to their contribution to scientific knowledge but that factors such as sex and seniority may have some negative effect, delaying promotion and decreasing one's chances to enter prestigious institutions (e.g., Long, 1978; Long et al., 1993). In hierarchical academic systems the prestige of previous institutions also has an effect lasting throughout a career (e.g., Crane, 1965; Long et al., 1993). This prestige effect corresponds to higher social capital that enables access to elite networks (Burris, 2004). This type of social capital (or network size) can also increase with mobility, which could therefore contribute positively to career advancement (Pezzoni et al., 2012).

2.1 Evidence of the Role of Training Prestige for Appointment and Promotion

As academics aim to enter the best departments and departments aim to hire the most promising staff, their choices and opportunities are limited (Hoare, 1994). In highly elitist academic markets such as the United States and Japan, selection starts at an early stage, whereby the best students enroll in the best undergraduate programs, have the best opportunities for entering the best PhD programs, and thus gain an advantage for promotion and hiring in one of the top graduate institutions. The choice of the PhD location hence becomes a tactic of professional socialization that allows access to elite networks and gives early advantages for a later academic career (Burris, 2004).

Several empirical papers have previously considered the prestige of PhD granting and hiring institutions to study early career advancement in the United States. Most of these studies found that the prestige of the PhD program is more relevant for obtaining a first position than the level of productivity during PhD training (Baldi, 1995; Crane, 1965, 1970; Long, 1978). Also, a study by Chan, Chen, & Steiner (2002) found the rank of the PhD-granting institution enhances opportunities for entering a higher-ranked institution. Analyzing a sample of neural network researchers, Debackere & Rappa (1995) suggested that prestige seems to matter most early in a scientist's career and then becomes nonsignificant during later career stages. This impact of institutional prestige thus declines along the career path, and productivity becomes at least equally as important (Long, 1978).

However, the prestige culture in academia still favors certain elite institutions. Even in the United States, where mobility is generally encouraged, PhD exchange networks have developed between universities that reinforce traditional ranking structures (Burris, 2004). In a recent paper Kim, Morse, & Zingales (2009) found that this prestige culture in the United States and its agglomeration effects are still very strong, which may create mobility obstacles for academic researchers. In Japan, as well, a highly hierarchical system of universities is in place, and PhD education is said to affect appointment and promotion later in the career (Yamanoi, 2007).[2]

2.2 Evidence of the Role of Mobility for Hiring and Promotion

Assuming that mobility can facilitate career progression by giving access to a larger job market is reasonable. The speed of promotion can be increased, particularly if an academic is able to use her bargaining power with the potential new employer by moving into a higher position at a new institution. Young academics from top institutions especially can use the prestige of their institution to gain promotion elsewhere (Oyer, 2008). Mobility to a more prestigious environment, on the other hand, may not be linked to promotion. Chan et al. (2002) found that very few academics are able to move to a higher-ranked institution and that these few exceptional scientists are two times more productive than the average academic at the destination university.

The role of mobility for promotion also is affected by different domestic labor markets for academics (Gaughan & Robin, 2004). In particular, the role of social ties may differ between countries. In countries that provide early institutional commitment in terms of permanent positions, mobility may be discouraged (Cruz & Sanz, 2010); indeed, there is some evidence in France, Spain, and Italy that inbred faculty (those employed at the same institution from which they graduated) are promoted sooner (Cruz & Sanz, 2010; Gaughan & Robin, 2004; Pezzoni et al., 2012), whereas the contrary is true for the United States and Mexico (Hargens & Farr, 1973; Horta et al., 2010). In the United States, however, promotion is still conditioned by the previous commitment to the home organization. For example, Long et al. (1993) showed that changing affiliations can reset the tenure clock, resulting in a delayed promotion for job-mobile academics. Life-long contracts and the importance of scholarly networks for increasing one's chances to be hired and promoted may therefore endorse immobility in a system that provides stable employment, as is the case in most of Europe and Japan (Cruz & Sanz, 2010; Stephan, 2012).

---

2. See Section 3 for a more thorough discussion.

2.3 Evidence of the Role of International Research Stays for Hiring and Promotion

In addition to job mobility, the role of research visits by means of visiting fellowships and secondments, along with the role of postdoctoral mobility in research careers and knowledge transfer, has been highlighted in recent years. Several papers found that those who participated in international mobility perform better and have a larger international network than their peers who have not been internationally mobile (Canibano et al., 2008; Franzoni, Scellato, & Stephan, 2012; Jonkers, 2011; Scellato, Franzoni, & Stephan, 2012).

Especially in the early stages of a career, international mobility can provide training in leading research groups. Postdoctoral international mobility has been argued to have a positive effect on research careers and may increase chances to be hired by a prestigious institution (Stephan & Ma, 2005; Su, 2011). Musselin (2004), for example, found that academics participating in postdoctoral visits perceive their international mobility as a personal strategy aimed at improving their career prospects back home. Some studies have focused specifically on international postdoctoral mobility and found that it has a positive effect on performance, career, and networks (Horta, 2009; Zubieta, 2009).

There is, however, evidence that not all internationally mobile academics benefit from their experience. Jonkers (2011) reported that early career academics in Argentina are promoted later than their nonmobile peers who are equally as productive, and Cruz & Sanz (2010) found that young returnees in Spain are less likely to gain a permanent position following their postdoctorate than those who have not been internationally mobile. These studies show that not all types of international mobility may increase an academic's chances for hiring and promotion because of a loss of social ties and the difficulty of incorporating the knowledge acquired abroad (Melin, 2005).

3. THE JAPANESE EMPLOYMENT AND SCIENCE SYSTEM

3.1 The Japanese Employment System

Many scholars firmly believe that Japan's employment system is characterized by lifetime employment and age-based reward (including promotion). In the public sector in particular and in large firms, these mechanisms were perceived as prevailing. In the academic professions as well we should largely expect lifetime employment in a single university and promotion that is primarily based on age, leaving little room for mobility and research efforts.

A closer look at employment data and recent reviews, however, shows that these mechanisms are far less common than previously thought. Griffiths (2004) points out that while the average duration of employment in the same company is much higher in Japan than in countries like the United States and United Kingdom, it is comparable to figures from Germany, France, and

Spain. Further, while labor fluctuation is perhaps lower than in the United States or Europe, there is a very high degree of internal mobility within the company or within a group of affiliated companies. In Japan an interlocked system of related companies (*keiretsu*) allows firms within the group to move employees between them. Thus the effective mobility, through either temporary placements in other firms or permanent changes in employer, is much higher than is apparent.

Griffiths (2004) also challenged the common belief of a primarily age-based reward system. He acknowledged that promotion occurs very late in the career of a Japanese employee, indicating that it might be exclusively linked to age. However, studies have shown that these promotions are signaled to the employees much earlier in their career through job rotation and higher basic wages or higher bonuses (see Griffiths, 2004).

3.2 The Japanese Academic Employment System

Japan has three types of institutions that offer 4-year courses and postgraduate education: national, public, and private universities. In 2012, the 86 national universities employed 101,522 academic staff and the 92 public universities employed 27,344 (full- and part-time staff; MEXT, 2012). National universities are financed by the central government and public universities by regional and central governments. Their employees were government employees until reforms in 2004 and thus fell under the public servants law. The majority of students and academic staff, however, can be found at the 605 private universities that in 2012 employed 240,012 academic staff (MEXT, 2012). Private universities, although theoretically sovereign institutions that are financed primarily through student fees, also are affected by government control in terms of enrollment and organization (Shimbori, 1981). Though only about 10% of their finances come from the government (figure for fiscal year 2008; Statistics Bureau, 2012, p. 724), they are heavily affected by its regulation of national universities with which they need to compete, an endeavor made difficult by the heavy government subsidy and low tuition fees of national universities (Akabayashi & Naoi, 2004).

The Japanese employment system discussed above also extends into the university sector. Surveys of the Japanese university system describe it as highly elitist with an established hierarchy that limits any transition of academics between universities and thus cripples overall mobility (Horta et al., 2011; Shimbori, 1981). Looking at employment statistics we can see that the average duration of employment is higher for academics than for university graduates in general (15 years vs 12.5 years in 2010) but is the same as that of other high-skill professions (e.g., architects, engineers, and teachers) with the exception of medical doctors (4.6 years) (Statistics Bureau, 2012, pp. 518–520). However, Japanese universities have their equivalent of the *keiretsu* found among companies, an alma mater–based form of patronage for graduates of one's university, called *gakubatsu* (literally: "school tie"), which was gradually institutionalized. Similar to the internal movement of employees inside a *keiretsu*, graduates are placed in a university with links to their degree institution, thus reinforcing the *gakubatsu*. The university hierarchy is dominated by the University of Tokyo, followed by other national universities and a few old private universities. This structure is reinforced by the fact that the majority of postgraduate and specifically doctoral education is done in the few national universities. While private institutions have consistently accounted for 75–80% of undergraduate students in the past 25 years, they produced only 23% of PhDs in 2010. The national universities, on the other hand, provide just 20% of undergraduate education but produce 70% of doctoral students (Statistics Bureau, 2012, pp. 714–715). In 2001 11% of the academic workforce had graduated from the University of Tokyo alone (Yamanoi, 2007). The increase in the number of postgraduate students, however, which has tripled in the past 20 years while the number of university teachers increased by only 50% (Statistics Bureau, 2012, pp. 714–715), makes the competition for academic positions much tougher and thus may have led to a more transparent hiring process. While positions were filled internally before the 1990s, often without being advertised publicly, by 2000 this changed and the recruitment process became more open. This is particularly reflected in the increasing number of Japanese academics with PhDs from abroad (Yamanoi, 2007).

Japanese universities largely have a three-level promotion system, with professor at the top, then associate professor, and finally assistant professor, lecturer (instructor), or assistant. In 2012 40% of all full-time academic positions were professorships, 24% were associate professorships, and 36% were in the lower ranks (MEXT, 2012).[3] Promotion decisions in Japan are largely made at the departmental level (Teichler, Arimoto, & Cummings, 2013). It has further been claimed that promotion is primarily based on seniority, with minor adjustments for education and performance (Shimbori, 1981; Takahashi & Takahashi, 2009). This is particularly true for national and public universities, which, until recently, fell under the public servant laws. Moreover, before 1990 the academic labor market was characterized by a chair structure (*koza*), where promotion was possible only if a chair resigned. This system was challenged when other academic structures were introduced, for example, allowing for fixed-term appointments (Yamanoi, 2007). In April 2004 a reform to incorporate these national and public universities removed the public servant status from academics and allowed greater freedom in determining recruitment, wages, and promotion. Nevertheless, the old structures prevail and in 2005 only 3.4% of full-time academics were hired on a fixed-term basis (Huang, 2006).

---

3. Part-time positions are not included in the statistics but are the most common type of appointment for junior staff.

3.3 Careers and Mobility

While Japanese academics are not entirely immobile, policymakers have long realized that the cross-organizational flow of academics lacks flexibility and is heavily constrained by a rigid social structure (e.g., *keiretsu*). Among others, the practice of inbreeding has been regarded as a serious impediment (Yamanoi, 2007). The Japanese Ministry for Education (MEXT) reported that inbred academics who assumed professorship in the same university where they earned their degree accounted for about 62% of all faculty members in graduate schools in 1998 (MEXT, 2003b). Arguing that inbreeding deters scientific competitiveness, the Science and Technology Basic Plan initiated the restructuring of the career system, especially for young academics (NISTEP and MRI, 2005). For example, national universities were allowed to employ faculty members on fixed-term contracts from 1997; in particular, permanent employment for entry positions was gradually replaced by fixed-term contracts with the intention to increase mobility. Further, the second-term plan published in 2001 urged national universities to employ faculty members through open competition. In 2003 the largest national fellowship for postdoctorates in Japan prohibited its fellows from staying in the same laboratories where they completed their PhD theses.[4] In 2006 a tenure-track system, modeled on the American system, was introduced so that young academics could obtain entry positions without social ties with incumbents (Morichika & Shibayama, 2015). Despite these efforts, the rigidity of the Japanese academic market largely remains, and further policy reform seems to be needed.

While the above-mentioned changes have primarily addressed the lack of domestic mobility, policies for international mobility have a long history in Japan. MEXT implemented several programs for research visits abroad starting in the late nineteenth century. The primary objective of these programs was the quick absorption of knowledge from and catching up with other developed countries, but their emphasis has shifted toward the promotion of academic and educational exchange in general (Tsuji, 2010). The government task force for faculty development recently published its future vision, in which the necessity of early career research experience in foreign institutions is stressed as a means for increasing global competitiveness (MEXT, 2003a, 2009).

Many of these government faculty development programs provide fellowships for research stays or travel funds for conference attendance; according to government statistics, approximately 7000 university faculty members were sent abroad every year in the 1990s (MEXT, 1990). Importantly, many of them were allowed to visit a foreign institution while on leave from their home institution. These stays differ from sabbaticals in that sabbaticals are given to senior scholars more as a reward rather than as part of faculty development for younger scholars. Further, they differ from postdoctoral stays in terms of job security.

---

4. Furthermore, from 2016 it will prohibit fellows from staying in the same university (http://www.jsps.go.jp/j-pd/data/seido_kaizen.pdf).

The programs aim "to dispatch university faculty members to foreign research institutions, encourage them to concentrate on their research, and improve their research capabilities" (MEXT, 1980). The major government-sponsored program for research visits was called the "Overseas Research Scholars Program," which started as early as 1882.

A recent analysis of academic articles in peer-reviewed journals and affiliation details of academics on Scopus found that 30% of academics who published under a Japanese affiliation at least once spent up to 2 years outside Japan, and 10% stayed abroad for more than 2 years (BIS, 2013). These shares are lower than those for other academic markets (e.g., the United Kingdom or the United States) but are comparable to those of some European countries. The results of the study show that international research visits are widespread among Japanese academics and are a more important means of international mobility than permanent migration. The most important partner for international exchanges and collaborations is the United States, as evidenced by the large number of articles coauthored by US authors (BIS, 2013).

4. DATA AND DESCRIPTIVE STATISTICS

4.1 Data Collection

The data used in this chapter were collected as part of a survey conducted in 2010. The survey was addressed to full professors in the fields of biology and bioscience who received a grant-in-aid (GiA) at least once between 2006 and 2009. GiA is the largest and primary funding source for academics in Japan, amounting to ¥200 billion (US$2.4 billion) in 2010. This sampling criterion allows us to effectively eliminate from the sampling frame faculty members who are not active in research. The field of bioscience is one of the most globally integrated (BIS, 2013). In 2010 professors in biology-related fields accounted for 45% of all GiA awardees. We identified 1378 professors in the database who fulfilled the criteria. From this population we selected 1080 professors in the top 56 universities.[5] After reviewing research fields and affiliations on university websites, we arrived at a final sample of 900 academics.[6]

Questionnaires were sent via the post to the 900 academics in May 2010. A reminder was sent 1 month later. Participants had to fill in the paper-based questionnaires and send them back by post. We received 400 responses by August 2010, thus achieving a response rate of 44%. Although this represents a good

---

5. We chose the 56 universities that had a minimum number of professors in the field of biosciences. In Japan about 50 national universities have life science departments, and our sample covers most of them and a few private or public universities.

6. The majority of the excluded 180 academics were those who had either retired or moved to universities outside our sample population. We also dropped foreign academics to avoid translation of the questionnaire. Though comparison between foreign and Japanese academics may be of interest, we believed that meaningful comparison would be difficult because of the very small number of foreign faculty members in Japan.

response rate, there may be a concern of respondent bias. The original survey did not indicate that the data would be used for the analysis of mobility and career advancement, mitigating this risk. In addition, to examine nonresponse bias, we randomly selected 50 nonrespondents and found no significant difference between the response and nonresponse groups in terms of productivity, organizational rank, and sex ($p > 0.1$).[7]

Curriculum vitae (CV) information was collected from ReaD, a career database created by a governmental agency, where academics voluntarily deposit their CV information. The data in ReaD are completely structured and thus particularly useful for career analysis. Because data registration in ReaD is not mandatory and information may not be complete, we completed CVs with information from the professors' personal websites. All CVs were verified with information collected through the questionnaire survey, which included questions about the year of the PhD and years of promotion. Full CVs were available for 370 academics, who in 2010 worked at 56 different universities in Japan.

CVs provide a rich source of longitudinal information that covers the major dimensions of an academic's career as well as their research contacts. While some of the dimensions of mobility can be inferred from bibliometric data, most of an academic's activities may not be observed using traditional data sources, particularly if they do not involve publications in scientific journals. CVs are particularly useful in the analysis of academic careers because they inform about job transitions and also allow reliable publication data to be gathered. Using data collected from CVs in addition to pure bibliographic measures improves the accuracy of the data because mismatches arising from name similarities and changes in academics' institutional affiliations can be avoided. Several academics have recently taken to analyzing CVs to study the impact of mobility on academic productivity and career progression (Canibano & Bozeman, 2009).

Data taken from CVs include all career information starting from the year of the first degree (a bachelors). It comprises a comprehensive listing of all positions, including visiting stays. In addition, publication data was collected from the Web of Science.

4.2 Career Statistics

Of the 370 professors for whom full CVs were available, only 12 are women, which represents 3.2% of the sample (3% of the total sample of 900 are women). The average professor finished his undergraduate studies in 1977 and his PhD in 1983. The average age of professors in 2010 is 54 years. As discussed earlier, doctoral courses are highly concentrated, and promotion is directly linked to training in one of the elite institutions in Japan. In our sample 91% of professors received their doctorate from a national university (336 professors), 26% from the University

---

7. For the nonrespondents, we collected publication data from the Web of Science and learned their rank and gender from curriculum vitae (available through ReaD) and personal websites.

of Tokyo alone. Just 3% of doctoral degrees came from public universities (10 professors), 5% from a private universities (17 professors), and 2% received their degree abroad (7 professors). Fifty-eight professors in the sample have a degree in medicine and may behave differently from the rest of the sample because of spells as medical staff in hospitals with lower levels of research activity.

We defined positions as the three career steps described earlier: assistant professor (or lecturer), associate professor, and professor. Descriptive statistics at the time of appointment to each of the three position types are reported in Table 1. On average, professors finished their PhD at the age of 28 and took up their first position as assistant professor at the age of 29. They were promoted to the position of associate professor at the age of 37 and to full professor at 44 (see Table 1). The mean promotion age is lower for professors with a medical degree (35 years to associate professor and 41 years to full professor).

We had to consider that not all professors in our sample follow this strict career path. In fact, 45 academics never assumed the position of an assistant professor, but took up other types of appointments and entered the standard academic career as associate professors ($n = 27$) at an average age of 36 or as full professor ($n = 18$) at an average age of 43. Moreover, 34 professors in our sample were promoted from the rank of an assistant to that of a full professor without the intermediate step of an associate professor at an average age of 40.

Focusing on the 325 professors who started their careers as assistant professors, we found that 79% took up a position at one of the national universities, 4% at public universities, 12% at private universities, 3% at public research organizations that follow academic career steps, and 2% at foreign institutions.

4.2.1 University Rank

We assumed that appointment and promotion is more difficult to achieve at top institutions and therefore introduced a ranking. The Japanese university ranking is headed by the seven preimperial universities (Tokyo, Kyoto, Osaka, Tohoku, Hokkaido, Nagoya, and Kyushu). We can distinguish the University of Tokyo from the other six because it receives twice as much public funding in the biosciences compared with the second-ranked institution (Kyoto). We further ranked all institutions based on GiA funding received by a university in the field of bioscience in the previous 5 years to create a time-variant rank measure that covers all the years 1972–2010. Funding values were normalized linearly, dividing each value by the maximum amount received in the sample. Thus we have a one-to-one relationship between the original and normalized values. The University of Tokyo represents the value 1,[8] and all other universities are defined as a share of this. The ranking confirms the positions of the other six preimperial universities in the top 7. Based on this index we assigned each academic a PhD

---

8. In the early 1970s Kyoto received the most funding and represents the value of 1.

TABLE 1 Descriptive Statistics at the Time of Appointment to Each Academic Rank

	Appointment to Assistant Professor (n = 325[a])		Promotion to Associate Professor (n = 300)		Promotion to Full Professor (n = 365)	
	Mean	SD	Mean	SD	Mean	SD
University rank	0.34	0.37	0.26	0.31	0.25	0.30
Top 7 universities (0/1)	0.49	0.50	0.42	0.49	0.38	0.49
Tokyo (0/1)	0.15	0.36	0.09	0.28	0.09	0.28
Age	28.60	3.02	36.69	3.60	43.59	4.38
Years since PhD	0.62	3.44	8.67	3.71	15.55	4.37
Years since initial appointment	0.00	0.00	8.23	4.00	14.99	5.03
Female sex (0/1)	0.03	0.17	0.03	0.18	0.03	0.18
Medical degree (0/1)	0.17	0.37	0.14	0.35	0.16	0.37
PhD Tokyo (0/1)	0.23	0.42	0.24	0.43	0.25	0.43
PhD top 2–7 (0/1)	0.59	0.49	0.59	0.49	0.57	0.50
PhD other (0/1)	0.18	0.38	0.17	0.38	0.18	0.39
Initial position at Tokyo (0/1)			0.14	0.35	0.14	0.34
Initial position at top 2–7 (0/1)			0.34	0.47	0.30	0.46
Initial position at other (0/1)			0.46	0.50	0.51	0.50
Initial position at public research organization (PRO) (0/1)			0.02	0.14	0.02	0.14
Initial position abroad (0/1)					0.03	0.18
Postdoctoral degree abroad (0/1)	0.18	0.39	0.04	0.20	0.20	0.40
Past job mobility (0/1)			0.18	0.38	0.72	0.45
Promotion mobility (0/1)			0.49	0.50	0.47	0.50
Visiting stay abroad (0/1)			0.35	0.48	0.20	0.40
Publication stock	13.96	24.50	47.17	61.35	93.18	120.72
Average citations	28.89	52.90	32.15	26.59	33.85	26.41
Funding stock	0.16	0.60	4.73	5.34	24.80	27.52

[a]The number of observations differs for each career stage: 325 professors started their career as an assistant professor, 300 experienced promotion to associate professor, and 365 experienced promotion to full professor.

ranking (representing the rank of the PhD institution in the year of the PhD) and a time-variant university ranking. The mean rank for all universities in Japan is 0.05 and that of the top 7 universities is 0.5. The mean PhD rank is 0.4, indicating that most academics receive their PhDs from one of the top universities. The mean rank among institutions in 2010 is 0.3, indicating a slight downward mobility.

4.2.2 Inbreeding

Academic inbreeding is widely defined as the practice of universities hiring their own graduates and is assumed to be widely spread in Japan (Horta et al., 2011). In our sample 146 academics were initially hired by their PhD institutions and another 53 academics moved back to their PhD institution after a short period elsewhere. In accordance with previous studies in the US context (e.g., Burris, 2004), we found that inbreeding is more prevalent among elite institutions. Figure 1 shows the distribution of professors by PhD degree among the different types of institutions in years 1, 5, 10, and 15 after the PhD. The graph clearly shows the dominance of top institutions and the high degree of inbreeding at the top. More than 80% of new hires (year 1) at the University of Tokyo received their PhD from the same institution. For the other six elite institutions, this share is still 78%. Lower-rank institutions mostly hire out of the pool of top graduates, partly out of necessity because of less developed postgraduate programs. After 10 years, which corresponds approximately to the time of associate professorship for most of the professors in the sample, 58% of professors at the University of Tokyo and 75% at the other top 7 institutions also received their PhD from one of the top institutions. In year 15, the median time of appointment to full professor, this share increased to 68% and 80%, respectively, whereas the share of those with a PhD from lower-ranked institutions decreased. If we also consider only those professors

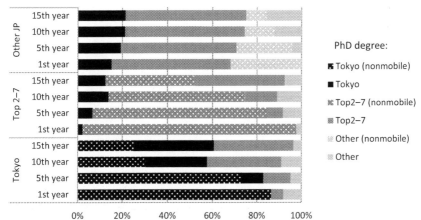

FIGURE 1   Distribution of PhD degrees by institution type in years since PhD.

who never moved but stayed at the same university since the start of their career, we found that after 15 years, approximately 50% of inbred academics at one of the top 7 universities are "pure inbred" (nonmobile), having gained no experience outside their PhD institution.

4.2.3 Mobility Paths

To measure the job mobility of these professors, we defined a move as a change of position that occurred after an academic's first appointment as assistant professor. The move has to be permanent, with no return to the original institution within 3 years of the initial move. Some of these appointments may be research fellow appointments at foreign institutions, but because they are held for at least 3 years and academics do not return to their original institutions, they are considered job mobility.

We identified three main job mobility patterns before promotion to full professor:

1. Those who do not change universities (107 academics)
2. Those who move at the assistant level (170 academics)
3. Those who move at the associate level (171 academics; including 78 from group 2)

The group of immobile academics constitutes just 29% of the sample, indicating a very high degree of mobility among university professors in Japan. This contradicts Shimbori (1981) and Horta et al. (2011), who argue that the Japanese system limits mobility. This high percentage of mobile could be a result of our sample selection, which included only full professors at research-intensive universities. The 263 mobile professors moved 424 times before being promoted to full professor. Academics moved 277 times to gain promotion. Table 2 shows that, of those mobile at assistant professor level, 57% move to be promoted to associate or full professor; among those mobile at the associate professor level, 75% move to gain the position of full professor. Thus mobility in Japan is closely linked to promotion opportunities.

Table 3 shows that, overall, 39% of assistant professors moved to gain promotion, whereas the remaining 61% were promoted internally. At the associate

TABLE 2 Promotion Patterns of Mobile Academics

	With Promotion	Without Promotion
Assistant's move	127 (57%)	96 (43%)
Associate's move	150 (75%)	51 (25%)
Total	277 (61%)	147 (39%)

TABLE 3 Mobility Patterns of Promoted Academics

	Moved	Not Moved
Promotion from assistant to associate/full professor	127 (39%)	201 (61%)
Promotion from associate to full professor	150 (45%)	186 (55%)

professor level, 45% moved for promotion, whereas 55% were promoted to full professor in their home department. This indicates that there still is a general tendency to fill professorial positions with internal candidates rather than hiring external candidates.

4.2.4 Visiting Research Stays and Postdoctorates

In addition to career mobility, we observed short-term mobility or visiting research stays. We defined a research stay as a move to another university or public research institution of up to 3 years that is usually followed by a return to the original institution. We do not include postdoctoral appointments, only research stays that occur after an academic has been appointed as an assistant professor. Research stays could theoretically be very similar to postdoctoral appointments; however, they are marked by a return to the original institution and the original position, indicating that they were solely intended as visiting fellowships. This type of mobility is fairly common among Japanese academics. In our sample 24% of professors (79 academics) spent some time as researchers or visiting fellows at other institutions, usually outside Japan (95% of cases). The majority of these research stays happened early during an academic's career: 80% of visiting fellows were assistant professors. Only one academic in our sample was a visiting fellow after his promotion to full professor. This may be because of the increased administrative and teaching commitments of full professors, which do not allow them to leave their institutions for more than a few weeks.

In comparison, postdoctoral fellowships, which are defined as research stays of up to 4 years starting just after completion of the PhD, were taken up by 118 academics in the sample. In contrast to visiting research stays, these postdoctoral appointments are distributed evenly across Japanese and foreign institutions, with 60% of appointments abroad. In 23 cases professors were appointed postdoctoral academics in the same institutions that rewarded their PhD. In 20 cases professors were offered a position as an assistant professor in the institution upon completion of their postdoctoral research. Sixteen academics later also took up visiting research fellowships.

4.2.5 Other Variables

We collected the number of publications for each professor from the Web of Science. Publications may be positively associated with promotions, though

Takahashi & Takahashi (2009) did not find this to be the case for a sample of Japanese economists. However, their sample was mainly drawn from education-oriented institutions, where merit may have less of an effect on promotion. Instead, performance may play a greater role at research universities, which are the focus of this chapter. Each professor published, on average, seven publications per year during the observation period. In addition, we collected the number of citations received by each publication as a quality measure. Publications receive, on average, 30 citations, a number significantly higher than the world and Japan average for citations in biological sciences (BIS, 2013), indicating that academics in our sample are high performers. In our estimations we used the stock of publications and the average number of citations up to the year before promotion to measure an academic's productivity. Upon appointment to their first permanent position, academics have already published 14 articles and receive, on average, 29 citations; at the time of promotion to professor the number of accumulated publications is 93 and the average citation counts is 34 (Table 1).

We also have detailed information on GiA funding received by each academic in each year. The amount of funding was split across years and investigators, and each professor received an average of ¥5 million/year. Again, we used a stock measure up to the year before promotion. Upon promotion to associate professor, academics had received approximately ¥5 million, and upon promotion to full professor ¥25 million.

4.3 Descriptive Analysis

Table 1 shows summary statistics for all variables used in our empirical analysis. It shows statistics for academics when they take up their first permanent position and at the time of promotion to associate professor and time of promotion to full professor. The statistics show that the mean rank of the employing institution decreases with time, indicating a general downward mobility trend among academics following their PhD, as indicated in Figure 1. The share of academics employed by one of the top institutions thus also decreased from 49% to 38%.

Table 4 shows various performance, age, and ranking measures by type of mobility for academics promoted to full professor. The results indicate that academics who have been job-mobile since entering their first employment are promoted to full professor significantly earlier than academics who do not move. They also receive significantly more citations, which may be indicative of their larger network. Inbred academics, on the other hand (those who are promoted to full professor at their PhD institution), are significantly more likely to hold an appointment at a highly ranked university. This again indicates that mobility in Japan is generally downward. These inbred academics also publish more and receive more funding, which may be a result of their position at a top institution.

For academics engaging in research visits, we found no difference compared with those who do not engage in this kind of mobility. Postdoctoral stays

TABLE 4 Descriptive Statistics for Mobility Types at the Time of Promotion to Full Professor

	Mobile		Inbred		Visit		Postdoctorate Abroad	
	Yes (n=262)	No (n=102)	Yes (n=87)	No (n=277)	Yes (n=73)	No (n=291)	Yes (n=73)	No (n=291)
Years since PhD	15.13	16.64***	16.17	15.36	14.85	15.73	16.11	15.42
Years since first job	14.42	16.44***	15.11	14.95	15.04	14.97	12.25	15.60***
Publication stock	97.90	81.05	115.21	86.26*	97.40	92.12	105.40	90.12
Average citations	36.18	27.85***	34.72	33.57	33.77	33.87	40.90	32.08**
Funding stock	25.80	22.24	29.65	23.28*	24.76	24.81	25.92	24.52
Rank of PhD university	0.55	0.53	0.56	0.54	0.56	0.54	0.55	0.54
Current University rank	0.25	0.26	0.49	0.18***	0.27	0.25	0.27	0.25

Note: Mean comparison test: *** $p<0.01$, ** $p<0.05$, * $p<0.1$.

abroad, however, were accompanied by significantly more citations, which may again point toward a positive network effect. However, there is no difference in time until promotion.

Figure 1 shows that a large share of academics move down between their initial appointment and the later career years. Table 5 looks in more detail at the mobility patterns of Japanese academics in terms of the university of initial appointment and the university of promotion to full professorship. For example, nine professors took up their first position at an institution other than one in the top 7 but gained their professorship at the University of Tokyo. Table 5 then compares various performance and age measures at the time of promotion to full professor, as well as PhD ranking measures for each origin–destination pair. The table shows that academics who do not change university rank are promoted later on average than those who are mobile. Further, academics at lower-ranked institutions who are able to move into the top 7 have an above-average productivity and attract significantly more citations and funding than their peers who remain in a low-ranked university. In addition, they do not perform any different, on average, than those who start their career in the top 7. The summary statistics further show that those who get promoted to professor at the University of Tokyo already have a PhD from a significantly higher-ranked institution. In terms of performance measures we found no difference between those in the top 7 who remain in the top and those who pass down into lower ranks. The main difference can be found in the ranking of their PhD institution and in the amount of funding they attract, which may indicate some remaining prestige effects from the PhD.

5. REGRESSION ANALYSIS

5.1 Initial Placement

As a first step we estimated the initial placement of academics in their first position as assistant professor. Table 6 estimates first an ordinary least squares model with university rank as the dependent variable; second, two probit models are used to measure the propensity to enter one of the top 7 universities or the top university. We found that academics with a PhD from one of the top 7 universities enter a higher-ranked institution. When looking at the propensity to enter one of the top 7 specifically compared with one of the other Japanese universities, we again confirmed that a PhD from one of the top universities is the main explanatory factor. This is in line with previous research in the United States that found the graduate school to be the single most important predictor of initial appointment at a top institution (see Crane, 1965, 1970). For the University of Tokyo, this elitism is even more pronounced because primarily its own graduates are hired. Postdoctoral stays and performance have no or little importance for the rank of the first position. Average citations

TABLE 5 Descriptive Statistics for Origin–Destination[a] Groups of Academics at Time of Promotion to Full Professor

#	Origin–Destination Pair	Academics (n)	Years since PhD	Years since First Job	Publication Stock	Average Citations	Funding Stock	Rank of PhD University
1	Other→Other	141	15.65	15.79	66.21	27.30	14.89	0.46
2	Other→Top 2–7	34	14.88	14.48	109.68***	38.61***	28.70***	0.46
3	Other→Tokyo	9	15.11	14.2	105.56*	59.49***	36.04***	0.86***
4	Top 2–7→Other	47	15.34	14.47	119.62°°°	35.40°°	25.50°°°	0.4
5	Top 2–7→Top 2–7	55	16.58°	16.47**	87.64	34.73	31.82	0.54***
6	Top 2–7→Tokyo	7	14.86	14.86	83.71	34.21	48.31**	0.61**,°
7	Tokyo→Other	24	14.46	13.42°°	114.63°°	37.44°°	24.74°°°	0.84°°°
8	Tokyo→Top 2–7	12	13	11.08°	119.83	44.81	32.57	0.88°°°
9	Tokyo→Tokyo	13	16.38	14.38	186.54	32.76	48.53**	0.98°

[a]Origin–destination pairs are defined as movement from first job to job of full professor.

Mean comparison for those starting in the same university. Base categories are 1, 4, and 7 (e.g., 2 and 7 (e.g., 2 and 3 are compared to 1): *** $p < 0.01$, ** $p < 0.05$, * $p < 0.1$.

Mean comparison for those becoming full professor in the same university. Base categories are 1, 2, and 3 (e.g., 4 and 7 are compared to 1): °°° $p < 0.01$, °° $p < 0.05$, ° $p < 0.1$.

TABLE 6 Initial Job Placement as an Assistant Professor

Dependent Variable	Rank		Top7		Tokyo	
Method	OLS		Probit		Probit	
	dy/dx	SE	dy/dx	SE	dy/dx	SE
Years since PhD	0.009	0.007	0.008	0.010	0.017**	0.007
Female sex (0/1)	0.053	0.084	0.054	0.153	-0.046	0.107
Medical degree (0/1)	0.096**	0.047	0.209**	0.081	0.067	0.048
Publication stock	-0.000	0.001	0.001	0.001	-0.000	0.001
Average citations	0.001***	0.000	0.001*	0.001	0.000	0.000
Funding stock	-0.059	0.053	-0.060	0.068	-0.038	0.042
Postdoctorate abroad (0/1)	-0.033	0.059	0.036	0.080	-0.053	0.045
PhD from University of Tokyo (0/1)	0.513***	0.060	0.526***	0.069	0.526***	0.062
PhD from a top 2–7 university (0/1)	0.226***	0.034	0.495***	0.053	0.010	0.027
Observations	306		306		306	
Adjusted (pseudo) R^2	0.2131		0.2139		0.4215	

Note: We controlled for the year of PhD. Professors that entered institutions outside our ranking (e.g., foreign universities or PROs) are excluded. *** $p<0.01$, ** $p<0.05$, * $p<0.1$. OLS, ordinary least squares; SE, robust standard error.

before the first appointment are associated with entry into a higher-ranked university; however, the magnitude of the effect is very small. The female dummy is insignificant, and medical researchers are found at higher-ranked institutions.

5.2 Placement as Associate and Full Professors

In addition to the initial placement, we were interested in where academics get promoted to associate and full professor, whether the PhD school remains an important predictor, and in the role of mobility for promotion rank or whether merit becomes more important. Table 7 shows that not the PhD institutions but initial placement in a top university has a positive effect on the rank of the university at the time of promotion to associate professor, as has a placement with a university abroad. A PhD from the University of Tokyo still increases the probability of gaining an associate professorship at a higher-ranked university (though not the University of Tokyo itself). In addition, visiting research stays abroad have a positive effect on placement in one of the top 7 institutions, whereas postdoctoral appointments do not affect later placement. Mobility during the assistant professorship also has no significant impact, but mobility during the year of promotion is associated with a decrease in rank. This indicates that Japanese academics indeed move down to gain promotion, something that also was observed in studies of the United States (Long, 1978). In terms of performance, publication quality is of importance for gaining associate professorship in a higher-ranked university. The number of citations received before promotion to associate professor also has a positive significant effect, but the magnitude of the effect is very small. Again, this corroborates to prior findings in the US context (Long, 1978; Oyer, 2008). The female dummy is still insignificant.

Table 8 gives the results for job placement at the time of promotion to full professor. We found that the advantage of initial placement remains: Academics who started at one of the top universities or at a university abroad also become full professor at a top institution. In addition, we still found a weak positive effect of a PhD from the University of Tokyo and the top 2–7 universities. This indicates that PhD networks and prestige still matter for promotion to full professor, especially for promotion within one of the preimperial universities, with local faculty having some promotion advantage (Yamanoi, 2007). Performance in terms of citations and funding acquisition also has a positive significant effect on placement at a top university. Still, the magnitudes of these effects remain small and do not offer strong support for a position allocation based on merit. Past mobility has no effect; however, those who move in the year of promotion to full professor tend to move to a lower-ranked university, again confirming US evidence of the link between advancement in rank and downward mobility (Long, 1978). Professors with a medical degree are no longer more likely to be found at higher ranked

TABLE 7 Job Placement as Associate Professor

Dependent Variable	Rank		Top7		Tokyo	
Method	OLS		Probit		Probit	
	dy/dx	SE	dy/dx	SE	dy/dx	SE
Years since PhD	0.013***	0.004	0.008	0.006	0.013***	0.004
Female sex (0/1)	−0.066	0.062	0.110	0.124	Dropped	
Medical degree (0/1)	0.136***	0.048	0.158**	0.067	0.122***	0.033
Publication stock	0.000	0.000	0.000	0.000	0.000	0.000
Average citations	0.002***	0.001	0.003***	0.001	0.001***	0.000
Funding stock	0.006	0.004	0.011**	0.005	0.003	0.002
Postdoctorate abroad (0/1)	0.011	0.040	0.061	0.068	−0.042	0.029
Past job mobility (0/1)	0.001	0.055	−0.060	0.072	0.027	0.033
Promotion mobility (0/1)	−0.172***	0.061	−0.139*	0.082	−0.118***	0.045
Visiting stay abroad (0/1)	0.013	0.040	0.092*	0.055	−0.026	0.032
PhD from the University of Tokyo (0/1)	0.111*	0.063	0.200**	0.088	0.157***	0.058
PhD from a top 2–7 university (0/1)	0.031	0.038	0.104	0.074	0.033	0.026
Initial position at University of Tokyo	0.326***	0.076	0.302***	0.102	0.224***	0.086
Initial position at top 2–7 university	0.196***	0.039	0.511***	0.062	−0.018	0.033
Initial position at PRO	0.031	0.105	0.149	0.223	Dropped	
Abroad	0.505***	0.141	0.640***	0.118	0.482***	0.166
Observations	280		280		265	
Adjusted (pseudo) R^2	0.2505		0.3658		0.4650	

Note: We controlled for the year of PhD. Professors that gain promotion at institutions outside our ranking (e.g., foreign universities or PROs) are excluded. *** $p<0.01$, ** $p<0.05$, * $p<0.1$; Cases are dropped in the Tokyo probit estimation because of collinearity/perfect prediction; OLS, ordinary least squares; SE, robust standard error.

TABLE 8 Job Placement as a Full Professor

Dependent Variable	Rank		Top7		Tokyo	
Method	OLS		Probit		Probit	
	dy/dx	SE	dy/dx	SE	dy/dx	SE
Years since PhD	-0.004	0.004	-0.017***	0.006	-0.006	0.004
Female sex (0/1)	0.129**	0.056	0.292***	0.107	Dropped	
Medical degree (0/1)	-0.041	0.044	-0.104	0.074	0.043	0.039
Publication stock	0.000**	0.000	0.000	0.000	0.000	0.000
Average citations	0.002***	0.001	0.002**	0.001	0.001*	0.000
Funding stock	0.003***	0.001	0.005***	0.001	0.002***	0.000
Postdoctorate abroad (0/1)	0.027	0.034	0.071	0.059	0.005	0.033
Past job mobility (0/1)	0.003	0.040	-0.041	0.060	0.048	0.031
Promotion mobility (0/1)	-0.084**	0.042	-0.041	0.061	-0.103***	0.035
Visiting stay abroad (0/1)	0.002	0.038	0.057	0.053	-0.006	0.037
PhD from University of Tokyo (0/1)	0.072	0.052	0.112	0.082	0.188***	0.049
PhD from a top 2–7 university (0/1)	0.068*	0.037	0.200***	0.070	0.042*	0.023
Initial position at University of Tokyo	0.203***	0.065	0.284***	0.085	0.103*	0.054
Initial position at top 2–7 university	0.202***	0.035	0.234***	0.060	0.036	0.036
Initial position at PRO	0.007	0.090	0.060	0.151	Dropped	
Initial position abroad	0.241**	0.112	0.378***	0.139	0.207*	0.112
Observations	361		361		342	
Adjusted (pseudo) R^2	0.2671		0.2136		0.3125	

Note: We controlled for year of PhD. Professors who gain promotion at institutions outside our ranking (e.g., foreign universities or PROs) are excluded. *** $p < 0.01$, ** $p < 0.05$, * $p < 0.1$; cases are dropped in the Tokyo probit estimation because of collinearity/perfect prediction; OLD, ordinary least squares; SE, robust standard error.

institutions; however, female academics have a higher propensity to be placed in a top university as full professors, though not at the University of Tokyo, where we found no female professors.

5.3 Duration until Promotion

In addition to placement within prestigious environments, we estimated the time until promotion and expect an earlier promotion for academics who choose to move out of their home institution, and especially those moving downward (Fernandez-Zubieta, Geuna, & Lawson, Chapter 4, discusses the issue of downward mobility). The descriptive statistics showed that the majority of job changes are accompanied by promotion to a better position. This is true particularly for transitions to lower-ranked institutions. In addition, we expect academics with mobility experience to have a larger network and to gain faster promotion because of their knowledge of open positions. On the other hand, it also has been argued that inbred academics, or academics with long-term ties to an institution, may find gaining promotion easier.

We estimated a duration model of career promotion as a function of job transition, taking into account past and current mobility events. We assumed that each researcher is subject to the probability of being promoted conditional on her status of being an assistant or associate professor. We therefore estimated our promotion equation separately for assistant professors who are promoted to associate professors and associate professors who are promoted to full professors. In the duration analysis a researcher is at risk of being promoted to associate professor from the beginning of her career and at risk of being promoted to full professor as soon as he becomes associate professor. We made use of a Cox proportional hazard model where the dependent variable is the time that elapses from PhD until promotion. The same model evaluated the effects of inbreeding, postdoctoral stays, and international research visits on promotion speed. Performance stock measures were used to control for a merit effect on promotion. Age and its square term were included to control for a possible age effect on promotion. Sex, PhD, and university type indicators were used as controls. All regressions also included year dummies. The results are displayed in Table 9.

The results for promotion to associate professor show that merit (publications, citations, and funding) has no significant effect on promotion duration. This confirms prior research from Japan; promotion is not accelerated through better performance. However, because we are looking only at full professors who have successfully applied for research funding, we are already looking at the best performers and therefore might not find an additional performance effect. Age, on the other hand, is highly significant, indicating that seniority has a major impact on being promoted.

TABLE 9 Survival Analysis: Risk of Being Promoted in Year *t* after the PhD

	Associate		Full Professor	
Female sex (0/1)	0.065	(0.226)	−0.232	(0.292)
Age	1.609***	(0.430)	0.904**	(0.376)
Age²	−0.020***	(0.006)	−0.009**	(0.004)
Medical degree (0/1)	0.136	(0.186)	0.529***	(0.185)
Publication stock	−0.000	(0.001)	0.001	(0.001)
Average citations	0.001	(0.002)	0.004*	(0.002)
Funding stock	0.021	(0.013)	0.002	(0.003)
Postdoctorate abroad (0/1)	0.213	(0.133)	−0.067	(0.147)
Past job mobility (0/1)	−0.131	(0.179)	0.124	(0.170)
Promotion mobility (0/1)	1.676***	(0.177)	2.069***	(0.142)
Inbred (0/1)	−0.122	(0.111)	0.193	(0.143)
Visiting stay abroad (0/1)	0.703***	(0.184)	0.550***	(0.160)
PhD from University of Tokyo (0/1)	0.123	(0.189)	−0.020	(0.233)
PhD from a top 2–7 university (0/1)	−0.038	(0.178)	0.001	(0.181)
Initial position at University of Tokyo	−0.355	(0.266)	−0.213	(0.234)
Initial position at a top 2–7 university	−0.073	(0.147)	−0.372**	(0.150)
Initial position at PRO	0.197	(0.268)	−0.025	(0.314)
Initial position abroad	0.045	(0.232)	−0.631*	(0.339)
Current university rank	0.139	(0.240)	0.119	(0.217)
Observations	2339		4431	
IDs	323		365	
Log-likelihood	−1205.739		−986.557	

Coefficients are reported. Year fixed effects are included. Robust standard errors are in parentheses; * $p<0.01$, ** $p<0.05$, *** $p<0.1$.

Turning to mobility, we see that past mobility does not predict promotion, but mobility in the same year has a strong positive effect. Thus mobility is only beneficial to promotion if the researcher can use his bargaining power to gain a higher position. It also indicates that Japanese academics are willing to move if this increases promotion speed.

Inbreeding has no significant effect on promotion speed. Thus being at the university that awarded the PhD does not provide an additional promotion advantage, which is in line with findings for the United States and Mexico (Hargens & Farr, 1973; Horta et al., 2010).

International research visits have a strong positive effect, indicating that these academics benefit from their stay and are promoted faster. Postdoctoral stays, on the other hand, have no significant effect. Instead, they could be an indicator of an academics' struggle to find a permanent position after receiving the PhD or the difficulty of reentry as a result of the close-knit scholarly network in Japan.

Looking at regression 2, which measures the years until promotion to full professor, the picture is slightly different. While seniority is still the most important factor, merit, as measured through average citation counts, also has a positive effect on reducing duration until promotion. Thus merit is indeed important for advancing to the rank of a full professor, a promotion usually accompanied by responsibility for a large research group.

Mobility in the year of promotion is still highly significant. Academics are able to exploit their bargaining power for a better position when changing institutions or are willing to change institutions only if offered a better position. Research visits remain positive and significant, indicating some positive long-term advantages associated with such visits.

Both regressions take into account the rank of the current institution, which is insignificant. Thus academics do not wait longer for promotion at top universities. As for control variables, we found no difference between men and women in terms of promotion duration. We further saw that the PhD institution plays no important role in the speed of promotion. Academics with a degree in medicine are promoted to full professor earlier than other bioscience academics.

6. CONCLUSIONS

This chapter investigated the effect of early career job transition and short-term mobility on a researcher's probability of placement at a highly ranked institution and of promotion. Because gaining promotion and a prestigious environment are the premise for access to resources and higher wages, fast career progression and appointment in a top-ranked university are two of the main objectives of an academic. Still, the analysis of career and mobility has received little attention, perhaps because both are assumed to be closely linked to productivity (Allison & Long, 1990; Long et al., 1993). However, especially at the start of an academic's career, promotion and hiring decisions often are made based on gender, seniority, and the prestige of previous institutions (Crane, 1965, 1970).

We focused on the case of bioscience in Japan and assembled data on the full academic careers of 370 professors. We found that the prestige of the PhD institution is the best predictor of initial placement and that inbreeding is more common at prestigious institutions. This confirms evidence from the United States that shows that the prestige of the doctoral training institution is the most important predictor for later positions in a top university (e.g., Crane, 1965, 1970). The choice of the PhD location in Japan too becomes a strategic choice that allows access to elite networks and gives early advantages for an academic's later career.

Merit, on the other hand, does not determine promotion duration for early career academics or their initial placement, but it does predict promotion to full professor. It also affects the propensity to be placed in a highly ranked university at middle to late career stages, although the magnitude of these effects was very small in findings that confirm those in the US context (e.g., Long, 1978).

Mobility only reduces the time until promotion if the move is itself accompanied by the promotion. However, we also saw that this mobility results in a promotion in a lower-ranked university, indicating the strategic decision to move down for promotion gains. This finding again corroborates previous research in the US context (e.g., Long, 1978).

We also found that research visits decrease the time until promotion. To shed light on the question of why research visits increase promotion speed, Lawson & Shibayama (2015) looked at their effects on publication performance and found only weak evidence for performance increases. Instead, benefits in terms of teaching and access to external networks may represent more important achievements. Also, these academics may have better existing networks, which may help with mobility and with promotion (see Pezzoni et al., 2012). These visits, however, do not affect access to prestigious institutions within Japan. This indicates that visits may be primarily valued within the sending institution, which is confirmed by Lawson & Shibayama (2015), who found that academics participating in such visits are less likely to move to a different university within Japan.

Some limitations of our results should be understood. By limiting our analysis to a sample of full professors in Japan, we are not able to investigate those who have not been promoted. Our results may therefore underestimate the effect of mobility on promotion, and we could expect even stronger effects compared with those who do not get promoted. Further, some studies have shown that inbred academics do not gain promotion as easily (e.g., Horta et al., 2010). The effect of inbreeding may be negative if we had considered academics who did not gain promotion (Morichika & Shibayama, 2015). Future analysis should therefore consider a more diverse population.

Finally, a better understanding of mobility and career opportunities of individual scientists may also help to evaluate recent reforms in Japan that touch on many aspects of academic life, including recruitment and promotion. A series of reforms during the past two decades, which encouraged and supported universities to adopt a tenure-track system and introduced more fixed-term positions, sought to address problems of inbreeding and localism in the Japanese career system. However, the strict hierarchy of the Japanese academic system discourages mobility at the top. Academics who move out to conform to the new requirements aim to return to the institution of their PhD, as shown by the increase in inbred faculty at full professor level, rendering reforms ineffective. Also, an unintended consequence could be that good academics from top institutions get pushed out of Japan to avoid moving to a lower-ranked institution. Instead, a reform that targets the strict hierarchy in Japan could be more efficient for increasing mobility. Greater autonomy (e.g., in hiring decisions and in setting wages) and greater accountability of institutions (through grants and assessment) were identified as effective means of increasing the performance of universities (Aghion, Dewatripont, Hoxby, Mas-Colell, & Sapir, 2010) and could as a result increase the mobility of academics. Japan established a national evaluation system in 2008, aiming at distributing future funding based on the research quality of national and public universities (Murata, 2008), which could address some of these issues. However, private institutions, with their dependence on tuition fees, would still lack any additional incentives to compete in research.

Evaluating the effects of these various reforms on academic careers in Japan will be the task of future research. CV analysis was useful for obtaining the exact time of recruitment and promotion, but improved measures of networks may further aid future analysis. This research will be important in moving forward the discussion of the Japanese academic career system but beyond this can inform the policy debate on current changes in Europe, as well.

ACKNOWLEDGMENTS

Cornelia Lawson acknowledges financial support through the European Commission (FP7) Project "An Observatorium for Science in Society based in Social Models—SISOB" (no. 266588), the Collegio Carlo Alberto Project "Researcher Mobility and Scientific Performance", and the University of Nottingham International Collaboration Fund. Sotaro Shibayama acknowledges financial support from the Konosuke Matsushita Memorial Foundation and Grant-in-Aid for Research Activity Start-up of the Japan Society for the Promotion of Science (no. 23810004).[9]

REFERENCES

Aghion, P., Dewatripont, M., Hoxby, C., Mas-Colell, A., & Sapir, A. (2010). The governance and performance of universities: evidence from Europe and the US. *Economic Policy, 25*, 7–59.

Akabayashi, H., & Naoi, M. (2004). Why is there no Harvard among Japanese private universities? In *Econometric society far eastern meetings*, no. 726.

Allison, P. D., & Long, J. S. (1990). Departmental effects on scientific productivity. *American Sociological Review, 55*, 469–478.

Baldi, S. (1995). Prestige determinants of first academic job for new sociology Ph.D.s: 1985–1992. *Sociological Quarterly, 36*, 777–789.

BIS (Department for Business, Innovation and Skills). (2013). *Performance of the UK research base: International comparison–2013*. Available online (22.04.14) https://www.gov.uk/government/publications/performance-of-the-uk-research-base-international-comparison-2013.

Burris, V. (2004). The academic caste system: prestige hierarchies in PhD exchange networks. *American Sociological Review, 69*, 239–264.

Canibano, C., & Bozeman, B. (2009). Curriculum vitae method in science policy and research evaluation: the state-of-the-art. *Research Evaluation, 18*, 86–94.

---

9. Some of the material presented in this chapter is also discussed in Lawson & Shibayama (2015).

Canibano, C., Otamendi, J., & Andujar, I. (2008). Measuring and assessing researcher mobility from CV analysis: the case of the Ramón y Cajal programme in Spain. *Research Evaluation*, *17*, 17–31.

Chan, K. C., Chen, C. R., & Steiner, T. L. (2002). Production in the finance literature, institutional reputation, and labor mobility in academia: a global perspective. *Financial Management*, *31*, 131–156.

Crane, D. (1965). Scientists at major and minor universities. A study of productivity and recognition. *American Sociological Review*, *30*, 699–714.

Crane, D. (1970). The academic marketplace revisited: a study of faculty mobility using the Cartter ratings. *The American Journal of Sociology*, *75*, 953–964.

Cruz, L., & Sanz, L. (2010). Mobility versus job stability: assessing tenure and productivity outcomes. *Research Policy*, *39*, 27–38.

Debackere, K., & Rappa, M. A. (1995). Scientists at major and minor universities: mobility along the prestige continuum. *Research Policy*, *24*, 137–150.

Fernandez-Zubieta, A., Geuna, A., & Lawson C. (2015). Mobility and productivity of research scientists. In A. Geuna (Ed.), *Global mobility of research scientists: The economics of who GOES where and why*. San Diego, CA: Academic Press. (Chapter 4).

Franzoni, C., Scellato, G., & Stephan, P. (2012). *The mover's advantage: Scientific performance of mobile academics*. NBER Working Paper 18577.

Gaughan, M., & Robin, S. (2004). National science training policy and early scientific careers in France and the United States. *Research Policy*, *33*, 109–122.

Griffiths, A. (2004). The Japanese employment system: image and reality in an evolving labour market. *Economia*, *55*, 1–30.

Hargens, L. L., & Farr, G. M. (1973). An examination of recent hypotheses about institutional inbreeding. *American Journal of Sociology*, *78*, 1381–1402.

Hoare, A. G. (1994). Transferred skills and university excellence?: An exploratory analysis of the geography of mobility of UK academic staff. *Geografiska Annaler: Series B, Human Geography*, *76*, 143–160.

Horta, H. (2009). Holding a post-doctoral position before becoming a faculty member: does it bring benefits for the scholarly enterprise? *Higher Education*, *58*, 689–721.

Horta, H., Sato, M., & Yonezawa, A. (2011). Academic inbreeding: exploring its characteristics and rationale in Japanese universities using a qualitative perspective. *Asia Pacific Education Review*, *12*, 35–44.

Horta, H., Veloso, F. M., & Grediaga, R. (2010). Navel gazing: academic inbreeding and scientific productivity. *Management Science*, *56*, 414–429.

Huang, F. (2006). The academic profession in Japan: major characteristics and new changes. In *Reports of changing academic profession project workshop on quality, relevance, and governance in the changing academia: International perspectives. COE publication series* (Vol. 20). Hiroshima: Research Institute for Higher Education, Hiroshima University.

Jonkers, K. (2011). Mobility, productivity, gender and career development of Argentinean life scientists. *Research Evaluation*, *20*, 411–421.

Kim, E. H., Morse, A., & Zingales, L. (2009). Are elite universities losing their competitive edge. *Journal of Financial Economics*, *93*, 353–381.

Lawson, C., & Shibayama, S. (2015). *International research visits and careers: An analysis of bioscience academics in Japan*. Science and Public Policy, forthcoming.

Long, J. S. (1978). Productivity and academic position in the scientific career. *American Sociological Review*, *43*, 889–908.

Long, J. S., Allison, P. D., & McGinnis, R. (1993). Rank advancement in academic careers: sex differences and the effects of productivity. *American Sociological Review, 58*, 703–722.

Melin, G. (2005). The dark side of mobility: negative experiences of doing a postdoc period abroad. *Research Evaluation, 14*, 229–237.

MEXT. (1980). *Kyoiku hakusho (education white paper)*. Tokyo: MEXT. Available online http://www.mext.go.jp/b_menu/hakusho/html/hpad198001/index.html. Accessed 28.04.14 (in Japanese).

MEXT. (1990). *Kyoiku hakusho (education white paper)*. Tokyo: MEXT. Available online http://www.mext.go.jp/b_menu/hakusho/html/hpad199001/index.html. Accessed 28.04.14 (in Japanese).

MEXT. (2003a). *For the development of researchers for the global competition.* Tokyo: MEXT. Available online http://www.mext.go.jp/b_menu/shingi/gijyutu/gijyutu10/toushin/03063001.htm. Accessed 28.04.14 (in Japanese).

MEXT. (2003b). *Central Council for Education – University Committee: Agenda for the 2nd steering group on University Staff Organisation.* Tokyo: MEXT. Available online http://www.mext.go.jp/b_menu/shingi/chukyo/chukyo4/004/gijiroku/020501ga.pdf. Accessed 28.04.14 (in Japanese).

MEXT. (2009). *For the development of human resources driving the knowledge-based society.* Tokyo: MEXT. Available online http://www.mext.go.jp/b_menu/shingi/gijyutu/gijyutu10/toushin/attach/1287784.htm. Accessed 28.04.14 (in Japanese).

MEXT. (2012). *Statistical abstracts 2012 edition 1.9 universities and junior colleges.* Tokyo: MEXT. Available online http://www.mext.go.jp/english/statistics/1302965.htm. Accessed 10.10.14.

Morichika, N., & Shibayama, S. (2015). Impact of inbreeding on scientific productivity: A case study of a Japanese university department. *Research Evaluation, 24*, 146–157.

Murata, N. (2008). Evaluation system for national university corporations in Japan – its research. Aspect. In *Workshop on the science of science policy.* Arlington, VI: National Science Foundation.

Musselin, C. (2004). Towards a European academic labour market? Some lessons drawn from empirical studies on academic mobility. *Higher Education, 48*, 55–78.

NISTEP and MRI. (2005). *Study for evaluating the achievements of the S&T basic plans in Japan: Achievements and issues of major policies for S&T human resources training program.* NISTEP Report. Tokyo: NISTEP.

OECD. (2000). *Mobilising human resources for innovation.* Paris: OECD.

OECD. (2008). *The global competition for talent: Mobility of the highly skilled.* Paris: OECD.

Oyer, P. (2008). Ability and employer learning: evidence from the economist labor market. *Journal of Japanese and International Economies, 22*, 268–289.

Pezzoni, M., Sterzi, V., & Lissoni, F. (2012). Career progress in centralized academic systems: an analysis of French and Italian physicists. *Research Policy, 41*(2012), 704–719.

Scellato, G., Franzoni, C., & Stephan, P. (2012). *Mobile scientists and international networks* NBER Working Paper 18613.

Shimbori, M. (1981). The Japanese academic profession. *Higher Education, 10*, 75–87.

Statistics Bureau. (2012). *Japan statistical yearbook.* Tokyo: Statistical Research and Training Institute, Ministry of Internal Affairs and Communication.

Stephan, P. (2012). *How economics shapes science.* Cambridge: Harvard University Press.

Stephan, P. E., & Ma, J. (2005). The increased frequency and duration of the postdoctorate career stage. *The American Economic Review, 95*, 71–75.

Su, X. (2011). Postdoctoral training, departmental prestige and scientists' research productivity. *The Journal of Technology Transfer, 36,* 275–291.

Takahashi, S., & Takahashi, A. M. (2009). *Gender promotion differences in economics departments in Japan: A duration analysis* GSIR WP no. EAPO 09-4.

Teichler, U., Arimoto, A., & Cummings, W. K. (2013). *The changing academy – The changing academic profession in international comparative perspective.* Dordrecht: Springer.

Tsuji, N. (2010). *Transition of objectives of research abroad in modern Japan.* Tokyo: Toshindo Publishing.

Yamanoi, A. (2007). *Academic marketplace in Japan.* Tokyo: Tamagawa University Press.

Zubieta, A. F. (2009). Recognition and weak ties: is there a positive effect of postdoctoral position on academic performance and career development? *Research Evaluation, 18,* 105–115.

Chapter 10

Moving Out of Academic Research: Why Do Scientists Stop Doing Research?

Aldo Geuna[1,2], Sotaro Shibayama[3]

[1]*Department of Economics and Statistics Cognetti De Martiis, Università di Torino, Turin, Italy;*
[2]*BRICK, Collegio Carlo Alberto, Moncalieri, Turin, Italy;* [3]*Research Center for Advanced Science and Technology, University of Tokyo, Meguro-ku, Tokyo, Japan*

Chapter Outline

1. INTRODUCTION

Academic research is extremely competitive, and its "up-or-out" nature inevitably results in a proportion of academics leaving a research career after initial involvement. Although this selection process is fundamental in explaining the highly skewed scientific production in academia (Lotka, 1926), we know little about what characterizes exit from academic research. Most of the sociological and economic literature that analyzes science concentrates on explaining success and focuses on the performance of academic stars. However, if the selection mechanisms are imperfect, for example, if selection is driven by criteria other than merit, then the investment in human capital will be used inefficiently. Policy makers and scientific communities have expressed concern over these issues. Gender and ethnicity discrimination are examples of biased selection criteria. Wolfinger, Mason, & Goulden (2009) indicate that female PhDs are disproportionately more likely to be employed as nontenured faculty and to exit the paid labor force, even when controlling for academic productivity (Kaminski & Geisler, 2012), while Ginther et al. (2011) show that US National Institutes of Health (NIH) grants are less likely to be awarded to certain ethnicities. Such discrimination could exclude potential talent from continuing an academic research career after completion of the PhD or expedite mobility out of an academic research career. There are other factors that can also discourage promising researchers from pursuing an academic research career after completion of their doctoral study. Donowitz, Germino, Cominelli, & Anderson (2007) suggest that American physician-scientists tend to favor lucrative practitioner careers and are discouraged by the unstable system of funding for junior researchers. In addition, the number of academic positions open to junior researchers in the US, EU, and Japan has failed to keep pace with the numbers of new doctoral graduates with the result that even the most capable are opting for nonacademic research jobs (NISTEP 2009a; Stephan, 2012).

The present study tries to shed more light on the process that induces academics to leave active research, by examining the determinants of academic research exit based on a sample of Japanese academics. We define "researcher exit" here as the case of an academic researcher abandoning research after some period either to take up an academic position that focuses on nonresearch activities, such as teaching or administration, or to move into industry. There are several potential determinants of exit from an academic research career; we focus on individual, institutional, and geographical factors, drawing on the literature on academic mobility (e.g., Allison & Long, 1990; Chan, Chen, & Steiner, 2002; Crespi, Geuna, & Nesta, 2006, 2007), search theory models (e.g., Burdett, 1978; Jovanovic, 1979; Mortensen & Pissarides, 1994), and policy research on academic career design (e.g., Gaughan & Robin, 2004; Ginther & Kahn, 2004; Long, Allison, & McGinnis, 1993).

The prior empirical literature on academic careers is based mostly on the US and Europe. With the exception of some research on higher education (Arimoto, 2011; Teichler, Arimoto, & Cummings, 2013; Yamanoi, 2007), the Japanese academic labor market has been understudied. Our main aim in this chapter is to offer a comprehensive analysis of exit among Japanese academic researchers. We employ a sample of 14,000 PhD graduates in hard sciences (all scientific fields except social sciences and humanities), who obtained their doctoral degrees in the period 1985–1989. The data source is the Japanese National Library's PhD degree database. We follow the careers of the sample graduates over 20 years (from 1990 to 2010) using the Japanese national research grant program, Grants-in-Aid (GiA), data.[1] Our econometric models suggest that the determinants of exit from an academic research career include scientific productivity and academic network that are negatively correlated with moving out of academic research, and that female researchers and researchers in less-prestigious universities have a higher probability of exiting from academic research. The findings suggest that the determinants of moving from academia are contingent on scientific field and career stage, and that the selection process in Japan is, at least partly, based on merit but may also be based on gender and university prestige, resulting in the unintended exit of potentially talented researchers.

2. CAREER PATH AND EXIT FROM ACADEMIC RESEARCH CAREER

In Japan and other advanced countries, the professional career of an academic researcher starts after completion of postgraduate-level education (e.g., PhD degree). Some doctoral graduates choose to pursue an academic career and continue to do research and teaching in academia, others focus mainly (or only) on teaching, and some choose research or nonresearch jobs in industry.

We consider the critical points in the academic research career path as those moments where the probability of leaving an academic research career is higher. Exit can be regarded as a type of mobility toward nonacademic research employment, which may occur at various points in an academic research career. In some countries such as France and the UK, there are special PhD programs that allow students financed by companies to pursue more focused research projects that are aligned to the firms' interests. It is not surprising that most of these students continue their career in industry. If we exclude these cases, the three most important decision times are: (1) after PhD graduation, (2) at the time of consideration for a tenured/permanent position, and (3) after obtaining a permanent position. At these moments, academics might be tempted to leave the academic labor market as the result of a job offer from a company or might decide to focus completely on teaching and/or administration and give up research activity. However, the probability of moving to a job in industry is small due to the specificities of the Japanese science market; for example, in 2004 only 0.1% of academics moved from a job in a university to an industry job (METI, 2006).[2] In what follows we discuss the three main moments when the risk of leaving an academic research career is higher, in the context of Japan.

In most OECD countries, students have completed their doctoral research by the time they reach their early thirties; the median age of graduation is 33 in the US, 31 in Switzerland, and 32 in Japan (Auriol, 2010). Most PhD graduates who intend to pursue a career in academic research spend their first period after graduation in a temporary position, such as a postdoc, before achieving their

---

1. GiA is the primary national research funding system in Japan.
2. See Section 4 for information on the Japanese academic context.

first assistant professor (or equivalent) position (Auriol, Misu, & Freeman, 2013). For example, in European countries such as Germany, the Netherlands, and Spain, the percentage of doctoral graduates on temporary contracts within the 5 years after graduation is around 40% (Auriol et al., 2013). In Japan, since 2005 doctoral graduates are awarded an assistant professor position after 5 or 6 years of postdoc employment on average, with only 15% of PhDs achieving this position immediately after graduation (Yamanoi, 2007, Chapter 12). The postdoc period has been extending in most countries (Stephan, 2012). For example, in the US in 2006, only 15% of biology PhDs were in tenure-track positions 6 years after graduation, compared to 55% in 1973 (Stephan, 2012). This discouraging and risky career prospect can dissuade even excellent academics from pursuing an academic research career. Among a sample of about 4000 PhD students in US tier one research universities, Sauermann & Roach (2012) show that an academic research career is considered attractive by only about one-third of respondents in life sciences and physics. Other careers such as academic teaching, civil service, employment in an established firm, or a start-up are perceived as extremely attractive by a large share of PhDs students; for example, 53% of chemistry PhDs considered a job in an established company as the most attractive career path.

A few studies have examined the determinants of career choice at this early stage. Gaughan & Robin (2004) use US and French data and suggest that the prestige of the undergraduate institution is associated with the likelihood of obtaining the first tenure-track position. Similarly, Debackere & Rappa (1995) show that the prestige of the graduate school for American neural network scientists is significantly correlated with the prestige of the first employer.

For those PhDs who survive the postdoc period and manage to secure an assistant professor position, the second critical point in the academic research career is the time at which the faculty member is considered for a tenured (permanent) position. In the US, tenure is usually awarded 7–9 years after initial hire (Stephan, 2012). In other countries, the system is less structured and rolling or temporary contracts over periods of 4–8 years are common. Failure to obtain tenure can often result in job mobility to a lower-ranked university with more or only teaching duties, a move to a job in business, or exit from the market. A few studies have analyzed the probability of being awarded tenure. First, in a sample of biochemistry graduates from US universities, productivity measured by publication count is found to be positively associated with promotion from assistant to associate professor (with tenure) and to full professor (Long et al., 1993). Second, there is an important gender difference; several studies indicate that females are less likely to be given tenure and have to wait longer for the offer of a permanent position (e.g., Ginther & Kahn, 2004; Long et al., 1993). Wolfinger et al. (2009) examine the contract types of first employment and suggest that female PhDs in the US are less likely to obtain tenured positions and more likely to exit the labor force. Third, academic mobility across institutions has an influence. Although mobility can contribute to researchers' social capital and productivity, Long et al. (1993) and Cruz-Castro & Sanz-Menendez (2010) suggest that mobility delays promotion possibly because the "tenure clock" is continually being reset.

Finally, academic researchers that have obtained a tenured position (associate professorship) may still choose to leave a research career to move to a job in a business organization or to refocus their academic profile toward a teaching and administrative position.

3. DETERMINANTS OF EXIT

This study examines exit from academic research drawing on search theory in labor economics (Burdett, 1978; Jovanovic, 1979; Mortensen & Pissarides, 1994). Exiting from an academic research career depends on the probability of receiving an offer (and accepting it) to pursue a career in academic research compared to academic teaching, administration, or industry. We identify individual, institutional, and geographical factors correlated to persistence in an academic research job.

3.1 Individual Factor

3.1.1 Scientific Productivity

The productivity of academics should affect their value in the labor market. Research organizations try to retain productive employees and to dismiss less productive employees (Becker, 1962). Highly productive academics have greater chances of both employment in a prestigious university (Allison & Long, 1987) and of promotion (Long et al., 1993). These studies suggest consistently that the opportunity for a job in academic research should be higher for more productive academics who consequently have a lower probability of leaving an academic career (Brewer, 1996). In parallel with their research responsibilities, academics usually engage in nonresearch activities such as teaching and administration. Some academics choose (or are forced) to concentrate on nonresearch jobs in academia and to give up their researcher careers. The expertise required for teaching, administration, and research may coincide to a degree, so productive researchers could become productive teachers or good administrators. This raises the question of whether higher research productivity leads to a higher chance of a teaching or administration job offer. In relation to social status, salary, etc., academics seem to gain higher utility from a research job than from pure teaching or administration responsibilities.[3] Thus, we hypothesize that productive researchers are unlikely to become teachers

---

3. Top executive administrative positions (e.g., provost, dean) may be both prestigious and lucrative. Researchers who leave research for such senior positions are regarded as examples of voluntary exit from academic research. However, the number of these job opportunities is limited. In Japan, executive administrators are often appointed from among professors within the university with some rotation pattern.

or administrators and have a low probability of exit. However, we recognize that there are also a few cases in which extremely productive researchers become excellent administrators.[4]

In some scientific fields where science and technology overlap, such as transfer and Pasteur-quadrant sciences (e.g., biomedical, software engineering), academic research expertise can be relevant for industry research. Thus, productive academics may attract job offers from business (Lazear, 1984; Murnane, Singer, Willett, Kemple, & Olsen, 1991). Stern (2004) and Sauermann & Roach (2014) suggest that scientists may choose industry jobs if the accompanying higher salaries compensate sufficiently for loss of freedom to do the research they like and to publish. Zucker, Darby, & Torero (2002) show that productive (measured by citations to their publications) academics are more likely to move to an industry job in the US biotech field. Thus, if the requirements for the industry job are academic research expertise, the effect of scientific productivity on exit could be positive.

3.1.2 Funding Inputs

Academics need research funding in order to undertake research. In many countries, noncompetitive block grants have been replaced by competitive funds. Since academics' capacity to raise competitive funding is correlated with their productivity (Dasgupta & David, 1994), we would expect the availability of competitive funds to be negatively correlated with the probability of exit since this type of funding is a research input. Even controlling for scientific productivity, stable funding could have a mitigating effect on exit. Academic research in the natural sciences, in particular, is heavily dependent on large research funding support for laboratory costs and the salaries of PhDs and postdocs. Thus, securing funding is a major concern for laboratory heads (Shibayama, Baba, & Walsh, 2015; Stephan, 2012). Secure funding should ensure a continuing research career (Donowitz et al., 2007; Zerhouni, 2006) and increase its expected utility, thereby reducing potential exit. Thus, we expect that competitive funding inputs are negatively associated with the likelihood of exit.

3.1.3 Gender

It is well known that women are underrepresented in academia. For example, Auriol et al. (2013) show that less than 40% of PhD graduates in most OECD countries are female. In Japan, the gender imbalance is particularly pronounced[5] with women accounting for only 26% of all PhD graduates in 2006 (NISTEP 2009a). Female researchers are more likely to have child

---

4. See, for example, the case of David Baltimore, Nobel laureate and President of the California Institute of Technology (Caltech) from 1997 to 2006.

5. Japan, ranked 21st in the UN's gender inequality index, lags behind most OECD countries for improving the gender gap, (http://hdr.undp.org/en/statistics/gii).

rearing and domestic responsibilities that are likely to cause earlier exit. Female researchers are less likely to obtain tenure and to take longer to achieve it (Ginther & Kahn, 2004; Long et al., 1993; Wolfinger et al., 2009). For example, although the situation has improved over recent decades, in 2010 in the US, females accounted for 44%, 37%, and 22%, respectively, of assistant, associate, and full professor positions (National Science Board, 2014, Chapter 5). The statistics for Japan show that, in the natural sciences, only 15.7% of assistant professors are female and a mere 3.8% achieve the position of full professor (NISTEP 2009b, pp. 2–16). Based on these findings, we expect that females are more likely than males to exit an academic research career.

3.1.4 Academic Career

Search theory shows that length of employment in the same organization stabilizes relations between employee and employer, and reduces job quit (Farber, 1994; Jovanovic, 1979). In the academic context, Crespi et al. (2007) show that the longer the academic remains in one university, the less likely he/she will move from academia to industry. This would seem to support the negative relationship between tenure and exit. However, it is also plausible that academic institutions appoint researchers with long tenure but diminished research excellence to nonresearch positions. Thus, tenure could be correlated either positively or negatively with exit.

Job rank (assistant, associate, full professor, etc.) should also affect exit. Promotion is usually associated with research performance; greater seniority equates with greater propensity to do research. In addition, seniority brings greater job security and a higher salary, resulting in greater expected utility from an academic research career. Overall, we expect that job rank is negatively associated with the likelihood of exit.

3.1.5 Academic Network

When academics are well embedded in a scientific community and have good connections with other academics, they are kept apprised of job vacancies. Zucker et al. (2002) show that the academic's external network, measured by the proportion of coauthors from different institutions, leads to mobility from academia to industry. Also, Crespi et al. (2007) indicate that network, measured by collaboration with external organizations, facilitates mobility from universities to public research organizations (PROs). Applying this evidence to the academic network, one can expect that researchers with good individual academic network connections will also be better informed about academic research job opportunities, which consequently will reduce the likelihood of exit. This may be particularly true in the Japanese context where human relationships (connections) play an important role in the recruitment of academics (Yamanoi, 2007).

3.2 Institutional Factor

3.2.1 Research Organization

An institutional factor that is known to influence academic career is organizational prestige. Undergraduate or graduate study at a prestigious organization is found to be a good predictor of future academic employment (Gaughan & Robin, 2004) and promotion (Long et al., 1993). In addition, it has been suggested that prior experience in an excellent organization leads to future employment in a prestigious organization (Allison & Long, 1987; Debackere & Rappa, 1995). These studies imply that organizational prestige should increase job offers for academic researchers and lead to higher expected utility, lowering the likelihood of exit.

Prestige is a complex concept that encompasses several factors. First, prestige is associated with the availability of resources for research. In general, prestigious organizations have more and larger sources of revenue, can invest more generously in research, and can maintain better facilities for individual researchers to conduct state-of-the-art research. This should increase the expected utility of an academic research career. A second factor is the institutional academic network. Prestigious organizations can employ excellent researchers and attract excellent external collaborators. This provides individual academics with advantages in the form of opportunities for intellectual interactions with peers and access to their social capital. Thus, we expect that institutional capital, measured as funding input and institutional academic network (peer effects and social capital), will be negatively correlated with exit.

3.2.2 Scientific Fields

In the context of academic research, individual academics have an affiliation with their particular university and become deeply embedded in their respective scientific fields. Thus, their career paths should be affected by the characteristics of their field. These include academia–industry linkages that can increase job offers from industry and are particularly important in Pasteur-quadrant sciences (compared to pure basic science) (Stokes, 1997), whereas mobility between academia and business involves lower transaction costs and is more common, resulting in higher levels of exit. Field growth is another factor; in expanding fields, employment is more likely to increase and the enhanced job prospects should improve the expected utility of an academic research career. Therefore, the probability of exit will be higher in Pasteur-quadrant scientific fields, and field growth will be negatively associated with exit.

3.3 Geographical/Labor Market Factors

In general, a career change involves a different workplace. A geographical change incurs search and moving costs, so job vacancies in the same geographical vicinity should be associated with a higher likelihood of a job change.

Disentangling types of employers, Zucker et al. (2002) show that mobility from academia to industry is positively associated with the number of biotech firms and negatively associated with the number of top-rated universities in the area. The effect of concentration of universities is unclear because universities offer both research and teaching jobs. In an attempt to disentangle these two types of employment opportunities, we expect that the local concentration of research-intensive universities will be negatively correlated with exit, while local concentration of teaching-oriented universities will be positively correlated with exit. We control also for the size of the local labor market and supply of qualified researchers.

4. CONTEXT OF JAPANESE ACADEMIA

Japan has three types of universities—national, regional (i.e., city and prefectural), and private—that offer 4-year degree courses and postgraduate education. In 1985 (our sample is composed of academics who obtained a PhD degree in 1985–1989), Japan had 95 national, 34 regional, and 331 private universities,[6] with national universities focused on academic research and most private universities focused on teaching. In 1985, 73% of undergraduate students were enrolled in private universities and 24% in national universities, while 38% of graduate students were enrolled in private or regional universities and 62% in national universities. In terms of research funding, in 1985, national universities received 77% (decreased to 67% in 2010) of the total GiA budget, the primary national research funding system in Japan. Among national universities, the seven pre-imperial universities (Tokyo, Kyoto, Osaka, Tohoku, Hokkaido, Kyushu, and Nagoya) are considered exceptionally prestigious for both research and education. Academic research is also conducted in PROs (e.g., RIKEN).[7] In 2004, PROs employed approximately 10% of researchers and universities 90% (METI, 2006, p. 264).

Japanese universities have a three-level promotion system from the entry position of assistant professor or lecturer, to associate professor, and finally full professor.[8] Currently, before being appointed to an entry position, academics—especially in natural sciences—must spend a few years as a postdoc. In 2005, the average postdoc period was 5 or 6 years (Yamanoi, 2007, Chapter 12). In the 1980s, postdocs were less common, and young academics were often appointed as assistants or lecturers directly after graduation. According to a national survey of natural scientists (NISTEP, 2009b), among respondents aged 26–36 years in 1990, 23.5% had held a postdoc position and 70.5% had not. Among the former, approximately 80% spent 3 years or less as a postdoc.

---

6. School Survey conducted by the Ministry of Education, Culture, Sports, Science and Technology (MEXT; http://www.e-stat.go.jp/).

7. http://www.riken.jp/en/

8. The position of assistant professor was officially introduced in Japanese universities in 2007. Previous to this, the position was designated "assistant" (Watanabe, 2011).

Japan's academic system has a few relevant features. First, it used to be characterized by lifetime employment (Shimbori, 1981; Takahashi & Takahashi, 2009). Until a series of reforms in the 2000s allowed temporary employment, entry positions were mostly permanent (Watanabe, 2011). Second, many Japanese universities operate a hierarchical "chair" system (Yamanoi, 2007). The system used to be, and sometimes still is, led by a full professor (the "chair"), responsible for a small team of junior researchers in entry positions and perhaps an associate professor. Thus, while junior researchers in entry positions were cleared of unemployment risk, they had to (and have to) compete to be promoted and win a position of an independent researcher. Third, Japan's employment practice is characterized by high rigidity and very low cross-sectoral mobility. According to a government statistic (METI, 2006, p. 264), in 2004, only 1.1% of researchers (8800 out of 790,900) moved across the three sectors of industry, government, and academia. In the same year, 97.4% of 291,100 university researchers were not mobile, 2.3% moved between two universities, 0.11% moved to industry, and 0.15% moved to government (i.e., PROs). Thus, industry is a less frequent destination for academics who leave university employment, and exit is more likely due to academics giving up research and remaining in academia in a teaching or administrative position.

5. DATA DESCRIPTION AND VARIABLE MEASUREMENT

5.1 Sample and Data

Our sample is composed of a cohort of 13,776 PhD graduates who were awarded a PhD degree in hard science (all scientific fields except social sciences and humanities) in the period 1985–1989.[9] We focus on the 1985–1989 cohort because a reform to the funding system allowed significantly more junior researchers to obtain grants since the mid-1980s (the number of junior grantees in 1980–1984 is about half the number in 1985–1989). This allows us to trace academic careers more precisely for up to 20 years. The data on PhD graduates were obtained from the Japanese National Library database[10] that provides full names, degree field, year of degree award, etc.

To trace careers and identify exit from an academic research career, we exploit the GiA program database. The GiA program is the largest source of funding

---

9. We exclude social sciences and the humanities because our theoretical framework to explain exit from academic research does not apply to these fields. PhD graduates from these fields account for 3.2%. We also exclude foreign-born graduates because name matching (explained later) for foreigners is difficult for nonunique notations of foreign names in Japanese characters and because nonnative Japanese graduates are unlikely to pursue an academic career in Japan (Franzoni, Scellato, & Stephan, 2012). Foreign students account for 7.3% of all PhD graduates. Finally, we do not include so-called paper-based PhDs who are awarded the degree on the basis of their research output (often based on corporate research experience) with no course work requirement; paper-based degrees are usually awarded to senior researchers, and their inclusion would bias the analysis.

10. Universities are obliged to archive all PhD dissertations in the National Library. The library creates electronic data upon receiving dissertations. There is open access to the database (http://opac.ndl.go.jp/).

for academic research in Japan and covers all scientific fields and all ranks of researchers.[11] A survey of GiA grantees in 2006 indicates that only 3% of academic researchers depended for the majority of their research budget on funding sources other than GiA, and that this rate differs between fields with a maximum of 13% in engineering (Iida, 2007, Chapter 6).[12] Thus, we can reasonably assume that researchers who have never received GiA funding, or have not continued to receive it, most likely stopped doing academic research.[13] For each grant award, the database provides full names of grantees,[14] grant size, affiliations, collaborators, associated publications after completion of the grant, fields of research, etc.

We created two datasets; the first includes cross-sectional information for all 13,776 PhD graduates, and the second includes information on 5,599 GiA grantees for the period 1990–2012. We linked the two databases on the basis of full names of PhD graduates and GiA grantees and found 5,599 matches among the 13,776 PhD graduates.[15] We consider that unmatched PhD graduates who never received GiA funding exited before embarking on a professional academic research career (pre-employment exit).

We built an unbalanced panel that consists of the matched 5,599 PhD graduates who have received GiA funding at least once, and trace their career until exit or up to 2010. We consider that an academic who appeared in the GiA database but then disappeared has exited from an academic research career after a spell of academic employment (post-employment exit). Although the two original databases do not provide information on age, we can assume that PhD degrees were awarded at around 26–31 years of age (NISTEP, 2009a). Since the retirement age in most universities in Japan was 60 (although this has now been extended), it is unlikely that researchers that exited our sample after having started an academic research career would be retired since they should be around 57 years old in 2010.

5.2 Dependent Variables

For pre-employment exit, we prepared a dummy variable that takes the value of "0" if a PhD graduate is matched with the funding database and "1"

---

11. General information on GiA can be accessed from the MEXT website (http://www.mext.go.jp/a_menu/shinkou/hojyo/main5_a5.htm). Kneller (2010) and Asonuma (2002) provide overviews of the GiA and the general budgetary structure in Japanese universities. The GiA database provides information on all grants awarded under the system since 1965, covering 210,000 university researchers.

12. Among the top seven national universities, about 84% of full and associate professors received GiA funding at least once in the period 2001–2005 (Shibayama, 2011). Our exit measure might be less reliable for researchers in private universities, where dependence on GiA is lower.

13. GiA grants are also awarded to researchers in PROs. Since PRO researchers are less dependent on competitive funding, our data might miss very active researchers in PROs and overstate exit. However, we believe that this effect is limited because of the higher mobility from PROs to universities (10%) and much lower mobility from universities to PROs (0.1%) (METI, 2006, p. 264).

14. The database includes two types of grantees: principal investigator (one or more) and members.

15. Name ambiguity is not a serious problem since full names in Chinese characters are available in both databases. For some common names, we differentiate by year of graduation and funding and scientific field.

otherwise. The matching rate is 41%, and thus, the rate of pre-employment exit is 59%.

For post-employment exit, we prepared a dummy variable that is coded "1" for the last year the academic received a grant from GiA and "0" otherwise. We used the year 2012 version of the GiA database and regard academics whose latest record in the database occurred in 2010 or later as survivors, on the assumption that research-active academics are funded at least once in 5 years.[16]

5.3 Independent Variables

We prepared several independent variables for the individual, institutional, and geographical factors discussed above, drawing on the funding database and other public data sources. To analyze pre-employment exit, we took the year of PhD graduation as the measurement year.

For individual level measures, we include eight variables. The funding database provides the number of publications resulting from each funded project. By dividing this publication count by the number of project members and project duration, we can compute a yearly publication count for each academic. Since publication count can differ by field and year, we standardized this measure by field/year mean and standard deviation. We then compute the accumulated count of publications prior to each year (pub stock). We divided funding amount for each project by the number of project members and project duration, and summed them for each year, for each academic, to compute a yearly funding input. We standardized this by the field/year mean and standard deviation to compute stock value (fund stock). We coded a dummy variable (female) of "1" for female and "0" for male. For academic career, we computed the number of years of employment each academic had in a university (job tenure). For academic rank, we constructed two dummy variables: the variable *full prof* takes the value "1" for full professor, and the variable *associate prof* takes the value "1" for associate professor. For academic network, we counted the cumulative number of cograntees related to a researcher's GiA funding (#cograntee), and we also controlled for the number of universities to which a researcher was affiliated (mobility).

We constructed four variables for institutional factors. The top seven national universities in Japan are regarded as prestigious research-intensive universities. To measure organizational prestige, we included a dummy variable that scores "1" for the top seven universities, and "0" otherwise (top7). University-level funding input was computed as follows. We first computed the GiA funds for each intersection of university, field, and year, and then total funds for each field/year. We divided the former by the latter to calculate the proportion of funding distributed to each university (%univ fund). To measure the importance of the institutional academic network of the grantee university (as a proxy for peer effects and social

---

16. Most funding is for 3–5-year periods.

capital), we counted the number of GiA grantees (only principal investigators) in each year in the same university and the same field (#researcher). To estimate field growth, we counted the number of grantees (only principal investigators) in each year and each field, and calculated the annual growth rate (field growth).

Finally, for geographic factors, we constructed four variables at the level of the 47 prefectures. We collected the number of jobs in national universities located in each prefecture as a proxy for academic research jobs (#national university employment) and the number of jobs in private universities as a proxy for teaching-oriented job opportunities (#private university employment).[17] This is based on the assumption that national universities tend to be research-intensive and private universities tend to be teaching oriented. We also collected employment numbers for each prefecture as a measure of employment opportunities in the private sector (#industrial employment).[18] Finally, we took the number of PhD graduates in universities in the same prefecture to measure the labor supply (#PhD graduate).

6. ECONOMETRIC MODEL AND RESULTS

The structure of our data allowed us to analyze exit at a few distinct moments: (1) immediately after PhD graduation (pre-employment exit), (2) after the academic embarks on a professional researcher career (post-employment exit), divided into (2a) before achieving a tenured position, that is, assistant professor (pre-tenure exit), and (2b) after achieving tenure, that is, associate or full professor (post-tenure exit).[19] Section 6.1 presents the estimations for exit at moment (1) drawing on cross-sectional data for 13,776 PhD graduates and estimates the likelihood of pre-employment exit by logit regressions.

In Sections 6.2 and 6.3 we examined exit at moments (2a) and (2b). We used panel data for the whole careers of the 5,599 PhD graduates who received GiA funding at least once. We estimated the likelihood of post-employment exit by survival analysis, drawing on a duration model that allowed us to analyze a point event (referred to as a failure event) that occurs after a certain period of time (spell length). The average spell length is 17 years. We drew on a discrete approach based on the complementary log–log (cloglog) model.[20] Based on

---

17. Source: School Survey conducted by the MEXT (http://www.mext.go.jp/b_menu/toukei/chousa01/kihon/1267995.htm).

18. Labor Survey conducted by the Ministry of Internal Affairs and Communications (http://www.stat.go.jp/data/roudou/index.htm). Since data are available from 1997, data for the years 1985–1996 are imputed from year 1997. Employment numbers have been stable since the late 1990s.

19. As discussed above, assistant professor positions were mostly permanent in the past. Thus, in our empirical setting, tenured position has the meaning of being granted the promotion to associate professor academic rank that is usually associated to a tenured position in the United States.

20. A continuous approach can be employed. A Cox (1972) semiparametric model yields a similar pattern of results.

Prentice & Gloeckler (1978), the discrete hazard time for individual i in time interval t to exit is estimated by the following function:

$$h_{it} = 1 - \exp\{ - \exp(\beta X_i + \theta (t))\}$$

where h_{it} is the hazard rate and $\theta(t)$ is the baseline hazard function with spell duration (Jenkins, 1995). A set of time dummy variables is included to capture the unobserved time-varying effect on the likelihood of exit.

6.1 Pre-Employment Exit

We first examined *pre-employment exit* defined by no award of GiA funding. Table 1 presents basic information on exit by field, university, and gender. Table 1(A) provides a breakdown by PhD degree field: Medicine (49.1%), Engineering (15.4%), Science (16.0%), Dentistry (10.0%), Agriculture (5.9%), and Pharmacy (3.6%). Exit rates differ substantially by field. PhDs in Engineering and Science show relatively low exit rate (~51%) or the highest rate of survival in an academic research career. Three medical fields (Medicine, Dentistry, Pharmacy) show high exit rates (>60%), probably because of substantial demand for their labor in practitioner jobs (doctors, dentists, pharmacists, etc.).

Table 1(B) provides a breakdown by PhD awarding university. During 1985–1989, 142 universities awarded at least one PhD degree in hard sciences. The top seven universities accounted for 37.6% of PhDs, and their exit rates are somewhat lower (<50%). Lower-ranked universities show higher exit rates, implying that more academic research jobs are given to graduates from top universities.

Table 1(C) provides a breakdown by gender and field. The proportion of females in all PhD graduates is 7.7%. In all fields, exit rates are higher for females (73.5%) than males (58.2%). The gender difference is greatest in Agriculture (1.44 times more for females than males) and least in Pharmacy (1.11 times). The three fields with the highest exit rates for female scientists are Agriculture (78%), Medicine (77%), and Pharmacy (71%).

Table 2 shows the regression results. We regress pre-employment exit using a logit regression model. Table 10A.1 provides descriptive statistics and correlations for the variables. Model 1 suggests that females are significantly more likely to exit before employment. This effect remains strong after introducing other factors in Models 2 and 3.

Model 2 includes institutional factors and suggests two determinants of exit. Affiliation during PhD training has a significant effect; graduates from top universities are less likely to exit, which is consistent with our hypothesis and summary data. Moreover, the number of researchers who received a GiA grant in the same university and field, proxy for institutional academic network, decreases the likelihood of exit. This may be because they help PhD graduates find employment through their large research network or because research-active departments have greater capacity to employ PhD graduates on a temporary basis.

TABLE 1 Description of Pre-Employment Exit

(A) By Field

PhD Field	#Graduate		#Matched		%Exit
Science	2202	(16.0%)	1068	(19.1%)	51.5
Engineering	2120	(15.4%)	1049	(18.7%)	50.5
Agriculture	817	(5.9%)	356	(6.4%)	56.4
Pharmacy	497	(3.6%)	175	(3.1%)	64.8
Medicine	6762	(49.1%)	2416	(43.2%)	64.3
Dentistry	1378	(10.0%)	535	(9.6%)	61.2
Total	13,776	(100.0%)	5599	(100.0%)	59.4

(B) By University

Rank	University	#Graduate		#Matched		%Exit
1	U Tokyo	1317	(9.6%)	643	(11.5%)	51.2
2	Kyoto U	1030	(7.5%)	507	(9.1%)	50.8
3	Osaka U	704	(5.1%)	365	(6.5%)	48.2
4	Tohoku U	607	(4.4%)	302	(5.4%)	50.2
5	Kyushu U	553	(4.0%)	298	(5.3%)	46.1
6	Hokkaido U	509	(3.7%)	226	(4.0%)	55.6
7	Nagoya U	459	(3.3%)	241	(4.3%)	47.5
	Top 7	5179	(37.6%)	2582	(46.1%)	50.1
10	Tsukuba U	294	(2.1%)	119	(2.1%)	59.5
20	Keio U	164	(1.2%)	74	(1.3%)	54.9
30	Tokyo Jikei Med U	118	(0.9%)	59	(1.1%)	50.0
40	Akita U	92	(0.7%)	28	(0.5%)	69.6
50	Hamamatsu Med U	68	(0.5%)	23	(0.4%)	66.2
	Total	13,776	(100.0%)	5599	(100.0%)	59.4

Continued

TABLE 1 Description of Pre-Employment Exit—cont'd

(C) By Gender

| PhD Field | #Graduate | | | #Matched | | | %Exit | | |
	Male	Female	%Female	Male	Female	%Female	Male	Female	%Exit Female/Male
Science	2053	149	6.8	1016	52	4.9	50.5	65.1	1.29
Engineering	2055	65	3.1	1024	25	2.4	50.2	61.5	1.23
Agriculture	740	77	9.4	339	17	4.8	54.2	77.9	1.44
Pharmacy	452	45	9.1	162	13	7.4	64.2	71.1	1.11
Medicine	6150	612	9.1	2277	139	5.8	63.0	77.3	1.23

Notes: Ranked by the number of PhD graduates.

TABLE 2 Prediction of Pre-Employment Exit

	Model 1			Model 2			Model 3		
Individual factors									
graduation year	0.021	*	(0.012)	0.025		(0.020)	0.015		(0.021)
female	0.688	***	(0.072)	0.653	***	(0.073)	0.650	***	(0.073)
Institutional factors									
top7				−0.173	***	(0.060)	−0.189	***	(0.061)
ln(#researcher)				−0.252	***	(0.030)	−0.244	***	(0.032)
field growth				0.026		(0.136)	0.016		(0.136)
field dummies				YES			YES		
Geographical factors									
ln(#national univ employment)							−0.223	***	(0.073)
ln(#private univ employment)							0.049	**	(0.020)
ln(#industrial employment)							−0.014		(0.047)
ln(#PhD graduate)							0.108	*	(0.060)
χ^2 test	102.927	***		510.962	***		537.174	***	
Log likelihood	−9254.68			−9050.67			−9037.56		
N	13,776			13,776			13,776		

Notes: Logit regressions. Unstandardized coefficients (standard errors in parentheses). Two-tailed test.
*$p<0.1$;
**$p<0.05$;
***$p<0.01$.

Field dummies are collectively significant. The fields of Dentistry and Engineering show the lowest exit propensity while Medicine shows the highest propensity. Since career structure might differ with scientific field, we ran the same set of regressions separately for each field. The statistical significance varies across fields, but the sign of the correlation is mostly consistent with the aggregate results (see Table 10A.2 for summary results).

Model 3 also includes geographical factors. Employment in research-intensive national universities has a negative effect, suggesting that the availability of academic research jobs in the vicinity reduces the likelihood of exit, as hypothesized. In contrast, and as expected, employment in teaching-oriented private universities increases the likelihood of exit (move to a teaching-oriented job). Employment in industry does not have a significant effect. Finally, a large number of graduates from the same geographical area facilitates exit perhaps due to oversupply and competition for research jobs.

6.2 Post-Employment Exit

For academics who do not exit immediately after graduation (i.e., awarded funding at least once), we compute survivor functions (Figure 1). Figure 1(A) illustrates the function for the whole sample, indicating that academic exit was steady, with 40% persisting after 25 years in research. Job ranks at the time of exit, or final position of survivors, are full professor (40%), associate professor (22%), and assistants or lecturer (38%).

We computed survivor functions for a few sample subsets. Figure 1(B) highlights field differences based on funding fields.[21] Funding fields consist of Clinical Medicine (35.1%), Engineering (15.1%), Mathematics and Physics (11.1%), Dentistry (10.6%), Biology (7.9%), Agriculture (5.7%), Chemistry (4.5%), and Pharmacy (2.3%). The survivor function shows particularly rapid exit in Clinical Medicine and Dentistry followed by Pharmacy. The other fields follow a similar trend with about 60% remaining after 25 years. In terms of PhD affiliation, the top seven universities account for 50% of those PhD graduates who remain in academic research. Graduates from these universities are significantly less likely to leave than those from other universities (Figure 1(C)). Finally, females, who account for 7.7% of those PhD graduates who remain in academic research, are more likely to exit than males (Figure 1(D)).

Table 3 shows the regression results for post-employment exit. Table 10A.1 provides descriptive statistics and correlations for the variables. Model 1 includes only individual-level factors. Publication stock has a significantly negative coefficient, suggesting that high performers tend to continue in academic research. This effect is consistent after controlling for other factors in Models 2 and 3. Funding

---

21. For those academics who did not exit immediately after graduation, we distinguish fields in slightly more detail drawing on the GiA database. Medicine is split into Basic Medicine and Clinical Medicine; Science is split into Biology, Chemistry, Mathematics, and Physics.

input has a negative coefficient, implying that larger yearly research funding for individual academics facilitates long-term engagement in academic research. Though Model 1 shows a negative sign for female, it turns insignificant when we control for institutional and geographical factors (Models 2 and 3). Job tenure has a negative effect on mobility; that is, academics who stay for longer in the same university are less likely to exit. Seniority reduces the likelihood of exit; that is, assistant professors are more likely to exit than associate professors, and associate professors are more likely to exit than full professors, which is in line with our hypothesis. For the individual network effect, the number of cograntees shows significantly positive coefficients, which is contrary to our expectation that a larger academic network helps job search. This result is discussed further in Section 6.3. Finally, previous mobility has a negative coefficient, suggesting that mobile academics tend to remain in academic research for longer. However, this effect decreases when we control for institutional and geographical factors (Model 3). One interpretation of this result is that mobility might be forced rather than voluntary, and that lower performers who are less likely to be granted tenured positions need to move to lower-ranked institutions to obtain more secure and teaching-oriented jobs.

In relation to institutional factors, our results suggest that academics in prestigious universities (top7) tend to stay longer in academic research, which supports our hypothesis. The coefficient of number of researchers in the same university and same field is significantly negative, showing a decreasing likelihood of exit and confirming the presence of an institutional peer and social capital effect.[22] As for funding input at the university level, we find a small positive correlation with exit, contrary to our hypothesis, which largely disappears in Model 3. After controlling for social capital and peer effects (#researcher) and organizational prestige (top7), resource input may have only a limited impact on the likelihood of exit.

Among field-related factors, Model 2 shows that field growth has a significantly negative coefficient. This suggests that in expanding fields, exit is less frequent, although when we control for geographic/labor market characteristics (Model 3), the effect becomes smaller. The field dummies collectively are significant. Among the nine fields, for post-employment exit we observe a relatively low propensity in Biology, Mathematics and Physics, and Pharmacy, and high propensity in Clinical Medicine and Dentistry. We examined field difference by running the regressions separately for each field (see Table 10A.2 for summary results).

Model 3 includes geographical factors. We observe a negative coefficient of number of jobs in national universities, suggesting that a higher number of

---

22. The number of researchers may be confounded by the size factor, since we control for the proportion of funding distributed to the university (%univ fund), we can interpret the number of researchers in the field in the university as a proxy for social capital and peer effect.

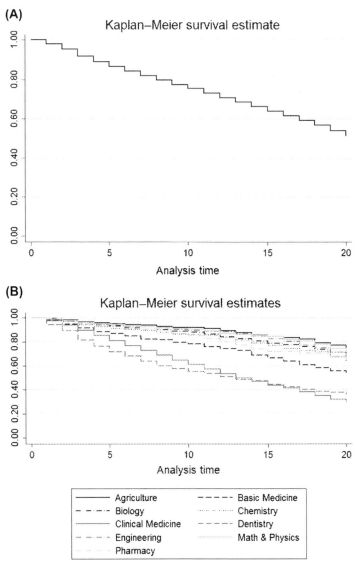

FIGURE 1   Survivor functions (*N*=5,264), (A) whole sample, (B) scientific fields, (C) PhD universities (top7 vs others), (D) gender (female vs male).

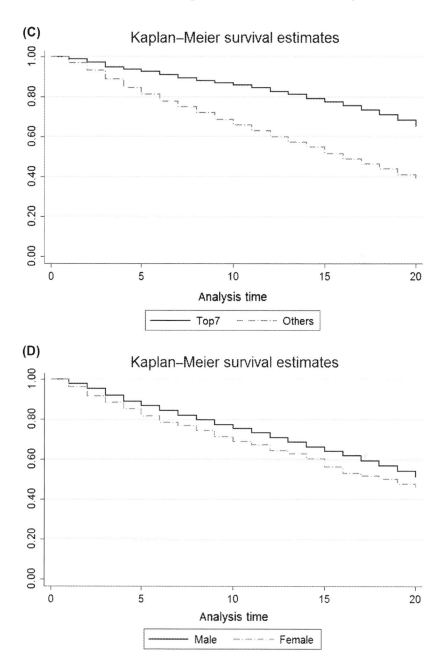

FIGURE 1 Cont'd

TABLE 3 Prediction of Post-Employment Exit

	Model 1		Model 2		Model 3	
Individual factors						
pub stock	-0.027	*** (0.005)	-0.032	*** (0.005)	-0.041	*** (0.005)
fund stock	-0.019	*** (0.005)	-0.009	* (0.004)	-0.015	*** (0.005)
female	-0.268	*** (0.086)	-0.094	(0.087)	0.045	(0.087)
job tenure	-0.050	*** (0.005)	-0.025	*** (0.006)	-0.011	* (0.006)
associate prof	-0.644	*** (0.058)	-0.578	*** (0.058)	-0.370	*** (0.058)
full prof	-0.892	*** (0.077)	-0.980	*** (0.077)	-0.704	*** (0.078)
mobility	-0.323	*** (0.048)	-0.565	*** (0.053)	-0.134	** (0.054)
ln(#cograntee)	0.119	*** (0.021)	0.243	*** (0.022)	0.231	*** (0.023)
Institutional factors						
top7			-0.197	*** (0.071)	-0.272	*** (0.072)
%univ fund			0.023	** (0.010)	-0.001	(0.012)
ln(#researcher)			-0.591	*** (0.020)	-0.245	*** (0.028)
field growth			-1.521	*** (0.190)	-0.601	** (0.239)
field dummies			YES		YES	
Geographical factors						
ln(#national univ employment)					-0.568	*** (0.045)
ln(#private univ employment)					0.066	*** (0.023)
ln(#industrial employment)					-0.429	*** (0.038)
ln(#PhD graduate)					0.504	*** (0.042)
χ^2 test	30,402.90	***	29,968.97	***	29,933.20	***
Log likelihood	-13,749.33		-12,434.98		-11,849.05	
N	93,474		93,474		93,474	

Notes: Complementary log-log model. Unstandardized coefficients (standard errors in parentheses). Two-tailed test.
*$p<0.1$;
**$p<0.05$;
***$p<0.01$.

researcher positions facilitates an academic career. We observe a positive coefficient of number of jobs in private universities, suggesting that the higher the number of teaching positions, the shorter the time taken for academics to leave academic research and accept a job in a teaching university. Model 3 indicates also that more PhD graduates from the same geographical area increase the likelihood of exit, suggesting the effect of oversupply. Finally, the number of jobs in industry has a negative coefficient. This effect is particularly strong for Biology, Engineering, and Basic Medicine (see Table 10A.2), maybe indicating that the presence of a proximate sizable industry sector increases the chances of industry funding allowing researchers to continue doing research.

Figure 2 depicts the estimated baseline hazard functions according to the predictions in Model 3, Table 3, for the set of PhD graduates who received GiA funding at least once. To draw the graphs, we averaged the predictions of the dependent variables for each subgroup. The *cloglog* models include dummy variables for each time period (year), which collectively are strongly significant. Figure 2(A) indicates that the probability of exit is initially relatively high, then it decreases, and after about 10 years starts to increase. By the end of the period, the probability of exit is similar to the initial level. The early peak represents researchers who are trying to develop an academic research career—probably during their postdoctoral or assistant professorship period—prior to obtaining a tenured position. The later increase in the hazard rate would seem to correspond to academics leaving research and moving to nonresearch jobs.

Figure 2(B) compares initial affiliations and shows that the likelihood of exit from academic research is lower throughout the whole career for academics who graduated from a prestigious university. Figure 2(C) compares gender effects, and shows a much higher exit probability in the early and later career stages for females.

6.3 Career-Stage Differences

Table 4 compares two career stages: (1) before obtaining a tenured position, that is, assistant professor (Model 1) and (2) after achieving a tenured position, that is, associate and full professor (Model 2). Scientific productivity is found to decrease the probability of exit in both stages. Funding stock, as expected, has a negative effect in both stages. We find that females are more likely to exit (though insignificant) during the junior stage, but if they obtain a tenured position, their likelihood of exit is smaller than that of males (Takahashi & Takahashi, 2009, 2010). Job tenure shows a negative effect turning insignificant in the senior stage, implying that academics might be assigned nonresearch jobs after very long employment. Mobility has a negative effect only in the senior stage. The observed mobility might be largely forced and associated with low performance in the junior stage.[23] The number of cograntees is negatively correlated to exit in the senior

---

23. Mobility and performance are negatively correlated during the junior stage.

career phase, indicating that the individual academic network exerts a moderating impact on exit only when the researcher has achieved a senior position and a well-developed, consolidated academic network.

Among institutional factors, university prestige is influential only during the junior stage, suggesting that tenure is more often awarded to graduates from top universities who may be benefiting from institutional prestige. The number of researchers in the same university decreases the likelihood of exit particularly at senior levels, once again indicating that positive network effects are relevant only for senior academics. Geographic/labor market control factors have a similar effect in both stages, although the number of jobs in private universities is significantly correlated only with exit by assistant professors, indicating that the choice to take up a career in a more teaching-oriented university is usually made at an early stage.

7. CONCLUSIONS

This chapter has examined the individual-level determinants of exit from an academic research career, controlling for institutional and geographic/labor market influencing factors, informed by the literature on academic mobility and academic careers (e.g., Allison & Long, 1990; Crespi, Geuna, & Nesta, 2006) and search theory in labor economics (e.g., Mortensen & Pissarides, 1994). The up-or-out nature of an academic research career results in some academic researchers being forced to abandon an academic research career despite huge investments such as fellowships and supervisory support. This career selection process might be compromised by biased selection criteria, or a badly designed academic system, leading to unintended exit. Although this is a practical concern (e.g., Cyranoski, Gilbert, Ledford, Nayar, & Yahia, 2011; Donowitz et al., 2007; Ginther et al., 2011), few studies have examined exit from academia. The study described in this chapter is an attempt to fill this gap, based on a sample of Japanese academics in hard sciences.

The results confirm that productive academics are more likely to continue to do research, suggesting that the selection process is based at least partly on merit, which is in line with the literature on academic careers (Allison & Long, 1987; Becker, 1962; Long et al., 1993). From a search theory perspective, the opposite effect is also plausible—that productive researchers attract offers of industry jobs or nonresearch jobs in academia; however, the results do not support this argument. Thus, scientific productivity increases job opportunities in academic research significantly more than other jobs. Coupled with the very low mobility from academia to industry in Japan (METI, 2006), this result might suggest that the demand for labor from industry is not adequately addressed by the academic system.

We also examined the impact of individual-level funding and found that funding decreases the likelihood of exit. With regard to discrimination in the selection process, our results show that females are more likely to exit an academic research career than males, which is consistent with the

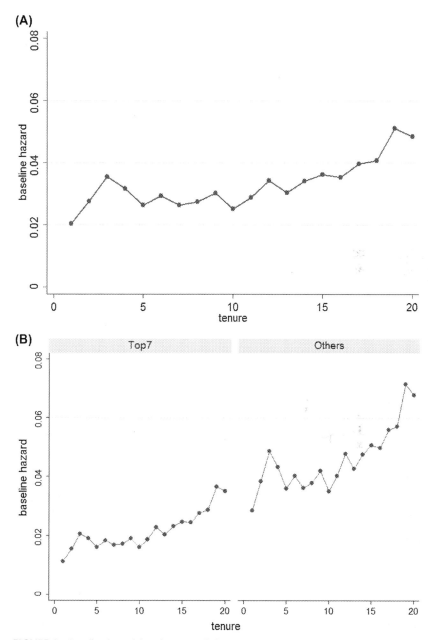

FIGURE 2 Baseline hazard function, (A) whole sample, (B) PhD universities (top7 vs others), (C) gender (male vs female).

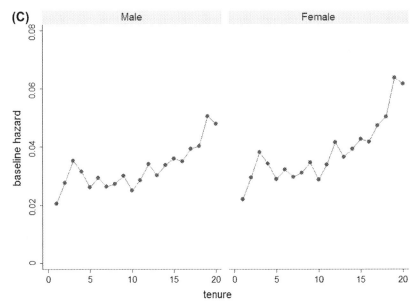

FIGURE 2 Cont'd

findings for other countries (e.g., Ginther & Kahn, 2004; Long et al., 1993). We found that this effect is especially strong immediately after graduation (73.5% for females vs 58.2% for males), less strong during the junior stage (3.9% vs 3.2%), and is reversed during the senior career stage (2.3% vs 2.8%).[24] However, the share of active female researchers at senior level (associate and full professor) is very low (4.4%). The Japanese government has implemented several policies to try to mitigate the gender gap, but it seems that further intervention is needed. We found also that the number of cograntees decreases the likelihood of exit only after award of a tenured position, suggesting that the effect of individual social capital may be moderated by seniority.

In relation to institutional factors, as Gaughan & Robin (2004) and Debackere & Rappa (1995) imply, academics in prestigious universities are less likely to exit at the start of their careers (50% for the top seven vs 65% for the rest) and during the assistant professor period (1.5% vs 4.2%).[25] Since academic inbreeding is common, particularly in high-ranked universities in Japan (Yamanoi, 2007), our result might indicate that opportunities for academics whose careers start in low-ranked universities are unreasonably hampered. From a science policy perspective, mobility across institutions should be facilitated so that talented researchers have more equal access to the institutional capital of prestigious

24. Predictions are based, respectively, on Model 3 Table 2, Model 1 Table 4, and Model 2 Table 4.
25. Predictions are based, respectively, on Model 3 Table 2 and Model 1 Table 4.

TABLE 4 Prediction of Post-Employment Exit by Career-Stage

	Model 1 (Pre-Tenure)			Model 2 (Post-Tenure)		
Individual factors						
pub stock	−0.024	***	(0.008)	−0.047	***	(0.007)
fund stock	−0.013	*	(0.008)	−0.011	*	(0.006)
female	0.109		(0.098)	−0.355	*	(0.196)
job tenure	−0.030	**	(0.013)	−0.002		(0.007)
full prof				−0.376	***	(0.073)
mobility	−0.015		(0.089)	−0.258	***	(0.073)
ln(#cograntee)	0.374	***	(0.029)	−0.133	***	(0.038)
Institutional factors						
top7	−0.360	***	(0.084)	−0.029		(0.143)
%univ fund	−0.031	**	(0.015)	0.029		(0.020)
ln(#researcher)	−0.081	**	(0.041)	−0.359	***	(0.039)
field growth	−0.695	**	(0.298)	−0.065		(0.411)
field dummies	YES			YES		
Geographical factors						
ln(#national univ employment)	−0.687	***	(0.056)	−0.336	***	(0.082)
ln(#private univ employment)	0.077	***	(0.026)	0.000		(0.046)
ln(#industrial employment)	−0.452	***	(0.047)	−0.325	***	(0.070)
ln(#PhD graduate)	0.584	***	(0.054)	0.366	***	(0.075)
χ^2 test	18,155.60	***		10,850.07	***	
Log likelihood	−7463.89			−4197.72		
N	57072			36402		

Notes: Complementary log–log model. Unstandardized coefficients (standard errors in parentheses).
Two-tailed test.
*$p < 0.1$;
**$p < 0.05$;
***$p < 0.01$.

universities or so that institutional capital at low-ranked universities is boosted. Our results suggest also that the number of researchers in the same workplace reduces exit at either entry or senior (associate and full professor) level. This effect is significant even after controlling for the size of university-level funding input, implying that social capital plays a pivotal role. Importantly, this effect is negligible in the pre-tenure term, suggesting that institutional social capital can help in the identification of entry positions for students, or may help in continuing academic research activities after tenure, but does not play a significant role at assistant professor level.

Among geographical factors, employment opportunities related to teaching jobs at prefecture level facilitates the exit of assistant professors, suggesting academics' move from research to teaching jobs within academia especially during the early phase of their career.

Overall, these results imply that the selection process in Japan is based at least in part on merit but might be compromised due to unfair selection or inequality between genders and among institutions, resulting in unintended exit.

We also found some evidence that senior academics (associate and full professor) are more able to benefit from positive individual and institutional network effects. In other words, junior academics searching for tenured positions can be unreasonably forced to exit due to social network effects favoring senior academics. The network effect also extends to the senior academic's students in relation to their first placements, implying that the social capital of senior academics can influence who joins academia.

These findings should be interpreted with care. Due to the structure of the data, the destination of academics after leaving research is not completely clear. The study in this chapter assumes, based on Japanese mobility statistics, that most academics leaving research become university teachers or administrators (rather than industry employees) or exit the labor force. However, the data might include different types of exit and also might include false exit (e.g., death, emigration). This study draws on a large sample in a first attempt to examine the main characteristics of exit from an academic research career. Future research should address the limitations outlined above by studying a smaller, more-detailed sample (e.g., survey data). The specificity of our sample is also a limitation. Country and time specificities need to be considered because career progress is heavily dependent on the design of the academic system. Future research should examine exit from an academic research career in different national and historical contexts.

ACKNOWLEDGMENTS

The authors are grateful to Paula Stephan and Satoshi P. Watanabe for comments and suggestions. We are grateful for financial support from the Konosuke Matsushita Memorial Foundation, the Grant-in-Aid for Research Activity Start-up of Japan Society for the Promotion of Science (#23810004) and the Collegio Carlo Alberto Project "Researcher Mobility and Scientific Performance." Sotaro Shibayama acknowledges Yasunori Baba's generous support for this project.

REFERENCES

Allison, P. D., & Long, J. S. (1987). Interuniversity mobility of academic scientists. *American Sociological Review*, *52*, 643–652.

Allison, P. D., & Long, J. S. (1990). Departmental effects on scientific productivity. *American Sociological Review*, *55*, 469–478.

Arimoto, A. (2011). Japan: effects of changing governance and management on the academic profession. In W. Locke, W. Cummings, & D. Fisher (Eds.), *Changing governance and management in higher education: The perspectives of the academy* (pp. 281–320). Dordrecht: Springer.

Asonuma, A. (2002). Finance reform in Japanese higher education. *Higher Education*, *43*, 109–126.

Auriol, L. (2010). Careers of doctorate holders: employment and mobility patterns. In *OECD science, technology and industry working papers*. Paris: Organisation for Economic Cooperation and Development. 2010/04.

Auriol, L., Misu, M., & Freeman, R. A. (2013). Careers of doctorate holders: analysis of labour market and mobility indicators. In *OECD science, technology and industry working papers*. Paris: Organisation for Economic Cooperation and Development.

Becker, G. (1962). Investment in human capital: a theoretical analysis. *Journal of Political Economy*, *70*, 9–49.

Brewer, D. J. (1996). Career paths and quit decisions: evidence from teaching. *Journal of Labor Economics*, *14*, 313–339.

Burdett, K. (1978). Theory of employee job search and quit rates. *American Economic Review*, *68*, 212–220.

Chan, K. C., Chen, C. R., & Steiner, T. L. (2002). Production in the finance literature, institutional reputation, and labor mobility in academia: a global perspective. *Financial Management*, *31*, 131–156.

Cox, D. R. (1972). Regression models and life-tables. *Journal of the Royal Statistical Society Series B-Statistical Methodology*, *34*, 187–220.

Crespi, G. A., Geuna, A., & Nesta, L. J. J. (2006). Labour mobility of academic inventors: career decision and knowledge transfer. In *EUI working papers*. European University Institute. RSCAS No. 2006/06.

Crespi, G. A., Geuna, A., & Nesta, L. J. J. (2007). The mobility of university inventors in Europe. *Journal of Technology Transfer*, *32*, 195–215.

Cruz-Castro, L., & Sanz-Menendez, L. (2010). Mobility versus job stability: assessing tenure and productivity outcomes. *Research Policy*, *39*, 27–38.

Cyranoski, D., Gilbert, N., Ledford, H., Nayar, A., & Yahia, M. (2011). The PhD factory. *Nature*, *472*, 276–279.

Dasgupta, P., & David, P. A. (1994). Toward a new economics of science. *Research Policy*, *23*, 487–521.

Debackere, K., & Rappa, M. A. (1995). Scientists at major and minor universities–mobility along the prestige continuum. *Research Policy*, *24*, 137–150.

Donowitz, M., Germino, G., Cominelli, F., & Anderson, J. M. (2007). The attrition of young physician-scientists: problems and potential solutions. *Gastroenterology*, *132*, 477–480.

Farber, H. S. (1994). The analysis of interfirm worker mobility. *Journal of Labor Economics*, *12*, 554–593.

Franzoni, C., Scellato, G., & Stephan, P. (2012). Foreign-born scientists: mobility patterns for 16 countries. *Nature Biotechnology*, *30*, 1250–1253.

Gaughan, M., & Robin, S. (2004). National science training policy and early scientific careers in France and the United States. *Research Policy*, *33*, 569–581.

Ginther, D. K., & Kahn, S. (2004). Women in economics: moving up or falling off the academic career ladder? *Journal of Economic Perspectives*, *18*, 193–214.

Ginther, D. K., Schaffer, W. T., Schnell, J., Masimore, B., Liu, F., Haak, L. L., et al. (2011). Race, ethnicity, and NIH research awards. *Science*, *333*, 1015–1019.

Iida, M. (2007). *The history of GiA*. Tokyo: The Science News Ltd.

Jenkins, S. P. (1995). Easy estimation methods for discrete-time duration models. *Oxford Bulletin of Economics and Statistics*, *57*, 129–138.

Jovanovic, B. (1979). Job matching and the theory of turnover. *Journal of Political Economy*, *87*, 972–990.

Kaminski, D., & Geisler, C. (2012). Survival analysis of faculty retention in science and engineering by gender. *Science*, *335*, 864–866.

Kneller, R. (2010). The changing governance of Japanese public science. In R. Whitley, J. Gläser, & L. Engwall (Eds.), *Reconfiguring knowledge production: Changing authority relations in the sciences and their consequences for intellectual innovation* (pp. 110–145). Oxford: Oxford University Press.

Lazear, E. P. (1984). Raids and offermatching. In *NBER working paper*. 1419. Cambridge, MA: National Bureau of Economic Research.

Long, J. S., Allison, P. D., & McGinnis, R. (1993). Rank advancement in academic careers–sex-differences and the effects of productivity. *American Sociological Review, 58*, 703–722.

Lotka, A. J. (1926). The frequency distribution of scientific productivity. *Journal of the Washington Academy of Science, 16*, 317–323.

Ministry of Economy Trade and Industry (METI). (2006). *New economic growth strategies*. Tokyo: METI.

Mortensen, D. T., & Pissarides, C. A. (1994). Job creation and job destruction in the theory of unemployment. *Review of Economic Studies, 61*, 397–415.

Murnane, R. J., Singer, J. D., Willett, J. B., Kemple, J., & Olsen, R. (1991). *Who will teach? Policies that matter*. Cambridge, MA: Harvard University Press.

National Institute of Science and Technology Policy (NISTEP). (2009a). Career trends survey of recent doctoral graduates. *NISTEP report* (Vol. 126). Tokyo: NISTEP.

National Institute of Science and Technology Policy (NISTEP). (2009b). A survey about mobility of researchers and diversity of research organizations. *NISTEP report* (Vol. 123). Tokyo: NISTEP.

National Science Board. (2014). *Science and engineering indicators 2014*. Arlington VA: National Science Foundation.

Prentice, R. L., & Gloeckler, L. A. (1978). Regression-analysis of grouped survival data with application to breast-cancer data. *Biometrics, 34*, 57–67.

Sauermann, H., & Roach, M. (2012). Taste for science, taste for commercialization, and hybrid scientists. In *DRUID 2012. Presented on June 19–21*. Copenhagen, Denmark.

Sauermann, H., & Roach, M. (2014). Not all scientists pay to be scientists: PhDs' preferences for publishing in industrial employment. *Research Policy, 43*, 32–47.

Shibayama, S. (2011). Distribution of academic research funds: a case of Japanese national research grant. *Scientometrics, 88*, 43–60.

Shibayama, S., Baba, Y., & Walsh, J.P. (2015). Organizational design of university laboratories: task allocation and lab performance in Japanese bioscience laboratories. *Research Policy, 44*, 610–622.

Shimbori, M. (1981). The Japanese academic profession. *Higher Education, 10*, 75–87.

Stephan, P. E. (2012). *How economics shapes science*. Cambridge, MA: Harvard University Press.

Stern, S. (2004). Do scientists pay to be scientists? *Management Science, 50*, 835–853.

Stokes, D. E. (1997). *Pasteurs quadrant: Basic science and technological innovation*. Washington D.C.: Brookings Institution Press.

Takahashi, S., & Takahashi, A. M. (2009). Gender promotion differences in economics departments in Japan: A duration analysis. In *GSIR working papers, EAP09–4*.

Takahashi, A. M., & Takahashi, S. (2010). The effect of refereed articles on salary, promotion and labor mobility: the case of Japanese economists. *Economics Bulletin, 30*, 330–350.

Teichler, U., Arimoto, A., & Cummings, W. K. (2013). *The changing academy–The changing academic profession in international comparative perspective*. Dordrecht: Springer.

Watanabe, S. P. (2011). Impacts of university education reform on faculty perceptions of workload. *Asia Pacific Journal of Education, 31*, 407–420.

Wolfinger, N. H., Mason, M. A., & Goulden, M. (2009). Stay in the game: gender, family formation and alternative trajectories in the academic life course. *Social Forces, 87*, 1591–1621.

Yamanoi, A. (2007). *Academic marketplace in Japan*. Tokyo: Tamagawa University Press.

Zerhouni, E. A. (2006). Research funding–NIH in the post-doubling era: realities and strategies. *Science, 314*, 1088–1090.

Zucker, L. G., Darby, M. R., & Torero, M. (2002). Labor mobility from academe to commerce. *Journal of Labor Economics, 20*, 629–660.

TABLE 10A.1 Descriptive Statistics and Correlation

(A) Pre-Employment Exit

	Variable	Mean	S.D.	Min	Max	1	2	3	4	5	6	7	8	9
1.	pre-employment dropout	0.59	0.49	0.00	1.00									
2.	graduation year	1987	1.41	1985	1989	0.02								
3.	female	0.08	0.27	0.00	1.00	0.08	0.02							
4.	top7	0.38	0.48	0.00	1.00	-0.15	-0.03	-0.02						
5.	ln(#researcher)	4.19	1.04	0.00	6.12	-0.16	0.01	-0.03	0.71					
6.	field growth	0.14	0.21	-0.09	0.54	-0.02	-0.77	-0.02	0.04	0.02				
7.	ln(#national univ employment)	7.84	0.83	5.81	8.76	-0.02	-0.03	0.01	0.12	0.16	0.02			
8.	ln(#private univ employment)	7.80	0.91	5.06	8.92	-0.07	-0.03	-0.01	0.30	0.36	0.02	0.79		
9.	ln(#industrial employment)	7.75	2.22	0.00	10.21	-0.02	-0.02	0.00	0.20	0.23	0.01	0.87	0.81	
10.	ln(#PhD graduate)	5.28	1.33	0.69	7.04	-0.05	0.05	0.00	0.29	0.32	-0.03	0.83	0.95	0.88

(B) Post-Employment Exit

	Variable	Mean	S.D.	Min	Max	1	2	3	4	5	6	7	8	9	10	11	12	13	14	15	16
1.	post-employment dropout	0.03	0.18	0.00	1.00																
2.	pub stock	0.27	7.16	-12.88	100.94	-0.05															
3.	fund stock	0.50	7.76	-13.42	186.16	-0.04	0.67														
4.	female	0.05	0.21	0.00	1.00	0.01	-0.01	-0.02													
5.	job tenure	7.88	6.47	1.00	77.00	0.03	0.04	0.05	-0.01												
6.	associate prof	0.65	0.48	0.00	1.00	0.01	-0.18	-0.16	0.04	-0.40											
7.	full prof	0.24	0.43	0.00	1.00	-0.01	0.03	0.03	-0.03	0.18	-0.69										
8.	mobility	1.26	0.79	0.00	8.00	-0.01	0.13	0.06	-0.01	-0.08	-0.50	0.26									
9.	ln(#cograntee)	1.38	1.16	0.00	5.01	0.01	0.33	0.35	-0.02	0.46	-0.58	0.30	0.40								
10.	top7	0.35	0.48	0.00	1.00	-0.06	0.12	0.17	-0.03	0.05	0.06	-0.03	-0.20	0.06							
11.	%univ fund	3.69	4.25	0.00	26.48	-0.06	0.11	0.18	-0.01	0.03	0.09	-0.05	-0.21	0.05	0.72						
12.	ln(#researcher)	3.79	1.24	0.69	6.06	-0.03	0.10	0.16	-0.04	0.13	0.12	-0.05	-0.31	0.06	0.61	0.67					
13.	field growth	0.04	0.11	-0.20	0.73	-0.02	-0.03	-0.02	0.01	-0.29	0.26	0.04	-0.18	-0.26	0.02	0.03	0.06				
14.	ln(#national univ employment)	7.81	0.91	5.06	9.05	-0.03	0.06	0.10	0.00	0.10	0.04	-0.03	-0.11	0.05	0.32	0.45	0.03	0.06			
15.	ln(#private univ employment)	7.82	2.08	0.00	10.49	-0.02	0.04	0.07	0.00	0.07	-0.01	-0.01	-0.05	0.07	0.22	0.36	0.23	0.32	0.83		
16.	ln(#industrial employment)	7.75	0.86	5.75	8.79	-0.02	0.02	0.04	0.01	0.04	0.07	-0.04	-0.09	-0.02	0.17	0.30	0.18	0.23	0.79	0.88	
17.	ln(#PhD graduate)	5.74	1.44	0.69	8.17	-0.01	0.07	0.11	0.00	0.27	-0.12	0.05	-0.01	0.20	0.28	0.39	0.28	-0.11	-0.01	-0.04	0.00

Notes: N = 13,776. For time-variant variables, we use the value of each variable at graduation year.
Notes: N = 93,474.

APPENDIX 2

TABLE 10A.2 Summary of Predictions by Career-Stage by Field

	(A) Pre-Employment Exit						
	All Fields	Science	Engineering	Agriculture	Pharmaceutical	Medicine	Dentistry
Individual factors							
graduation year							
female	+++	+++	+	+++		+++	++
Institutional factors							
top7	---						
ln(#researcher)	---	-	-	----		---	---
field growth							++
Geographical factors							
ln(#national univ employment)	---					-	
ln(#private univ employment)	++					+++	+++
ln(#industrial employment)					--		
ln(#PhD graduate)	+						--

(B) Post-Employment Exit

	All Fields		Math&Physics		Biology		Chemistry		Engineering		Agriculture		Pharmacy		Basic Medicine		Clinical Medicine		Dentistry	
	1	2	1	2	1	2	1	2	1	2	1	2	1	2	1	2	1	2	1	2
Individual factors																				
pub stock		---		---						–									–	
fund stock	–	–				++	+			–		–		+				–		
female		–								–	+		+++	–						
job tenure	–												+							
full prof	n.a.	---	n.a.		n.a.	–	n.a.	---	n.a.		n.a.		n.a.		n.a.		n.a.		n.a.	---
mobility		---				–						–								---
ln(#cograntee)	+++	---		–					+++	---					++	–	+++	–	+++	---
Institutional factors																				
top7	–	–						–			–			–			–		–	–
%univ fund	–	–				+			+											
ln(#researcher)	---	---	---	---		–											–	–		
field growth	–					+	–		–	–		–					–			
Geographical factors																				
ln(#national univ employment)	–	---	–		–		–				–		–				–			
ln(#private univ employment)	+++	---							–								+++			
ln(#industrial employment)	---	---	–			–	–				–						–		–	
ln(#PhD graduate)	+++	+++	+++	++	+			++	+++	+++	+++	++	+++	+++	+++		+++	++	+++	---

Notes: +/– p<0.1; ++/– – p<0.05; +++/– – – p<0.01. Column 1 corresponds to pre-tenure exit and column 2 to post-tenure exit.

Index

Note: Page numbers followed by "f" or "t" indicates figures and tables respectively.

who move	from where	to where	consequence (d.v.)

- students (undergraduate, graduate)
- particularly PhD

- researchers (incl. post-doc)

- All countries
- region
- intra-Europe

- U.S.
- UK
- Europe
- extra-Europe

- research productivity (publications)

- collaboration

- improve something (e.g. publications)

motivation
- earning
- career

·